ABYSS OF REASON

Abyss of Reason
Cultural Movements, Revelations, and Betrayals

DANIEL COTTOM

New York   Oxford
OXFORD UNIVERSITY PRESS
1991

Oxford University Press

Oxford   New York   Toronto
Delhi   Bombay   Calcutta   Madras   Karachi
Petaling Jaya   Singapore   Hong Kong   Tokyo
Nairobi   Dar es Salaam   Cape Town
Melbourne   Auckland

and associated companies in
Berlin   Ibadan

Library of Congress Cataloging-in-Publication Data
Cottom, Daniel.
Abyss of reason : cultural movements, revelations, and betrayals /
Dan Cottom.
p. cm.   Includes bibliographical references and index.
ISBN 0-19-506857-2
1. Surrealism (Literature)   2. Spiritualism in literature.
3. Criticism — History — 20th century.   I. Title.
PN56.S87C68   1991   809′.91 — dc20   90-44015

Chapters 2 and 9 originally appeared, in different forms, in *Critical Inquiry* 14 (© 1988 by the University
of Chicago) and *Critical Inquiry* 16 (© 1989 by the University of Chicago), respectively.

2 4 6 8 9 7 5 3 1

Printed in the United States of America
on acid-free paper

For Deborah,
for everything

Acknowledgments

I'd like to thank Charlie Baxter, Ross Pudaloff, Henry Golemba, David Leverenz, John Leavey, Jack Perlette, Alistair Duckworth, Mel New, Elizabeth Langland, Carol Flinn, Brandy Kershner, Michelle Lekas, and Alex Menocal for their helpful readings of various parts of this book.

And I'd like to thank Nancy Armstrong, Jochen Schulte-Sasse, and Stanley Fish, for tender mercies of a professional sort, and the editors and publishers of *Critical Inquiry,* where earlier versions of chapters 2 and 9 first appeared.

Sonia Tergas and Melanie S. Davis were a great help to me in my search for obscure texts. Also, for their aid in tracking down artworks and permissions, I'd like to acknowledge Antoinette Rezé-Huré and Alain Sayag of the Centre Georges Pompidou; Roswitha Neu-Kock of the Museen der Stadt Köln; Sigrid Bertuleit of the Hamburger Kunsthalle; Michael Sweeney of Burgh Hill House; Agnieszka Lukinska and Anna Krems of the Fondation Jean Arp und Sophie Taeuber-Arp; Peter Seidel of the Staats- und Universitätsbibliothek in Hamburg; Bill Valerio of Art Resource; Katia Steiglitz of ARS; Eva Lindstrom of the Moderna Museet, Skeppsholmen; Cecile Brunner of the Kunsthaus Zürich; Giselle Ollinger-Zinque of the Musées Royaux des Beaux-Arts de Belgique; Jules Roland of the Centre Culturel de Bruxelles; Elisabeth Raabe of Arche Verlag, Zürich; Thomas D. Grischkowsky and Ruth Priever of the Museum of Modern Art; and Graham Langton of the Tate Gallery.

Gainesville, Florida   D. C.
January 1991

Contents

ABYSS OF REASON

Introduction

He who fights with monsters should look to it that he himself does not become a monster. And when you gaze long into an abyss the abyss also gazes into you.

FRIEDRICH NIETZSCHE, *Beyond Good and Evil*[1]

A century after Emanuel Swedenborg's colloquies with angels, on the last day of March in 1848—a year distinguished by a westering plague of cholera, the California gold rush, the failure of the Chartists' "Great Petition" to the English Parliament, and the spectacle of revolutions and counterrevolutions among the *anciens régimes* of Europe—a few residents of the small town of Hydesville, New York witnessed what many would later describe as the dawn of a new age of miracles. The experiences that began in the presence of Margaret and Kate Fox came to be called "the Rochester knockings," after the nearby city, and these knockings opened the door onto modern spiritualism. This was a cultural movement devoted to communications between living persons and those who had passed beyond the veil, to the Other Side, or (in the name made famous by Andrew Jackson Davis, the Poughkeepsie Seer) to the "Summerland."

Three-quarters of a century later, in Paris, on the 15th of October in the year 1924—a year that saw Benito Mussolini consolidating his power over Italy, Adolf Hitler killing time in prison by dictating *Mein Kampf* to Rudolf Hess, Vladimir Ilyich Lenin and Woodrow Wilson going to their graves, and a jazzy mood lighting up certain social circles in the United States and abroad—a former medical officer in the First World War, André Breton, published a manifesto proclaiming a new revolution. He told of a reign of dreams, unfettered imagination, willing unconsciousness, insanely pure spirit. "Columbus had to set out with madmen in order to discover

America,"[2] he wrote, repeating an image used by the spiritualists of bygone years to defend their seeming eccentricity. Thus was surrealism, a cultural movement devoted to communication between the human spirit and the world beyond the façade of reality, officially given a name and local habitation.

The differences between the two movements were many, but perhaps the most obvious were in the kind of crowd they attracted. Modern spiritualism cast its net wide: while generally a middle-class and plebeian affair, it was patronized by an emperor and empress, various noblemen, a number of well-known literary figures, and others among the elite classes of Europe, America, and other parts of the world. "Quietly stealing on from fireside to fireside," wrote William Howitt, "without pretence, without parade, it has gone up from the middle ranks of life to the highest aristocratic regions, and down to the humblest abodes of working men."[3] By contrast, while those who called themselves surrealists came from various backgrounds, almost all were young artists and intellectuals, many of whom had already participated in the avant-garde shenanigans of dada.

This difference in social background is magnified by the disparities in scope of the two movements. Spiritualism was a popular affair, attracting many adherents in the United States, Britain, France, Germany, Spain, Russia, and other countries. Moreover, all of these people actually participated in the movement. This was not a case, as with the experiences of Bernadette Soubirous at Lourdes in 1858, of a vision being granted to one and taken on faith by those who followed. The spiritualist press liked to claim three million persons sharing in the new dispensation; and even if this number was exaggerated, the influence of the movement was sufficiently widespread to inspire comments such as the following editorial reflection in the May 1853 issue of *Harper's*:

> What are we coming to, in this enlightened era? Are we gradually turning into a nation of Spiritual Rappers, or believers in Spiritual Rappings? One would think so, to hear of the hundreds of "spiritual circles" that are forming, or have been formed, in different places, north, south, east, and west; of the distinguished men and "strong-minded women" who are announcing their adhesion to all the alleged "mysteries" of the delusion, and particularly the marvelous matters involved in this wonderful and supernatural "*Ism*."[4]

The situation with surrealism could hardly have been more different, with the group that actively contributed to the movement comprising at most a few dozen, whose doings were centered primarily, though not exclusively, in Paris.[5] They received little publicity outside their own circle; and until the movement as such had practically disappeared, their journals and books never had a circulation anywhere close to that enjoyed by many spiritualist works. One can read the entire oeuvres of writers who lived in Paris during the twenties and thirties and find scarcely a passing allusion to surrealism, while writers in the second half of the nineteenth century — Fanny Trollope, Charles Dickens, Elizabeth Barrett Browning, Leo Tolstoy, Victor Hugo, Nathaniel Hawthorne, Harriet Beecher Stowe, Henry James, and William Dean Howells, among others — showed much more awareness of spiritualism as a cultural phenomenon that had to be addressed. The possible relation between spiritualism and the revolutions of 1848 was noticed not only by S. B. Brittan's proselytizing newspaper, *The Spiritual Telegraph*, but also by Karl Marx in the opening pages of *The Eighteenth Brumaire of Louis Bonaparte*, which are replete with references to revenants, miracles, and the awakening of the dead.[6]

Because of attitudes encouraging wide participation while frustrating domination by any one individual or organized body, spiritualism tended to be democratic in orientation; despite their professed sympathies with the masses, the surrealists defined themselves as a superior and authoritarian few. As Victor Crastre has written of their movement, all "attempts at vulgarization went against its singular genius."[7] Moreover, most spiritualist mediums were said to be female, many women were among its believers, and women's rights were often among its goals, as when Victoria Woodhull ran for president of the United States on the Cosmo-Political Party ticket. In contrast, while allowing for the participation of women such as Meret Oppenheim, Gisèle Prassinos, Leonora Carrington, and, more peripherally, Frida Kahlo, surrealism as a cultural movement was both male and patriarchal.

Modern spiritualism sought to be an open movement, one that welcomed anyone who sought the truth. In fact, its participants were happy to claim kinship even with many of those who most vigorously opposed them. The surrealist style of approaching the world was very different, with the members of this group often showing themselves to be jealous of its identity and determined to maintain its exclusivity against all pretenders and *arrivistes*. Surrealism was censorious where spiritualism was celebratory, aggressive where spiritualism was placating, and angry where spiritualism was sentimental. Spiritualism was founded on pathos, surrealism on pathology. If spiritualism sat in shadowed rooms and dreamed of light, surrealism, pregnant with darkness, walked the noonday streets of the city, hoping to inspire alarms and diversions. "To the exterior world," wrote Roger Callois, "already woven of signs of recognition, is added the secret language of the personal abyss that diurnal controls serve to stifle and travesty."[8]

Under the leadership of Breton, the surrealists sought purity and were eager to condemn or expel those who did not meet their standards; the spiritualist movement was so loosely organized that it could not possibly recognize any heterodoxy except a total disbelief in the possibility of an afterlife. Elaborately disciplined and calculatedly intransigent, the surrealists cultivated an attitude of wildness, unpredictability, fury, and rebellion, whereas the spiritualists generally sought to reject such terms when they were applied to their movement, arguing that no one was more respectable and circumspect than they. The surrealists were self-confidently intellectual, sufficiently so that they could laugh in the face of professors and wise men; anxiously and defensively, the spiritualists labored to claim intellectual credentials for themselves. Ironically, surrealism eventually gained respectability, becoming a recognized artistic movement and style, suitable for canonical representation in museums and textbooks; equally ironically, the spiritualism that so desperately sought acceptance quickly became a kooky footnote (if so much as that) in standard histories of the nineteenth century.

Despite these and other differences between the two, they do bear some resemblance to each other. It is not for nothing that "abyss" is a word that crops up repeatedly in the rhetoric of both movements, just as it does today in works of critical theory. In the first place, insiders and outsiders alike perceived both movements as being opposed to the dominant cultures of the societies from which they emerged. More specifically, both movements placed themselves in opposition to the established institutions of scientific authority in their day, and yet both often presented themselves as systematic investigations that would show up the limitations, faults, or lies of the prevailing opinion among the respectable. Both challenged common sense as a measure of experience while simultaneously attacking the way knowledge was institutionalized in school philosophy. Just as spiritualists defended their beliefs by comparing the incredulity that greeted them to the similar reception initially given the electric telegraph and other scientific achievements, Breton defended the works of surrealism, arguing that those who condemned as an abstraction "every form not currently registered by the eye" failed to realize that "the contour of the filament of an electric lamp would have appeared the apex of abstraction" just a century earlier.[9] Galileo's legendary whisper of defiance, *"E pur si muove!"* ("And yet it moves!"), was frequently quoted by spiritualists; and it was cited as well in one of Breton's essays.[10]

Furthermore, in denigrating positivism and its fellow traveller, the aesthetics of realism, both movements challenged the forms of art that were privileged in their day. While claiming to be equal or superior to science, both claimed that they were doing what the best art had always done or at least what it should have been doing. They were equally opposed to what is broadly termed "high art" or "culture" in the Arnoldian sense, and yet both would sometimes try to lean on its prestige. As the spiritualists believed they could ferret out support for their beliefs in the works of contemporary writers such as Walt Whitman, Alfred Tennyson, and even Charles Dickens (who thought the movement preposterous), the surrealists would claim a kinship with people who had little or no direct involvement in their program, such as Pablo Picasso and Raymond Roussel.

In their historical postures, too, these movements bore some resemblance to each other. Looking back, spiritualists saw anticipations of their movement in Mother Ann Lee's "Shaking Quakers," or Shakers; in the millenarian Irvingites of early Victorian England; in Frederica Hauffé, the "Seeress of Prevorst" publicized by Dr. Justinus Kerner in the early nineteenth century; and in a host of historical figures, including Jacob Boehme, Jesus Christ, the Witch of Endor, and Socrates.[11] Similarly, Breton's "Manifesto of Surrealism" claimed that his was the party of William Shakespeare and Dante Alighieri, of the Marquis de Sade and Edgar Allen Poe, and of Edward Young and Jonathan Swift, among others. The two movements even had one hero in common: Charles Fourier, the self-dubbed "Messiah of Reason" and designer of socialist utopias.

Spiritualists and surrealists further resembled each other in the emphasis they placed on the value of passivity and unconsciousness. In their early stages especially, both movements included trance-speaking and trance-writing among their characteristic practices. And the connection was more than coincidental: in Breton's early days, his reading included works by Frederic W. H. Myers and Theodore Flournoy, two supporters of spiritualism, and by Pierre Janet and Hippolyte Taine, students of the mind who had devoted lengthy critical studies to this phenomenon. In one of his late essays ("The Pearl Is Spoiled for My Eyes . . . "), Breton was still remembering this connection between his movement and the earlier one when he extended a footnote to Éliphas Lévi, a nineteenth-century writer who was interested in spiritualism and the occult (although Lévi saw the former as an inauthentic version of the latter).

Other notable similarities between these two movements include their sense of personal identity as an elusive and problematic thing; their desire to analyze the workings of communication, which both considered to be fraught with perplexities even in its most ordinary forms; their related concern with appropriating certain key terms to their own ends, such as "medium" and "purity"; their interest in reconceiving their notions of everyday objects, as with the spiritualists' speaking tables or Meret Oppenheim's *Fur-Covered Cup, Plate, and Spoon* (1936); and their fascination with the phenomena of doubles, uncanniness, revelation, and betrayal.

One might even argue that spiritualism and surrealism have shared something of the same fate. When read today, many surrealist writings are likely to inspire the same reaction that spiritualist writings will receive: a very little goes a very long way. Surrealism was a more consciously artistic movement and has been granted much more scholarly attention than spiritualism, but it still seems fair to say that the bulk of the writing produced by both movements was destined for a quick fall into the archives. And as previously noted, the directions in which spiritualism and surrealism fell were equally ironic in relation to the pronounced intentions of their supporters.

In isolation, these intersections may appear to be of marginal importance at best, since surrealism was indebted much more obviously to such ancestral influences as the outrageous lives of Arthur Rimbaud and Alfred Jarry, the

symbolist experiments of Stéphane Mallarmé and Paul Valéry, the dada
experience, Freud's work on dreams, and Guillaume Apollinaire's poetics.
Yet the surrealists themselves suggested a portrayal of their movement in
relation to spiritualism. Aragon, for instance, in *The Peasant of Paris*, while
describing a nighttime visit to the Parc des Buttes-Chaumont in the company
of Breton and Marcel Noll, thought sympathetically of the spiritualists' moving tables when he affirmed the surrealists' turbulent, ecstatic, rapturous
version of love:

> They used to tell me that love is laughable. They told me, "It's simple," and
> explained to me the mechanism of my heart. So it seems. They told me that I
> ought not to believe in miracles; if the tables turned, it was because someone
> shoved them with his foot. . . .
>   However, you didn't take into account my credulity. . . . Me, I've seen the great
> pale ghost, with its broken chains, leaving the crypt. But they haven't sensed the
> divinity of that woman. . . . You see, their eyes don't catch the inexplicable.

Or such references to spiritualism could be played strictly for laughs, as in
the absurdist dialogue of Roger Vitrac's *The Mysteries of Love*:

> *Patrick*:   It turns. It turns.
>   *Lea*:   What turns?
> *Patrick*:   Not the table, certainly.[12]

In any event, the earlier movement communicated with the later one in all
sorts of ways, big and little, direct and indirect. René Crevel, who led the
surrealists into their experiments with trances in the *temps des sommeils*, did
so after having been inspired by a visit to a medium; a medium turns up in
Leonora Carrington's story, "Little Francis"; a surrealist journal of the 1950s
was called *Medium*. Alfred Jarry, one of the surrealists' heroes, dedicated
the ninth chapter of his *Deeds and Opinions of Doctor Faustroll, Pataphysi-
cian*, to William Crookes, the famous English scientist and spiritualist;[13] the
father of Victor Brauner, one of the artists associated with surrealism, was a
spiritualist; one of Brauner's more famous works was a *Wolf-Table* (1939–
47) that might well be seen as an allusion to the tables of the spiritualists.
  Even fleeting references are significant insofar as they show a marked
awareness of spiritualism among the surrealists at a time when the older
movement no longer aroused the attention it had once enjoyed. Although it
had not completely disappeared by the early years of the new century—
it continued to influence artists such as Sweden's Hilma af Klint and the
Bohemian-born Frantisek Kupka, and it was still current enough when
Thomas Mann wrote *The Magic Mountain* to play an important role near
the end of that novel—spiritualism had become either the equivalent of a
parlor game or simply an embarrassment as far as most people were con-

cerned. For just this reason, the relationship between spiritualism and surrealism proved disturbing to Walter Benjamin, leading him to ask, "Who would not wish to see these adoptive children of revolution most rigorously severed from all the goings-on in the conventicles of down-at-heel dowagers, retired majors, and *émigré* profiteers?"[14] Freud was another who might have made Benjamin unhappy by his refusal to dismiss spiritualism as a low thing. "The 'Uncanny'" is only one of several essays in which Freud touched upon the subject of spiritualism, observing that placards in "our great cities . . . announce lectures that undertake to tell us how to get into touch with the souls of the departed"; Freud went on to note that "not a few of the notable and penetrating minds among our men of science have come to the conclusion, especially towards the close of their lives, that a contact of this kind is not impossible."[15]

As in many other aspects of the surrealist movement, Breton assumed a leading role in cultivating this awareness of spiritualism. His first "Manifesto of Surrealism," like another early work, "The Entrance of the Mediums," did consider that a "materialist attitude" was beneficial insofar as it countered "some ludicrous tendencies of spiritualism"—a point he was still prepared to expatiate on late in his life.[16] However, spiritualism also came to serve him as an impetus toward creativity. It appears in this role in the "Second Manifesto of Surrealism"—"I demand, once again, that we efface ourselves before the mediums"—and, most remarkably, in his "Letter to the Seers," a paean to mediums that simply refuses to countenance the suggestion that their purposes could be at odds with the surrealists'. "They tell me," Breton writes in a characteristic passage, "that you have offered your services to help certain police investigations succeed, but this is not possible: either there has been some usurpation or it is false."[17]

So surrealism certainly had some acknowledged affiliations with spiritualism and some distinct resemblances in its practices and motivations, but it is important to remember the divergences as well. Aside from the points sketched out above, the historical relation between the movements is not very extensive; how participants in the later movement came into contact with or learned about the earlier one may certainly be an interesting question for some purposes, but it is not really my concern here. This is not a study of influences and borrowings, of patterns and appropriations. Nor is it, strictly speaking, a comparative study; I have not devised a scheme to measure the two movements in relation to each other. The motivation for bringing them together under one cover has more to do with questioning than with establishing foundations of knowledge. I do not approach history here as a ground, a court of last resort, but rather as a torn, disputed, demanding space and time that gives our understanding no choice but to be at once and indivisibly historical, cultural, and political. The justification for studying these two movements together is that the differences between them, as much as the connections, allow me to explore the complexities of cultural movements and their implications for the study of culture in any of its aspects: literary, artistic, philosophical, scientific, religious, and so on.

Modern spiritualism and surrealism are not representative in the sense of providing us with a model of all possible cultural movements, but their pairing does yield a range of provocative material for working through the issues with which criticism in all sorts of fields today remains preoccupied. Most broadly, they provide a frame within which many modern cultural movements, especially those that have objected to the privileges of reason and science, have composed themselves. The alternatives that set the frame are a fascination with the depths of the universe or with the depths of consciousness: a search for revelation from beyond or from within. At the same time these movements challenged such distinctions, for both investigated how the "within" might become the "beyond," the "beyond" the "within," and both the seeming "in itself" of the things of our world. Thus, when Breton wrote of the "nauseating terminology" of spiritualism,[18] the strength of his disgust measured the difficulty of distinguishing surrealism's "inward" from spiritualism's "outward" orientation. The surrealists also recognized this difficulty in their conception of dialectic and especially in their notion of "objective chance," or of that which appears unpredictably and yet with a sense of inevitable necessity, thus knotting together the impulses of interiority and exteriority as if to assure us of their ultimate union. In this as in other respects, the pairing of modern spiritualism and surrealism leads to a focus on a history shot through with contradictory movements that are likely to be oversimplified or overlooked in our more usual perspectives on the past. Martin Heidegger came at this point from another direction when he wrote of "the basic movements of human beings (*Dasein*) that have occurred, movements which apparently are no longer movements because they are past," adding, "But a movement need not be gone just because it cannot be established; it can also be in the state of quiescence."[19] The renewed attention in recent years to Heidegger's involvement in the National Socialist movement, along with the subsequent shifts in his and others' reputations, only makes his words on this subject all the more compelling.

How can one address *movements*, the meaning of movements? For this is what is most interesting about spiritualism and surrealism: that they were movements of cultural interpretation composed by groups, which may still challenge—if we give them the chance—the approaches to interpretation that critics usually find to be legitimate. When intellectuals are in the act of writing, we are almost always physically isolated, and we generally profess an ideal of cautious, temperate, open-minded, and socially responsible inquiry. To allow these cultural movements the possibility of communicating, of making sense, must raise questions about this isolation, this ideal, and the way they both inform what we take to be knowledge. To address cultural movements *as* movements is to see interpretation in terms of urgencies, pulsions, gestures, historical desires, struggling oppositions, and impromptu

deviations. This perspective differs from a concentration on individual intentions, careers, propositions, and works; it differs also from critical enter-
prises that take "culture," "society," or similar terms to be descriptions of
historical totalities; and while it is indebted to various strains of poststructur-
alist thought, it differs from approaches that so thoroughly subordinate
semiotic passion, action, and event to the claims of philosophical rigor that
they may seem unable to comprehend that this rigor is often completely
beside the point. As Paul Feyerabend says in a different but related context,
"And what is the use of an argument that leaves people unmoved?"[20]

If cultural critics, like cultural movements, are always bound to be in a
vexed position, at once sustained and buffeted by the turmoil of the events,
languages, institutions, and social practices in which they find themselves,
then the idea that criticism should be devoted above all else to bringing order
to a subject is very dubious. To put it simply, this call to order may use
the names of intellectual responsibility and professional discipline to cloak
defensive attitudes, sly rationalizations, and narcissistic hallucinations. Nietzsche, who wrote in the heyday of spiritualism and would one day be named an
admired ancestor of the surrealists, addressed this issue when he argued, "Very
belatedly (only now) is it dawning on men that in their belief in language they
have propagated a monstrous error. Fortunately, it is too late to be able to
revoke the development of reason, which rests on that belief."[21]

Of course, Nietzsche's "fortunately" is ironic, or more than ironic, something like a rhetorical abyss. Appropriately so. By leading us to approach
history in terms of signifying forces, as opposed to truths or essences or facts,
an attention to movements should put criticism into the midst of wrenching
debates, where we must try to catch contexts, rules, and meanings on the fly,
even as they are being constructed, construed, contested, and torn apart —
often all at the same time. To devote criticism to the question of cultural
movements is thus to work *through* and *among* movements. It is always to
consider what it means, what it could possibly mean, to be in one position
rather than another; to have one vision rather than other possible visions; to
seize on this meaning as opposed to that or on history wrought in one
uncertain way as opposed to other ways of uncertainty.

Such a criticism will have its peculiar difficulties. For one thing, movements at least seem more difficult to outline than specific texts and lives.
Not only are their shapes uncertain at any given time, but they do not provide
us with clearly punctuated beginnings and ends of the sort one at least seems
to have when dealing with works and lives. The differences here are more
apparent than real, but still these differences do call for some preliminary
clarification.

First, I wish to note that I have generally confined myself to modern
spiritualism in the second half of the nineteenth century and to surrealism
between the world wars. In both cases, arguments can and have been made
for seeing these movements as extending beyond these boundaries, and I will

touch upon some of these arguments in the course of my study; but I have stuck with the periods during which modern spiritualism and surrealism were seen contemporaneously, by adherents and outsiders alike, as taking on and maintaining a recognizable form. In terms of certain beliefs and practices, spiritualism certainly lived into (and still survives in) the twentieth century, but it is very unlike the mass movement that began to decline in the last quarter of the nineteenth century; similarly, surrealism after the Second World War, whatever interest it may hold, was extremely different from what the movement had been earlier, even taking into account all the twists and turns between 1924 and 1940. Judgments of boundaries like these are always tactical, and I present mine as such. For the purposes of this study, I think they pay off, but I know they must also limit me in some ways.

A related difficulty arises when I write of spiritualism or surrealism through what traditional rhetoric would call a personification. "Surrealism did this," I will write, or "Spiritualism took this idea to be false," as if either movement could ever have been a coherent agent, all of one mind in its attitudes and exertions. Again, the difference from the problems faced by critics dealing with individual authors or texts is more apparent than real, for the "personification" involved in thus evoking a group does not differ radically from the rhetoric involved in the uses of proper names or titles. Certainly the differences among persons, texts, and cultural movements are many, but they do not extend to persons and texts possessing an unproblematic unity that movements lack. Still, I have tried to correct for this personifying tendency by concentrating on the ways the movements under consideration were riven by differences, uncertainties, and divergent impulses; when I generalize about spiritualism or surrealism, it should be remembered that I am generalizing, not essentializing, as I trust my arguments throughout the book will make clear.

I do not write as a partisan of either movement, but this is not to say that I write disinterestedly or indifferently. It will quickly become apparent that my spiritualism is neither the Fox sisters' nor Henry James's and that my surrealism is neither Breton's nor, say, Jean-Paul Sartre's, in the attack he made on it after World War II. As I have noted here and as I have argued elsewhere,[22] the production of knowledge is always political, whether or not one acknowledges and tries to work through the implications of this aspect of intellectual life; I have not tried to survey these movements with impartiality, nor do I believe it is possible to do so. As we all must, I have plunged in.

Consider first the case of spiritualism. The question with which most people in the nineteenth century would start — whether the manifestations came from departed human spirits, other supernatural powers, hitherto unrecognized natural agencies, or the machinations of impostors — is really the least important for us today. Of course it is possible for us to discredit the phenomena involved in this cultural movement if we care to do so, just as it is possible for contemporary savants, when they get the likes of Uri Geller into a controlled environment, to show their seemingly extraordinary powers as very dispiriting trickery. This kind of criticism has been historically important (G. H. Lewes, Michael Faraday, and, curiously enough, P. T. Barnum are among the relevant nineteenth-century debunkers); but by now this labor is largely beside the point, even if we consider distant relations of modern spiritualism such as the "New Age" movement that arose in the United States in the 1980s. The difficulty is not in discounting spiritualist phenomena: the difficulty is rather in crediting them.

The problem modern spiritualism poses for our understanding today is that of explaining how seriously it was taken. The attitude most intellectuals today are likely to take is that of W. V. Quine and J. S. Ullian in their popular introduction to logic, *The Web of Belief*: "A person might have a moderately amusing time playing with a ouija board, but if he drifts into the belief that it is a *bona fide* avenue to discovery then something has gone amiss."[23] The attitude of Quine and Ullian can itself be said to be moderately amusing as long as we remain within the domain of logic, but it fails us as soon as we want to think about what underlies its boundaries and how those boundaries are drawn in the first place. Then we can no longer dismiss spiritualism; then we need to figure out what meaning these mediumistic communications could have had for those they excited and those who were antagonized by them. In this regard, the precise mechanism of the table-rappings and other manifestations becomes less important than the experiences, discourses, and practices—the cultural movement—that developed around them. Unless we believe that logic can correct history, we must acknowledge that the issue of empirical verification has no necessary precedence over the issue of meaning, which may actually constitute a telling critique of the tendency to identify empiricism with truth. I am not so concerned with the origins of spiritualism, then—the Fox sisters in upstate New York, Mrs. W. R. Hayden's first visit to England, Daniel Dunglas Home's incursions into France and Russia—as I am in the cultural appeal and power, the evident meaning, that this movement proved to have.

The case is similar with surrealism. Today, for anyone so inclined, it is easy enough to dismantle the pretensions of this movement. Philosophically, it may appear as a characteristic modernist rehash of romantic images, ideas, and themes that simply will not withstand close examination. Although surrealism has been of more account aesthetically than spiritualism, earning itself a secure place in the canons of modern art and literature, this significance has generally entailed the surrender of all the power that the surrealists saw as their works' very reason for being. Salvador Dali's images appear on mass-produced postcards in museum *tchotchke* shops; the galleries that hang René Magritte's paintings and the libraries that shelve nice editions of Paul Eluard's collected writings do not dream for a moment that these works will cause a stir. In other respects as well—its posturing as a political avant-garde, its "good-girls-like-bad-boys" approach to sexuality, its flirtation with the aesthetics of violence — surrealism is likely to appear as a movement that never had much backing it up.

Conclusions such as these are not so much wrong as overly convenient. Our intellectual routines parade themselves as the necessary conclusions of our judgment, and so we comfortably come to terms with everything about a movement *except* the movement: the suggestion (however crude, brutal, childish, or ultimately ineffective) of meaningful change.

I have no particular desire to praise surrealism, and I do not write about spiritualism because I "like" it; but I do want a critical practice that will not allow intellectual convenience or professional cynicism to set its agenda. Criticism should look to find its directions through the dissatisfactions, the possible *and* the impossible desires, through which culture is articulated as lived history. Then we may appreciate the conditions through which desire, possible and impossible, becomes desire; and we may then work our way toward an understanding of the politics of imagination and the demands of historical commitment. We should not expect a simplifying or transcendent order, then, but difficulties, contradictions, challenges, excesses, excuses, compromises, failures, arbitrary assertions . . . signs of movement, in movement. Signs that are not authoritative, signs that show up authority.

Since both were widely perceived as movements opposed to the dominant cultures of their day, spiritualism and surrealism might be seen as partaking of this critical attitude. Such a conclusion was suggested, for instance, by Crevel's praise of Dali:

> Dali specifies: "Idealists without participating in any ideal." This formula condemns idealist or matterist satisfactions that put all thought to sleep. Dialectical materialism, alone in rendering to notions the movement of which metaphysical analysis has defrauded them, sucks up this chloroform. Then, images and concepts to link up, to metamorphose, to collapse the water-tight bulkheads. Whence revolution in understanding, today the prelude, tomorrow (in virtue of the law of universal reciprocity that evades quibbles over causality and hides the shadow of details heaped up into obstacles) reflex-reflection of the living Revolution, of the lived Revolution.[24]

But what is revolutionary from one perspective may be conservative or reactionary from another, and the fact that a movement is marginalized or oppositional is certainly no guarantee that it will be particularly perceptive, productive, or kind. A movement can go backward as well as forward; and as I have noted, I do not address spiritualism and surrealism because I want either movement to appear especially likable, virtuous, or politically correct. What I do argue is that both movements, even and sometimes especially when they were most foolish, overweening, fraudulent, reprehensible, or unreasonable, had something meaningful to say about reason and the world of reason.

To put it simply, those involved in both movements recognized that reason had been oversold. But this is putting it much too simply. To stop at this point would be to overlook how reason was bound to be oversold because it was always as much overreaching desire as it was controlled logic and recorded experience. Although it may be pretty to think that we could separate "good reason" from "bad reason"—the reason that lives up to its ideal from that which is "misapplied" or "perverted"—such an approach will not do. Neither philosophical argument nor historical evidence (even assuming that we can separate the two) is able to justify this distinction. The possibility of doing so is an article of faith with many, but only an article of faith.

As an ideal, reason leads to its own undoing when it finds that its definitive rejection of dogma must finally disturb its reliance on experience because it cannot provide experience with a foundation, whether in essences, structures, or time, that is undogmatic. In other words, the motivating ideal of reason founders upon the demonstrable historicity of reason. Sooner or later, reason is driven back upon persuasion, logic upon rhetoric, fact upon value, truth upon sovereignty—at which point it turns out that these were not radically distinct in the first place. The differences between them can then be seen to be historically and materially, not logically or philosophically, justified. What reason comes to see (if I may continue for a moment with this personification) is that its motivation has never been innocent, neutral, universal, purely logical, or divine. It has been human; and like any other human invention, reason can always be translated from a given context to another and yet, for all of us, is always implicated in specific historical conditions, institutions, conflicts, experiences, and movements that are bound to make any translation also a betrayal. Reason has its ins and outs, and they are not always conscious of and consistent with each other. In any given moment, the principles of reason that are supposed to hang together and preserve each other—transcendence, universality, logical consistency, and so on—are just as likely to be at each other's throats, not even waiting for the enemy to hang them separately.

To say so is not to deny all that reason has done and can do. In the accomplishments of modern science and technology, in many modern institutions of education and medicine and law and polity, and in the lives of innumerable people who have felt that reason helped to emancipate them from local, traditional, accidental, or arbitrary constraints, the importance of reason is so obvious that I am embarrassed even to have to mention it. I do so only because any criticism that questions the historical claims of reason is liable to be perceived, in the present intellectual climate, as an "attack" on reason. Of course, this study is nothing of the kind. To attack reason one first must suppose that it is subject to attack: that it is something other than a rhetorical device, a personification, used to give a seeming unity to all sorts of cultural objects, forms, and practices that are ultimately incommensurable and irreducible to a common spirit. It makes no more sense to attack "reason," in the abstract, than it does to attack "humanity": what could one possibly mean?

The accusation of irrationalism is a way around the recognition of the historical, cultural, and political implications of reason. As Michel Foucault and others have argued, to assume that one who does not worship reason must necessarily be recommending irrationality is to adopt, unthinkingly, precisely the discourse of reason about which one is supposedly inquiring. Historically, this discourse has been defined, in part, through a distinction between reason and unreason in which the horrible (but also attractive) image of the latter term is premised upon the idealization of the former; so as long as one merely turns to irrationality, one is still supporting the transcendent figure of reason. As I shall argue, this consideration posed a problem for modern spiritualism and surrealism; but a problem faced by a movement should not be mistaken for the entire reality of that movement. Irrationality is reason's device, reason's game. To say that spiritualism and surrealism were irrational might be to blame or to praise them, depending on one's attitude; but in either case the attitude would be self-defeating, confined within the metaphysics of the rationalism it seems to be looking beyond. As in a Magritte canvas, one would see a window painted in the painted image of a wall and yet believe that one was looking through transparent window-panes to the assurance of a reality beyond representation.

But might this criticism be too convenient, too easy? Is there not a danger of "going native," as the English phrase so tellingly puts it? That is, a danger of adopting the values and practices of the subject from which one is supposed to keep a certain distance, the enabling distance of any critical perspective?

"Going native" is a paradoxical idiom. To the children of Western imperial adventure, it signifies its seeming opposite, "returning as an alien." A similar paradox lurks in the image of critical distance, for this distance is supposed to convey the truest intimacy with one's subject. The simplest answer to questions such as those above, then, is that they are logically incoherent. They cannot expect meaningful answers because they do not know what they are asking. These questions assume that we can have identification without differences, that we can know the alien and the native independently of each other; and these assumptions are contradicted in the very asking, which must rely on rhetorical devices such as paradox to do the work of reason that is supposed to be independent of such logically irresponsible vehicles. In figures such as "going native" or "critical distance," then, we may observe how the supposed clarity of reason may in fact be the opacity of the dogmatic word.

However, questions such as those I raised above are misguided in an even more basic way. Where they err most profoundly is in the assumption that at some time and place reason has actually lived up to its name, maintaining assured perspectives, distances, and distinctions. As Nietzsche argued, this assumption may be as central and as important to our lives as it is wholly unsupported by anything but our linguistic habits. This is another cause for thinking that the designation of irrationality is more convenient than illuminating when it is applied to cultural movements: because this term assumes that reason owns itself, is true to itself, professes itself, even though we can never find an exemplification of reason that is not haunted by an alien familiar, shadowed by a double identity, committed to its own usurpation in the form of an inevitably triumphing but eternally postponed ideal. Reason, it is fair to say, has always been in communication with ghosts. ("Making a picture," Max Ernst noted, "is like creating a ghost.")[25] Spiritualism and surrealism were movements that investigated this insistent strangeness and strange insistence of reason.

Therefore, it may be misleading to call modern spiritualism and surrealism "responses" or "alternatives" to reason. The problem with such terms is that they tend to characterize reason as a monolithic entity attacked from without when, in fact, these movements emerged at least as much "within" as "without" reason, challenging the very possibility of such a distinction. A better characterization would describe them as interpretations of reason; for this phrase suggests historical turnings, refigurations, without implying that reason need ever have had an original or singular direction, reflection, or "picture."

In social terms, this amounts to saying that spiritualism and surrealism were both defined, in part, through a struggle over the delineation of an "inside" and an "outside" in certain areas of culture—a struggle epitomized by the question of who would control the name and historical legacy of reason. In the introduction to his *Spiritualist Philosophy: The Spirits' Book*, which quickly became a definitive guide to French "spiritism," Hippolyte Léon Denizard Rivail made this struggle explicit:

He who believes his reason to be infallible is very near to error. Even those whose ideas are of the falsest profess to base them on reason. . . . They who formerly rejected the admirable discoveries that are the glory of the human mind did so in the name of reason; for what men call reason is often only pride disguised. . . .

Similarly, L. Alphonse Cahagnet commanded, "Let it not . . . be supposed that a clairvoyant who struggles at your feet is hallucinated; he is the centre of reason, while we stand around the circle." A comparable passage from the writings of the surrealists may be taken from Breton's essay, "The Crisis of the Object":

By applying the Hegelian adage, "All that is real is rational, and all that is rational is real," we can expect that rationality will match in every respect the course of reality. In effect, contemporary reason proposes nothing so much as the continual assimilation of the irrational, an assimilation during which rationality is called to a ceaseless reorganization of itself so that it may at once grow and be strengthened. Given this understanding, it must be said that *surrealism* is necessarily accompanied by a *surrationalism* that doubles and measures it.[26]

In challenging what they perceived as an institutionalized orthodoxy, and thus in seeking to grasp the role and even the name of reason for their own purposes, spiritualists and surrealists addressed reason as power, persuasion, and trope. Where the ideal of reason was supposed to stand, they saw the politics of reason; where reason was supposed to be law, they made room for invention, discovery, desire, and art; where nothing was supposed to be, they found meaning. The reason that others regarded as a commanding abstraction, they saw as sign, symbol, metaphor, icon; as lure, weapon, and prize; as wish, alienation, and uncanny compulsion; as the promise and frustration of the world.

To point out that reason is a word is not to say that it is "just a word." On the contrary, this gesture raises far-reaching questions as to how human beings are implicated in language. To say there is no absolute ground to reason, that reason in this sense is abyssal, is not to suggest that there is no ground at all. What this statement does mean is that all our knowledge, including even the most strictly articulated empirical findings, serves as knowledge only in respect to historically limited discourses and discursive conditions, which can be justified, demonstrated, and communicated in various ways but which can never be simply self-evident.

Inevitably, then, cultural movements that challenge what is taken to be knowledge will be inquiries into the situation, creation, and communication of meaning. These movements will be semiotic experiments. As such, some will be of more interest than others, depending on how and why we take them up; but it would indeed be stupidly prideful to see them only as instances of irrationality or nonsense.

In struggling over the name of reason, spiritualism and surrealism asked how communication works. They considered how things could come to have or to lose meaning. They sought to learn how words like "reason" get under our skin, into our very spirit . . . and how we may come to know, or fail to know, what a spirit is and why this word, spirit, may represent us, may even *be* us. It is not incidental to spiritualism that some of its critics saw its source in what they presumed to be an inherent weakness in the physiology of women;[27] similarly, it is important to remember that surrealism was inspired in large part by Freud's reconception of sexuality and remapping of the human body. As I will be concerned to show, these cultural movements responded to other identifiable forces, such as positivism, realism, and communism; but they also argued more generally over the definition of experience and reality. What we perceive was at stake in these movements, as well as how we perceive it and what we do with our perceptions. They were concerned with the life of our words, the intentions of our languages. They spoke to the history we are willing to recognize, the history that imposes upon us, and that which we may create anew. In this way they addressed the historical complexity of reason as philosophical conception, method of discovery, institutional understanding, discursive logic, popular image, and physical sense. Neither movement came close to addressing all that might be considered to fall under the history of reason (and I do not presume to be able to do better in this regard); but in the way they investigated reason, they explored important questions in science, philosophy, art, psychology, history, linguistics, and other fields of knowledge, including fields without a name.

To point out that reason is a word is to raise the question of culture, the question of human definition, without the assurance of a given answer. If individuals and movements are never totally free of this question (else we would be lusterless stones) and if no one can ever raise this question in a totally new way (since the price of this accomplishment would have to be a psychotic inaccessibility to history and communication), spiritualism and surrealism are still notable for their telling interrogation of the definitively modern faith in reason. Like dada, which Tristan Tzara once described as "a virgin microbe that insinuates itself, with the insistence of the air, into all the spaces that reason has not been able to stuff full of words or conventions,"[28] these movements sought for what reason had missed, for what was missing in reason or in "truth with its interminable procession/ of puerile evidence" (Eluard).[29] Neither movement could boast of any "serious" philosophers, as the academic locution would have it, but both were (in the academic phrase) "doing philosophy" in ways that posed a meaningful challenge to the sense of seriousness characteristic of intellectuals. This "sense," this way of perceiving, this meaning, this word . . . what was it, really? Was it really as pressing, as unavoidable, as necessary as it seemed?

Just as it would be misleading to characterize these movements as responses or alternatives to reason, so would it be confusing to characterize the groups involved as marginal, countercultural, or dissident parties, groups "out of the mainstream." To describe them in this way is to assume an assuredly dominant point of view, but one of the questions posed by these movements was whether orthodox reason and the dominant culture *were really there*. A popular charge against both movements was that their participants were too credulous (toward ghosts, dreams, magic, leaders . . .), but those involved in spiritualism and surrealism would quickly return the charge, arguing that it was the parties opposed to them who were overly credulous (toward science, the educational system, their senses, their leaders . . .). The debate was not an empty one: as I try to show in the chapters that follow, it communicated some of the most important turnings through which knowledge was implicated in belief, authority in history, language in human flesh, for those who lived within the societies in which these movements arose.

Reason (to return to the personification) wants to insist on its centrality even when it allows that human beings may be refractory in recognizing its rights. This consideration was recognized by J. B. Ferguson, a supporter of modern spiritualism, and by Ralph Waldo Emerson, a decided skeptic. In his *Spirit Communion*, adopting the voice of a "worthy and venerable friend," Ferguson told of the confidence reason had placed in itself, a confidence with which it tried to shove all else to the margins of being—until it had to confront the force of modern spiritualism:

> Before the rising sun of science, literature, and a superior knowledge of man's five-senses rationality, ghosts had been driven to the obscurity of the negro quarters, or had sought a retreat in the imperfectly developed craniums of a few of the old women of a rapidly-being-forgotten age. If they showed themselves by day, the intellectual beat their brains out with Scott's Demonology, and Abercrombie's Metaphysics, and Collier's Phrenology; and the multitude rehearsed anew the old horse, and goose, and cow tales. If they assailed the dull ear of night by unearthly noises, rats and moaning night-birds solved the mystery, and the ghost was laid forever and aye.

Although from an opposing standpoint, Emerson offered a very similar characterization of reason, in relation to which, he argued, spiritualism appeared as an alien, vulgar, destructive, and notably feminine "gypsy principle":

> The insinuation is that the known eternal laws of morals and of matter are sometimes corrupted or evaded by this gypsy principle, which chooses favorites, and works in the dark for their behalf; as if the laws of the Father of the universe were sometimes balked and eluded by a meddlesome Aunt of the universe for her pets. . . . It is a midsummer-madness, corrupting all who hold the tenet.[30]

Reason is proleptic as well as evangelical, as imperial in its promise as it is determinedly humble in any particular position or assertion; as Emerson says, it is patriarchal will, law, order; and so surrealism, like spiritualism, was likely to appear a negligible affair in relation to it. Consider only how easy it is to mock the grandiose ambitions of the surrealists from the standpoint of a historian today, for whom the movement may appear as the affair of a few excitable artists and intellectuals whose doings, in comparison to other events transpiring between the world wars, are very small potatoes indeed. Yet it was precisely this tendency to deny centrality to any experience that did not conform to the world of reason that spiritualism and surrealism both were determined to oppose. Participants in both movements asserted that the world was with them, and still with them no matter how many persons said otherwise, no matter how irrational such movements might seem. To measure the significance of these movements by an intellectual convenience such as "historical context" or "the judgment of history" is then to beg the question, for their greatest provocation was to propose that the world of reason, as it was commonly understood, was a construction relevant only to an extremely limited domain of human experience.

This book is an attempt to work through spiritualism and surrealism. It takes its title, *Abyss of Reason*, from Cahagnet, the nineteenth-century author of *The Secrets of the Future Life Unveiled* and other works on spiritualism; but as I have noted, I trust that this title also engages the concerns of contemporary criticism and theory. In writing of spiritualism and surrealism, I do not try to idealize these movements, to reflect upon them as objects of dispassionate scrutiny, or to trace their origins, growth, and decline. My aim has been to entertain their suggestiveness as cultural movements, to work through them in this sense, as opposed to thinking upon, about, against, or with them. However works of cultural criticism are presented, it seems to me that this is the approach taken by those I would emulate, by which I mean those that try to show us how a confrontation with the monsters and abysses of reason may lead us to discover other, more satisfying worlds in that which we call the world.

2

On the Dignity of Tables

The media *are, we understand, multiplying day by day to such an extent, that presently no live man will be sure of his side-board, and no dead man will be sure of his soul.*

We do not mean to speak too flippantly of what the very respectable media *will tell us we do not comprehend; and we only object to the matter that it takes off so much from the dignity of the spirits.*

Harper's (1852)[1]

Soon after modern spiritualism announced itself with the "Rochester knockings" of 1848, tables took on a new and controversial life. No longer were they content to live out their days impassively upholding dishes and glasses and silverware, vases, papers and novels, bibelots, elbows, or weary heads. They were changed: they began to move. Tables all over the United States and then in England, France, and other countries commenced rapping, knocking, tilting, turning, tipping, dancing, levitating, and even "thrilling"— though this last was uncommon. So Mrs. Sophia Elizabeth De Morgan said in her discussion of Daniel Dunglas Home, probably the most famous nineteenth-century medium:

It is only in Mr. Home's presence that I have witnessed that very curious appearance, or process, the *thrilling* of the table. This takes place for some seconds, perhaps more, before it rises from the floor. The last time I witnessed this phenomenon, an acute surgeon present said that this *thrilling*, the genuineness of which was unmistakable, was exactly like what takes place in that affection of the muscles called *subsultus tendinum*.[2]

And the tables did still more. Their actions were a language; and so they came to symbolize "the 'movement,' as it has been called,"[3] of modern spiritualism. Spirits had chosen the table as an organ of speech.

Customarily viewed as objects of economics, aesthetics, utility, diversion, tradition, or even theology (in the case of church artifacts), the tables of this age demanded a different kind of attention. After 1848, as Professor De Morgan joked in the preface to his wife's book, "London and Paris were running after tables in a new sense,"[4] not to gamble at them but to gambol with them. These things had become both exciting and disturbing. Whatever one might think about reports of spiritual communications, the conception of tables had changed. For spiritualists and their opponents alike, the table had become a moral object.

Only a few years ago, watching an interview on television, many of us laughed when Barbara Walters asked a famous actress to imagine her metamorphosis—if she were a tree, what kind would Katharine Hepburn be?—but at the time of which I write, hundreds of thousands were seriously arguing about what kind of persons tables might be. This was not the kind of argument that can be predicted, and it may be difficult for us today to imagine that it could ever have been proposed; and yet it was a real, passionate controversy, with a scope that extended from the outermost reaches of the universe into the very grain of the furniture in people's homes. For roughly thirty years, until spiritualism declined in the last two decades of the century, tables were burdened with a responsibility no one had ever before dreamed they might have. Their dignity was in question: their *human* integrity. Even people who refused to believe they spoke made tables responsible for the character they would have if they did speak.

This change in the table as an object of discourse might be insignificant if it concerned only an odd digression in cultural history called "modern spiritualism," a movement that could be regarded as a mere fad, something like the popular pastime of playing with hula hoops in the United States of the 1950s. However, this nineteenth-century table speaks of more than an old-fashioned "other world" historically distant from the beliefs that most of those reading this book will hold. This table is also a fable, a story of culture and its contending forces. It tells of historical conflicts over people, objects, words, and ways of thinking that have been extraordinarily influential and yet are apt to go unnoticed. Unlike the hula hoop, the nineteenth-century table was an extraordinarily provocative object; and by showing how controversial ordinary things could be, spiritualism exposed occult powers within many areas of nineteenth-century reason, including religion, science, art, education, and philosophy. Although Theodor Adorno has argued that human beings "do not possess dignity as they do furnishings,"[5] these nineteenth-century tables, when they were characterized in human terms, came to show how human beings are in a very real sense the findings, the divinings, of things.

To opponents of spiritualism, the table was *infra dig* as a medium for spiritual communications simply because it was such a commonplace piece of furniture. Although Alfred Tennyson attended seances and was very interested in spiritualism in his later years, this was the reason he opposed the belief of his brother, Frederick, on at least one occasion. "I am convinced," he said, "that God and the ghosts of men would choose something other than mere table-legs through which to speak to the heart of man."[6] More commonly, people showed their contempt for the movement by refusing even to care whether its phenomena were real. It was sufficient that the rappings and other manifestations were undignified; having established this point, one need say nothing more about them. Count Agenor de Gasparin was among those who were infuriated by this condescending argument, which, he argued, is really no argument — this "objection that is only an exclamation, a shrug of the shoulders."[7]

Anthony Trollope offered a polite version of this response in writing to a close friend, Kate Field, the lecturer, advocate of women's rights, and author of *Planchette's Diary*: "But when tables rap, and boards write, and dead young women come and tickle my knee under a big table, I find the manifestations to be unworthy of the previous grand ceremony of death."[8] Like Charles Dickens and George Eliot in England, Henry David Thoreau, Nathaniel Hawthorne, and Ralph Waldo Emerson in America were less restrained. Thoreau wrote to his sister of "spirits which the very bull-frogs in our meadows would blackball." "To hold intercourse with spirits of this order," said Hawthorne's Miles Coverdale, "we must stoop, and grovel in some element more vile than earthly dust." "Why look so wistfully in a corner?" Emerson asked; and he concluded, "These adepts have mistaken flatulency for inspiration."[9] For these writers the accusation of indignity was sufficient to explode the phenomena; and this way of thinking remained popular, appearing sometimes even in places where spiritualist hypotheses were given some credence, as one can see from Marie Corelli's *A Romance of Two Worlds*, which was published near the end of the century. ("Your reason will at once tell you that disembodied spirits never become so undignified as to upset furniture or rap on tables," says Heliobas, a medium, to Corelli's heroine.)[10] Harriet Martineau reported one version of a widespread jest that epitomizes this accusation of indignity: "An eminent literary man said lately that he never was afraid of dying before; but that he now could not endure the idea of being summoned by students of spirit-rapping to talk such nonsense as their ghosts are made to do."[11] In a different sense than the spiritualists intended, this popular movement must have seemed heaven-sent to Mortimer Thomson, the American humorist, who promptly dispatched Q. K. Philander Doesticks and his friends, Bull Dogge and Damphool, to attend a seance. "Being sated with the ordinary common-place things of every-day life," reported Doesticks, tongue ostentatiously in cheek, "and having heard a great deal about the mysterious communications telegraphed to this, our ignorant sphere, by wise and benignant spirits of bliss, through the dignified medium of old chairs, wash-stands, and card-tables, we three . . . determined to put ourselves in communication with the next world. . . . "[12]

The irony in all this is that tables ceased to be ordinary as soon as they were accused of being so. If anything is ordinary, it is that which goes without saying. Therefore, what is ordinary is wholly imaginary and yet as material as tables or, say, the acoustic waves that create the sound of rapping in human ears. The ordinary is the background or the frame that encloses consciousness without itself seeming to suffer enclosure. In this respect it is the invisible agency of meaning—that dubious spirit—and any scrutiny is bound to transform it, subtly or dramatically, into something else. Even the very fact that it is subjected to scrutiny shows that a change in the object has occurred. In a sense it *has* moved, regardless of its physical placement or stability, for it has *drawn attention*.

In this situation, in which the ordinary turns remarkable, the representational status of objects is strikingly demonstrated; and perhaps more clearly than anywhere else, it is in such demonstrations (or "*demon*strations")[13] that social struggles are recorded. Certainly the implications of such struggles in modern spiritualism did not go unnoticed. Although John Tyndall, the scientist, could compare "the degrading spiritualistic phenomena" to Frankenstein's monster without seeming to remember all the furious criticisms of familial relations, scientific self-absorption, and political and economic affairs that Mary Shelley had made her creature articulate, not everyone was so obtuse.[14] For instance, one Calvinist divine argued that the spiritualists intended "to inaugurate the vile sentiments of Tom Paine, his compeers and pilferers, as the only true principles compatible with the 'rights of man'" and thus "to effect radical changes in the *social and commercial world*."[15]

The table that can become an image of degradation has entered into relations very different from those customary to it. For many opponents of spiritualism, this change violated boundaries or upset categories. Institutions were confounded—church, home, clinic, laboratory, court of law—as angels spoke to humankind, issued information and regulations, blessed sensitive individuals with the power of healing, solicited experiments and testimony, and claimed to represent natural law as surely as Michael Faraday's theory of electromagnetism. Varieties of discourse were promiscuously exchanged: sacred, sentimental, philosophical, conversational, literary, you name it, all tossed higgledy-piggledy together in spiritualists' speeches, tracts, books, and newspapers. In *The Spiritualists and the Detectives*, Allan Pinkerton emphasized this aspect of the movement when he described Mrs. Winslow, a supposed medium, "mingling her vile catch-words with scraps of spiritualistic sayings, snatches of holy songs, couplets of roystering ballads, and crowning the hideousness of the whole with countless Bible quotations."[16] His characterization was tendentious, but it could not be said to be entirely inaccurate as a representation of the spiritualists' usual style. (Writing to Robert Owen, the industrialist and socialist, Samuel Clarke of Beaverton, Illinois told of "a divine spiritual influence," of the "holy and true," of "beautiful visions," and then concluded bathetically, "You have pain in your right side, extending from the liver to the kidney, rather acute, just above the hips, and so in your spinal column, the calf of your leg aches—with a curious sensation about the ears"—to which Owen solemnly appended the note, when he published the letter in his *Millenial Gazette*, "It is true I had this pain in the right side and the sensation in the left leg.")[17] Rhetorically and otherwise, the spiritualist movement put conventional forms of authority into question while raising into prominence unlettered Americans, hysterical girls, charlatans, pretenders, "low adventurers,"[18] all sorts of shady characters usually expected to remain in the background of society. Compared by Reuben Briggs Davenport to the "bastard faith" of Islam,[19] spiritualism was compared by others to the infamous cult of Mormonism, as it was termed, and to other outbreaks of beliefs presumed to be alien, unnatural, lascivious, or in some other wise intolerable.

The sense of taste was assaulted at every turn. Even the most ordinary of practices could come to seem extraordinary in the context of these phenomena. ("The most interminable game at beggar-my-neighbor," wrote Henry Morley in Dickens's *Household Words*, "is not half so dull and stupid as the knocking out of long and foolish sentences from the A. B. C. D. card of a Rapper.")[20] To those most struck by the sense of degradation, the entire world might seem to have been turned upside-down by "this spiritual carnival,"[21] as when Faraday wrote to the *Times* to complain of people who refer "to the rotation of the earth, as if the earth revolved round the leg of a table."[22] There was no telling to what ends this movement might go. "Fathers and mothers," exclaimed a M. Bonjean, "if you do not desire to develop premature feelings in your daughters, husbands who regard the peace of your wives, *be mistrustful of the magnetic chain in general*, and of the dancing of tables in particular."[23] If less apocalyptic than Bonjean's, Henry James's characterization of the movement in *The Bostonians* was just as certain of its vulgarity and perversity (despite the fact that the elder Henry James had been strongly influenced by Emanuel Swedenborg's mysticism as well as by the socialisms of Owen and Charles Fourier).

The problem was not that the supernatural was sacrosanct. In literature alone it had played wildly varied roles in the hundred years preceding the birth of modern spiritualism. In works like Horace Walpole's *Castle of Otranto* and Matthew Lewis's *The Monk*, it was dramatized as an exotic mystery; in Ann Radcliffe's Gothic novels, in which spirits always turn out to be natural phenomena mistakenly apprehended, it was rationalized. Like others of the romantics, Walter Scott subscribed to reason and yet exploited irrational superstitions to provide his work with the *frisson* of romance; and as modern spiritualism was making its existence known, George Eliot was treating the supernatural as an entirely historical phenomenon and thus making it the subject of psychological study. As even this cursory inventory should be sufficient to indicate, spiritualism was not upsetting simply because it played fast and loose with traditional conceptions of the supernatural.

The reason must be found elsewhere. What distinguished modern spiritualism, what made it so controversial, is the way it vulgarized the supernatural and everything pertaining to it. Spiritualists turned nature, the supernatural, human beings, and the entire universe into public scenes unregulated by social and sacramental conventions.[24] They found unmediated truth in objects and other phenomena accessible to all. (Someone named Henry Novra even published a book called *Spirit Rapping made Easy*.)[25] This is the great pathos of modern spiritualism, which made it intolerable to so many: that immediacy should be so ordinary, so graceless, nothing more than common life. It was revelation on the cheap, and one might so describe it and provoke no dissent from believers. As Novra suggested, this movement was unapologetically *easy*. (Speaking of the process involved in materializing a spirit, a guardian angel in Florence Marryat's *The Dead Man's Message* says, "It is very easy"; it is "only like turning on an electric light, and turning it off again.")[26] Spiritualism brought "the knowledge that immortality means no gauzy abstraction, but *real human* life."[27]

Spiritualists did not think communication a simple thing; their literature bulged with theories about the myriad ways messages between living people and those on the other side might go astray or fall prey to misinterpretation, ambiguity, and outright fraud. Nonetheless, this movement did give access to communication to virtually everyone, and on the simplest of terms. In fact, having first become popularized in the United States, spiritualism was often seen as being stamped with the principles, or the excesses, of this nation; as in the wordplay of a believer of the 1890s, spiritualism was "democratic" because it could be "demonstrated to anyone."[28] With a quasi-Pentecostal trust, spiritualists often remarked that any group of six or eight people who gathered together regularly would find that at least one of them was a medium and so would receive otherworldly communications.

In this movement ultimate reality was a rap on a table or a popular tune played on the accordion. It abandoned traditional conceptions of sublimity, although it still might trade on this discourse; and it shrugged off the intense practices involved in discerning and examining the state of one's soul. Everything was brought to the surface, as in a painting whose frame dissolves into the picture even as the picture is absorbed into the world beyond the frame. The result, as Hawthorne put it, was "a sentimental surface with no bottom beneath it."[29] In effect, spiritualism guaranteed familiarity no matter whence one approached it and no matter how unlooked-for its manifestations might be. This reassuring familiarity-in-strangeness is nicely captured in R. Laurence Moore's comment that many spiritualists "seemed to be greatly relieved to learn that spirits wore clothes."[30] Epes Sargent took it to be a proof of spiritualism that a spirit, during a seance, had "been known to cut its finger with a knife, then to borrow a handkerchief to wind around the wound, and, at the end of the sitting, to return the handkerchief marked with blood";[31] not for a moment did he suspect that this plain evidence might be turned against his position.

It seemed that spiritualism (or spiritism, the preferred term for the French version) positively encouraged vulgarity. Speaking through Home, Dr. John Elliotson, the recently deceased scientist and mesmeric experimenter, described the human spirit as "a jack-in-the-box"; and this image, which he admitted was "very homely,"[32] marks the usual style of spiritualist practices. In enumerating the spiritualist phenomena in America that preceded the Fox sisters' discoveries, William Howitt did not hesitate to include among their number "the Kentucky Jerks."[33] Before one of the three university commissions that investigated the phenomena in the United States, spirits at one seance could not manage to say much more than "Hello folks," "Oh I am a big slugger," and "How is your nose Doc."[34] In some seances, as with the Davenport brothers, spirits not only talked but also ate and drank with notable gusto; the spirits that spoke during Home's trances were given to saying, "When Daniel recovers give him some bottled porter!"[35] The spirits were simply heedless of decorum: in the period before Madame Blavatsky abjured spiritualism in favor of theosophy, the powers in her presence once embarrassed a lady by rapping on her false teeth.[36]

Although spiritualism soon developed (as the contemporary idiom would have it) far beyond its initial knockings, with the popularizing of spirit cabinets in the late 1860s and with materializations of entire persons in the succeeding decade, it never achieved greater dignity. All its paraphernalia of tables, cabinets, ropes, bells, slates, planchettes, musical instruments, megaphones, pencils, curtains, robes, turbans, drapery, and darkness only stuck it all the more tightly to the trivial surfaces of things. "They move chairs, &c.; but it is nowhere suggested that the mediums move furniture half as well as day-laborers and porters," wrote one commentator.[37] Satirizing this diminution of the sublime, Robert Browning, a long-suffering witness to his wife's enthusiasm, had "Mr. Sludge, 'The Medium,'" say, "We find great things are made of little things, / And little things go lessening till at last / Comes God behind them."[38]

By making the most trivial objects resound with portentous significance, spiritualism made common experience the measure and limit of every cultural pretension. Everyday things become the ultimate texts, texts of the ultimate. Thus, after listing the various kinds of spiritual knockings he had heard, Adin Ballou wrote, "And I am as certain that these sounds were not made by any conscious mortal agency, as I am of the best authenticated facts in the common transactions of life."[39] It might seem paradoxical, then, that outsiders and opponents were wont to seize on the freakishness of spiritualist manifestations: all those speaking tables, writings appearing out of nowhere, bodies possessed by ghostly controls, turtles and freshly cut flowers dropping into locked rooms, departed spirits tugging on gentlemen's trousers. These critics laughed, however, only because the manifestations were not marvelous enough. They seemed ridiculous, not marvelous, because they insisted on clinging to common objects such as tables, turtles, and trousers. More incredible than the Ultramontane Catholic, said George Beard, is "the victim of dark *séances*, where a slight movement of the hand, or a well-directed kick, would reveal, even to a non-expert, the baldness, the grotesqueness, and vulgarity of the performance."[40]

Occultists agreed at least in this respect with those who criticized spiritualism on scientific or commensensical grounds. By regarding condescendingly what they took to be the puerilities or ignorant misapprehensions of spiritualism, Madame Blavatsky, Edward Bulwer-Lytton, Éliphas Lévi, and other nineteenth-century occultists prepared the way for William Butler Yeats to complain that it was too "vague and obvious" in its faith, not "incredible" enough; and so he wrote disparagingly of "the women speaking unknown tongues, the barbers and weavers expounding Divine revelation with all the vulgarity of their servitude, the tables that move or respond with raps."[41] In his fifteenth-century *Oration on the Dignity of Man*, Pico della Mirandola had been concerned to maintain the philosophical and religious traditions separating profane from esoteric knowledge; and when the dignity of tables became an issue in the nineteenth century, a similar concern was involved. It is significant in this respect that nineteenth-century spiritualists would often explicitly contrast their movement's democratic orientation to the more hierarchical, insular, and dictatorial forms of occult movements.[42] While spiritualists quarreled with some of their opponents over the grounds of middle-class respectability, this related conflict was played out in the relations between spiritualism and occultism. To a traditional model of judgment, which favored a social and cultural elite, spiritualism opposed the demotic forms of judgment seemingly encouraged by this increasingly middle-class age. To the critics of spiritualism, the idea that such a profane, lawless knowledge could be professed in the modern world was simply staggering.

Spiritualism admitted the existence of another world, but there was nothing new in this idea. Nor was there anything new in an attention to humble objects, which one could find in the practices of several Catholic and Protestant movements, including the more classic spiritualism of the Swedenborgian New Church.[43] The controversy over modern spiritualism grew so fierce only because of the unsettling irony that this movement's adherence to the surface of things was radically opposed to the everyday world—the human world—the world supposed to guarantee meaning. This movement made spiritual ideas speak through the stupidest objects and people while at the same time suggesting that this ordinary world, the world that goes without saying, might actually be unreliable and disoriented: a world, in Emerson's outraged conclusion, with "no police, no foot-rule, no sanity, —nothing but whim and whim creative."[44]

If you take the world to be capable of such surprises, you may or may not believe in John Jones's account of his "SHELL BATTERY" or in Dr. William Gregory's report of a discovery in animal sympathy that resulted in a "projected Snail Telegraph, or, as it is called by the inventors, the Pasilalinic

Telegraph";[45] but you will find nothing laughable on the surface of these things. If you reject this attitude, as the extensive literature that treated spiritualism as an occasion of comedy attests, any association with this movement will appear unbearably low, in all senses of the word, despite all the eminent people who identified themselves with it. And of course there were many notable people on the spiritualist roll call, even if one follows the usual practice of dismissing Robert Owen as a man in his dotage: Elizabeth Barrett Browning, Laurence Oliphant, Alfred Russel Wallace, Harriet Beecher Stowe, Mary Todd Lincoln, William Lloyd Garrison, Victor Hugo, Alexander Dumas *père*, Emperor Napoleon III and Empress Eugénie, Tsar Alexander II, and many others. If one adds those who were at least half-believers, such as William Thackeray, John Ruskin, William James, and Elizabeth Stuart Phelps, the list gets even longer; and the list of those who attended seances encompasses staunch unbelievers such as George Eliot and T. H. Huxley along with others as diverse as Queen Victoria and Frederick Douglass.

Mark Twain was infuriated by the sickly sweet vision of heaven popularized by Elizabeth Stuart Phelps in *The Gates Ajar* (a book that led some to claim her unequivocally for the spiritualist ranks), but the judgment that sentimentality is a kind of weakness is not self-evident. In fact, spiritualism could be described as the courage to reject orthodox faith in favor of sentimental knowledge. While spiritualism may be seen as growing out of other popular movements — phrenology, mesmerism, millenarianism, and, especially in the United States, the reaction against Calvinism — it was distinguished even from this background by its claim to a form of communication available to all and dependent on no authority beyond its public manifestations. Spiritualism had its mediums, but they were not looked upon as interpretive authorities. In this regard they differed from the teachers of phrenology and mesmerism as much as they did from orthodox religious leaders. Mediums were characterized above all else by their passivity and unconsciousness. Any role beyond this was only in the nature of imparting tradecraft ("three knocks mean yes," "the spirits find darkness more congenial," "unbelievers disturb the harmony of the group"). Interpretation had no place; public experience was everything. One of the most common moves in spiritualist rhetoric was to say that one did not urge others to believe anything: one simply urged them to investigate for themselves.

This aspect of spiritualism may seem to parody the science of the day, with its emphasis on physics and physical experiments. Spiritualism took its name from its opposition to materialism, and many spiritualists did claim that they were dealing with discoveries in natural law and that scientists who disdained them were neglecting their own principles. More was at stake, however, as some on both sides of the issue recognized. After all, at the same time as it challenged science, this movement might also be seen as mocking the sentimentality to be found in the fiction of Dickens, Eliot, and yes, even Twain. Spiritualists would sometimes cite death scenes in Dickens's works in support of their own experiences; and considering how thoroughly Dickens loathed spiritualism, is it possible to distinguish this homage from infuriating satire? Dickens likes ghost stories, complained Elizabeth Barrett Browning, "as long as they are impossible."[46]

The spiritualist rejection of faith went beyond orthodox religion, aesthetic privilege, and scientific belief. It was a threat to the very notion of culture, and at just the time when it had become peculiarly vulnerable as a result of middle-class questioning of the traditional liberal arts as the foundation of knowledge and values. It threatened culture by insulting one of the most dramatic developments in nineteenth-century social history: the incipient professionalism of science, medicine, education, and the arts. The *nouveau sage* in these fields, who wanted to codify them in the modern form of natural law and rational organization, was troubled, on the one hand, by the traditional educated elite and, on the other, by unprofessional members of the middle classes. Brian Wynne has described the conflict between the Cambridge physicists and other scientists in this era, in which the Cambridge party, with its social base among the upper classes, disputed with the utilitarians and the professionalizers "the authority to socially interpret reality for society at large";[47] and spiritualism was another party to this dispute, coming at the professionalizers from within their own household, as it were, and thus virtually asking to be stigmatized as a vulgar and backward force.

In this respect, although the parallel is by no means exact, one might compare this treatment of spiritualism to the reception given Gustave Courbet's art at about the same time. Courbet, too, was often castigated for the supposed vulgarity of his work, which, like the claims of the spiritualists, was deliberately fashioned to oppose established notions of propriety. And just as many spiritualists saw their faith as part of a general movement of reform, so did Courbet conceive of his art in terms of socialist beliefs. It might seem perverse thus to link the great nineteenth-century realist with the spiritualist movement, which developed in explicit opposition to realist aesthetics; but as I will argue, one of the telling features of the history of spiritualism is the way it may lead us to see a curious intimacy between realism and anti-realism in nineteenth-century culture, as in the friendship between Courbet and Charles Baudelaire, or as in the relation between the scientist, William Crookes, and the spirit, Katie King.

The associations between spiritualism and other nineteenth-century movements — abolitionism, Fourierism, campaigns for women's rights, and so on — are apt to overshadow this more obscurely identified connection with professionalism, as they do in Artemus Ward's comic description of the crowd at a convention of free lovers: "They was likewise spirit rappers and high presher reformers on gineral principles."[48] However, the conflict with professionalism may have a greater political importance, since it involves the centralization and bureaucratization of knowledge that characterizes all

modern states.[49] To some extent, this conflict had been rehearsed by mesmerists and other unorthodox practitioners of science in the late eighteenth and
early nineteenth centuries, when they complained about the bigotry of the
established academies; and it is important to note that many spiritualists
had experimented with animal magnetism and similar phenomena before
devoting themselves to the other world. However, the new impetus toward
professionalism, as it was coupled with an increasing demand for widespread
and scientifically grounded systems of education, gave this complaint about
exclusionary practices a focus that was at once more specific and more wide-
ranging in its application.

For this reason, despite the differences in their social origins and ideological conclusions, we find agreement on this point between Faraday, the com-
moner ("I think the system of education that could leave the mental condition
of the public body in the state in which this subject has found it must
have been greatly deficient in some very important principle"), and Tolstoy's
well-born hero in *Anna Karenina* ("'My opinion,' answered Levin, 'is only
that this table-rapping simply proves that educated society — so-called — is
no higher than the peasants'").[50] Both recognized that modern spiritualism
challenged the very organization of meaning in modern life, which was coming to be determined by the relations between a nation's system of education
and its other institutions. Even as traditional Christianity was becoming a
shaky ground, a new faith was being demanded by professionals and experts
and by the assumptions from which they derived their authority — assumptions that were as invisible as ghosts to most people. Hence Wallace's argument, which bears some resemblance to discussions of the nature of certainty
in Ludwig Wittgenstein's later works:

> The almost universal belief in gravitation and the undulatory theory of light does
> not render them in any degree more probable, because very few indeed of the
> believers have tested the facts which most convincingly demonstrate those theories,
> or are able to follow out the reasoning by which they are demonstrated. It is for
> the most part a blind belief accepted upon authority. But with these spiritual
> phenomena the case is very different. They are to most men so new, so strange, so
> incredible, so opposed to their whole habit of thought, so apparently opposed to
> the pervading scientific spirit of the age, that they cannot and do not accept them
> on second-hand evidence, as they do almost every other kind of knowledge.[51]

Emerson wrote very much to the point when he noted that the "supposed
power" of spiritualism "is not the power to which we build churches, or
make liturgies and prayers, or which we regard in passing laws, or found
college professorships to expound."[52] And yet, as Ann Braude notes, Emerson's opposition to spiritualism was particularly ironic in light of the fact
that this movement drew many of its followers from those who had once
flocked to his inspiring lectures.[53]

Even where professionalism tended not to be explicitly codified, as in the arts, a quite elaborate faith was demanded in the understanding of tradition, of the spirit of the author's work, of taste, and of similar critical articles. "The responsibility of the writer becomes heavier and heavier — does it not? — as the world grows older and the voices of the dead more numerous," wrote George Eliot, who would not countenance spiritual communications except through the medium of the philosophical history she made into the stuff of her art.[54] Possessing this kind of faith, opponents of spiritualism laughed at the "noodles and ninny-hammers"[55] who disseminated the posthumous scribblings of writers like Benjamin Franklin and Percy Bysshe Shelley (particularly busy spooks at the time); rejecting it, spiritualists accepted the writings and the signatures that they saw on the table in front of them. For what could be more real than these if one considered, as did J. B. Ferguson, that "tables, chairs, crockery, carpets and the like are not to be dosed by doctors, nor converted, nor terrified by clergymen, nor reasoned with by philosophers, nor ridiculed by any body. They do not care for drugs, nor theologies, nor rationales, nor public opinion."[56] In responding to the accusation of indignity (as Ferguson was in this passage), one might argue that it was actually the spirits' cleverness to recognize that dignity, especially in its professional form, was an elaborate apparatus designed to delude humanity. It is within this crucial conflict over professionalism that it becomes possible to understand why popular stereotypes so frequently highlighted the association between the believers in spiritualism and socialist, feminist, and abolitionist reform movements. These other movements were likely to be seen — for instance, by the younger Henry James — as equally undignified in their own right; and so the stereotype developed even though the association of spiritualists with these other movements was frequent but by no means universal. It was not for nothing that the author of *Lucy Boston: Or, Woman's Rights and Spiritualism*, drew a parallel between the two movements in his subtitle as "the two greatest humbugs of modern times."[57] Nor is it insignificant that this work features among its characters a racist caricature of a black female servant.

Immanuel Kant, who in his younger days wrote a treatise arguing against belief in ghosts, also had something to say in his mature work about the multitudes who could be expected to resist the professional discipline and the systematic grounding of empiricism that he conceived his work to represent. Though antedating the spiritualist movement, his analysis bears quoting at some length, for it lays out very clearly the attitudes with which the spiritualists would have to contend. What should be observed is that even though Kant accuses the common crowd of an error, "transcendental dogmatism," which he elsewhere argues to be characteristic of virtually all philosophers before his "Copernican revolution," he does not conclude, as one reasonably might, that these people, like philosophers, need to rethink their approach to things. Instead, he offers a description of the emotional or motivating ground [*Bewegungsgrund*] of the crowd—a description that tells us more, perhaps, about the territory that this philosopher sought to occupy.

It may seem "very extraordinary," Kant begins,

> that empiricism should be utterly unpopular. We should be inclined to believe, that the common understanding would receive it with pleasure—promising as it does to satisfy it without passing the bounds of experience and its connected order; while transcendental dogmatism obliges it to rise to conceptions which far surpass the intelligence and ability of the most practiced thinkers. But in this, in truth, is to be found its real motive. For the common understanding thus finds itself in a situation where not even the most learned can have the advantage of it. If it understands little or nothing about these transcendental conceptions, no one can boast of understanding any more; and although it may not express itself in so scholastically correct a manner as others, it can busy itself with reasoning and arguments without end, wandering among mere ideas, about which one can always be very eloquent, because we know nothing about them; while, in the observation and investigation of nature, it would be forced to remain dumb and to confess its utter ignorance. Thus ease [*Gemächlichkeit*] and vanity form of themselves strong recommendations of these principles. . . . And, at last, all speculative interests disappear before the practical interests which [the common understanding] holds dear; and it fancies that it understands and knows what its necessities and hopes incite it to assume or to believe. Thus the empiricism of transcendentally idealizing reason is robbed of all popularity; and, however prejudiced it may be to the highest practical principles, there is no fear that it will ever pass the limits of the schools, or acquire any favour or influence in society or with the multitude.[58]

It should be noted first how Kant simply assumes that education will continue to be confined to a privileged few, for this uncritical conception indicates the kind of "practical interests" that the philosopher, like the people of whom he writes, confuses with truth. In imagining the emotional grounds of the popular mentality, Kant blithely ignores the historical and institutional grounds of his own work. Second, note that he does *imagine* the common mind, even though he presents his description as if it ought to be the outcome of empirically tested experience. To put it simply, Kant argues against dogmatic theories by offering the same and thus undoes his argument for reason in the very act of articulating it. (It pays to remember Nietzsche's taunting analysis: "Kant wanted to prove, in a way that would dumbfound the common man, that the common man was right: that was the secret joke of his soul.")[59] Third, Kant imagines the common mind as being preoccupied with the concerns of power, prestige, and rank, which are assumed to corrupt a properly philosophical orientation—"robbing" it of popularity—even though Kant's work in its entirety suggests that these concerns exterior to the school walls have formerly been inside them and continue to inhabit them even to the present day, insofar as students and faculty do not immediately accept the justice of his *Critique*. This is only one of many respects in which Kant's conception of philosophical discipline can be seen as failing to deny its relationship to "practical interests." Finally, it is notable that Kant imagines the popular mind as being captivated by a desire for ease, for in this characterization he translates what might be an active opposition, resistance, or alternative to academic authority into a directionless passivity, which later in the century might well be criticized as excessive "sentimentality." In its emphasis on the people's practical interests and on their desire for advantage, his own description tends to contradict his suggestion that the wish for mere "ease" is behind this popular way of thinking; but this concept of ease serves a crucial rhetorical function for Kant, since it effectively strips away not only empirical truth but also any meaning from the thinking of most people, which then in fact seems less like thinking than like the movement of animal impulses.

Of course, one must be careful in relating Kant's argument to spiritualism. The most obvious complication is that spiritualists generally contended that they were, in fact, committed to experience and empirical tests. Nonetheless, Kant's characterization of the common understanding is significant for the way it anticipated the shape of the debates around spiritualism, especially as the power of articulation and the articulation of power would be thematized around the centers of personal character, social tone, professional authority, rhetorical persuasion, and undisciplined desire.

The issue was the power of meaning. What "spirits" would be allowed to have meaning and what would their designated media be in this modern age, when the spirits of science, of reason, of progress, and of various other agencies were accepted with much less controversy than the spirits of the dead? "In private conversation," argued a writer in a spiritualist journal, scientific investigators "adopt the idioms of Spiritualists, and unwittingly give expression to the fact that they entertain the same convictions as to the existence of spirits, their agency as mediums, and their communion with those in the flesh."[60]

Keenly perceiving, but rejecting, the spiritualist emphasis on the surface of things, Wilhelm Wundt recalled that "scientific authority is not a property which [can] be set down in the description of a person."[61] To scientists' demands for competent and expert witnesses, though, spiritualists responded with demands for the recognition of the respectability of their witnesses. Of Faraday's critical letter on this subject to the *Times*, Elizabeth Barrett Browning commented that it simply ignored the facts—a contention that is unassailable, as Katherine H. Porter commented, "if one accepts her concept of a fact as something told by a person whom she trusted."[62] This kind of response, which in its most egregious form led to the spiritualist habit of listing the aristocratic personages who had shown favor to their cause, had obvious limitations, especially if one was concerned to link spiritualism to other "progressive" causes. Those willing to argue that spiritualism "will not molest Mr. [sic] Grundy in the smallest degree, and that all spiritualists who think it will do so, are mere excrescences on the great body of 'respectable' spiritualists,"[63] would tend to make this movement the stuff of parlor games and timid little bookshops instead of the motivation for imaginative criticism and cultural revision that it could sometimes be. Nonetheless, there was a critical movement even in this appeal to respectability insofar as this served to combat the assumed authority of those individuals who, like Kant, thought they could simply dismiss from meaning any testimony that did not fit their specifications for truth. As a long-term strategy, the appeal to respectability was certainly self-defeating; but it was understandable in a cultural context in which truth was conceived to bear an intimate relationship to the capacity for pitying condescension, as in Kant's work or (to leap across space, time, and genre) James Russell Lowell's "The Unhappy Lot of Mr. Knott," which characterized the common understanding by saying, "Each of the miscellaneous rout / Brought his, or her, own little doubt, / And wished to pump the spirits out, / Through his or her own private spout / Into his or her decanter."[64] To measure the full force of this condescension, its essential imbrication with the establishment of reason, and the implications of this relation for the phenomena of the spiritualist movement, one need only contrast the massively patronizing characterization of women in Kant's *Anthropology* to the role of women among spiritualists, who accepted them as mediums and often linked their spiritual powers to a concern with women's suffrage, the right to divorce, and similar causes.

Spiritualists contested the professional spirit of authority by appealing to the public and to public experience, and they went still further. Emma Hardinge Britten complained of "the persistent opposition directed against this movement from the enemies who may be classified as the would-be monopolists of all knowledge, in religion, science, and literature." Andrew Jackson Davis specifically instanced lawyers, physicians, and clergymen as characters inimical to a spiritualized society (although he did offer hope for their eventual reform). Charles Hammond said that not only preachers, "but lawyers, doctors, schools, colleges, and books, are wrong." Dr. John Ashburner inveighed against "the dictators of science in England" and "the narrow bigotry of professional cliques"; L. Alphonse Cahagnet referred to people "too educated to descend to such beliefs" as he represented.[65] After records of experiments that suggested the reality of spiritualistic phenomena had been published by "Professor Zöllner, the well-known excellent astrophysicist" and other academic colleagues, Dr. Hermann Ulrici of the University of Halle was prepared to admit that spiritualism "had achieved the dignity of a scientific question";[66] but most spiritualists were not about to stand around waiting for such a go-ahead.

Yet this was not a know-nothing movement. When advocates like Davis and Cahagnet boasted of their humble selves, it was only to establish the supernatural credentials of their communications by seeming to eliminate the possibility of imposture. As a movement, spiritualism was opposed to both professionalism and common sense. This was what was so distinctive about its vulgarity, and so frustrating to its opponents: that it would not respond to reason because it claimed to represent reason. It used the rhetoric of enlightenment in the service of a cause that appeared as the opposite of enlightenment, as superstitious prejudice, to those who claimed to be the spiritual heirs of Bacon, Descartes, Locke, Kant, and Voltaire. In doing so it exposed reason as an apparatus of institutions, traditions, texts, practices, personal relationships, and common sense that was unified and coherent only as long as it was represented as an imperceptible spirit. Spiritualism had to be rejected as an indignity because otherwise it would utter, write, rap, or in some other way say "reason." It would show the meaning reason could not bear: the meaning of its own social existence and power.

To be sure, many people simply concentrated on unmasking spiritualist fraud or, like G. H. Lewes, on explaining the errors in reasoning that lent credence to the "base and debasing" practices of this movement.[67] The general insistence on the unbearable indignity of the movement, however, indicates that the organization of meaning was an issue more important than the question of how far the phenomena were genuine. Although on one occasion he devised a test to unmask Mrs. Hayden, even Lewes did not really concern himself with the question of truth or falsity: he simply pointed out that proper evidence and scientific procedure were wanting. Lewes then saw fit to characterize Mrs. Hayden, the medium famous for being the first to come to England, as speaking of the spirits "without awe, but with implicit confidence—as if they had been pet monkeys"; and yet this way of speaking, which made Mrs. Hayden an object of disdain to Lewes, was precisely what spiritualists celebrated. Newton Crosland wrote, "When we asked the spirits why they manifested themselves by moving tables, their answer was significant and in these words: 'If we came with more solemnity, we should awe you too much.'" Crosland went on to ask, "Who among us shallow mortals can venture to decide what is or is not consistent with angelic dignity?"[68]

The issue was how, when, and where communication would be allowed to take place and would be granted the power of meaning. This issue was marked on the one hand by the objection that spiritualist communications were improper and, on the other, by the diversion of communication from its ordinary practices and media into trance utterances, the rapping out of words letter by letter, automatic writing, spirit drawing, the "psychographic" inscription of stigmata in human flesh, and similar performances.[69] Spiritualism was bending discourse into forms at once bizarre and reassuring, into familiarity-in-strangeness, at the very time when professionals were insisting that their practices aspire to a disinterested and neutral form, as in the artistic code of realism that Lewes and George Eliot, among others, were helping to promulgate. And while this relation to professionalism does not exhaustively explain spiritualism, it does become especially important when one considers the way spiritualist communications would be characterized in relation to ordinary language. The choice of anecdotes was significant when John Nevil

Maskelyne, the magician, ridiculed seances by describing how "a 'control,' in answer to the question, 'Are you the spirit of Lindley Murray?' shall reply 'I are,' to the immense satisfaction of the faithful."[70] Spiritualism was suspect because it was thought to be wrong, but more importantly because it upset linguistic as well as other social and ideological relations.

Earlier in the nineteenth century, in criticizing the supposed certainty of sense experience and the assumptions of phrenology, Hegel had anticipated some of the major issues involved in modern spiritualism. "They speak of the 'existence' of external objects," he wrote,

> which can be more precisely characterized as actual, absolutely particular, wholly personal, individual things, each of them not like anything or anyone else; this is the existence which they say has absolute certainty and truth. They "mean" this bit of paper I am writing on, or rather have written on: but they do not say what they "mean". If they really wanted to say this bit of paper which they "mean", and they wanted to say so, that is impossible, because the This of sense, which is "meant", cannot be reached by language, which belongs to consciousness, i.e. to what is inherently universal. In the very attempt to say it, it would, therefore, crumble in their hands; those who [had] begun to describe it would not be able to finish doing so: they would have to hand it over to others, who would themselves in the last resort have to confess to speaking about a thing that has no being. . . . Consequently what is called unspeakable is nothing else than what is untrue, irrational, something barely and simply "meant".

Phrenology, he wrote, drawing on this critique, "conceals from itself the ignominiousness of such an irrational crude thought as that of taking a bone for the reality of self-consciousness." His criticism of those who thought they could find truth in individuals who were mesmerized followed the same lines, but from the direction of subjectivity rather than objectivity. Such individuals, he argued, were in a condition of unreflective subjectivity and thus were passively submitting themselves to the shrunken reality of their merely individual, empirically particular personality, with the result being an abdication of their true spirituality.[71]

There may be no getting past this criticism as long as one assumes that meaning must be rational—and that *reason* must be rational—but these assumptions were put to the test by modern spiritualism. Occasionally, they were questioned explicitly, as in the words of an American medium, Selden J. Finney ("Spiritualism destroys the sensationalism of English philosophers, the subjective atheism of Spencer, and the materialism of the French encyclopedists; while, on the other hand, it corrects the too ideal tendencies of Hegelianism in Germany").[72] More often, it was simply by the style of its practices that spiritualism repelled the irony of philosophical idealism, the grammar of culture, the regularities of science—the modern ideal of professional discipline in all its forms—in favor of "a household religion," as it was dubbed by the Reverend Charles Beecher, the brother of Harriet Beecher

Stowe.[73] As Hegel had foreseen, the dignity of reason was being thrown out of the game. If tables, trumpets, ordinary Joes, children's slates, and all the rest of the furniture of our lives could become philosophical mouthpieces, other objects—the objects of science, philosophy, religion, art—might appear as nothing more than the furniture of professional people, who gathered around it to be moved by the sorts of spirits they happened to prefer. "Don't speak to us of those vulgar fingers stupidly resting upon the tables!" Gasparin mockingly imagined a critic of spiritualism as shouting. "Don't speak to us of these heterodox experiences in which none of our consecrated apparatuses is involved!"[74] And to the prophet, the usual reward: Hegel actually came to be popularly associated with spiritualist doctrines, as in Yeats's *A Vision*, Thomas Mann's essay on "An Experience in the Occult," and Isaac Bashevis Singer's short story, "The Séance."[75]

This threat to professional dignity also loomed from other directions. The criticism writers like Dickens received from others who thought themselves more serious, such as Eliot, also suggested that sentimentality that got out of hand was more than an affront to taste. Even within polite literature, sentimentality taken beyond a certain (and yet indefinite) limit could seem a cruel satire of reason and an ontological threat. There were still other sources from which this disturbingly excessive sentimentality might appear, such as "politics" and "charity," but spiritualism provided the most dramatic demonstrations. By provoking reason to defend its dignity while refusing to characterize their own position as that of irrationality, ignorance, or common sense, spiritualists drove reason to face the frustrating weakness of its discourse and thus the embarrassing complicity of its power with social privilege.

If reason is not distinguishable through its opposition to unreason, but instead is opposed to vulgarity, it cannot be what nineteenth-century thinkers wanted it to be. One could always say that the mediums produced the raps and other manifestations themselves, but to say so would come uncomfortably close to the stultifying statement that Hegel produced the words of his *Phenomenology* himself. ("Mediums cheat certainly," said Elizabeth Barrett Browning. "So do people who are not mediums.")[76] If one understood anything of Hegel, one had to understand that his words were not "his" words, but a medium that was supposed to exceed the individual's meaning; in this respect, it would not be unfair to call his work "ghostwriting," especially considering that his key word, "*Geist*," means "ghost" as well as "spirit."

With spiritualism, then, the case was similar. Were all its manifestations to be attributed to the fakery that even its supporters admitted would enter into things sometimes, this knowledge would still be an insufficient basis for addressing the movement, which manifestly exceeded the intentions and control of any individual. As supporters often argued, fraud on such a scale was simply unthinkable. The very idea would "reduce all history to a gigantic fiction, and destroy every appeal to its decision on any question whatever."[77] The problem was that in spiritualism reason faced a social phenomenon, not an individual thing or a securely framed text, and so found itself driven back upon its own social status—its dignity—and thus upon the compromising limits to its meaning. In effect, spiritualism pressured those who claimed to speak for reason to recognize the unstable rhetorical structuring of their discourse. After all, it is not even self-evident that fraud disqualifies a practice from meaning, morality, and truth, as George Eliot recognized, perhaps unwarily, in her portrait of Savonarola in *Romola*.

This is not to say that spiritualists always rejected the accusation that their practices lacked dignity. Their responses were varied. Some, like Charles Beecher, took what others called indignity and interpreted it as a welcome end to melodrama. "I used to think ghosts big things," said the Reverend Charles Maurice Davies, "but that was before I knew them. I should think no more of meeting a ghost now than a donkey on a dark night, and would infinitely sooner tackle a spirit than a burglar." Elizabeth Barrett Browning turned this attitude into a Romantic aesthetic:

> The common objection of the degradation of knocking with the legs of the table, and the ridicule of the position for a spirit, &c., &c., I don't enter into at all. Twice I have been present at table-experiments, and each time I was deeply impressed— impressed, that's the word for it! The panting and shivering of that dead dumb wood, the human emotion conveyed through it—by what? had to me a greater significance than the St. Peter's of this Rome. O poet! do you not know that poetry is not confined to the clipped alleys, no, nor to the blue tops of 'Parnassus hill'?

Others, like Home and Ballou, brought the issue into the realm of moral homilies. Surprise was out of place: there was nothing anomalous in the role of the tables. "God is a better judge than we are what is fitted for humanity," said Home while in a trance; "immense results may spring from trivial things. The steam from a kettle is a small thing, but look at the locomotive!" Ballou was even more emphatic: "Is not all nature full of such *undignified* demonstrations? Look at man's *generation, birth, nutrition, excrementation, medication*, and *dissolution*." Allan Kardec gave similar explanations but was willing to admit that the genesis of modern spiritualism seemed tailor-made for attracting the contempt of people who were supposed to be "keen and cultivated minds":

> Without reflecting that the movement referred to might be communicated to every object, the idea of *tables* became associated with it in the general mind, doubtless because a table, being the most convenient object upon which to experiment, and also because people can place themselves round a table more conveniently than round any other piece of furniture, was generally employed in the experiments. . . .

But Robert Hare would have nothing to do with such temporizing. Throughout Christendom now, as in ancient times, he exclaimed, the table still draws about it the inmates of every human dwelling, at all seasons and in every kind of weather. . . .

At tables, moreover, conferences are held, contracts and deeds are signed. . . .

. . . It was at a table the Declaration of Independence was signed. . . .

And so on.[78]

There were many other responses to the accusation of indignity, including those of a large number of spiritualists, such as Laurence Oliphant, Thomas Shorter, and Gerald Massey, who themselves rejected most physical manifestations as vulgarities while encouraging instead the "higher manifestations" involved in trance-speaking and other practices. It is important to note the variety of responses because spiritualism was as heterogeneous in its own actors, actions, motivations, conclusions, and uses as it was heterodox in relation to the dominant religious, artistic, scientific, and philosophical orders of the day. The bottom line was minimal—a belief in the persistence of individuality after death and in the possibility of its communication with the living—and beyond that the possibilities were deliberately left open. Although some attempts were made to organize mediums and believers, they had little success; and almost all spiritualists boasted of the movement's antipathy to dogma, dictators, and institutionalization. In this regard it was less a meaningful movement than an occasion for meaning. To generalize any further would be to adopt Hegelian modes of thought and miss seeing why spiritualism was such a crux for nineteenth-century reason: because it lacked any unity beyond these simple assumptions that were consistent with cultural tradition to the point of utter banality. Even its emphases on the persistence of personality after death and on the possible existence of multiple worlds suggest this refusal of totality. Spiritualism was everything reason and the rationalized professions were laboring not to be, everything they wanted to overlook, or to survey and repress at the same time. It was popular, unhierarchical, inconsistent, disorganized, idiosyncratic, uneducated, uncultivated, and so, in short, undignified. And when it sometimes seemed to escape this character, as in the patronage it attracted from crowned heads or some literary celebrities and "respectable" professionals, these examples only persuaded critics of spiritualism that reason was bound to be (in Kant's formula) robbed of the popularity it deserved. They would demand, again, that one distinguish between competent and respectable witnesses; but again, the call for this distinction would be fundamentally rhetorical (since competence is not self-defining) and thus would prove disturbing to the foundations of reason.

Just as it played fast and loose with the things of this world, allowing tables to speak or trumpets to levitate, spiritualism was itself a problematic object. It could no more be called an institution than it could be called a "thing"; and if it was most easily addressed as a movement, it was one that had no ascertainable shape or boundaries or end. It might well be seen (and

often was) as an infectious disease or a funny but disconcerting joke. It was
so difficult to pin down because it was, in effect, a mass semiotic exercise. In
inventing a ground for meaning that ran both within and without the territory of reason, it interrogated the materiality of reason through the cultural
media of accordions, roses, mountebanks, and every kind of table one could
imagine.

In the second half of the nineteenth century, for spiritualists and their
detractors alike, tables became texts, tables of values. Emerging at last from
their submersion in ordinariness, which for so long had seemed to make
them exemplary philosophical objects (as they would still be, for instance,
in the fourth of Edmund Husserl's *Cartesian Meditations* and in Martin
Heidegger's *Being and Time*), tables began to display, as in a tableau, the
mystery of things. In other words, they displayed their own historicity as
things and so refused any longer to act as the passive servants of philosophy.
("Think of a kitchen table," says Andrew when he instructs Lily in philosophy in *To the Lighthouse*.)[79] In rebelling against their enslavement to particular domestic, economic, and symbolic functions, tables fought against the
fate of being consumed in their signification, signifiers sacrificed to the
signified. However one judged them, their demonstrations proved that tables
were representations, not simple things of this world, and further established
that representations — tables of classifications, codes, laws, evaluations —
could turn, *did* turn, no matter how long it took for people to notice their
turnings, and no matter how often these turnings were forgotten. For the
spiritualists, remember, history did not cease even with one's death — spirits
could continue to "progress" after their entrance into the other world, and
they might be expected to continue an active interest in the affairs of the
living.

When the tables turned, escaping their ordinary decorum, purposes, and
placements, *of course* they talked. For their turning was saying that they
were other things, and they had to articulate this otherness. As many spiritualists noted, the table as such was unnecessary to the seance; virtually any
other thing could take its place, or it could be eliminated entirely; and so the
tables said. They insisted that they might be other than they were. They might
be the medium of otherwordly communications, a way by which people from
the past spoke to living persons, and thus texts of inexhaustible historical
meaning. The text was frequently trivial, to be sure, likely to be mistaken,
open to misunderstanding and cynical manipulation, and yet *telling*, if only
because of its undeniable persuasiveness.

During this period in the nineteenth century, tables refused to be tabled,
to have their consideration set aside or postponed under the excuse of business as usual. By speaking up, they revealed the tablings, the spatial and
temporal displacements — the historical movements — that are always at work
in the world supposed to be mute, fixed, unchanging, unquestionable, or in
some other way "ordinary." Their mystery lay in asserting — I must carry this

word just a bit further — that we can never put all our cards on the table, for ancestral voices speak through the simplest things with which we surround ourselves or by which we find ourselves surrounded. The tables spoke of pastness inhabiting the present, of unconscious determinations within the universe of consciousness, and of the way judgments of possibility are bound to be shattered by the very process of their communication. And yet they communicated this sense of things — and here, again, is the crucial difference from other religious movements and from philosophical reason — by remaining tables, not symbolic, transformed, or transubstantiated matter. Here, the tables said, right here and now (what does Hegel know anyway?) is history. History is these rappings, these turnings, these thrillings.

Of course (it would be the ordinary thing to do) I could rephrase the foregoing description so that I did not attribute grammatical agency to these nineteenth-century tables. As it is, I might almost seem to be implying that I believe they "actually" rapped and tipped and danced on their own or, to be more exact, at the instigation of otherworldly spirits. But there is an important respect in which the description as I have offered it is more true than the other way of putting the matter. For describing tables in this way reminds us of what the spiritualist movement reminded the nineteenth century, that objects are never simply inanimate and speechless things. As far back as we go with objects and as much as we may try to strip them down to an essence, what we find are the experiences, forms, and movements of our values, from the primary distinction of objects from our subjectivity through all the articulations that define our grounding in history. Just such considerations led Karl Marx to complain that rather than being undignified, the spiritualists' tables were only too tame:

> The form of wood, for instance, is altered, by making a table out of it. Yet, for all that the table continues to be that common, every-day thing, wood. But, so soon as it steps forth as a commodity, it is changed into something transcendent. It not only stands with its feet on the ground, but, in relation to all other commodities, it stands on its head, and evolves out of its wooden brain grotesque ideas, far more wonderful than "table-turning" ever was.[80]

To take objects as the spiritualists did is to say that we are always being taken by objects. It is to say that through objects, we are always being remanded into the past and the future, transported or carried away from ourselves, forever reminded that things have been and can still be conceived otherwise than however we happen to be conceiving them. Plato, who made the table a philosophical example in Book 10 of *The Republic*, conceived of objects in such a way that he could propose, in Book 9 of *The Laws*, to put a rock on trial if it should fall and kill a human being: through spiritualism, Victorians were led through the implications of such a moment in reason, though generally without ever encountering a reference to this philosopher.

They were reminded as well that for Aristotle things did not move in obedience to Newtonian gravity but rather in accordance with their own proper
natures, which made each thing seek out its natural place in the universe;
they were reminded in advance that after Albert Einstein, the world would
again become composed of very different sorts of things. In this respect,
these tables were truly surreal objects *avant la lettre*, anticipating the way
the surrealists would both support and rewrite Marx by opposing dreamy
things to the things of science and commodity production. (The table, in
surrealism, often suggested the bed, a place of copulation and creativity
presumed to be at odds with tables of law.) And while it might be objected,
from Marxist or surrealist or other standpoints, that this spiritualist understanding was still an alienated or precritical one, we must consider to what
extent understanding can be the point here and to what extent spiritualism
placed one beyond or beside that point. As opposed to simply assuming that
the spiritualists lacked an adequate language for critical analysis, we should
consider the criticism they may have been working out in another—not necessarily a lesser—language.

It is evident that these cautions are not overly generous if one considers,
for instance, how many spiritualists were also abolitionists who received
messages from their mediums that spoke of the necessity and coming triumph
of emancipation. The debate over the human integrity of tables was significantly related to the debate over the humanity of Americans of African
descent; in challenging the orthodox definitions in the one case, people often
had to fight against the same institutions, codes of respectability, and assertions of professional authority as in the other. And though one might be
tempted to see the spiritualist movement as more of a diversion than the
abolitionist movement, as a less serious or pressing or respectable cause, to
regard it in this way would be a mistake. By itself, the general overlapping
of the two movements should suggest that the distinction between direct and
diversionary movements, between movements of practical reform and those
that are spiritual or utopian, may be misleading. Certainly distinctions are
called for, but this simplistic form of categorization only reinforces those in
the nineteenth century and in our own time who would mock any movement
critical of the dominant culture by portraying those involved in it as being
blown about by whatever -isms or -ologies happen to be popular at the
moment. The distinction between critical and naive approaches to things
easily ceases to be critical and instead turns out to be little more than a
professional tone, a cultural style, or a sense of something like "dignity."
And while it is unquestionable that modern spiritualism was often a clumsily
articulated movement, one that grasped after the otherness of historicity
with the crude tools of rapping knuckles and surreptitiously lifted knees and
simple conjurors' tricks, this diversion or delusion was also a way into the
heart of things. It led many people who had no other path into a critique of
patriarchy, racism, or Calvinist dogmatism while more generally spurring

them to combat the mutism to which eminent cultural figures would have liked to condemn the everyday life of the common understanding.

If in developing this point I have touched only tangentially on what seems to many the most obvious feature of modern spiritualism, the desire to communicate with the beloved dead, I do so deliberately. First of all, this feature is not as obvious as it is generally taken to be (witness the emphasis in spiritualist proceedings on communications with famous persons from the past or with persons entirely unknown to the assembled company). And even more important, the groping criticism of things that I have just described was in fact largely definitive of the spiritualists' conception of life after death. Although social criticism might have been far from the mind of this or that individual longing to get into contact with his late Uncle Ralph, the spiritualist movement and the opposition it aroused both demonstrated that these quarrels over the dead, like quarrels over the dead wood of the table, turned on issues that extended into every aspect of contemporary culture.

So as the long history of philosophical attempts to come to terms with it may suggest, the table is a thing that is extremely complex in its banality. Heidegger raised this point near the beginning of one of his works (*What Is a Thing?*) and, like the spiritualists, raised it in relation to science:

Another example: The English physicist and astronomer Eddington once said of his table that every thing of this kind—the table, the chair, etc.—has a double. Table number one is the table known since his childhood; table number two is the "scientific table." This scientific table, that is, the table which science defines in its thingness, consists, according to the atomic physics of today, not of wood but mostly of empty space; in this emptiness electrical charges are distributed here and there, which are rushing back and forth at great velocity. Which one now is the true table, number one or number two? Or are both true? In the sense of what truth? What truth mediates between the two?[81]

Even in this passage, the table has more than one double. In addition to the everyday thing and the thing of science, it is also (as both Heidegger and Eddington recognized) the thing of philosophical exemplification, and it is other things as well (for instance, a name, "the table"). Following turnings suggested by Heidegger's work, one might try to improve on Eddington by arguing that a double is no simple thing, either; that as soon as a thing has one double, it has others; that the table disclosed by history, philosophical and otherwise, is fluid, like the movement of waters or luminiferous ethers or social forces.

It would be stupid to suggest unanimity between modern spiritualism and Heidegger's philosophy; but before I retrace a crucial distinction, I want to entertain their convergence a bit further. As with my earlier references to Kant and Hegel, this comparison will speak of philosophy's relation to that which exists both beyond and within the school walls: to that which these walls overlook.

Consider Heidegger's essay, "The Thing." This work, too, begins with a dramatic distinction between its ends and the ends of modern science. "Science always encounters only what *its* kind of representation has admitted beforehand as an object possible for science" (170).[82] Like spiritualism, this essay has an aura of millenarianism, with its foreboding opening on the influence of technology, including the hydrogen bomb, "whose triggering, thought through to its utmost potential, might be enough to snuff out all life on earth" (166). Again like spiritualism, it has a pervasive but decidedly ambiguous religious tone. And it resists systematization at least as much as the nineteenth-century movement did: the essay insists on the impossibility of achieving its objective and is at once social criticism, phenomenological analysis, etymological meditation, and romantic poem.

As spiritualists would, this essay dilates upon communications between mortals and spirits:

Earth and sky dwell in the gift of the outpouring. In the gift of the outpouring earth and sky, divinities and mortals dwell *together all at once*. These four, at one because of what they themselves are, belong together. Preceding everything that is present, they are enfolded into a single fourfold. (173)

This essay and spiritualism are both concerned with ordinary objects (in the passage above, Heidegger focuses on the one that dominates this essay, the jug). And Heidegger's essay is also a drama of representation, which, like the spiritualist drama, breaks with semiotic conventions while explaining the necessity and difficulty of such a break. Its concerns go beyond the question of scientific representation to the issue of representation as such:

This appropriating mirror-play of the simple onefold of earth and sky, divinities and mortals, we call the world. The world presences by worlding. That means: the world's worlding cannot be explained by anything else nor can it be fathomed through anything else. This impossibility does not lie in the inability of our human thinking to explain and fathom in this way. Rather, the inexplicable and unfathomable character of the world's worlding lies in this, that causes and grounds remain unsuitable for the world's worlding. As soon as human cognition here calls for an explanation, it fails to transcend the world's nature, and falls short of it. The human will to explain just does not reach to the simpleness of the simple onefold of worlding. (179–80)

I do not bring spiritualism into the company of Heidegger and philosophy in order to dignify it. As some spiritualists recognized, dignity can be a poisoned gift. Nor do I mean to suggest an inversion in their positions, an elevation of the vulgar over the refined. Such a turn would be misleading. Although spiritualism had its reformist and revolutionary elements, it was not generally the carnival, the upsetting of distinctions, or the revolt of the low against the ruling powers that its most distressed opponents took it to be. As previously noted, most spiritualists were eager to assert their respectability and to enumerate the persons from high society who had condescended to share their company. Nor am I suggesting that spiritualism anticipated Heideggerianism, as in the recent academic jokes along this line ("He's writing a book on the influence of Derrida on Shakespeare," and so on).

The comparison does bring out how persistent the animosity of reason toward vulgarity may be: so persistent that it influenced a philosopher who was out to destroy metaphysics. In comparison to the tawdry objects of the spiritualists' regard, one need only consider Heidegger's list of iconic things — "the jug and the bench, the footbridge and the plow . . . tree and pond . . . brook and hill . . . book and picture, crown and cross" (182) — to see how much of Kant and Hegel was still in the twentieth-century philosopher. Heidegger's are dignified things, every one of them, while the planes, radios, bombs, and other equipment he mentions at the beginning of the essay are synecdoches for representation, which occludes things. Thus, his romantic attitude is not adventitious in relation to his thought about language and things in this essay but is inseparable from it. It is not representation in general but his dignity that interferes with the disclosure of the thing as a thing. "Dignity" is also a representation, but not one he ever thinks to question in this essay. Like Jacques Derrida's, his notion of play has no room for pratfalls.

But still this is not the reason for my comparison: to use spiritualism to say about Heidegger something not especially new. The more interesting point returns to the intersection of the modern phenomenon of professionalism with the issue of dignity and the social organization of meaning. If social struggles are played out in dramatic demonstrations of representation, as I have argued, then there is no ultimate ground to meaning. Meaning is a political activity. It is always conflictual and so can neither escape nor rest assured in the conditions of representation. Given this understanding, Heidegger's insistence that there is no form of representation that can allow things to appear as the things they are expresses symbolic control even as it pleads epistemological compunction. On this point spiritualism can tell us something, for it is precisely the kind of thing that sticks to and yet escapes from Heidegger's language — the kind of thing he cannot let be.

The speechlessness of Heidegger's things contrasts sharply with the world of spiritualism, all alive as it was with chattering bric-a-brac. When tables began to communicate in the middle of the nineteenth century, what they communicated was the indignity of metaphor. They did not make the metaphor of the spirit a literal reality; instead, for all practical purposes they collapsed the distinction between the surface of things and "the other side," between the ground and the representation of meaning. (So Georgiana Houghton said her spirit photographs had taught her "that our clothing in the hereafter is literally woven from the emanations of our life upon earth, thus the numberless texts in Scripture bearing on the subject are not to be considered as merely figures of speech, but as promises to be fulfilled, such as in the last chapter of Proverbs, 'Strength and honour are her *clothing*, and *she shall rejoice in the time to come.*'")[83] Though still an affair fraught with all sorts of problems, communication was immediate, intimate, ultimate, and open to all. It gave pleasure by showing that the ordinary is imaginary: that even the school walls of religion, literature, and philosophy, which were usually privileged to regulate the extent of this perception, were imaginary.

Spiritualism was not all ecstasy, *jouissance*, or anything of the sort. Being political, meaning can never be grounded or totalized in this way. If one gave more attention to biographies than I have here, one could say a great deal about the gross disparity between the sense of things suggested by spiritualism and the experiences of those involved in this movement.[84] By the same token, I do not mean to imply that spiritualism bore some inherent or necessary relation to progressive social causes. The historical connection it did have with such causes is certainly significant, as I have tried to argue, but this is not a significance guaranteed by something in the nature of spiritualism; as Alan Gauld has noted in relation to Bill Hickock's experience with seances, "The spirits who warned Wild Bill of impending danger and guided the aim of his double-action .44s can hardly have come from the same spheres as the reformed generals who lectured the Quaker, Isaac Post, on pacifism and the wickedness of war."[85]

The point is that spiritualism communicated the indignity of metaphor to those opponents of the movement who identified with the growing authority of professionalism: hence the need to retort that tables were undignified. Emerson had anticipated this problem in *Representative Men* when he complained that "Swedenborg's revelation is a confounding of planes, – a capital offense in so learned a categorist. This is to carry the law of surface into the plane of substance, to carry individualism and its fopperies into the realm of essences and generals, – which is dislocation and chaos."[86] The meaning of spiritualism was so insufferable to its critics because the control of metaphor, the delineation and protection of the distinction between literal and metaphorical meaning, was passing into the hands of professionals at this time; and this desire for metaphorical control persists in Heidegger's writing. Even though he set out to reject the very concept of metaphor,[87] it survived in his desire for totality: in the hierarchy he could not surrender in the distance, or difference, of Being from representation. Only imagine someone confusing Heidegger's essay, "The Thing," with the 1950s science-fiction movie of the same title, in which James Arness plays a weedy extraterrestrial threatening a scientific outpost in the arctic, and one can begin to appreciate something of the very real challenge that spiritualism once posed and may yet continue to pose to respectable thinkers. Heidegger's things are speechless because his philosophical dignity, the dignity of metaphor, cannot let things like words be. Or (in other words) his fear of vulgarity turns his words into unsatisfying objects of representation as soon as they leave his mouth, his hand, his table.

"The Thing," one might say, is a variety of discursive procedures that explore the social conditions of philosophical meaning around the middle of the twentieth century; the spiritualism that flourished a century earlier, one might say, was an essay on things.

3

The Experience of Personation

At present there is no vocabulary invented which can describe the experiences of these more highly sensitised persons; and even if there were, it would be incomprehensible to any except to those who had attained the same degree of susceptibility. Just as there is no equivalent in the language of a tribe of African negroes for the word "hysteria," and it would be extremely difficult to convey to the mind of a Hottentot the idea which it represents, so there is no term by which those who are conscious of a new condition of sensibility, can describe their sensations to those who still remain in the old condition of denseness.

LAURENCE OLIPHANT[1]

It is almost impossible to lay down absolute rules, to regulate the almost infinite variety of human culture and conditions.

J. B. FERGUSON, "Rules for Receiving Spirit-Teaching"[2]

In work that calls for innovation and improvisation, people sometimes get stuck. The experience of writing is exemplary. (That is, if one ignores its more specialized distresses — at work, most of us cannot excuse ourselves by raising a hand to a suffering brow and complaining that we are "blocked.") It is a common experience for writers stalled at a certain point in their progress to spend hours and even days worrying at the troublesome spot, writing and crumpling page after page, only to realize that all this time they have been on the wrong track. Suddenly they know how to go on with their work, and all the intervening writing then seems to have been a pointless detour around the obvious next step. It was all wrong: a lapse in their thinking, a waste of time, a failure to grasp things in the right way. They wonder how they could have lost themselves so completely when the solution was right there under their noses — or, with a bit more experience, they may wonder why this kind of frustration seems unavoidable.

It is tempting to see spiritualism as a deviation on a larger, cultural scale. It is treated in this way in most studies of nineteenth-century literature and in most general histories of the age. When mentioned at all, it appears as an oddity akin to Victorian fashions in crinolines or whiskers. Even those who think that this movement deserves more attention are likely to believe that its participants were mystified about their activity. Writers may find meaning beckoning around the movement as a whole or peeking out of the shadows it has let fall onto other areas of society, but they usually conclude that its own scribblings missed the point. All those interminable accounts of seances may be seen as the stuff of an interesting situation, but that is all. By themselves, they are not really work.

This was the attitude taken by Hippolyte Taine in his influential study of the mind:

> The more bizarre a fact is, the more instructive it is. In this regard, the "spiritual" manifestations . . . put us on the track of discoveries by showing us the coexistence at the same instant, in the same individual, of two thoughts, two wills, two distinct actions, one of which he is aware of, while he is not aware of the other and attributes it to invisible beings. The human mind is thus a theater in which several different works are playing at the same time, on different planes, only one of which is illuminated.[3]

This attitude has its advantages, as one can see from the works of Taine and the other students of psychology, including Sigmund Freud, who found spiritualism of interest. In this era, when the study of psychology was being reformed on an empirical, experimental, and professional basis, spiritualism did indeed furnish its practitioners with instructive material for the analysis of mental processes. However, the assumption that observers like Taine must have had more awareness than the mediums can also be misleading, especially in its reduction of a complex social phenomenon to an instance of individual psychology. Even if one agreed that the minds of mediums were explained by Taine and the others (such as Alfred Binet, Pierre Janet, and William Carpenter) who elaborated theories of "unconscious cerebration," the practices that had grown up around these mediums would still await understanding. And then another question would arise: the question of the detour.

Taine assumed that spiritualism communicated despite itself. It could put us on the right track because it was so bizarre, but it was not meaningful discourse in its own right. It communicated as a symptom, not as an argument; it did not know its own meaning. This is the attitude of reason, and this is the point where one might consider more closely reason's frustrations. For here the student of psychology seems even more trusting than the devotees of spiritualism. Unlike Taine, spiritualists did not believe in the existence of a strict boundary between bizarre and rational phenomena. Sir William Crookes was typical in adopting the old saying, "I never said it was possible, I only said it was true."[4] Furthermore, spiritualists lacked the faith in meaning that allowed Taine, through all the complexities of his analysis, to be confident that he understood how words made sense.

Taine was committed to an inductive, associationist, sensationalist psychology influenced by John Stuart Mill, among others. He attributed the conception of ideas as spirit to Descartes and regarded it as an error that ought to be submitted to rational explanation. Through the following illustration, Taine traced the etiology of this error:

> If a page is in manuscript, we have more difficulty in understanding its sense than if it is printed; part of our attention goes to the exterior form of the characters, instead of going entirely to their sense; we notice not only how these signs are used, but also their individual peculiarities. But, after a while, these no longer strike us; no longer novel, they are no longer odd; no longer odd, they are no longer noticed; from that point on, with the manuscript as with the printed page, it seems to us that we no longer follow the words, but rather pure ideas. One now sees why, in our reasonings and all our superior operations, the word, although present, should appear absent.

For Taine as for other psychologists of this era, words are always present to consciousness. By the same token, although it may no longer be conceived of as a metaphysical agent, human identity is still a reliable presence on the whole. With the vividness characteristic of his style, Taine compared

> the secret elaboration of which the ordinary effect is consciousness to the march of the slave who, after the games of the circus, crossed the whole arena with an egg in his hand, among the tired lions and the tigers in repose; if he arrived at the other side, he was liberated. So the spirit advances across the hurly-burly of monstrous deliriums and howling follies, almost always with impunity, to sit in truthful consciousness and exact memory.[5]

Spiritualists were not so sure, and their difference from Taine was not simply the difference between sickness and analysis or even between idealism and empiricism. They made their spirit at least as concrete as Taine's, displaying for all the world to see the presence of writing on slates, drawings on paper, or knocks on wood. They also showed these signs to be ineradicably particular, derived from historically identifiable individuals. However, in insisting on a spiritual agency in these communications, they denied that words are ever entirely present to the understanding. They denied that the materiality of signs could furnish one with the stable referential ground on which Taine believed he could vanquish Descartes. The spiritualists' words were not simple and simply resting on the page for the eye to follow. Nor did identity find the security to which Taine destined it, as far as spiritualists were concerned. For them meaning came in the form of a drama that evaded any definitive analysis.

Unquestionably, this way with words was self-serving. One of the most striking aspects of spiritualism was the relentlessness of its apologetics. The Seybert Commission of the University of Pennsylvania was bemused that Thomas R. Hazard, a spiritualist adviser to its investigation, said "that the true spirit in which to approach the study of Spiritualism is 'an entire willingness to be deceived,'"[6] but this candor was not at all extraordinary. A common argument among mediums was that an intense use of the eyes or a concentration on any of the senses, on the part of those gathered in a seance, would be likely to inhibit any possible manifestations. "The table requires to be taken gaily, and with spirit," wrote Count Agénor de Gasparin; tables, he said, "demand at the beginning, singing, with amusing and easy exercises . . . [and] if they are met by preoccupation or nervous excitement, they are very apt to get *sulky*."[7]

There was just no escaping this kind of confidence. William Henry Harrison, the founder of a prominent newspaper, *The Spiritualist*, and a publisher of many spiritualist works, noted with excruciatingly unselfconscious candor that "in a circle with truly affectionate and truthful people, where such a proposition as that of tying the medium or holding each other would be thought degrading by everybody present, manifestations are witnessed in the light which cannot be obtained with equal power under other conditions."[8] When magicians like Harry Kellar duplicated the performances of mediums, some spiritualists were so impressed that they claimed Kellar and the others were not really magicians at all but rather highly developed mediums perversely denying their true nature by pretending to be engaged in artifice. As early as 1850, when Dr. Charles A. Lee of Bowdoin College toured New York with a man who could manipulate his toe joints to produce raps like the Fox sisters', this tendency became apparent; for many in his audiences insisted on understanding this performance as confirmation of the modern-day miracle.[9] To the same effect but from the opposite direction, when two magicians in London began giving regular performances at which they sought to debunk spiritualist manifestations, one outraged believer tried to support his cause by demonstrating to his fellow spiritualists how the conjurors achieved their effects. The Reverend Charles Maurice Davies doubted the wisdom of this exposé ("Illogical people will not see the force of Dr. Sexton's argument, and will possibly think it 'proves too much'");[10] but Dr. Sexton's imperviousness to the possibility of any irony illustrates this movement's redoubtable capacity for self-justification.

Many spiritualists were not in the least disconcerted even when mediums were seized in the act of pretending to be etheric spirits. Such "exposures" did hurt the movement and contributed greatly to its eventual decline; but as soon as they began to be publicized, claims that trickery had some legitimacy became conventional in spiritualist discourse. So Robert Browning's Mr. Sludge argued that "every cheat's inspired, and every lie / Quick with a germ of truth."[11] The most common version of this excuse was that mediums were fallible and extremely sensitive human beings and therefore were liable to resort to imposture when they lost their powers, which were notoriously unpredictable. This is the argument of the wife of the medium in Laurence Oliphant's *Masollam*. She explains that Mr. Masollam must "supplement the peculiar gifts which he really possesses, with subterfuges and *coups de théâtre* carefully prepared, and likely to strike the imagination, based often upon information which he has acquired by ordinary means."[12] In *The Undiscovered Country*, William Dean Howells showed how elaborate the argument could become when he had Dr. Boynton explain trickery as "solicitation":

"I have gone to the very bottom of this matter, and I find that in almost all cases there is a degree of solicitation on the part of the mediums; that where this is most daring the results are most valuable; and what I wish now to establish as the central principle of spiritistic science is the principle of solicitationism. If the disembodied spirits do not voluntarily approach, invite them; if they cannot manifest their presence, show them by example the ways and means of so doing."[13]

While arguments like these were self-serving, to say so is not to say the last word about them. After all, these intellectual contortions were no more elaborate than those practiced in orthodox theology, philosophy, political theory, and kindred forms of discourse. They were generally less sophisticated, or more vulgar, but for this reason they could be more difficult to dismiss. While a thoroughgoing materialist might be able to understand how an intelligent human being could fall for the blandishments of Cartesian idealism or Thomistic hairsplitting (and this was a time when scholarly scientific work could still refer to God without any self-consciousness), spiritualism was a different matter. It cried out to be treated as a sick patient rather than a meaningful discourse. Otherwise, it threatened the very concept of rational communication—a point not lost on Robert Browning. In his "Mr. Sludge" (which exposes much more than spiritualism), Browning observed that the seance could exhibit an embarrassing bond between the persuasiveness and the vulnerability of language; and John Tyndall came to a similar conclusion when he worried about spiritualism playing upon the "logical feebleness of science," which renders it "perfectly powerless in the presence of this frame of mind."[14] By demonstrating how one could extend to practically infinite lengths the practice of interpreting appearances as signs (of physical forces, of God's providence, and so on), the seance could suggest that all rational discourse followed a logic of endless circularity and self-confirming redundancy. Like *Don Quixote*, spiritualism could show how the world is enmeshed in words that are never entirely present to us unless we are suffering a hallucination.

By making the occult speak openly, spiritualism also made public the practices of interpretation that give words the effect of presence and materiality. It suggested that words are never entirely present or self-evident by insisting that communication is always interpretation that is subject to irreducible uncertainties. This is the reigning paradox of spiritualism: that its insistence on immediacy, on personal experience, was supported by reference to a compromising medium. It opposed the Enlightenment faith in words in the service of the Enlightenment faith in reason. While rationalists brought words and reason together through their faith in logical discourse, legal forms, and reformed social institutions, words and reason were split asunder by the spiritualists' desire for communication. Spiritualists had such a strong devotion to communication that they could hardly trust at all to words. They were so fully attached to reason that they could not pass that point where its directions were indirections: where the path of truth was the detour of experience.

At times the basic drama of spiritualism might seem identical to the pattern of conventional spiritual autobiography. As in this pattern, the spiritualist narrative almost always began with doubt. So G. H. Lewes commented, "There is probably not a single convert who does not assure his listeners that he began by being incredulous of the facts narrated by spiritualists."[15] In seances as in spiritualist literature, this initial skepticism served the same function as the frequent emphasis on the youth, ignorance, innocence, femininity, or naiveté of the mediums. It both heightened the dramatic conflict and argued for the truth of its outcome. "The facts beat me," said Alfred Russel Wallace. "They compelled me to accept them *as facts* long before I could accept the spiritualist explanation of them."[16] In spiritualist literature, this initial unwillingness was often redoubled in the professed reluctance of individuals to continue with this disturbing business even after they had become convinced of its truth. The oldest of the Fox sisters, Leah, emphasized that they were just as reluctant to shoulder the burden of mediumship as they had been to welcome the idea of spirits in the first place. Similarly, William Stainton Moses recorded his prolonged struggles to maintain his Anglican beliefs against the challenge posed by the spirits; other examples are innumerable.[17]

All the basic elements of spiritual autobiography appear in the spiritualists' narratives of their experiences: doubt, supernatural visitations, conversion, fanaticism, backsliding, and repentance. Nonetheless, spiritualist narrative differed radically from the tradition of spiritual autobiography. As the examples of "Christian spiritualists" indicate, the difference was not that this narrative necessarily involved heterodox belief. Indeed, Christian spiritualists often claimed that they were more orthodox than the orthodox because they did not blanch at the literal word of Biblical miracles; in this respect, spiritualism was an effort to salvage faith from science by arguing that "scepticism is frequently more credulous than faith."[18] If anything, these Christian spiritualists were seen by their critics as believing too well, identifying with an aspect of tradition that was being politely discredited elsewhere in society. In the fiction, science, philosophy, and theology of the mid-nineteenth century, it was generally taken for granted that the age of miracles was long gone and that even the eighteenth-century notion of Providence was rather passé—more a poetic image than a definite historical reality. In opposing what it might term "the reigning materialism of the age" or "the spirit of skepticism and unbelief," spiritualism could then boast that it was the true inheritor or restorer of religion; but still its difference from tradition lay elsewhere. After all, John Bunyan had been opposed to the reigning social and religious authorities of his day, and attempts by religionists to out-orthodox each other were quite common in the nineteenth century, which witnessed the growth of the Oxford and Evangelical movements; in this regard spiritualism was nothing new under the sun.

The spiritualist drama *was* different, however, because of the dramatic way it communicated the difficulty of communication. When critics such as Lewes, Tyndall, T. H. Huxley, and Wilhelm Wundt tried to confront spiritualism with the rigorous demands of scientific evidence, they failed to appreciate that spiritualism did not appeal only to experience. Although its drama asked people to encounter the phenomena for themselves, it appealed to experience as a form of representation. Its seemingly miraculous claims guaranteed that while it based itself on the immediate evidence of experience, it questioned what that evidence communicated. ("The truth is," wrote Judge J. W. Edmonds, "that a miracle, a marvel, a wonder never converted any one.")[19] Spiritualism made every fact a representation and so made meaning as debatable as facts were indubitable. While it made communication more important, it made interpretation less certain.

In this way spiritualism encouraged dissatisfaction with interpretive practices, scientific and otherwise, while offering a social situation in which people could explore the possibilities of communication. As one might gather from the multitude of witnesses, investigations, prosecutions, testimonies, and attempted proofs littering its history and literature from their inception, spiritual rappings opened a doorway into representation for people who felt it had not adequately represented them. Even as university commissions, courts of law, seances, essays, and more informal tribunals put spiritualism on trial, it tested the truth of representation. Its expressions of desire—to speak with the dead, to revise the prevailing images of the afterlife, and so on—were only the least threatening of its communications. Pitying, sneering, one could condescend to the recently bereaved who would accept silly scratchings on wood as a sign of their loved ones' presence. But spiritualism spurred riots as well as ridicule, antagonism and argument as well as condescension, because it communicated the extreme difficulty—even the utter improbability—of communication. As it showed how unpersuasive scientific evidence could be and thus how far the authority of science was a matter of irrational persuasion, it also threatened to expose language, behavior, character, individual persons, and the entirety of culture as unfounded representations. It was sometimes suggested that people who attended seances were subjected to a kind of mass mesmerism, but spiritualism suggested that involuntary persuasion vexed all communication and thus was neither so simple nor so isolated a concern. In fact, Gasparin argued that the most telling evidence for "the principle of suggestion" was to be found in the facility with which the adversaries of spiritualism lent themselves successively "to all the ideas which have been *suggested* against" it.[20]

The most famous of the difficulties raised by spiritualism was that of correct language. Noting the infelicities in spiritualist writings, who among the general populace could manage not to laugh? That is, if these people were not holding their noses in disgust. The spiritualists themselves were embarrassed. While trying to keep a straight face, Emma Hardinge said of this time that "even the most credulous of the well-educated Spiritualists had cause to mourn over the deterioration in grammar and orthography which befalls the exalted dead by a long residence in the spirit world."[21] (The old joke about Beethoven de-composing in the grave irresistably obtrudes itself.) If the movement could offer nothing better than these communications, many would say, then why should they waste their time on it? If it was this vulgar, it hardly mattered if the movement was true. "The only good that I can see in the demonstration of the truth of 'Spiritualism,'" said Huxley, "is to furnish an additional argument against suicide. Better live a crossing-sweeper than die and be made to talk twaddle by a 'medium' hired at a guinea a *séance*."[22]

Spiritualist diction was also found wanting. It was seen as a jargon, nonsensical as well as incorrect in form. "Just so soon as a man becums a reglar out & out Sperret rapper," said Artemus Ward in his *faux naif* style, "he leaves orf workin, lets his hare grow all over his fase & commensis spungin his livin out of other peple. He eats all the dickshunaries he can find & goze round chock full of big words, scarein the wimmin folks & little children & destroyin the piece of mind of evry famerlee he enters."[23] Humorists such as Ward, novelists such as John Hay (in *The Bread-winners: A Social Study*), reporters, and other sorts of observers all found spiritualism an attractive subject for burlesque. Although he had been one of the first to sponsor the Fox sisters' exhibitions, P. T. Barnum got in his licks, too:

Then shall all the blockheads in the nincompoopdome of disclosive procedure above the all-fired leather-fungus of Peter Nephninnygo, the gooseberry grinder, rise into the dome of the disclosure until coequaled and coextensive and conglomerate lumuxes in one comprehensive mux shall assimilate into nothing, and revolve like a bob-tailed pussy cat after the space where the tail was.[24]

One does not have to read far in spiritualist literature to find that even a satire as crude as Barnum's was outdone by the *bizarreries* of the originals it mocked. And yet this vulnerability was also a strength, a positive opportunity, since these problems in linguistic form led to an acute analysis of language. To some extent this recapitulated earlier analyses, such as the learning devised by Biblical exegetes to make sense of the spirit of words (some spiritualists even drew upon the findings of the contemporary Higher Criticism); but spiritualists did not simply reinvent the wheel. The difficulties they met in communicating with spirits were also difficulties in communications between living human beings, for they involved the same issues of reference, meaning, and truth. "Notice even the danger there is of mistakes occurring in the transmission of thoughts through the simple medium of words," said Clara Sherwood, with endearing simplicity; and John Jones urged more gruffly, "[L]et us not idiotize a German, because his raps are to *us* foolish; neither let us idiotize spirits, if they rap or speak at the family table; let us, if we wish their company, endeavour to understand their sounds."[25] Because the texts with which spiritualists concerned themselves were exchanges between individual human beings, some of whom just happened to be disembodied, their apologetics provides a revealing perspective on nineteenth-century society and discourse. "Let us clear our minds of distinctions between human beings and spirits," said William Wetmore Story. "We are all spirits; all our communications are spiritual."[26]

In the first place, then, spiritualism characterized communication as being at best an approximation to meaning. Spiritualism elided the difference between metaphorical and literal language, but it did so by insisting that one cannot be certain when this distinction may come into play. "For spirits," wrote Allan Kardec, "and especially for those of high degree, the idea is everything, the form is nothing . . . and it must therefore be very inconvenient for them to be obliged, in communicating with us, to make use of human speech."[27] This attitude made language a compromised medium, one "borrowed from earth," as a spirit told Moses;[28] but it also made language shimmer in its every syllable with otherworldly possibility. Just as "spirit" had turned out to be reality rather than metaphor, so might any figure of speech turn out to be instinct with truth and any worldly reality a mere figure of speech. As Anna Mary Howitt Watts noted, "the universal language of spirit-symbolism" was a necessary but chancy acquirement, since a word like "death" might be understood in a physical sense when it was intended quite otherwise.[29] No one could know for sure what this world was anymore: hence the impetus toward millenarianism in spiritualism, and also the impetus toward jargon. In this bastardized way with words and phrases, this casting about for an exotic mooring in language, one sees spiritualists exploring the implications of their conviction that language lacks a proper form. Like Watts or like Charles Beecher, who sought the principles "which underlie all figurative diction,"[30] many spiritualists thought that the most crucial task they faced was learning how to deal with the many ways in which communication could go wrong.

At a time "when the comparatively recent discovery of electricity, and other kindred mysteries of nature, seemed to open paths into the region of miracle," as Nathaniel Hawthorne put it in "The Birth-mark,"[31] spiritualists struggled especially with a discourse — of wonders, miracles, gifts, superhuman powers, and so on — that science had begun to appropriate from religion. They wanted to reappropriate this discourse, wresting it away from science, and so one of the most popular arguments in this movement was that contemporary scientific discoveries actually supported it. Here the spiritualist revision of language is particularly striking. It was not only "spirit" or "death" that confounded the distinction between literal and metaphorical meaning: scientific phenomena also appeared in various discursive roles through which the possibilities of the world could be explored and reformed. Science was made the stuff of illustration (messages sent through "the spiritual telegraph" were like words sent over Morse's electric wires),[32] comparison (table-rappings resembled telegraphic clickings and so bespoke the same natural laws), analogy (the darkness requested at seances was no more objectionable than the "dark chamber essential in the process of photography"),[33] deduction ("The clairvoyance of somnambules is therefore a miracle for 'enlightened' journalists, much as telegraphy is a miracle for savages"),[34] and prolepsis (the advent of the millenium was being signaled by the "extraordinary discovery of inventions to promote the union of nations, by railways, steam navigation, electric telegraphs, &c.").[35] In these ways and others, spiritualists sought to take "the achievements of physical science, very charming of course in their own limited way,"[36] and to use them for purposes seemingly designed to drive most scientists into decidedly unspiritual fits.

One could describe this treatment of science as a metaphorical or catachrestic use of its discoveries comparable to the popularization of terms like "relativity" in the twentieth century, but only at the risk of ignoring the questions spiritualism raised about metaphor, science, and the experience of the world. In exploring the possibilities of scientific discoveries as objects of discourse, spiritualism both displayed and criticized the cultural meaning of science. Just as some spiritualists claimed to be more orthodox than the orthodox, almost all spiritualists thought they were more scientific than the scientists; and through this attitude they suggested that the question of scientific fact could not be divorced from the question of scientific design. Although with very different premises and to a very different purpose, the spiritualists can be said to have agreed with Nietzsche that "science also rests on a faith" and that "there simply is no science 'without presuppositions.'"[37] To press this comparison too far would be to forget what is most provocative about spiritualism, its sentimental vulgarity, quite unlike the style for which Nietzsche strived; but still it is important to see the relation between the critiques of linguistic figuration in Nietzsche's works and in the spiritualist movement. Like Nietzsche, spiritualists were interested in what could be gained culturally through the assertion of unrationalized will, and they were interested as well in the idea that rational assertion at a certain level may be indistinguishable from or may even entail unconsciousness. More to the point at hand, spiritualists, like Nietzsche, would not allow scientific authority to be owned by scientists and confined to the procedures and logic being codified with increasing rigor throughout this century. As R. Laurence Moore puts it, "Spiritualists feared that anything science would not investigate would in the modern world become a matter of indifference."[38]

This attitude was a protest against professionalism, but it was also an attempt to figure out how one should inhabit a world radically changed by scientific inventions. According to an article published in 1868 in an English newspaper, the *Western Gazette*, "A generation that sees two men on opposite sides of the globe, conversing with each other by means of an ubiquitous agent, that is known only by its effects, can surely believe in almost anything, except the incorrectness of the multiplication-table."[39] Despite all their absurdities, frauds, disappointments, and yes, vulgarities, what spiritualists saw with exceptional distinctness was that the changes science had wrought in the world could not be isolated in the form of particular laws, theories, and technologies. The whole sense of things had changed since the eighteenth century in a way people had hardly begun to grasp. Conceptions of space, time, and physical agency had been transformed by inventions like the telegraph, and along with them conceptions of history and possibility.

The case of miracles was indicative of the general questioning of the world that was bound to follow such changes. "Had the electric telegraph been invented and employed for a brief period two thousand years ago," said Robert Dale Owen, who was Robert Owen's son and a prominent American writer, politician, and propagandist for spiritualism, "and had telegraphy then become one of the lost arts, the old records of its temporary triumph, how well attested soever, if unsupported by modern example, would have created but feeble belief to-day."[40] Thus, in the contemporary parlance, spiritualism was a "modern miracle" that was providing scientific confirmation of the special providences of ancient times.

Struggling to get a handle on this new world, spiritualists did often seem to be grasping science only as an ornament that they grafted onto outmoded or irrelevant beliefs. Although it was made before the Rochester knockings, a prophecy of Margaret Fuller's is a case in point: "[W]e have no doubt that in the course of fifty years a new spiritual circulation will be comprehended as clearly as the circulation of the blood is now."[41] Here Fuller might seem to be appropriating "circulation" as an image she can cut from the pages of scientific tomes and paste into a volume of spiritual concerns, much as Clifford Pyncheon in Hawthorne's *House of the Seven Gables* takes the telegraph to be virtually the same stuff as mesmerism, "rapping spirits," and spirituality in general. (His conclusion is that telegraphy deserves to be

"consecrated to high, deep, joyful, and holy missions.")[42] However, this idea
that spiritualists were trying to abuse science by treating it as "mere" rhetoric
rests on two assumptions specifically challenged by spiritualists: that there is
a language proper to science and that science is a property handed down
through an uncontested will. In effect, spiritualists argued that there could
be no *praescriptio proprietatis*; scientific truth was a word that might be
variously literal or metaphorical, depending on the circumstances in which it
was communicated. To the popular aphorism of the time—"ghosts have been
everywhere banished by the introduction of gaslight"[43]—they responded that
"gaslight," like "ghosts," was a word subject to interpretation; and they
treated scientific theories and things accordingly. They would not allow science to define itself as if it existed in isolation from the rest of the world and
from that world's desires.

One consequence was the machinery some spiritualists tried to bring to the
movement. John Rutter devised a "Magnetoscope" to prove that "we are
each of us surrounded by a magnetic sphere of force" that "is our medium of
communication with the spirits of our former friends." Rutter's contraption
involved a pendulum and a magnet; Robert Hare's "Spiritoscope" seems to
have been more elaborate. It manipulated weights, a pulley, a cord, and
various other devices around the key element, a circular disk designed to
receive messages. (The disk was imprinted with the letters of the alphabet,
musical notes, and some basic words and phrases, such as "I think so," "yes,"
and "I'll come again.") Crookes devised various apparatuses in the course of
his investigations, which he sought to distinguish from those of the "pseudo-
scientific spiritualist" who "talks glibly of all sciences and arts, overwhelming
the enquirer with terms like 'electro-biologize', 'psychologize', 'animal magnetism', &c.—a mere play upon words, showing ignorance rather than understanding."[44] The most publicized and notorious spiritualist machine, though,
was John M. Spear's "electrical infant," also known as "The New Motive
Power, Physical Saviour, Heaven's Last Best Gift to Man, New Creation,
The Great Spiritual Revelation of the Age, The Philosopher's Stone, The
Art of All Arts, The Science of All Sciences. . . . "[45]

A Universalist minister involved in the anti-slavery, peace, and temperance
movements before he became a medium in 1852, Spear had an inordinate
fascination with electricity. On more than one occasion, according to Emma
Hardinge, he "subjected himself to the most scathing ridicule from his contemporaries by seeking to promote the influence and control of spirits,
through the aid of copper and zinc batteries, so arranged about the person
as to form an armor, from which he expected the most extraordinary phenomenal results."[46] In High Rock, Massachusetts in 1854, Spear was moved
by spirits called "Electrizers" to have his disciples build a perpetual-motion
machine to which life would be communicated by a woman who had earlier
been impregnated by spirits. The machine was built; it was brought into
rapport with the woman in a ceremony that remains obscure and that

aroused lubricious speculation at the time; and then, according to Spear's followers, the machine began to move. If the turning table was the Model A, this was the Duesenberg. Had they been aware of it, the surrealists of the next century might have compared Spear's invention to the "Love Machine" ("*machine-à-inspirer-l'amour*") that Arthur Gough makes in Alfred Jarry's *The Supermale*—Gough, like Spear, having been inspired by Michael Faraday. Of course, one might also remember Mary Shelley's *Frankenstein*, Villiers de l'Isle-Adams's *The Future Eve* (in which Thomas Edison's recording of the song of a nightingale that has since died is described as "serious spiritism"),[47] Marcel Duchamp's *The Bride Laid Bare by Her Bachelors, Even*, and various other works that indicate how the image of humanity has been altered by the image of modern technology.

"It beats Joanna Southcott in funny absurdity, if not in blasphemy," said Barnum, who concluded that "if things like this are going to happen, the ladies will be afraid to sleep alone in the house if so much as a sewing-machine or apple-corer be about, and will not dare take solitary walks along any stream where there is a water power."[48] Like the orthography of spirits, this machine even discomfited other spiritualists. While defending it, Hardinge was disturbed by "the awkward and most injudicious claims of a human parentage for a material machine,"[49] and Andrew Jackson Davis thought the project deserving of some sympathy but believed the woman's pregnancy was psychosomatic. In the end, following much public ridicule and after it had been moved to Randolph, New York, the electrical infant was destroyed by a mob.

Spear's machine is interesting from a number of perspectives. As I have just noted, it may be seen to anticipate twentieth-century fantasies about the relations between technology and human life that have been mooted in art, popularized in movies like *The Demon Seed* (in which Julie Christie is raped by a computerized house), and elaborated in discussions about the limits, if such there may be, of artificial intelligence. In relation to nineteenth-century science, however, the most significant aspect of this invention was its appropriation of machinery as a form of language.

According to Davis's report, Spear regarded the new motive power as an artifact in which each wire was "precious, sacred, as a spiritual verse. Each plate of zinc and copper [was] clothed with symbolized meanings, corresponding throughout with the principles and parts involved in the living human organism."[50] Even aside from this description, the very idea of a machine in which human, technological, and spiritual realities would freely join suggests a belief that science is fundamentally a form of communication and so in any of its aspects is open to rhetorical manipulation. From this perspective, the new motive power was an attempt to grasp the cultural meaning and social influence that were formally distinguishable and yet practically inseparable from the power of science. It was not, as the likes of Kant would have it, a motive power of hopeless ignorance, outrageous arrogance, and would-be dogmatic ease. It was a meaningful attempt to grapple with the representational nature of the machine and of science in general (an attempt that today might be called a work of performance art). It concerned the alchemical aspect of modern science: its implication in dreams, desires, and fantasies that are social and political as well as individual. (Here a comparison with Shelley's *Frankenstein* becomes especially appropriate.) Spear's machine was an oddity even among spiritualist projects, and Spear's character begs for a diagnosis of schizophrenia; but still the meaning of his work is easily dismissed only if one ignores how fantastic a change science was bringing to the world at this time. On this point, Paul Feyerabend's argument about the futility of a priori distinctions between respectable theorists and scientific cranks becomes very interesting.[51] Spear's machine dramatized the perception that scientific reality is married to scientific metaphor, a perception with which Hawthorne and many other respectable writers were to struggle; philosophers of science, too, continue to seek an accommodation with this perception.

Still, for all the interest it held, the construction of machinery was not the usual way spiritualists would try to come to grips with the issue of metaphor and other linguistic complexities. Many other responses were possible. Some believers, like Beecher, sought language reform. Robert Owen thought this was necessary, and he also wanted to see a universal language established so as to facilitate communication all over the world. (He specified "the Anglo-Saxon" tongue.) Characteristically, Victoria Woodhull went even further, agreeing that there should be a universal language but suggesting an entirely new one called "Alwato."[52] In these and other cases, the shared conviction was that the current state of language was at best misleading and at worst quite literally maddening. Language, one might say, was an ill-designed machine. From this perspective, the linguistic improprieties that embarrassed spiritualism ought really to have embarrassed all those who communicated in correct and polished measures; and many spiritualists did not hesitate to come to this conclusion, which was at once critical and creative in relation to the polite standards of the time.

This concern with language was also expressed in relation to specific aspects of communication. One difficulty identified by spiritualists concerned the medium through which language was delivered. Already compromised as speech (or as writing, drawing, painting, or some other form of text presumed to be secondary to thought or pure spirit), communication was further straitened by the role of the mediums. Spiritualists often boasted that mediums spoke foreign languages, proffered information, and displayed a refinement that they could not possibly possess *in propria persona*. However, it became apparent early on that the spirit of Ben Franklin might misspell the same words that usually tripped up the medium taking his dictation, or that he might remember only those facts of colonial history that happened to coincide with the medium's schooling. ("All his interlocutors Swedenborgize," Emerson had noticed of the man many spiritualists adopted as an ancestor.)[53] When pressed on this point, spiritualists had a ready answer: "It is to be understood that a pipe can carry no more than its own diameter permits."[54] So said Arthur Conan Doyle, drawing on the kind of scientific analogy favored by spiritualists. If the analogy was inelegant, its very plainness could be convincing even to those who opposed this movement. "Spirits, I suppose, like earthly people, have to use such instruments as will answer their purposes," Hawthorne allowed, referring to Daniel Home, although he added that personally he would prefer not to hear from a dead friend "through the organism of a rogue and a charlatan."[55]

In addition to the constitution of the medium, his or her state of being at a particular time could affect the communications being made. Mediums were always enjoined to be utterly passive and so to be unconscious or neutral mediums. However, it was often seen that this was a state taxing to maintain and perhaps impossible to achieve to perfection. The strain could be awkward, and in a discussion of clairvoyants Dr. William Gregory rehearsed what would become a common spiritualist excuse: "I have some reason to believe that individuals, of whose power at times no doubt can reasonably be entertained, have, when over-fatigued, or by some chance, less lucid than usual, endeavored to cover failure by deceit." Even when deception was not at issue, bubbles in the glass of the medium could inflect or interrupt the communication. According to Charles Hammond, "the evil spirit who writes incorrect communications" is "the evil of self." J. B. Ferguson noted that the minds of mediums and those of spirits often mingle and that "the mixed communication is too often regarded as a pure spiritual document." In Moses's formulation,

> The purity of the spirit message depends much on the passivity of the medium and on the conditions under which the message is communicated. Hence, in your Bible there are traces here and there of the individuality of the medium; of errors caused by imperfect control; of the colour of his opinions; as well as of special peculiarities addressed to the special needs of the people to whom the message was first given, and for whose case it was primarily adapted.[56]

This argument accompanied the practice of referring to mediums as being "developing" or at a higher or lower stage of "development." As Hawthorne noted in his comparison to "earthly people," this defense of failure and error in spiritualist communications implied a disturbing argument about the nature of communication of all sorts. The word *development*, usually associated with the Victorian faith in progress, could be used to indicate that the proper interlocutor was as elusive as the proper language. Seriously raise the possibility that everyone may be at a different stage or in a different course of development in relation to everyone else, and all the world may be a scene of babbling tongues, with each utterance as resistant to communication as it is perfectly coherent to the individual producing it. The presumed universality of progressive development seemed far from reassuring if one could not also presume a basic uniformity in this progress. In the problematic communications of spiritualism, the rationalized translation of "Providence" into "progress" so characteristic of the nineteenth century confronted this incoherence in its own conception; and even writers like Hawthorne and Dickens, who did not subscribe uncritically to the notion of progress, could not accept this image of its dreamily chaotic meaning.

Another area explored by spiritualists was the scene of communication. Like the medium of language and the human medium through which speech and other forms of communication came, this social medium was fraught with difficulty. In one of its more querulous versions, this appeared in the complaints of spirits who spoke through Home and Moses to say that Derby Day, with its attendant frivolity and license, interfered with the messages they wished to transmit.[57] In one of its more subtle instances, this was the problem of cultural and historical tradition that bothered Frederic Myers when he was preparing to analyze the relation between Swedenborg and modern spiritualism. As he put it, the stumbling block was that "Swedenborg [was], in fact, a madman in most men's view"—a judgment that had "much to recommend it." But this was also a general worry in the nature of communication:

And here I meet with a kind of difficulty which is sure to present itself sooner or later to all persons who endeavour to present to the world what they regard as novel or important truths. There is sure to be some embarrassing likeness or travesty of the truth in the world already. There are sure to be sects or persons, past or present, holding something like the same beliefs on different grounds;— on grounds which one may find it equally difficult to endorse and to disavow.[58]

However it was addressed, the problem was one of determining and making allowances for changing contexts of communication, which are there before utterances—"always already there," as Derrida would say—with the maddening power to turn these utterances from their seeming intentions even though no perceptible change occurs in the form of the utterance itself.

Myers was not the only spiritualist who argued that communication in general was bedeviled by this difficulty. Hippolyte Rivail, for instance, made this point when discussing the inconsistencies in the opinions given by different spirits or through different mediums. "The contradictions," he said, "are not always as absolute as they may seem to be at first sight. Do we not see every day that men who are pursuing the same science give various definitions of the same thing; sometimes because they make use of different terms, sometimes because they consider it from different points of view, although the fundamental idea is the same in each case?" Similarly, Epes Sargent said that these communications, though various and sometimes conflicting, merely show that spirits, like mortals, are very fallible, and often very conceited individuals, many of them it may be, groping in a moral and intellectual darkness denser than that which encompasses many souls yet fettered by the flesh. It leaves us just where all codes and all revelations take us up; for the authority of a message, come whence it may, lies always in the completeness of its harmony, with the laws of our being as disclosed by the highest experiences of individuals and of the race.

Therefore, he predicted, "the supposed communications from the spirit-world will, we think, in this nineteenth century, be received as we receive communications through books, newspapers, and even weekly critical journals." A related argument, very common in spiritualist literature, held that it was always necessary to adapt one's discourse to one's audience. "Hence, spirits must either neglect one class in their communications, or write differently to benefit all classes. If they write differently, so as to instruct all classes, and develop all minds, what is wisdom to one may be esteemed folly by another."[59]

As was pointed out by Laroy Sunderland, a Swedenborgian hostile to much of what passed for spiritualism in his day, "where the method of communication is embarrassed with so very many difficulties, we must suppose it next to impossible to get pure, unadulterated truth." One might well ask how anyone could "publish books on this subject, and . . . encourage people to rely as much upon communications . . . as they would upon the advice of a 'kind, experienced parent.'"[60] But the very form of his question suggests the answer. Spiritualists could continue to send and receive messages despite endless quibbling over their meaning because they were facing the uncertainty they felt to be prevailing in all forms of communication, including even the loving discourse of a parent to a child. To withdraw from modern spiritualism because of the embarrassments to which its words were subject would have been equivalent to withdrawing from communication altogether. Such an action would have constituted an admission that all communication was a meaningless, or "spiritless," affair.

If one notices only the ontology adumbrated in the writings of spiritualists—the harmony of the spirit circles, the undead personalities, the celestial spheres, the channels of communication—one fails to observe that this representation of the universe was also an exploration of representation. By itself, this ontology would have been easy to dismiss. It could have been called a fable, a myth, or a simple delusion or lie. It was the critique of communication implicitly and explicitly made by modern spiritualism, in its undignified refusal to accept these kinds of generic distinctions, that made it so frustrating to more conventional proponents of reason.

This critique did not end with language, the spiritual medium, and the communicative context. The character and behavior of spirits were also matters inspiring much speculation. If the ambiguity of words, the capacity and conditions of the medium, and the conjugation of context were insufficient to explain disturbing features in communication, an answer might be sought in the nature of the spirits. Phenomena like those recounted by Janet were the most common impetus to such speculation among spiritualists: "[W]ho has not known families in tears, in despair, because the young girl of the household wanted to call forth angels and her hand, guided by the devil, wrote only obscenities?"[61] To Janet this was just a "laughable" example of the subconscious *idées fixes* to which he attributed different sorts of hysterical behavior, and even Swedenborgians like Sunderland and the elder Henry James would berate modern spiritualism for being too uncritical toward its messages: "[E]very one who has read Swedenborg with attention, a cool, dispassionate, scientific observer, knows very well that ghosts are up to any kind and degree of 'artful dodge' which suits their final purpose."[62] But spiritualists were not really oblivious to this problem in evaluating the spirits with which they were communicating—quite the contrary. E. W. Capron's analysis is representative:

It may be proper here to state that whatever may be the facts in regard to the wicked intent of any spirits, there is danger of great annoyance, and even injury, resulting from free communications with spirits of a coarse and undeveloped character. Either ignorantly or willfully—I am hardly able to decide which—they seek to get and keep control of the medium, making angular, discordant, and even vulgar and obscene communications.[63]

When spiritualistic or "pneumatological" theories are compared on this point to psychological explanations like Janet's, they may simply seem unbearably naive where they do not smell suspiciously of self-justification. This naiveté would lie in the way they project onto imaginary spirits expressions properly belonging to the medium. However, as naive as it is to assume the utter innocence of the medium, it may be more naive to assume that one can trace communication back to its proper origin within the minds of individual human beings.

"Never forget that there are tricksters and liars out of the flesh as well as in it," said Leah (Fox) Underhill.[64] If this assertion may be a convenient disguise for the medium's true character, it may also suggest the perception that the truth and meaning of communications do not lie wholly within individuals or individual words on a page. The belief that spirits speak to and through us may be more than an instance of hysteria, a defense of chicanery, an echo of outmoded theories of demonology, or a metaphor for other kinds of cultural inheritance (as in the description of ghosts in Henrik Ibsen's play).[65] It may be a perception of the contradictions in the relation between the vanishing pinpoint of individuality and the hallucinatory environment of universality. In other words, it may be an attempt to come to terms with the disparity between the spirit of reason and the meaningful experience of individuals. In dealing with spirits, Immanuel Hermann von

Fichte said, one may encounter an "objective, but falsified, 'lying' manifestation";[66] and in what respect did such a possibility differ from what one faced
in dealing with any other kind of experience? From this perspective, as a
representation of the experience of representation, spiritualism certainly was
often stupid and inchoate and tedious. However, it was also truth-seeking in
a way that was discredited for reasons having little to do with scientific truth.
Spiritualism was never really a threat to scientific truth, but it did prove a
real challenge to the forms of experience that the dominant ideologies of the
nineteenth century, including empiricism, wished to identify as necessarily
governing each and every individual.

   George Eliot's correspondence with Harriet Beecher Stowe is particularly
enlightening on this point. Stowe was influenced in part by her husband's
lifelong spiritual visions; and although she came to different conclusions
about modern spiritualism at different times, even at her most skeptical
she went well beyond the common nineteenth-century saying that "there's
something in it." In response to Stowe's conversations with a spirit claiming
to be Charlotte Brontë (which Stowe's brother, Charles Beecher, printed in
his *Spiritual Manifestations*), Eliot wrote as follows:

> *Your* experience with the *planchette* is amazing; but that the words which you
> found it to have written were dictated by the spirit of Charlotte Brontë is to me
> (whether rightly or not) so enormously improbable, that I could only accept it if
> every condition were laid bare, and every other explanation demonstrated to be
> impossible. If it were another spirit aping Charlotte Brontë—if here and there at
> rare spots and among   people of a certain temperament, or even at many spots
> among people of all temperaments, tricksy spirits are liable to rise up as a sort of
> earth-bubbles and set furniture in movement, and tell things which we either know
> already or should be as well without knowing—I must frankly confess that I have
> but a feeble interest in these doings, feeling my life very short for the supreme and
> awful revelations of a more orderly and intelligible kind which I shall die with an
> imperfect knowledge of. If there were miserable spirits whom we could help—
> then I think we should pause and have patience with their trivial-mindedness; but
> otherwise I don't feel bound to study them any more than I am bound to study the
> special follies of a particular phase of human society.[67]

Eliot was trying to be diplomatic in referring to the beliefs of a woman she
admired, and her strain seems evident in the equivocal and disconnected
language of this response. Her attitude was a fairly common one among
opponents of spiritualism; believers often expressed their outrage at this sort
of appeal to a tacit sense of probability, which they saw as begging the
question. Most interesting here, however, are the contrasts Eliot drew between Charlotte Brontë and "tricksy spirits" and, more generally, between
"revelations of a more orderly and intelligible kind" and "the special follies
of a particular phase of human society." These contrasts serve to enforce a
distinction, between rationality and bizarre or eccentric phenomena, that
spiritualism resolutely refused to observe. In assuming that "follies" are un-

worthy of study—are, in effect, meaningless—this response might well be seen as being more naive about the conditions of meaning and the complexities of experience than spiritualism ever was. Whether Eliot's attitude in her fiction is the same as in this letter is another question, but here, at least, her sense that the spirit of Brontë cannot be expected to converse with living human beings may seem surprisingly vulnerable. Rather than arguing against naiveté, Eliot seems to be arguing for a kind of faith, in individual propriety and in the propriety of rational knowledge, which is itself as naive as it is condescending.

Like the writer who finally finds the right track, reason wants to overlook trickeries and follies in order to preserve order and intelligibility; hence its frustration with a movement that claimed the title of reason while neither overcoming nor condescending to the contradictions of individual experience. Reason asserted the improbability of communication with spirits, but spiritualism trumped this assertion. It suggested the improbability of communication of any kind and so raised upsetting questions about the identity—the spirit—of reason.

All these complexities of communication were summarized in the issue of "personation." This term was sometimes applied to mediumistic possession (entranced mediums "personated" the spirits speaking through them, and one might even have a case of "Personation by a Table"),[68] but more often it described the behavior of spirits. To *personate* was to assume an identity, and much spiritualist discourse turned upon the problems raised by the invisibility of spirits. To put it simply, one could not be sure of a spirit's identity and so could not know how its communications should be interpreted. The medium's and the spirit's integrity were radically distinguished and yet inextricably knotted together in this issue of personation, for no one could devise an entirely satisfactory response to the question raised by the chairman of the Dialectical Committee: "How can you distinguish between a medium who is an impostor and a spirit that is a liar?"[69] The problem was not solved when spirits began to materialize in the form of hands, faces, entire bodies, or photographic images, for even the most solid and distinct of these manifestations could not eliminate the suspicion that identities were being falsely assumed. "Tell me all about the spirits, only not about what they say of *me*," wrote Elizabeth Barrett Browning to Fanny Haworth, who had sent her a spirit message purporting to come from her recently deceased father. "I am very interested. The drawback is, that without any sort of doubt they *personate falsely*."[70]

Théophile Gautier was one of many to point out that mediumistic communication might be comparable to the traditional literary concept of inspiration, and this parallel could be extended to encompass all the ills to which texts are heir, from stupidity to cupidinous irresponsibility to the ghostly abyss of false personation, which literary language would term "plagiarism."[71] Thus, the problem of personation was the problem of textuality. To define reference, truth, and meaning with any hope of accuracy, it seemed that at the very least one had to know who was talking. While psychologists like Taine sought to establish this identity through the reformulation of psychology as an empirical science, this did not really respond to the question spiritualism was asking. Even if one granted that "the spirit" speaking through the medium was only a metaphor, these psychologists (as Nietzsche recognized) failed to respond to the implications of their own idea that "identity" was spirit under another name—that identity was itself a figure of speech.

Even as they clung to the idea of distinct personal identities that persisted after death, spiritualists explored identity as a form of representation. Since the issue of personation suggested that identity might be nothing more or less than a figure of speech, a thing "detached by fiction," as even Taine was prepared to admit,[72] the question of who was speaking would become the question of what discourse was speaking. No wonder Taine wanted to assert a professional control over discourse; no wonder Binet would warn against the seductive appeal of spiritualist experiments by saying that "in each experience one always tends to lose a little of the unity of his thought and the clearness of his intellect."[73] Once confront the issue of personation, and one runs smack into the problem of the cultural order of representation.

It is significant in this regard that personation was most frequently discussed in relation to the famous spirits who solicited communication with the living. The basic difficulty posed by these spirits was the same as that posed by the Bible, as Stainton Moses regarded it: "None can accept the whole, because the whole is not homogeneous."[74] In contending with inconsistencies and the related problems of verbal forms or statements that did not seem to live up to the standards associated with the famous names to which they were attributed, spiritualists were unpacking, as if from a magician's kit, the practices of reason that establish meaningful communication. In addition to the assumptions that words are always present to consciousness and that identity is essentially a stable, consistent, and reliable factor in communication, these practices included those tacit and explicit cultural teachings that turned proper names into adjectives. After all, when someone like the narrator of Edward Bulwer-Lytton's "The Haunted and the Haunters" denied that communications purporting to come from the likes of Shakespeare could actually have come from him, he had to appeal to a recognizable "Shakespearean spirit" that was just as invisible as the spirit of which mediums spoke. In their disquisitions on personation, spiritualists explored the implications of this metaphorical life that was so essential a part of rational ideation. They acted out the figurative nature of rational experience. From this drama came their recognition of the complex relations between individual identity and social representation, as in the analysis of personation offered by Hippolyte Rivail ("Allan Kardec"):

Experience shows us that spirits of the same degree, of the same character, and animated by the same sentiments, are united in groups and families; but the number of spirits is incalculable, and we are so far from knowing them all, that the names of the immense majority of them are necessarily unknown to us. A spirit of the same category as Fénélon may therefore come to us in his name, and may even be sent by him as his representative; in which case he would naturally announce himself as Fénélon, because he is his equivalent, and able to supply his place, and because we need a name in order to fix our ideas in regard to him. And, after all, what does it matter whether a spirit be really Fénélon or not, if all he says is excellent, and such as Fénélon himself would be likely to say? . . .

It is certain, however, that the assumption of false names by spirits may give rise to numerous mistakes, may be a source of error and deception, and is, in fact, one of the most serious difficulties of practical spiritism.[75]

A common habit in nineteenth-century literature was to sprinkle one's writing with unattributed quotations from writers of the past both famous and obscure. The dead that spoke in modern spiritualism should be compared to these literary voices. In both cases people created a living past; in both cases problems might arise in orchestrating the conflicting possibilities that the dead presented to the understanding of the living. In claiming that the dead yet lived, spiritualism did not really claim more than did laborers in the mainstream of literature. All it claimed was a different interpretation of textual reality. The fact that this interpretation was forwarded through outright fraud and fantasy need not in any way detract from the recognition that spiritualism was, among other things, an exploration of representation that revealed and criticized assumptions of which reason was generally unconscious. After all, fraud and fantasy were acceptable literary practices; and if they seemed ridiculously out of place in the other disciplines, such as philosophy and science, with which spiritualists sought to be identified, spiritualism was able to show the considerable extent to which these disciplines, too, were literary. In other words, it was able to show their reliance on figures of speech in their institutionalization as disciplines and in their expressions of disciplinary authority. The state of unconsciousness sought by spiritualist mediums thus traced the detours in the progress of reason and challenged the attempt to isolate its practices from the dissonance of conflicting figures of speech. And as I have previously suggested, this revision of culture certainly had a political edge, which was nicely captured by the anonymous writer who commented, "Spiritualists admit that many messages . . . are worthless, and in some cases are untrue, but hold that the way to prevent false messages coming from the other world, is to cease sending untruthful people into it from this one."[76]

Consider in this respect what might be termed the most literary passage in Lewes's *Study of Psychology*. It appears near the end of the book, where he is occupied in defining "Human Knowledge":

The consolidations of convergent thought in Social Forms, scientific theories, works of Art, and, above all, Language, are incessantly acting on me. Ideas are forces: the existence of one determines our reception of others. Each novel impression has to be assimilated by the existing mass of residual impressions; each new conclusion has to be affiliated on the old, dovetailed into the rest, made congruent with the system of thought. In the great total of collective Experience, — as in that of the individual, — absurd perversions and wild fancies take their place beside exact correspondences of feeling and fact, and truths that are unshakable; it is a shifting mass of truth and error, for ever becoming more and more sifted and organised into permanent structures of germinating fertility or of fossilised barrenness. Our mental furniture shows the *bric à brac* of prejudice beside the fashion of the hour; our opinions are made up of shadowy associations, imperfect memories, echoes of other men's voices, mingling with the reactions of our own sensibility. Thus it is that a mass of incoherent and unreasoned premises are brought to bear on the evidence for any new opinion, as for any novel fact: this is the unrecognised standard by which the conclusion is determined. The most rational of men mingles with premises logically assignable obscure premises of which he can give no account.

Reason here does not seem such a prideful thing. It is so deeply implicated in an unreasoned culture and history that it can hardly account for itself. If progress is suggested by its "for ever becoming more and more sifted and organised into permanent structures," it is not assured by the result, which may be "germinating fertility" but may also be "fossilised barrenness." As this description indicates, it is not to be supposed that Lewes, Taine, or the other nineteenth-century proponents of scientific reason thought this to be a simple faculty. Nonetheless, they thought it antithetical to spiritualism. They recognized no community between their "mental furniture," with its "shadowy associations" and "echoes of other men's voices," and the speaking furniture of spiritualism. Directly following this passage, in fact, Lewes launched into an attack on this movement:

A deep longing for some direct proof of existence after death has made hundreds of people accept the grossest impostures of "Spiritualism," impostures which contradicted the most massive experiences of the race, and which had nothing to support them save this emotional credulity acting where direct knowledge was wholly absent. Because men did *not* know how the appearances were produced, — the means of knowledge being carefully withheld, — they willingly accepted the explanation which suited their preconceptions, disregarding the incongruous and often degrading circumstances which would otherwise have repelled their belief. And that this is so may be readily proved. For in the absence of all positive knowledge how the tables were moved, or the lights and flowers were produced, there could be no ground for concluding that these effects were produced by spirits. What data have we for supposing that spirits are thus occupied? All would reject the hypothesis that the agent was an invisible dragon, not because they know more about spirits than about dragons, but because the idea of the dragon is incongruous with their preconception and with their desire.[77]

Having just confessed to reason's ineradicable emotions, preconceptions, and desires, Lewes could yet dismiss spiritualism on precisely those grounds. He could do so without acknowledging any contradiction or uncertainty because he treated the discourse of spiritualism as a psychological symptom rather than a meaningful communication. He could prove that "spirits" might just as well be "dragons," were it not for an accident of cultural tradition, because he assumed he could isolate his own language from its psychological detours even while admitting that language never takes a direct route to its object. It is not logical that he should have found "spirits" more inadmissable than "forces" or "ideas," but logic was not the issue. It was not logic that decided where language terminated in a symptom—an irrational and *degrading* metaphor—and where it fought its way past such dragons to rescue the prize of elevating images.[78] Not logical order but the order of figuration was in question here.

In other words, the issue was the image of reason; and the image Lewes was determined to maintain was that of a power that mediated all psychological signs, or figures, into a general "experience of the race" that could be asserted without fear of meaningful contradiction. Reason neither provided nor administered the distinction between psychological symptoms and meaningful communications on which intellectuals like Lewes relied. On the contrary, this distinction formally defined reason, which figured in it as the capacity to distinguish and mediate conflicting subjectivities. Reason represented the way "the great total of collective Experience" was to be conceived and appropriated by individual persons, and they by it. Reason, then, was the issue of the social figures individuals personated or felt themselves to be. Contrary to its orthodox representation as the ultimate judge of, guide through, or legislator to experience, reason appears here as the issue of experience, which intellectuals like Lewes wanted to identify with their faith in certain forms of words and communication. To people like Lewes, reason was just this assumption that one could distinguish meaningful from deviant forms no matter how closely they were interrelated; and so they could not help but be frustrated by the image of reason suggested by spiritualism, which made communications so doubtful and experiences so incongruous.

Even while admitting its many and ineradicable flaws, reason was bound to uphold a certain image of itself in the form of culture. Culture was state-of-the-art reason. It was to provide guiding forms for the experience of the age. It is not surprising, then, to find that spiritualists were often struggling to conjure with the experience and the names of the past so as to formulate an alternative way of conceiving their relation to individuals in the present. This is perhaps what bothered the highly educated opponents of spiritualism most of all: that spiritualists would act in such an *uncultured* manner— would not recognize an established history to the conception and discussion of culture—as they articulated their sense of experience. To put it in the simplest possible terms, it was not what spiritualists said so much as the way they said it that was so frustrating. Style, too, is political, nothing more so.

The ways spiritualists conceived of the relation between the individual and the universal or the present and the past were not particularly original. Just as spiritualists' communications with famous historical figures might be seen as an unconscious imitation of certain literary protocols, banalities such as Robert Owen's reference to "the Spirits of our departed relatives and friends, who in the world of spirits are also assisted by the sages and prophets of olden times, and of all that is superior among them,"[79] might be seen as a crude attempt to formulate an image of culture such as that which appeared in Alfred Tennyson's "In Memoriam" or in the writings of Matthew Arnold. Even when the image was more elaborate, as in Charles Bray's *On Force* (a work, according to Wallace, that "labors under the great objection of being unintelligible"),[80] one might see a bizarre attempt to define the unexceptionable concept of the *Zeitgeist* or the spirit of the age:

When I speak then of a "thought" atmosphere, a "mental" atmosphere, or a "general" mind, I mean either mind or sentiency, or that condition of force which immediately precedes mind or consciousness, and which must exist in the brain, when from a slight pressure upon it, consciousness ceases.

To the transference of nervous force, and even mental states with it, from one body to another, and to the union of individual mind with the mental atmosphere, are owing I think it will be found, all the varied phenomena of somnambulism, mesmerism, and clairvoyance, and of what is called spiritualism.[81]

And at times there is hardly any difference between spiritualist suppositions and images that might be used by philosophical historians or by writers like George Eliot, as in Stephen Pearl Andrews's series of essays in *Woodhull and Claflin's Weekly*:

I believe that all men and things have spiritual emanations, which tend to aggregate into more attenuated reproductions of themselves, modified by conjunction with other emanations from other objects. How far these new ethereal personalities attain to an independent consciousness, and are really the "national angels" of particular peoples, remains to be discovered.[82]

But it would be a mistake to suppose that spiritualists were struggling to develop concepts at which smarter and better-educated people had already arrived, just as it would be misleading to think that spiritualists' explications of the problems of communication unknowingly recapitulated earlier hermeneutics. The conflict between spiritualists and their opponents suggested the more provocative thesis that reason might never arrive at the ends to which it already seemed to have arrived. In its conclusions reason might try to ignore the detours of experience, but conflicts over the articulation of experience would show that these conclusions were themselves detours, with no end in sight.

Quite movingly, this sense of experience was communicated by "Anna Suzanne" in a letter to Margaret (Fox) Kane. The occasion of this letter was a newspaper report of Margaret Kane's disavowal of the spiritualist movement and recantation of her own claims to mediumship, and it was quoted by a critic of spiritualism to illustrate the movement's destructiveness. The writer tells of having spent thousands of dollars on mediums, about whom she now has doubts; and yet these lines speak less to a disgust with fraud than to a problem of establishing identity that might just as well occur when trying to communicate with living persons. In this respect, they recall the themes of Alfred Tennyson's "In Memoriam":

> It is true that never once have I received a message or the token of a word that did not leave a still unsatisfied longing in my heart, a feeling that it was not really my loved one after all, who was speaking to me, or if it was my loved one, that he was changed, that I hardly knew him and that he hardly knew me. . . . The constant, the frequent pretended response, its unsatisfying meaning, the sense of distance and change between me and my loved one—oh! it has been horrible, horrible![83]

The spiritualist movement dramatized the trope of *prosopopoeia*, which in traditional rhetorical theory names the personification of inanimate things or the assignment of discursive presence to persons who are absent, unreal, or dead. Having thus described spiritualism, however, I must immediately suggest that this description be retracted. The problem is that this traditional rhetorical scheme turns upon the assumption that at the center of discourse there is a proper way of referring to things, in relation to which all other rhetorical forms are additions, ornaments, or distortions, whether strategic or inadvertent. One could call this case of proper reference the casket of propriety, for it encrypts within discourse a corpus of logical distinctions and relations between the animate and the inanimate, the human and the nonhuman, presence and absence, reality and unreality, and so on. This logical corpus is encrypted because it is supposed to govern the way discourse is interpreted and yet is not itself regarded as discourse that is subject to interpretation. Engraved in language, it governs from beyond the grave; proper reference *is* prosopopoeia.[84]

To make this statement, of course, is to suggest a deconstruction of traditional rhetorical theory that entails as well a surrender of the notion of person to the experience of personation. The power of suggestion in modern spiritualism had just this effect. In saying so I do not mean to slight the complexities and contradictions of the spiritualist movement, which counted among its advocates many who were terribly concerned to represent themselves as the most proper persons, correct speakers, and decorous writers imaginable. This is why I choose the nineteenth-century term *suggestion*, which tended to displace the logic of proper reference with a logic of persuasion that would eventually occupy the interests of Freud, among others. Suggestively, as living movement or turning of prosopopoeia, modern spiritualism desecrated the sacred grounds of discourse and effectively showed them to be cultural and political. Instead of being the abstract foundation of logical governance, they were shown to be grounds for rebellion. From this perspective, the relentless apologetics of the spiritualists, which might seem designed merely to be self-serving, appears instead as an attack on the tyranny of the self, the "person" of rhetoric and philosophy, which spiritualists wanted to oust in favor of an "other" identity, a purely *suggestive* identity. In dramatically undoing the seeming paradox of the living dead, in insisting on the openness and immediacy of this undoing, and in thus allowing supposedly inanimate tables to move and seemingly absent or imaginary worlds to be present at hand and perceptibly real, spiritualists were engaged in seeing what might appear when the logical distinction between literal and figurative language was collapsed and this tyrannical, unjustifiable person—this corpus of rational superstition—was brought back to life.

Like spiritualists, Taine and Lewes appealed to the authority of experience against all dogmas, desires, and preconceptions. Spiritualism, however, exposed the weak point in the way this appeal was forwarded by reason. In communicating the difficulty of communication, this movement showed that experience is cultural, not natural or logical, and that culture in its turn is chaotically overdetermined. In other words, it showed that the image of reason could not be sustained by the experience of reason alone. It demonstrated that meaningful experience was secondary to the cultural order it was supposed to originate, so that neither culture nor reason could ever find the experience necessary to ground its pretensions. This is what spiritualist writings said: that persons must struggle to communicate because experience commands reason by speaking in diverse, conflicting, infinitely suggestive tongues.

What made spiritualism vulgar, in its ungrammatical writings or in its banal desires or in its parroting of parodies of philosophy, religion, and literary tradition, was that it would not permit experience to speak with a single voice. (A ghostly spirit never comes singly, by itself: the numinous ghost is the very image of numerousness, of the absence of singularity haunting one's life, one's name, one's supposed identity.) Spiritualism treated culture as something that sported with persons and thus something with which these same persons could play, disassembling and reassembling it according to their desires.[85] Reason was not beyond this play but structured by it, as in the culturally assumed relations between logic and rhetoric or between interpretation and text. Within and through spiritualism, then, reason recognized how it fell short of its own image and desperately tried to catch up to this phantom, succeeding only in spinning out different images, images as trite and ridiculous as ghosts and yet, to many, excitingly new, as desirable as they were inconclusive or discomfiting, or even desirable *because* they were inconclusive and discomfiting. ("Paradoxical as the assertion may seem," wrote Louisa Lowe, "it is in the impurities, and above all, the inconsistencies and the incongruities of modern revelation that I find its chief value.")[86] In comparison to reason, spiritualism was most assuredly vulgar, and this vulgarity was the pathos of spiritualism; but spiritualism was the pathos of reason.

4

The Medium of Reason

"I am not talking to you now through the medium of custom, conventionalities, nor even of mortal flesh:—it is my spirit that addresses your spirit; just as if both had passed through the grave, and we stood at God's feet, equal—as we are!"

Jane Eyre to Edward Rochester[1]

The Only News I know
Is Bulletins all Day
From Immortality.

EMILY DICKINSON[2]

At a remarkable gathering between the years 1854 and 1857—the exact date does not come down to us—Robert Owen met with His Royal Highness the Duke of Kent, Thomas Jefferson, and Benjamin Franklin. Also in attendance, according to Owen's record of the event, were William Ellery Channing, Alexander Chalmers, Percy Bysshe Shelley, Lord Byron, and "several old prophets." Owen's account continues:

> [O]n this occasion the spirits of eight of my deceased relatives were also present. Each one communicated with me through distinct different raps, in their strongly marked characters as when in life upon earth.

> The object of these extraordinary communications from the invisible spheres of spirits is uniformly stated by each of these advanced spirits, when asked separately and at different times, to be to reform the world and to unite the population as one family of man.[3]

Owen's mind had been opened to spiritual intercourse by the famous Mrs. Hayden, who had landed on England's shore in 1853 as an ambassador with a double mission, from the New World and from the Other World. We do not know who guided Owen's conversations on this occasion, but in his last years the voice of reason spoke to him most tellingly through a medium of one sort or another. A human medium, that is—a man, woman, or child who had become a channel of communication between persons in our world and spirits departed from this life.

While Owen was turning to spiritualism, George Eliot was turning to the medium of art, especially the art of fiction. (It was in 1857 that she published her first story, "The Sad Fortunes of the Reverend Amos Barton," in *Blackwood's Magazine*.) Art was coming to represent to her the new form of religion that others were finding in spiritualism. She considered art to be sacred and absolutely vital to the communication of truth in the modern world. "I become more and more timid," she would write, "—with less daring to adopt any formula which does not get itself clothed for me in some human figure and individual experience, and perhaps that is a sign that if I help others to see at all it must be through that medium of art."[4]

Medium in these two instances is likely to seem a false cognate, not the proper material for cultural analysis. And any influence or literary borrowing between these two writers is certainly very unlikely. Nonetheless, Owen's dotty faith in mediums in his last years was closely related to Eliot's dignified conception of art and human life. This relation came about through the general employment of this term, the *medium*, in the physical science, psychology, philosophy, history, and art of the mid-nineteenth century. Despite the different twists given to this term in various fields, the basic conception of the medium was shared by all of them. As a figure of understanding, the medium straddled space, culture, communication, literature, and all other areas of potential thought and creation, at once opening and promising them to reason, submitting them all to the desire for enlightenment. The medium, then, was comparable in its assumed universality to terms such as "the body," "the spirit," "force," "truth," and "reason" itself.

In any age a term given so much power will reverberate with the stresses of historical conflict and change, much as the tables of this era shook and danced and rapped with the desire for communication; and the nineteenth-century medium was indeed very eloquent. As unlikely as it may seem, the relation between Owen and Eliot was real. Victorian spiritualism and art struggled over the possession of the medium and the discourse associated with it, and in this struggle we can trace the occult politics of knowledge in this time.

The medium witnessed to history in a much less obvious way than coinages like "the shopocracy," "cotton lords," and "the aristocracy of labor." These grimaced with the strain of adapting language to new conditions, but the medium presented an untroubled face to the world. It could seem inconspicuous, verily a neutral go-between, or a term so ubiquitous as to seem hardly a word at all. In its rhetorical pliancy (the medium of language, the medium of art, the medium of time, the social medium, and so on, ad infinitum), it could seem at once universal, endlessly versatile, and completely invisible. To some extent, it might be compared to "the gentleman," another term that looked quite ordinary while being subject to much grievance; and yet Victorians were very conscious of the changing fortunes of the gentleman, whereas their references to mediums generally passed without remark.

Even today, it must seem odd to write of this term as I am doing, to describe "the medium" doing this or that, even though it would not seem strange if I were to present other figures, such as "nature," in the same way. We are used to addressing many so-called abstractions as actual beings, as when we write sentences such as "Nature always drew Wordsworth into feelings of sadness and thoughts of duty"; but our expectations are different with the medium. It has been such a perfect servant, instantly appearing when called but otherwise fading into the furnishings in the background of our world, that we are still very unlikely to see it as a character in its own right. Noticing this figure requires some violence to our sense of language and history. To pay attention to it, we have to yank the rug out from under the relations of understanding in this time — as we may by turning our attention to the historical intersection of spiritualism and literature, Owen's medium and Eliot's. And to approach this intersection as something more than an unlikely play on words, we need first to consider the relations between spiritualism and the other disciplines of knowledge I have mentioned, with which it acted out a much more obvious rivalry than it displayed with literature.

In the field of physical science, a medium was a particular form, state, or arrangement of matter and thus any describable condition of objectivity. This usage supported the more specialized role of the medium as a term for the ether, which was a conception of the universal medium of matter that had originated in Aristotelian cosmology and was not to be finally discarded until the development of Einstein's theory of relativity in the twentieth century. In its universal role, the medium was vital to nineteenth-century science and yet so naked of definition that it could come to seem scandalous, as Auguste Comte recognized in his *Course in Positive Philosophy*. Those who "believe in caloric, in luminous ether, or electric fluids," he wrote, "have no right to despise the elementary spirits of Paracelsus, or to refuse to admit angels and genii."[5] Like electricity, the agency Joseph Priestley had considered a danger to philosophy because its invisibility could give rise to limitless speculation,[6] the medium played a role that might seem to drive empirical science far beyond itself, into the willful depths of the imagination. Even scientists who opposed spiritualism, such as Balfour Stewart and P. C. Tait, could find in the medium a way to blot out materialist objections to the Christian idea of life after death:

May we not regard ether or the medium as not merely a bridge between one portion of the visible universe and another, but also as a bridge between one order of things and another, forming as it were a species of cement, in virtue of which the various orders of the universe are welded together and made into one? In fine, what we generally call ether may be not a mere medium, but a medium *plus* the invisible order of things.[7]

It is but a step from Stewart and Tait's position to that of the British photographer who wrote, "My experiences have demonstrated that there exists in nature a fluid or an ether, which condenses under certain conditions and which, in this state, becomes visible to sensitive persons," to whom "it denotes the existence of an invisible intelligent force."[8]

Many spiritualists were well aware of how convenient, or sloppy, the scientific conception of the medium was. When the British photographer came to his conclusion, as when Théophile Gautier had the titular heroine of *Spirit* describe her environment beyond the grave as "the unfathomable ether,"[9] he was only following out a possibility already allowed by scientists; and some scientists were prepared to go all the way with him. For instance, Robert Hare, who had been a professor of chemistry at the University of Pennsylvania before he became a spiritualist, thought that the extreme speed of light and electricity through the "ethereal medium" furnished grounds for the inference "that the instrument of Divine will acts with still greater velocity."[10] Like Stewart and Tait, Hare could be described as a man probing the images at the limits of science for their logical implications; in this endeavor he also resembled Comte, who had decided to turn his positivism into a form of religion, notwithstanding his earlier criticism of the spiritualized language of science. In fact, Comte began to rewrite positivism as the Religion of Humanity during the same period when the spiritualist movement was sweeping across America and Europe, and this coincidence is significant. Comte had always thought that "positive" science was a necessary outgrowth of and control over the merely "negative" freedom of inquiry guaranteed to enlightened reason, but by this time he had come to believe in the further necessity of girding scientific understanding with ritual practices and an emotional, traditional, communal faith. This turn of his thinking, which met a sympathetic response in the writings of some of his erstwhile disciples, such as John Stuart Mill and George Eliot, resembles the turn that spiritualists gave to science when they read it as a language that actually supported them because they could regard its doings as being encompassed by their faith.

More commonly, however, spiritualists devoted themselves to harsh criticism of the imagistic limits of science, hoping thereby to discredit the apparent opposition between the established discipline and their beliefs. Referring to Priestley, Leibniz, Michael Faraday, T. H. Huxley, and Herbert Spencer, among others, Charles Beecher argued that the existence of spirits "seems no more incredible than the hypothesis of the existence of ultimate particles of matter."[11] The contention was that the agencies posited by orthodox scientists had no more ground beneath them than the spirits and were actually less credible. After all, they were arbitrary and abstract suppositions, unlike the familiar and ingratiating figures of spiritualism, which could call one by name and touch one's leg and speak in a style one could fondly identify. So Dr. George Sexton pointed out:

> The atoms themselves have never been cognised by any of the senses, and their existence, therefore, is purely hypothetical. . . . Of course the existence of these molecules is said to be arrived at by inference, or as a necessary means of explaining the phenomena that we do see and know; but then, why is the existence of other things — spirit, for example — denied on the very ground that such inferences are not allowable, if we would have anything like certainty in our conclusions?[12]

During the nineteenth century, the theory of "imponderable fluids" acting upon matter was replaced with theories of the ways dynamic forces like electricity and magnetism acted through material media, but spiritualists were not daunted by this tossing of invisible agents onto the rubbish heaps of history. Some, like Justinus Kerner and Samuel Guppy, stubbornly or ignorantly clung to the notion of imponderable substances. Others, like Dr. William Gregory, evaded the issue of specifying the spirits' physical nature. And as previously indicated, people such as Hare, Alfred Russel Wallace, Frederic Myers, and Johann Carl Friedrich Zöllner made the new theories work for them — milked them for all they were worth, in fact.[13] Here the common argument was that spiritualism was not anything supernatural at all. It was a new discovery in nature fully explicable by rational analogy from commonly accepted scientific images and truths. Thus, when Adin Ballou explained "Spiricity" as the "spiritual atmosphere, or element, serving as a medium of communication to conscious intelligences," he argued on the assumption that "the whole universe is one vast complication of mediumship." His argument continued, "Spirit works within and upon matter. Interior substances demonstrate themselves through exterior and grosser ones. The higher and lower throughout nature are linked together by intervening grades."[14] Even as it diverges from the orthodoxies of Victorian science, each sentence of this explanation mimics almost perfectly the language of that science.

Spiritualists would not allow the medium in the discourse of science to remain unconscious of its importance. This was their revelation: that this figure that spoke from science also spoke from other spheres of rational discourse, in fact consolidated all these spheres by its utterances, and so possessed an occult power in the judgment of meaningful communication among the educated classes. Its role in theoretical explanation was vital but abyssal, for it served as a kind of asylum of ignorance to which scientists and other thinkers could relegate all the unknowns, faults, failures, and compromises in their comprehension of things. As a result, the medium had become the figure through which the culturally constructed practices of physics and other fields were dissimulated and unnamed, represented only through their denial, and thus returned to cultural history as seemingly unmediated experiences, regularities, and laws. In this respect, the medium was truly the unrecognized voice of truth, a voice from the Other Side, and the font of all essential communication. And since all knowledge of what Victorians called the spirit of humanity also passed through this form of communication, humanity, too, depended on the speaking of the medium.

In other words, the spiritualists' practices symbolically awakened the medium to a consciousness of its rationally unfounded and potentially confounding role in rational discourse. The typical structure of a seance—in which seemingly ordinary persons fell into a state of unconsciousness, became mediums of communication beyond the usual constraints of time and space, and finally returned to their ordinary appearance—dramatized this awakening of the universal medium to an awareness of its role. So did the blossoming of different sorts of mediums that immediately followed the advent of modern spiritualism: rapping mediums, tilting mediums, trance mediums, speaking mediums, writing mediums, drawing mediums, healing mediums, clairvoyant mediums, clairaudiant mediums, physical force mediums (in whose presence objects were moved about), pointing mediums (who communicated by gestural signs), psychometric mediums (who divined one's character), universal mediums (who produced intellectual as well as material manifestations), and so on. One classification in *The Medium and Daybreak* listed twenty-four types, including the recondite "Pulsatory Medium" and "Duodynamic Medium";[15] this paper's correspondents even reported the existence of clairvoyant horses and bulls.

The lead article in the second issue of *The Medium and Daybreak* reflected on this question of how communication originated in, through, and beyond culture. The article was titled "My Name: 'The Medium and Daybreak,'" and in it the paper beseeched,

> I hope no one will object to my name. Whether such a thing as "spiritualism" exists or not is a question with some. Its numerous explanations are exceedingly conflicting; but there is no doubt as to the existence of a peculiar faculty of the human organism which has received the appellation of "mediumship." Man's organisation is a "medium" whereby he performs the functions necessary to life and thought; and, in other respects, human beings and the means which they use, are the "media" for purposes and processes beyond themselves. This is my position exactly. Many minds are busily engaged in the investigation of mediumship, its nature, cause, products, and results; and I desire to be a "medium" between them and the accomplishment of their labours.

Returning to this topic almost two years later, the paper pointed out that its form exemplified its philosophy:

It has always been our effort to make Spiritualists feel that this paper is *their* MEDIUM, and not the exponent of the views of one person or set of persons. Hence, our columns have been largely occupied with communications "to the Editor," thus allowing every Spiritualist who had a fact, a thought, or suggestion to offer, to occupy the same position as the Editor does himself.[16]

The whole universe being a vast complication of mediumship, there was no logical end to the activities that might be seen as a manifestation of the infinite. This universe might lift a piece of chalk and scrawl out a greeting or a bit of advice . . . give a stool a spin of sidereal significance . . . display heaven in a wildflower . . . or make any body speak. So Lizzie Doten, the spiritualist poet who served as a channel for Edgar Allen Poe, among others, could argue that Poe was a "medium for the general inspiration which sets like a current of living fire through the universe."[17]

As far as spiritualists were concerned, there was nothing irrational in such manifestations. On the contrary, they hoped to prove that reason was exactly what their opponents agreed it was, the ultimate medium, through which all of reality aspired to the condition of thought. To its advocates in the nineteenth century, reason seemed to have surpassed the doubts of David Hume, who had seen the necessity of a medium to justify causal reasoning but had confessed, "What that medium is . . . passes my comprehension."[18] For spiritualists, as for critics of spiritualism such as Eliot, one simply had to reason one's confidence, lest all intuitions should prove blind and all concepts empty. In effect, reason was the cunning transubstantiation of every possible medium into the all-encompassing ideal of continuous progress without which there seemed to be no assurance of meaning in any communication.

In dramatizing the power of the medium through their seances and other practices, spiritualists were certainly bad scientists, but they were often perceptive critics of the ideology of science. They were not wearing pots for hats, struggling to shoot the stolen guns they had reloaded with pebbles and dirt — savages clumsily imitating the actions of civilized men. They were more like a man Claude Lévi-Strauss described in *Tristes Tropiques*: the tribal leader who observed the anthropologist busily scribbling in his notebook and then imitated his gestures of writing and reading, thus impressing the tribe with his seeming mastery. Spiritualists were people seized by the tantalizing power that rushes from civilization's representation of itself. They reached out for and were haunted by an imagined origin of communication glimmering through the intentions of disparate individuals to convey particular meanings. Like so many in this time, the spiritualists were no longer satisfied with the access to this imaginary origin once symbolically provided by the established institutions of church and state; what set them apart from the crowd was their reluctance to relocate this origin in more modern and presumably reformed institutions of knowledge, among which could be counted both empirical science and realist art. Their skepticism toward interpretive authority even in its modern forms led them to regard scientific civilization as above all else a form of communication, an institution built of rhetorical figures, with its foundation established in the figure of the medium. And while spiritualists were often foolish in this way of grasping how communication worked in the modern world, their foolishness was also perspicacious, allowing them to see how their culture was likely to be occulted by its own discourse of scientific revelation. In this respect, it is impossible to distinguish the credulous belief of the spiritualists from their critical power, their stupidity from their wise disbelief.

The situation was similar in the field of psychology, which was being constituted as an inductive science at this time. The rivalry between this discipline and spiritualism was highlighted by the fact that "mesmerized," "biologized," and "psychologized" often appeared as interchangeable terms in spiritualist literature.[19] Moreover, this literature sometimes had "psychological" as a synonym for "spiritual" and "psychology" for "spiritualism," much as the nineteenth-century idiom characterized the person who fell easily into mesmeric trances as a "very psychological" individual. The professional discipline of psychology had to fight with spiritualism not only for credibility but for its very name.

Here, too, the argument was made that at the very least spiritualism was more believable than the theories offered by the opposing discipline. Thus, citing Carl du Prel (the author of *The Philosophy of Mysticism*) and presumably referring also to Faraday and to W. B. Carpenter (author of *The Principles of Mental Physiology* and of essays sharply critical of spiritualism), Alfred Russel Wallace mocked the "extraordinary theory of the 'second self' or 'unconscious *ego*'":

> But is this so-called explanation any real explanation, or anything more than a juggle of words which creates more difficulties than it solves? The conception of such a double personality in each of us, a second-self, which in most cases remains unknown to us all our lives, which is said to live an independent mental life, to have means of acquiring knowledge our normal self does not possess, to exhibit all the characteristics of a distinct individuality with a different character from our own, is surely a conception more ponderously difficult, more truly supernatural than that of a spirit world.[20]

And in this field, again, the figure of the medium was contested. "An organism when in action," said G. H. Lewes in his *Problems of Life and Mind*, "is only to be understood by understanding both it and the medium *from* which it draws its materials, and *on* which it reacts." It followed that "the organism of a Goethe in the social medium of the Carib would constitute a very superior Carib, but not a wide-sweeping intelligence with a sympathetic conscience." Lewes identified this medium as "culture" or "the general mind" and listed as its colloquial synonyms "*the* Mind, Common Sense, Collective

Consciousness, Thought (*Das Denken*), Reason, Spirit of the Age." What he excluded from this list was an Other World of angels or of personalized spirits by any other name. Just as he rejected what he saw as Hegel's "metaphysical fallacy" of treating mind as a real "*res completa*," so he opposed his conception of the medium as a cultural environment to the conception popularized by spiritualism.

If the difference was clear to Lewes, it may not be so obvious to one who compares his medium to the spiritualists'. His reference to Goethe serves as a good indication that Lewes's medium was not an objectively regarded substance or environment of pure reason. Like the spiritualists' medium, it spoke. It came to life as a historical character ("the *general mind*, or what we call the 'culture of the age,' is an historical growth"),[21] and it gave voice to ideas that ventriloquized those of the individual medium, the author, who was supposedly doing nothing but letting the truth speak through him. (For instance, it voiced Lewes's assumption that the civilization with which he identified was superior to societies that were non-European and nonwhite.) From this perspective, one can appreciate the effort toward a different sort of understanding in Frederic Myers's willing admission that "the 'humble thinkers' of the Stone Age" had been his "true precursors."[22] One may also appreciate that Myers's attempt to adapt psychology to spiritualism was not as revanchist a project as it might otherwise seem. As was the case with physics, more was at stake in the field of psychology than was admitted by those who imagined it could be a "pure" science, self-evident in its conception and self-determining in its historical development. No matter what they failed to comprehend, the spiritualists did grasp that imagination was involved in the workings of these sciences and that this imagination was liable to be limited or perverted, as by assumptions of racial inequality or historical destiny. This is not to say that the spiritualists' notions of progress were necessarily more innocent or just, but only that their hallucinations, delusions, projections, beliefs—call them what you will—effectively marked their recognition of comparable elements acting within but disavowed by the orthodox sciences.

In philosophy, the rivalry with spiritualism was also dramatically marked. Just as they grappled for the name of psychology while Lewes and others were trying to constitute it as a scientific discipline distinct from its academic tradition, spiritualists fought over the name of philosophy at a time when it was still striving to change from an *ancilla fidei* to a discipline distinct from theology. What was a thinker to do with someone like Elizabeth Barrett Browning, who actually thought that she understood modern philosophy and yet believed it could be refuted and returned to the faith of the dark ages because raps were heard around a table? The "whole theory of spiritualism," she wrote, "all the phenomena, are strikingly *confirmatory* of revelation; nothing strikes me more than that. Hume's argument against miracles (a strong argument) disappears before it, and Strauss's conclusions from *a priori* assertion of impossibility fall in pieces at once."[23]

It is the simplest thing in the world to claim the word "philosophy" for one's beliefs, and one does not necessarily pose a philosophical challenge of any moment by doing so. But given the extent to which spiritualists sought to fulfill the themes of the dominant philosophical tradition in the nineteenth century—themes of experiential testimony, experimental investigation, human progress, and guiding reason—it should not be surprising that this movement was not easy to dismiss. As Lewes obliquely recognized, spiritualism could even seem strikingly akin to Hegelianism. Was it not, like Hegel's influential philosophy, an attempt to weave the past together with the present and the future, to institute a universal culture and historical tradition, and to realize a structure for memory, perception, and anticipation that would conform to the structuring of all reality? And of course the importance of the medium to Hegel's thought could not be more clear (as J. B. Baillie indicated by often using this term to translate *"Elemente"* and sometimes *"Mitte,"* as well as *"Medium,"* in *The Phenomenology of Mind*). With its clinging to individual personalities, even to the very dialect of voices, spiritualism might seem a vaudeville Hegelianism while, on the other hand, Hegel's writing might sometimes seem distinguishable from laughable spiritualist formulations only by the rigorous discipline with which the formations of his syntax march forward. ("Spirit is alone reality. It is the inner being of the world, that which essentially is, and is *per se*; it assumes objective, determinate form, and enters into relations with itself—it is externality (otherness), and exists for self; and yet, in this determination, and in its otherness, it is still one with itself.")[24]

Alternatively, spiritualism, like Comteanism, might be seen as a philosophical attempt to accommodate the figures and practices of traditional Christianity to the ideology of modern science. Taking yet another approach, Du Prel attempted to fit spiritualist phenomena (mesmerism and seers such as Swedenborg) into academic philosophy in the Kantian tradition; and perhaps it is not even surprising to find that the spiritualist *Woodhull and Claflin's Weekly* included correspondence with Karl Marx among its statements on free love, suffragism, prostitution, scientific breeding, labor reform, language, and millenarianism. (Marx, too, was quite keen on developing a new conception of the medium, beginning with the so-called medium of exchange in economics.) In any event, spiritualism should be much more explicable when one sees that its visionary approach to science, psychology, and philosophy turned upon a revision of figures common to all these areas of intellectual endeavor, crucial to the knowledge they represented, and yet vulnerable to the charge of being dogmatic, inconsistent, irrational, or simply undertheorized.

It is for this reason that spiritualists did not usually present themselves as the enemies of these disciplines. Instead they saw themselves as crusaders coming to their rescue, striving to prove that their troubled language actually made sense. If the weakness of spiritualism as a way of thinking came from its premature abstractions—its drive to make raps, taps, words, and similar stuff leap across all intervening boundaries to the ultimate reaches of the universe—its strength lay in its recognition of how very far nineteenth-century discourse was from logically justifying the abstractions toward which it herded its sensations, observations, and testimonies. In criticizing "the worship of 'facts' that is so characteristic of nearly all empiricism," Paul Feyerabend has recently drawn attention to the strange intimacy that can exist between spiritual and scientific fact: "Indeed, the new idea of an unprejudiced *experience* that has been cleaned of all human opinion has much in common with the new idea of an unprejudiced *divine decree* that affects the faithful directly, and without mediation through papal declarations, church councils, philosophical speculation."[25] But already in the nineteenth century W. H. Lecky was arguing that the "number of persons who have a rational basis for their belief is probably infinitesimal" because reason is so overwhelmed by "old associations," "education," "foregone conclusions," "hereditary opinions," "illegitimate influences," and other sorts of irrationality. Like others of his age, such as Lewes and Mill, who were aware that "the process of reasoning is much more difficult than is commonly supposed," Lecky still managed to reserve a distinct place for reason in history. He said it was distinguishable by the "innumerable gradations of progress" in humanity's approach toward truth, and at least one reader cited his work as definitively establishing a "general progress of Rationalism" that obliged one not to believe in spiritualism.[26] However, the gingerly way this historian of rationalism handled his subject shows how difficult it was to distinguish the facts of progress from the fantasms of theory—and thus how scientific discourse of all sorts practically invited the speculations of spiritualism.

The rivalry between spiritualism and history is of a type with these other contests. In this connection, too, spiritualists would finger sore spots in the conventional discourse. As the Seybert Commission reluctantly observed, "There is apparent force in the argument that our national histories are founded, accepted, and trusted on evidence by no means as direct as that by which, it is claimed, the proofs of spiritual miracles are accompanied."[27] To a more positive end, spiritualism could take assumptions informing nineteenth-century historiography and tease their own doctrine out of them. They had no quarrel with those who conceived of history as a continuous and progressive process, which then would be taken to represent a human spirit that was essentially universal even though it had developed at an irregular pace among different individuals, peoples, and nations. Emma Hardinge Britten argued that "we may realise by careful research into the fanaticisms of the Irvingites, the abominations of Mormonism, the unnatural ascetisms of Shakerism, and the frenzied agonies of Irish Revivalism that 'all are but parts of one stupendous whole'—*differences of administration, but the same spirit working in all.*"[28] In his explanation of how the recent spiritual manifestations had come to be, Beecher noted, "This principle may be applied, not only to individuals, but to nations. The Jewish nation, for example, may be regarded as a kind of MEDIUM among nations—an organ of spiritual manifestations."[29]

To describe these rivalries is not to suggest that spiritualism actually was, as its apologists sometimes suggested, the victim of tyrants determined to repress the truths it was discovering. The point is that spiritualists were making significant discoveries, but of a kind we fail to see if we judge their work by a standard of truth that is not only inappropriate to their circumstances but also anachronistic in relation to the science, psychology, philosophy, and history of this time. Spiritualists were exploring the possibilities that came to life in the discourse of these disciplines of knowledge. In other words, they were not only acting as scientists, psychologists, philosophers, or historians but also, and more importantly, as rhetoricians or artists. ("They shall train themselves to go in public to become orators and oratresses," said Walt Whitman in "Mediums"—"Strong and sweet shall their tongues be, poems and materials of poems shall come from their lives. . . . ")[30] This understanding of their actions alters our view of this age's aesthetics and especially its literary aesthetics, since spiritualism was strongly oriented toward written publications. It is important even in considering the writing of someone like George Eliot, who was so opposed to spiritualism and whose words may seem so far removed from the writings spawned by this movement. It raises the most basic aesthetic questions: what is an artist, what is art?

In some respects the relations between spiritualism and nineteenth-century fiction are obvious. Spiritualist phenomena were a fictional subject in well-known works by famous authors (Nathaniel Hawthorne's *The Blithedale Romance*, William Dean Howell's *The Undiscovered Country*, Henry James's *The Bostonians*), in more obscure works by familiar authors (Herman Melville's "The Apple-Tree Table," Mark Twain's *Schoolhouse Hill*, Edward Bellamy's *Miss Ludington's Sister*), and in now-forgotten works by other authors who have lost whatever popularity they once had: T. S. Arthur's *The Angel and the Demon*, Orestes Brownson's *The Spirit-Rapper: An Autobiography*, Hamlin Garland's *The Tyranny of the Dark*, Margaret Oliphant's "The Open Door," Allan Pinkerton's *The Spiritualists and the Detectives*, and Bayard Taylor's *Hannah Thurston*, to name just a few. Spiritualism even made its way onto Broadway in the form of a ditty sung by Miss Mary Taylor, "The Rochester Knockings at Barnum's Hotel"; in England, a "Dark Séance Polka" was published.[31]

Furthermore, mediums acted as amanuenses for innumerable writers of the past, from Plato to Shakespeare to Poe, and diligently printed their posthumous works in journals and books. While cooler heads were wont to make jokes about the effects of decomposition on the grammar of departed luminaries, fervid believers in spiritualism were astounded by the quality of these works. Twain satirized this fervor in his description of a seance with an Indian "control," or guiding spirit:

Byron was the most active poet on the other side of the grave in those days, and the hardest one for a medium to get rid of. He reeled off several yards of poetry now, of his usual spiritual pattern—rhymy and jingly and all that, but not good, for his mind had decayed since he died. At the end of three-quarters of an hour he went away to hunt for a word that would rhyme with silver—good luck and a long riddance, Crazy Meadows said, for there wasn't any such word.[32]

Spiritualists would also refer to conventional literary works in order to amplify their own teachings. One, for instance, cited Longfellow's "Hiawatha" as a good description of Indian religion (which was often viewed as a form of spiritualism by those who sought to explain the popularity of Indian spirit controls in American seances).[33] At other times passages were lifted from famous works as unwitting examples of spiritualist teachings, as when Epes Sargent quoted Wordsworth's "The Prelude" and his "Intimations of Immortality" ode in the same chapter of *Planchette* for which he borrowed an epigraph from Alfred Tennyson.[34] Many believers observed "the rich store of *latent* or *unconscious* Spiritualism which English poetry, and especially modern English poetry, contains."[35] To this end, *The Medium and Daybreak* sometimes quoted without comment passages from writers such as Ralph Waldo Emerson, Thomas Carlyle, and Theodore Parker; and this effrontery did not go unpunished. William E. Aytoun was one of many critics who damned spiritualist writings as a blasphemous and "corrupted literature." Like others, he compared the interest in these works to an obsession with fairy tales and exotic stories "fondly cherished" in childhood and then reluctantly but necessarily abandoned "when a more intimate knowledge of the practical world forced upon us the painful conviction that we were doomed to wander outside of the gorgeous realms of enchantment."[36]

This is a clearly marked intersection, and the signs could be multiplied by many more examples, especially if one considered the other forms of art involved in spiritualism, including drawing, oratory, music, photography, and theatrical drama.[37] Yet unless one was joking about this movement, spiritualism was almost never seen as a rival of imaginative literature. It could be an affront but not a competitor. Spiritualists were bound to find that any evidence of artistry impugned their honesty, which was especially symbolized by the supposed naiveté and passivity of mediums; and opponents of the movement could only ridicule any suggestion that spiritualist performances bore more than a nominal relation to the performances of the artistic spirits they evoked, or indeed to the works of any legitimate artist.

On the one hand, spiritualists would defend themselves against any associations with artifice and would tax their opponents with such ties. His writing was "far from offering the interest of a novel," said L. Alphonse Cahagnet; it would be more interesting to the followers of science than to "the impassioned readers of the poetic descriptions in the novels of the day." Dr. J. M. Gully complained that writers of fiction "appear to be so used to inventing that they cannot believe that any one else can possibly be employed in stating facts," much as Elizabeth Barrett Browning criticized the "moral *lâcheté*" of Dickens, "who is so fond of ghost-stories, as long as they are impossible." Myers was upset that spirit communications had been made "a subject of ridicule, — as though it were a meaningless thing that B should appear to A who cares nothing about him," and added, "Of course the meaning belongs to the realm of science, not of romance." Warren Chase even went so far as to grouch about the taste for fiction demonstrated by the spirits themselves, complaining that the entertainment these creatures found amusing ended up confusing and imposing upon the mediums, who mistook their fiction for fact.[38]

On the other hand, critics of spiritualism would not associate it with literature unless they were making light of it or referring to fiction they considered juvenile or nonsensical. In a review of Henry Spicer's history of American spiritualism, a writer in *Blackwood's* jested, "In truth, this is a very serious revelation for authors. What would become of the living novelists were a new series of the Waverley tales to be spiritually communicated? Are they safe against Cervantes and Boccaccio? Not at all." A writer in *Fraser's Magazine* adopted a similar position, although for him it was no laughing matter: "The Rosicrucian theory of aërial beings which supplied the machinery of *Undine* and *The Rape of the Lock*, was more worthy of philosophical attention than Mr. Home's; and to locate spirits in chairs and tables would be a poor compensation for turning them out of trees, fountains, and brooks." Lewes portrayed spiritualism as literature *manqué* when he commented, "Virgil and Tennyson have given us talking oaks, without greatly disturbing our philosophy; we can accept the moving-tables only on a similar licence." While he also directed his satire to the middle classes' general approach to art, Robert Browning made a similar point when he had his Mr. Sludge confess of his mediumship, "It's fancying, fable-making, nonsense-work — / What never meant to be so very bad — / The knack of story-telling, brightening up / Each dull old bit of fact that drops its shine." It was even possible to accuse some spiritualists of the most elementary confusion over the nature of fiction: John Nevil Maskelyne pointed out that New York's Judge Edmonds, the most prominent of the early converts to American spiritualism, had written to the editor of a magazine to say he "had had several spiritual interviews with the defunct fictitious hero" of a story it had published. (To the same end, Maskelyne noted that the newspaper *The Spiritualist* had taken a story by Wilkie Collins to corroborate its beliefs.) At its most extreme, as in John Hay's *The Bread-winners*, this criticism portrayed spiritualism as a failure to grasp legitimate culture in any of its aspects. Hay's novel introduces a seance with this lurid warning:

> To one who has never attended one of these queer *cenacula*, it would be hard to comprehend the unhealthy and even nauseous character of the feeling and the conversation there prevalent. The usual decent restraints upon social intercourse seem removed. Subjects which the common consent of civilized creatures has

banished from mixed society are freely opened and discussed. To people like the
ordinary run of the believers in spiritism, the opera, the ballet, and the annual
Zola are unknown, and they must take their excitements where they can find
them. The dim light, the unhealthy commerce of fictitious ghosts, the unreality of
act and sentiment, the unwonted abandon, form an atmosphere in which these
second-hand mystics float away into a sphere where the morals and the manners
are altogether different from those of their working days.[39]

While spiritualists were happy to butt heads with professors of physics,
psychology, and kindred disciplines, and while those professors sometimes
stepped forward to grapple with the spiritualists, no such rivalry was acknowledged between spiritualism and art. The comparison was often made;
and yet as often as it was made, both sides declined to find any meaningful antagonism in it. Critics considered spiritualism to be nothing like true
art, and spiritualists usually found the "old ghost stories" to be "effete, stale
. . . nothing to the everyday events of the present generation that eats straw-
berries & cream in telling of them."[40]

Why, then, did believers in the movement and their opponents alike feel
called upon to deny that spiritualism was art? It would seem odd that the
question came up in the first place and then turned up again and again, as in
the title, "Stranger than Fiction," of Robert Bell's famous article for William
Thackeray's *Cornhill Magazine*. If both sides were reacting against assertions
of a rivalry between mediums and artists, then what was the origin of these
assertions? Where can one find an origin that had the effect of reality and
yet was treated as being wholly imaginary, disembodied from any particular
person, place, or thing?

The answer lies in art itself—in the voice of art—or, more precisely, in the
discourse of art at this time. The rivalry of mediums and artists had to be
denied on all sides because the very existence of spiritualism materialized a
profound contradiction in the Victorian conception of art. To put it simply,
mid-nineteenth-century art, in the form of realism, aspired to be a truthful
representation of natural reality in all its circumstantial particularity and yet
could forward this aspiration only by appealing to an idea of nature beyond
the limits of any particular perceptions, conventions, institutions, and faculties of communication. To appeal to this world, the everyday world, it also
had to appeal to an ironic, anti-literary, other world. Only by communications from this metaphysical realm could it create the effect of physical
reality. The most characteristic gesture of realism was to evoke and then
symbolically differentiate itself from an unnatural world, and yet this gesture
was its own contradiction; for in it the nature of realism was torn into
rhetorical and logical shreds.

Realism was never more itself than when Claude Monet, working *en plein
air* to capture the direct and living impression of a bare-limbed tree, had to
hire workers to strip all the leaves from his subject when it had the audacity

to bud during the darkness of one night, before his painting was finished. As the more sophisticated critics of the time were aware, the nature supposedly guiding realist artists and experimental scientists never simply gave itself to them but instead was a construction that emerged from their historical situations, social expectations, and individual desires. Spiritualism was one recognition of this unsettling condition of things, as symbolism was another. "Imagination is the queen of truth," said Charles Baudelaire, complaining that the idea of copying nature was stupid, "and *possibility* is one of the provinces of truth. It is positively allied with the infinite."[41]

It is only fitting that modern spiritualism developed alongside the popularization of photography; by this movement's second decade, a distinctly spiritualist photography was already established. Indeed, "spiritualist photography" is almost a redundancy, given that photography always turns upon the irretrievable past: upon what is absent, missing, and dead. Photographs do not preserve the appearance of moments from the past but the disappearance of these moments, as evidenced by the ghostly image. In this sense, photographs are always records of the beyond, and photography has always been at once the most realist and most spiritualist of artistic forms, as Hawthorne recognized when he associated photography and spiritualism in *The House of the Seven Gables*.[42] Although the terms of the two arguments differed, the way nineteenth-century artists strove to distinguish their work from the supposedly lesser or mechanical images of photography is closely related to the way they tried to separate themselves from spiritualism. In both cases, they saw something of themselves in these other forms of representation that they could not admit to seeing.

Realism could not help but see in spiritualism its own troubling, earnest, mocking double. With its domestication of the supernatural, spiritualism was doing the work of realist art and yet undermining the rhetorical forms, ideological grounds, and social habitation of that art. Because of the contradiction in its appeal to nature, realist art was bound silently to assert that spiritualism was like itself while at the same time calling for vociferous denials of this assertion. The fact that believers and disbelievers in communications from the Other World both said that spiritualists were not artists and yet gave radically different meanings to this statement does not mean that they had different conceptions of art. This difference *was* art, which identified itself with nature and yet could support this identification only by an ironic distancing of itself from nature. Turn the table one way, and you say spiritualists are not artists because they are fakes and fantasizers rather than truthtellers; turn it the other way, and you say they are not artists because they are truthtellers rather than fakes and fantasizers. In this dizzying manner, the encounter in the nineteenth century between spiritualism and art played out on the scale of an international cultural movement the tensions inherent in the dominant aesthetic theory of the time. And this drama was not just aesthetic: it was also the drama of nineteenth-century reason.

The effect of the realist conception of art was to repress the expression of idiosyncratic whim and desire within certain representational procedures. These were supposed to be neutral in regard to individuals. Properly used, they were to have the effect of nature. Through this way of thinking, realism was intimately allied with other middle-class forms of representation, most notably with empiricism. Given this perspective, one can see the contradiction involved in this art as an indication of a contemporary historical drama: a struggle for the possession of the soul of the middle classes.

In the relation between spiritualism and art in this time, we see the desires the middle classes had tried to repress from their conception of nature returning upon them in a ghostly form. Coming from beyond and yet from within the orthodox ideologies of the middle classes, this disruptive spirit threatened to upset everything from their vision of the starry universe to the tables, spouses, and children in their parlors. What the comparison of Owen's medium with George Eliot's makes clear is that spiritualism is the romance realism tried to expel from its boundaries, the intentionality and desire empiricism tried to transcend, the will to power middle-class ideologies vainly tried to contain within the rationalized guidelines of decorous social competition and gradual historical progress. Far from drawing together unrelated discourses, the comparison of nineteenth-century spiritualism and the literature of this time shows that they articulated a common problem: this cultural contradiction that is so simple to state and yet so immensely complex in its implications.[43]

By identifying art with natural reality, the credo of realism developed in the eighteenth and nineteenth centuries made art, in effect, the legitimate supernatural. At its most exalted, art was identified with religion, as when Elizabeth Barrett Browning said that poets were "the only truth-tellers now left to God."[44] Just as nineteenth-century writers were often dubbed latterday prophets and priests, art could be described as a substitute for religion, as a new form of religion, or, most complexly, as a mode of expression incorporating a rational comprehension of the historical motives, growth, and significance of religion. More generally, art came to be the legitimate supernatural in that it was understood to be the proper medium for the exercise of the powers traditionally attributed to the supernatural. In art one could manipulate human destinies, make people appear and disappear, see into the minds of others, hear the voices of the dead, levitate above this earth, do practically any godlike thing, and yet proceed under the assumption that the results represented ordinary nature.

As long as one read with this assumption, there was no contradiction in the fact that an uncompromising realist had begun her first novel by identifying her narrator with an occult practice often described by spiritualists:

With a single drop of ink for a mirror, the Egyptian sorcerer undertakes to reveal to any chance comer far-reaching visions of the past. This is what I undertake to

do for you, reader. With this drop of ink at the end of my pen, I will show you
the roomy workshop of Mr. Jonathan Burge, carpenter and builder, in the village
of Hayslope, as it appeared on the eighteenth of June, in the year of our Lord
1799. (3)[45]

In this opening to *Adam Bede*, Eliot was figuring the power of realism to
represent as natural reality its appropriation of godlike powers, spiritlike
figures, and otherworldly communications. Henry James made a similar
gesture in *The Bostonians*, in which the narrator finds himself "under the
necessity of imparting much occult information"[46] even as he prepares to
ridicule the pretensions to mystic knowledge among spiritualists. In realist
art the supernatural was transformed into representational conventions,
which were understood to be artificial and so might seem to pose no problem
of understanding.

Nonetheless, the contradiction in the figurative grounds of realism was
there all the while. The similarities between Charlotte Brontë's *Jane Eyre* and
spiritualist writings can show why it was almost predictable that spiritualism
should appear as the double of realism—and why one ought not to be surprised that Brontë was disturbed from her eternal rest by Harriet Beecher
Stowe's planchette. Graham Hough's observation about the problem of interpreting William Butler Yeats's beliefs is applicable here: "We can say, as a
number of scholars have, that *mystères littéraires*, mere poetic metaphors,
are often mistaken for *mystères cultuels*, objects of cult and devotion. But I
doubt whether the line between them can be so sharply drawn."[47]

Spiritualists often affiliated their movement with traditional gypsy lore,
and few adjustments are necessary to invent spiritualism out of a scene like
that in which Rochester disguises himself as a gypsy fortune-teller, "whose
talk, voice [and] manner" Jane describes as wrapping her "in a kind of
dream." ("One unexpected sentence came from her lips after another, till I
got involved in a web of mystification; and wondered what unseen spirit had
been sitting for weeks by my heart, watching its workings, and taking record
of every pulse" [250].)[48] Nor is spiritualism far away from Jane's passionate
claim at another point that her spirit is speaking directly to Rochester's, "just
as if both had passed through the grave, and we stood at God's feet, equal, —
as we are!" (318). The distance is even less if one remembers Jane's discussion
of presentiments, signs, and "sympathies," such as exist "between far-distant,
long-absent, wholly estranged relatives; asserting, notwithstanding their
alienation, the unity of the source to which each traces his origin" (276).
And it virtually disappears when Jane is released from St. John Rivers's
overpowering demands by the cry from Rochester that speeds its way to her
in defiance of the ordinary boundaries of time and space. These are also the
boundaries overcome in the theology of Jane's inspiring friend, Helen Burns:
"Besides this earth, and besides the race of men, there is an invisible world
and a kingdom of spirits: that world is round us, for it is everywhere; and
those spirits watch us, for they are commissioned to guard us" (81).

Appearing one year before the date usually given as the advent of modern spiritualism, *Jane Eyre* is no more typical of all nineteenth-century literature than is *Wuthering Heights*, which also suggests the existence of an other-worldly reality communicating with the natural world. Nevertheless, this novel wonderfully displays the way various kinds of discourse commonly found in nineteenth-century literature might take on life and jump the walls of realism. No wonder the man who helped to popularize "realism" as a critical term in England tempered his praise of *Jane Eyre* with a warning that Brontë should stay more primly within the bounds of ordinary reality. Lewes was insultingly arrogant, but at least he was perceptive in regard to his own concerns. *Jane Eyre* makes the individual soul of romantic discourse, the transcendent ego of Enlightenment rationality, the spirits of Christian and folk tradition, and the extraordinary powers involved in superstition and the occult all part of one medium that may blur, suspend, or utterly efface their categorical differences. Hence Rochester's habit of wondering whether Jane is real and his fondness for strewing her with epithets like "spirit," "fairy," and "witch." Through this kind of characterization, this realist work seems to be all but admitting that its nature is wholly rhetorical, and thoroughly equivocal to boot.

In a related way, characters in *Wuthering Heights* are frequently haunted by the sense that others are witches, imps, devils, or the like. It is as if they fail to recognize real people in these other characters and instead perceive them as fictive elements in the story of which they themselves play a part. It is this turn toward acknowledged artifice that is traditionally read as an incursion of the supernatural. In this case as in many examples of Gothic literature, supernatural effects are achieved through a self-reflexive emphasis on the literary work's formal conventions of character, incident, plot, and theme. For example, when Cathy says, "I *am* Heathcliff" (122),[49] it is as if she is saying, "The novel hereby suggests that you, the reader, acknowledge a thematic identity between the characteristics attributed to the figure 'Cathy' and those attributed to the figure 'Heathcliff.'" What differentiates this passage in the novel from my yawn-inducing paraphrase is that Cathy's words hover contextually between realist drama and the otherness of its grounds, refusing total satisfaction to either, unable to satisfy both, and so capable of striking readers with an uncanny or spiritual force. When Heathcliff picks up this theme, he adds to it a literal belief in spirits ("I know that ghosts *have* wandered on earth" [204]); but his literal addition is only an extended figuration of this insight that identity is assumed out of a fearsome gap between realist manifestations and rhetorical exposures. Heathcliff exclaims, "Be with me always — take any form — drive me mad! only *do* not leave me in this abyss, where I cannot find you! Oh God! it is unutterable! I *cannot* live without my life! I *cannot* live without my soul!" (204).

Tennyson's "In Memoriam," which was published in 1850 but written over a long period before that date, furnishes another useful comparison. Anyone who reads this poem is unlikely to be surprised to learn that Tennyson grew interested in spiritualism in his old age. The poem is related to spiritualism not only in its concern with otherworldly reality but also in its reaction against a wholly scientific and materialist view of nature. If at some points this series of lyrics finds no possibility of communication with the dead — "For this alone on Death I wreak / The wrath that gathers in my heart: / He put our lives so far apart / We cannot hear each other speak" (929)[50] — at others the narrator hears a whisper from Arthur Hallam that seems at least momentarily real: "So hold I commerce with the dead; / Or so methinks the dead would say; / Or so shall grief with symbols play / And pining life be fancy-fed" (935). As this passage indicates, Tennyson's poem is distinguished from the spiritualist literature of the second half of the nineteenth century by its final refusal to assert a spiritual communication that carries more weight than desire and emotional experience — a refusal given ritual force by Tennyson's formal submission of himself to Christian orthodoxy in his opening invocation. Still, the ecstatic experiences portrayed in stanzas 2 and 12, his reference to a "guardian angel" (902), his insistence upon the survival of personality after death, and all his obsessive musings upon "the spirit" might well be seen as something more than poetic fancies and religious beliefs. Such techniques, terms, and themes show the distress inherent in the nineteenth-century conception of nature in art as well as in science. They suggest that the drive toward a demystified experience does not result in a stable form of perception but rather in the garrulous proliferation of spiritual hypotheses.

Emily Dickinson's poems also suggest the contradiction haunting the nature of realism and returning upon it in the troubling form of spiritualism, even though appeals to the world beyond the grave generally receive no response in these poems. One cannot hear or touch spiritual reality:

Prayer is the little implement
Through which Men reach
Where Presence — is denied them.
They fling their Speech

By means of it — in God's Ear —
If then He hear —
This sums the Apparatus
Comprised in Prayer —. (1:338)

Despite the uncertainty thus described, her poems do share important references, terms, and perspectives with spiritualist discourse. They describe the vision after death seen by "our *developed* eyes" (1:48). They refer to mysterious melodies in the air: "Some — say — it is 'the Spheres' — at play!" (1:114). They contrast the physical sense of hearing to the "Spirit," which "is the

Conscious Ear" (2:559). And in addition to receiving "Bulletins all Day /
From Immortality," Dickinson also wrote posthumous poems, narrated by
characters beyond the grave, such as the famous one that begins, "Because I
could not stop for Death— / He kindly stopped for me" (2:546). Dickinson's
emphasis on the imperceptible nature of spiritual reality suggests that such
expressions are poetic license rather than ontological assertion, but her
poems press so insistently against this boundary that they might well be seen
as challenging its power. At the very least, these poems, like *Jane Eyre* and
"In Memoriam," show some of the more obvious grounds in nineteenth-
century discourse from which modern spiritualism would be constructed and
through which it would become an occulted rival of respectable literature
like Dickinson's.

Even more telling is the way Eliot sought to appropriate for realist literature the terms that spiritualists were also trying to claim. *Medium* is a good
case in point. It does yeoman work in *Middlemarch* in describing everything
from the historical era inhabited by its characters to their different modes of
perception. "A new Theresa will hardly have the opportunity of reforming a
conventual life," says the Finale, "any more than a new Antigone will spend
her heroic piety in daring all for the sake of a brother's burial: the medium
in which their ardent deeds took shape is forever gone" (2:427). The town of
Middlemarch itself is a "petty medium" that proves "too strong" for Lydgate's ideals (1:195), just as Tipton and Freshitt turn out to be "unfriendly
mediums" to Dorothea (1:38). What Lydgate had wanted, of course, was "a
medium for his work, a vehicle for his ideas" (1:87); but the mediums he
finds are not what he had expected. The case is similar with Dorothea when
she travels to Rome with Casaubon and is "humiliated to find herself a mere
victim of feeling, as if she could know nothing except through that medium"
(1:208), while Casaubon finds all the world around him "a dim and clogging
medium" (2:69).

As these examples indicate, a medium in Eliot's fiction is a channel for
communication and revelation, just as it is in the spiritualist writings of her
time. As the spiritualist universe was a vast complication of mediumship, so
is the universe in this novel. From one perspective, the modern world as a
whole is a medium; by the changes in perspective that Eliot announced as
vital to the practice of realist representation, a particular town, institution,
consciousness, or act becomes the medium through which a spirit speaks.
And "medium" is not the only term that voices the relation between Eliot's
writing and spiritualism. Very notable in this regard is "sympathy," which
occurs throughout Eliot's writings as a name for the highest sort of human
understanding. According to Eliot, it is at once a faculty developed through
hard experience and the knowledge constituted by the accumulated experience of suffering that one shares with all other human beings. In short, it is
what binds individuals to each other—and so it is in spiritualist writings. In
these writings and in the earlier discourse of mesmerism to which they are

indebted, "sympathy" is a technical term that names the phenomenon of one person sharing another's perceptions, sensations, feelings, or entire identity. Of course, sympathy also has other meanings and histories in this age; but in this term, too, modern spiritualism and Eliot's fiction intersect.

This intersection goes beyond the use of discrete terms. It also involves more extended images, as in Eliot's description of Dorothea's boudoir: "Nothing had been altered there; but while the summer had gradually advanced over the western fields beyond the avenue of elms, the bare room had gathered within it those memories of an inward life which fill the air as with a cloud of good or bad angels, the invisible yet active forms of our spiritual triumphs or our spiritual falls" (1:386). A similar passage refers to Lydgate's attempt to work for the new fever hospital and to carry out his associated researches despite the prejudice of the town: "Many thoughts cheered him at that time—and justly. A man conscious of enthusiasm for worthy aims is sustained under petty hostilities by the memory of great workers who had to fight their way not without words, and who hover in his mind as patron saints, invisibly helping" (2:30).

In passages like these, Eliot interprets spiritual figures as psychological phenomena. This would seem to be the slim but distinct difference between her art and spiritualism: that she treats spiritual figures as representations, not as agencies. Such is the practice articulated as realism, which might refer to the supernatural but would not allow for an order of causation outside of commonly accepted natural laws and probabilities. The problem, again, is that accepting this difference between realism and spiritualism means ignoring the figurative grounds to the nature of realism in much the same way as an audience may ignore the mechanisms employed by conjurors, con-artists, and mediums of all sorts.

Eliot invites us to smile at Rosamond's "superstitious" gesture of writing a note to her dead husband and sealing it within an envelope that she places in her desk (*"Do you not see now that I could not submit my soul to yours, by working hopelessly at what I have no belief in—Dorothea?"* [2:115]). However, the medium of her art is not merely decorated with spiritual figures; it is actually developed and supported on their basis. Just as characteristic as her reduction of the spirit to psychology are her unqualified evocations of spirits communicating through the normally impenetrable walls of space and time. For instance, after describing Dorothea's sudden appeal for Lydgate's wisdom when Casaubon first falls ill, Eliot dilates on Lydgate's reaction: "For years after Lydgate remembered the impression produced in him by this involuntary appeal—this cry from soul to soul, without other consciousness than their moving with kindred natures in the same embroiled medium, the same troublous fitfully illuminated life" (1:302). Or she describes Rosamond Vincy playing the piano: "A hidden soul seemed to be flowing forth from Rosamond's fingers; and so indeed it was, since souls live on in perpetual echoes, and to all fine expression there goes somewhere an originating activity, if it be only that of an interpreter" (1:167). Like the role played by words such as "medium" and "sympathy," this kind of passage gives the lie to the realist renunciation of supernatural machinery because it indicates the absence of neutrality, the failure to represent an uncontradictory nature, that exists in even the most pedestrian or unassuming of realist representations.

"Exposures" was the name given at this time to incidents that discredited spiritualism by proving the use of artifice in seances, but this proof could cut both ways. Spiritualism as a cultural movement might well be seen as an exposure of the faith in art necessary to the credo of realism and crucial as well to the social and physical sciences of this time. I do not slander the intentions of Eliot by saying so; like many others who pledged their art to nature, she was by no means ignorant of the contradictions at work in her aesthetics. She acknowledged them with particular clarity in one story, "The Lifted Veil," in which she dramatized clairvoyance and prevision. The narrator of this story compares his "double consciousness" (435) not only to the inspiration of great artists but also to ordinary ideation, and through this comparison the story may be seen as challenging the usual assumptions of realism. For present purposes, however, this confessedly extraordinary narrative is less interesting than the ways narratives that appeal to the grounds of ordinary human life can be seen to unveil supernatural presuppositions.

Silas Marner is Eliot's most interesting work in this regard, for it is explicitly designed to appropriate spiritualism to the cultural guidance represented by the genre of the realist novel. The inception of spiritualism, its opposition to science, and its subordination to the interpretive purposes of art are announced early on, when Eliot describes the nonconformist congregation of Lantern Yard to which Silas belongs. Having once fallen into a trance at a prayer meeting, Silas is viewed by his fellow worshipers as "a brother elected for a peculiar discipline" even though the spiritual significance of the trance is not immediately evident to any of them. "Silas was both sane and honest, though, as with many honest and fervent men, culture had not defined any channels for his sense of mystery, and so it spread itself over the proper pathway of inquiry and knowledge" (220–21).

The seizure, paralysis, limpness, or descent into unconsciousness that mediums typically underwent at the beginning of seances was often described as catalepsy. Being sane and honest, Silas is distinguished from run-of-the-mill spiritualists, as Eliot also indicates when she spies another character in the act of inventing a memory about a peddler suspected of stealing Silas's gold. ("'Well—stay—let me see,' said Mr. Snell, like a docile clairvoyant, who would really not make a mistake if she could help it" [276].) But despite his personal rectitude, Silas is assuredly not in one of the channels of proper cultural communication. To give him his honesty's reward, Eliot must move his spiritualist friends to reject him and then must nudge him toward his proper medium by causing a child to appear in his new home while he is suffering another of his attacks. Thus materialized, the child seems otherworldly to Marner but enters into his life by natural and even logical means, as Eliot's readers are made to understand. In this way Eliot gives the entranced Marner a message that has a spiritual effect and yet is a wholly natural reality. In other words, she gives him the dawning of cultural understanding in the form of a realist narrative personified by a blond-haired toddler. This understanding beckons Silas toward a proper relation with the past that hitherto had haunted him and yet had refused to speak its meaning to him: "The thoughts were strange to him now, like old friendships impossible to revive; and yet he had a dreamy feeling that this child was somehow a message come to him from that far-off life" (329–30). Through Eppie, then, at once materially and spiritually, the message is dictated and received:

In old days there were angels who came and took men by the hand and led them away from the city of destruction. We see no white-winged angels now. But yet men are led away from threatening destruction: a hand is put into theirs, which leads them forth gently towards a calm and bright land, so that they look no more backward; and the hand may be a little child's. (352)

Silas Marner shows that it was the *propriety* of art that was challenged by spiritualism. The rivalry between spiritualism and other disciplines of knowledge could be acknowledged more openly because all parties agreed on the testimony of experience, the importance of experiments, the goal of progress, and the guiding promise of reason. This rivalry involved disputes over the judgment of truth but not questions about the very mission of these disciplines, whereas the case was very different with art. Totally upsetting questions could not help but arise in the confrontation between spiritualism and art, for these two were bound to devalue each other, gripped as they were in the contradictory figuration of their imaginary origin.

Spiritualism claimed the license that art thought proper to itself, and in doing so it showed the dispossession within art's seeming propriety. In this sense of propriety, which finally was a matter of tone as much as anything else, an inflection of cultural assurance, art hid from itself its own irrationality, its otherworldliness, and its vulgarities and impostures. In effect, modern spiritualism was the extrusion of a disruptive difference already at work within art. It was art turned inside out and gaping at the seams. It was the vision of art as a practice that in its modern conception was dreadfully new, innovative, unsanctioned by historical continuities, and reliant upon communications from authorities that spoke dubiously and unsystematically. The rivalry between spiritualism and art was carried out covertly because it represented this repressed rivalry of art with itself—hence the way spiritualism appeared to be at once an imitation, a travesty, and a critique of the symbolic powers distinctive of art.

This rivalry was by no means all there was to spiritualism, as if it were only art's emanation, a kind of spooky Hegelian antithesis. And the rejection of realism did not necessarily signify a change in political attitudes; it was as likely to represent an aristocratic as a democratic stance, and it might appear reactionary (for instance, when artists appealed to the standards of the schools against innovators like Gustave Courbet) as easily as it might seem revolutionary (with the surrealists early in the next century). As I have tried to make clear, I also do not mean to suggest that realism (or empiricism, for that matter) was ever a rigidly defined system of ideas, commonly accepted without reservation or dissent. And I certainly am not suggesting that a realist conception of referentiality was ever or can ever be easily rejected, even by the most unorthodox artistic practices. On the contrary, my point has been to show how the relation between modern spiritualism and the nineteenth-century conception of art is peculiarly intriguing precisely because spiritualism is so difficult to untangle from art, historiography, philosophy, psychology, and physical science as these were defined in the nineteenth century, of which we are still the heirs, willing or not. Like Pearl, the child of Hester Prynne and the Reverend Dimmesdale in *The Scarlet Letter*, spiritualism was the contradictory issue that resulted from the coupling of truth with nature in this time.

This contradiction could erupt in a struggle over the possession of words even in a work like *The Blithedale Romance*, which is far from being an exemplar of realism, as its title announces. Although Hawthorne pleads in this work for an aesthetic freedom that would exempt him from a strict fidelity to nature, his work reproduces the rivalry between art and spiritualism. The fact that it should do so shows that the contradictory nature of realism was so gripping at this time that it might appear unavoidable even where one had sought deliberately to exclude it.

Hawthorne's preface first introduces the problem. "In the old countries," he says, "a certain conventional privilege seems to be awarded to the romancer; his work is not put exactly side by side with nature; and he is allowed a license with regard to every-day Probability," whereas in America "there is as yet no such Faery Land, so like the real world, that, in a suitable remoteness, one cannot well tell the difference, but with an atmosphere of strange enchantment, beheld through which the inhabitants have a propriety of their own" (1-2).[51] In the narrative that follows, Hawthorne addresses this problem by presenting a narrator who is continually concerned to win for art the rhetoric that otherwise would be claimed by representatives of "the spiritual world" (5). At its most simple, the effect involves a play on single words, as when Coverdale speaks of "the odd little guest, whom Hollingsworth had been the medium of introducing among us" (49). Here the play on "medium" is so unmarked that it may go unnoticed even if one guesses that this guest is the otherworldly Veiled Lady. "Medium" frequently reappears in the text, though, and so through repetition may call attention to its vital role. "Spheres" is another word that echoes in the narrative. Since it is used at times in its spiritualist sense and at others in its social connotation—"There are some spheres, the contact with which inevitably degrades the high, debases the pure, deforms the beautiful" (101) — one may begin to hear an allegorical resonance, a veritable music of the spheres, between the social and spiritual references. With similar results, Coverdale's narrative also seeks to wrest "spirit" away from questions of probability so that its aesthetic role can be dominant.

More dramatically, this desire to appropriate the rhetoric of spiritualism appears in incidents like the illness that afflicts Coverdale soon after his arrival at Blithedale. Like Jane Eyre's moments of passion, Silas's catalepsy, and the trances of mediums, this sickness suggests the transition of death and the ensuing consciousness of another world. ("My fit of illness had been an avenue between two existences. . . . In this respect, it was like death. And, as with death, too, it was good to have gone through it" [61].) In the ensuing drama, as in Eliot's work, this appropriation further appears in the way the narrator toys with the supernatural but does not allow it to reach beyond the boundaries of psychological phenomena. Although he refers to Hollingsworth's influence over Zenobia and Priscilla as "necromancy" (124) and states, "Our souls, after all, are not our own," Coverdale always turns this kind of description into psychological analysis: "We convey a property in [our souls] to those with whom we associate, but to what extent can never be known, until we feel the tug, the agony, of our abortive effort to resume an exclusive sway over ourselves" (194). By this same turn, Coverdale notes the existence of "a species of intuition — either a spiritual life, or the subtle recognition of a fact — which comes to us in a reduced state of the corporeal system," and so concludes, "Zenobia's sphere, I imagine, impressed itself powerfully on mine, and transformed me, during this period of my weakness, into something like a mesmerical clairvoyant" (46-7). While evoking the rhetoric and example of spiritualism, he converts them into the conventional ambiguities of art, bounded by psychology.

The process of Hawthorne's romance is epitomized by the way speculation is maintained about the character of Priscilla. Early in the story, Zenobia mocks Coverdale's "poetical" idea of her, tauntingly saying that he should "turn the affair into a ballad" with "supernatural machinery" and then dismissing the subject with the conclusion, "She is neither more nor less . . . than a seamstress from the city" (33). Ironically, Coverdale's feverish fantasies are then revived in chapter 13, "Zenobia's Legend," when Zenobia tells the Blithedale group a tale, "The Silvery Veil," that relates Priscilla's life in the transmogrified form of a supernatural story. But by the end of the romance, Priscilla's biography appears to be very well known; the questions that remain have more to do with Coverdale's character as a narrator than with the structuring of reality in the universe that he assumes for himself and his readers. Supernatural speculation has been turned from spiritualist demonstrations and manifestations to psychological figures employed for artistic effect. Although the supernatural is not categorically dismissed — else there would be no further play, no "romance," no epistemological elbow-room—its evocation in modern spiritualism is declared to be inappropriate to any desirable form of communication. In Coverdale's words, "The epoch of rapping spirits, and all the wonders that have followed in their train—such as tables, upset by invisible agencies, bells, self-tolled at funerals, and ghostly music, performed on jewsharps—had not yet arrived. Alas, my countrymen, methinks we have fallen on an evil age! . . . These goblins, if they exist at all, are but the shadows of past mortality, outcasts, mere refuse-stuff. . . . The less we have to say to them, the better; lest we share their fate!" (198–99).

This is the conclusion of *The Blithedale Romance*—but then it was also its beginning. Like *Silas Marner*, this work had announced at the outset its plan to appropriate the rhetoric of spiritualism to the cultural ends of art. Just as Coverdale's evocation of a proto-spiritualism characterized by exotic mystery serves to move spiritualism away from questions of ontology to questions of aesthetic convention, his pronounced indifference to the possibly miraculous truth of the Veiled Lady, when she is mentioned at the beginning of the romance, served to transform her from a metaphysical problem into a hermeneutic puzzle. As Coverdale set the scene, the Veiled Lady's "pretensions . . . whether miraculous or otherwise, [had] little to do with the . . . narrative," except in relation to a question he had decided to try out on her, concerning whether Blithedale would prove a success. "The response, by-the-by, was of the true Sibylline stamp, nonsensical in its first aspect, yet, on closer study, unfolding a variety of interpretations, one of which has certainly accorded with the event" (5–6).

Here as throughout *The Blithedale Romance* and many of Hawthorne's other works, fiction is constituted as the legitimate supernatural and yet seems compelled to exhibit its closeness to an illegitimate double. Compare the admonitory conclusion to "The Hall of Fantasy": "Let us be content, therefore, with merely an occasional visit, for the sake of spiritualizing the grossness of this actual life, and prefiguring to ourselves a state, in which the Idea shall be all in all" (185). Because fiction, or more particularly romance, is "occasional," diffident, self-deprecating, even willfully inconclusive, it can legitimately appropriate the rhetoric and practices of spiritualism. In fact, it must do so, because spiritualism poses such a threat to its propriety. Art must preserve meaningful communication, and thus a refined culture, by acting out its surrender of the power of ultimate explanation and its acceptance of the modesty of representational conventions. This is the politic move illustrated, to mention another example, in *The House of the Seven Gables* when Hawthorne writes about the Maules' reputation for inheriting the power of witchcraft: "Modern psychology, it may be, will endeavor to reduce these alleged necromancies within a system, instead of rejecting them as altogether fabulous" (26). This cautious deferral to science symbolically reasserts the union of art and nature.

The problem of Hawthorne's romance is then the problem of realism. It is not a happenstance that a realist ideologue like Eliot admired Hawthorne's work or that elements and techniques resembling those used in Hawthorne's romances appear in her fiction. I do not wish to deny Hawthorne's aesthetics any distinctiveness, but these examples should show that what he sought in a restoration of legitimacy to romance was a way to overcome the contradictory nature of realism. And it should be clear, too, that his work could not hope entirely to succeed at this task.

The weakness of the solution of romance is that its criticism of supernatural assertions is measured by the extent to which it concedes its own insignificance. The result is an art that can offer judgments and discriminations only by withdrawing itself from any specific reference to human life. This is a negative form of realism but a form of realism nonetheless. Hawthorne could not admit to a rivalry with spiritualism or "necromancies" any more than Eliot could. Like Eliot, he needed to call attention to this comparison and yet to deny its relevance. And the resulting works, like Eliot's, enact conflicts that illustrate the more general problem of reason among the educated classes of this time.

Viewed through the interplay of spiritualism and nineteenth-century literature, the problem of reason in this time can be described as the problem of the double. Spiritualism's appearance as the double of realism was so unsettling that spiritualists and their critics alike always remarked upon it and yet refused to recognize it. However obscurely, what they perceived in this confrontation was a contradiction that extended through their visions of art and nature to the very grounds of reason in this age. As William Lecky testified, reason could tolerate the intrusions of all sorts of dogma and nonsense and unthinking conviction as long as it did not have to swallow the "absurd" notion that it did not progress and so could not make discriminating judgments; but the image of the double could seem to put an end to any justification of progress and hierarchy. Putting difference in the place of identity, divergence in the place of development, it might turn the ultimate medium of reason into conflicting universes. The double would then be the face of a contradiction that could neither be repressed nor repelled. Its difference would shadow, haunt, degrade, and vulgarize, always alien and yet never alien enough, which is to say, always alien and yet familiar. In the double, in the works I have mentioned as in those of Poe, Robert Louis Stevenson, and Joseph Conrad, one can see the possibility of a historian like Feyerabend eventually following in the footsteps of Lecky, or of a psychologist like Freud coming to haunt Lewes, or of a philosopher like Jacques Derrida emerging like eerie ectoplasm from the dialectic of Hegel.[52]

Conrad's "The Secret Sharer" is especially interesting in this regard. Elsewhere, in a story called "The Black Mate," Conrad burlesqued spiritualism in a conventional way, portraying it as a belief proper to a ridiculous lower-middle-class fool. "The Secret Sharer" can also be read in a conventional way, as a tale of borderline psychology or troubling experience, but the comparison of spiritualism and nineteenth-century literature invites us to read it differently. In highlighting the spiritualist images involved in this work, this comparison can lead us to read it as a story of art that goes beyond the boundaries of any normal or abnormal psychology and thus beyond what the dominant culture of the nineteenth century defined as the necessary limits to the reading of literature.

Spiritualists often referred to the phenomena of doubles or *doppelgängers* as support for the beliefs. In itself this fact says nothing about Conrad's tale, but it becomes more interesting if one notices how "The Secret Sharer" is suffused with the images of spiritualism. The story, of course, involves a new captain on a ship, a stranger to its crew and to the position of leadership, who secretly rescues from the sea and then hides from the rest of the crew a young sailor who has committed murder on another ship. It is a "mysterious communication" (99) that the narrator feels between himself and Leggatt, the sailor who resembles him so seductively and yet disturbingly: "It was, in the night, as though I had been faced by my own reflection in the depths of a somber and immense mirror" (101).[53] Clairvoyance comes into play: as Leggatt tells his story, the narrator says, "I saw it all going on as though I were myself inside that other sleeping-suit" (102). The narrator's mind turns repeatedly to thoughts of witchcraft and ghosts; and not only does he imagine Leggatt as his "other self" (105), but when he is with him he also has "the confused sensation of being in two places at once" (111). He comments at another point, "That mental feeling of being in two places at once affected me physically as if the mood of secrecy had penetrated my very soul" (125). He even wonders if all his precautions in hiding Leggatt from his shipmates and from Leggatt's pursuers have been necessary: "Can it be, I asked myself, that he is not visible to other eyes than mine? It was like being haunted" (130). Finally, in helping Leggatt to escape, he violates the law, and not just the written statutes of England's navy. He breaks every code known to himself and his fellow sailors by deliberately and even perversely bringing his ship toward seemingly inevitable destruction before he finally separates himself from this other figure.

Although this story can be profitably read as a psychological thriller, it may be more challenging to view it as a dramatization of realist aesthetics *in extremis*. The doubleness here is then the rivalry of spiritualism and realism and thus the doubleness inherent in realism, which can appeal to a substantial and particularized nature only by a covert reliance on a host of supernatural assumptions, terms, and techniques.

In other words, this is then a story of fiction looking at itself. As the narrator receives this other character as his double and so comes to see himself in another body, another place, another life, and an entirely different story, realist fiction comes to the border of its own possibility and stops just short of destroying its apparent reference to natural reality. In a psychological reading, the narrator, who is in a position of peculiar uncertainty and stress, identifies with a fellow "stranger" and recognizes that this stranger's fate as a murderer and exile could very well be his own, so chancy is one's fate in the world of men and nature. (It is significant in this regard that the murder was precipitated by a monstrous storm at sea.) But in the present context, one can see this story as dramatizing the inescapable contradiction of realism, which must appeal to an other world in order to convey the effect of natural reality and yet must also differentiate itself from the other world. From this perspective, the narrator who so obsessively looks at, speaks with, and broods over his other self is confronting the literal possibility that he might figure as another character in another story. He is meditating on his own composition as a fictive character and thus on the composition of realist fiction itself, which is shown here to be bound to an otherness it can neither acknowledge, contain, nor repel. The story is then an experiment that tests how close the narrator can come to being absorbed by—revealed as—words on a printed page while still having the effect of a represented human being for readers imbued with the metaphysics of realism.

Here the complex relationship between nineteenth-century spiritualism and literature is taken about as far as it could go. No longer an antagonism or covert rivalry, in "The Secret Sharer" this relation has become an acknowledged complicity. This is, however, a most uneasy compact, which in Conrad's drama entails deep guilt and deathly risk and unresolved bewilderment. The nature that squeaks out of this tight spot is no longer the nature of Hawthorne and Eliot and Tennyson, and the art is now a medium that exemplifies reason only by lingering on its inevitable betrayal.

In Conrad's portrayal, this change does not imply a retreat, a return to miracles, and thus a rejection of "the distinctive mark of Rationalism," which Lecky described as the "attempt to explain away the miracles of Scripture."[54] Instead, reason itself begins to seem a kind of miracle—and thus it begins to recede into the faith, and the literature, of the past.

Wording the Subject
of Spiritualism

I've seen some men, veracious, nowise mad
Who have thought or dreamed, declared and testified
They heard the Dead a-ticking like a clock
Which strikes the hours of the eternities,
Beside them, with their natural ears, — and known
That human spirits feel the human way
And hate the unreasoning awe which waves them off
From possible communion.

ELIZABETH BARRETT BROWNING, *Aurora Leigh*[1]

Oh! abyss of our reason!

ALPHONSE CAHAGNET[2]

Modern spiritualism was a messy business. It seems exceptionally difficult to pin down even in comparison to the other cultural movements with which it consorted: mesmerism, abolitionism, Fourierism, Unitarianism, transcendentalism, all the rest. As spiritualists often remarked, their movement seemed to have a genius for disorganization. Trying to judge it today is like trying to nail Jello to a tree. It was not just a monstrous fraud, although trickery and charlatanism played a large part in it. Certainly it was not reasonable, and yet it cannot be dismissed as a wholly irrational belief unless one appeals to an unreasonable image of reason. It can hardly be taken seriously, but it was; and even within the movement, believers were hopelessly at odds with each other. Spiritualists did and did not believe in reincarnation, in life on other worlds, in Christianity, in physical demonstrations, in this particular message or that particular medium. To add to the frustration, their movement often seemed as purposeless as it was inchoate. Even if we were to grant the truth of all you assert, opponents scoffed, what difference would it make? Spiritualists resented this question (a frequent subtitle in their writings was *cui bono*? — "who profits?"); but still they were stuck with believing in divine revelations that could not be proven to change anything in this world, signs and portents that could be laughed off. It was all too chaotic.

But it may be that a mistaken way of understanding lures us into this confusion, which we then wrongly imagine to be distinctive of modern spiritualism. After all, this movement was more than a heap of beliefs, assertions, propositions, demonstrations, words. It was also wording: not speech but a way of speaking, not writing but a way of writing, not the seance but a way of gathering people together. The error in reducing spiritualism to a symptom of psychopathology should be evident, but it should be just as clear that we cannot take spiritualism "literally," as if it were that fabulous beast, a text that can make all its intentions clear. Even the conceptions of interpretation formulated within this movement militate against such an oversimplification.

The better course may be to recognize that the subject of spiritualism appears so difficult to word because the subject *was* wording. What this movement had to say of spirits was practically insignificant in comparison to the practices that composed its sayings. Even as their opponents said that spiritualist truths would not be worth the having, would make no difference to anyone or anything, spiritualists themselves often argued that their fundamental ideas of immortality were so open to discussion as to be completely undogmatic and so universal as to be banal, and not only in the context of Western and Christian nations. The issue was not their statements, which many freely admitted were nothing new, but the making of these statements, which opened a different view of things. The foundation of the movement was less important than its findings; the sense of discovery was what mattered, regardless of whether the modus operandi that shaped its participants' experiences could be called "legitimate." "In what are called enthusiasm and fanaticism," wrote William Howitt, "there is a spiritual orgasm which inspires, inflames, and attracts men, and gives them life and potency, whether for good or for ill, without which zeal would soon die out, and the energy of progression cease."[3]

Turning from spiritualism as speech to spiritualism as a way of speaking discloses a view that makes a difference, all the difference in the world. It shows modern spiritualism as an attempt to reinvent the human subject. In the practices of spiritualism, linguistic and otherwise, in the very drift and uncertainties of this movement, there appears a search for new definitions and configurations of human faculties. (Its association with phrenology becomes significant in this regard.) In considering the pathos of this search, we need to consider why it took on this character and what this character has to say about the social history of the nineteenth century.

In many ways language in modern spiritualism seemed to take on a life of its own and thus to foreground wording, or language as revealing attitude and action, while putting the given meaning of signs into the shade. Obviously the rappings that initiated the movement had this effect. Earlier, persons who spoke of communicating with the dead might be pious (in prayer), sentimental (in memory and imagination), or loony, if they neglected to phrase their assertions in a respectable way; but the rappings had a very different tendency. To those who were not believers, what the rappings purported to say was controversial primarily because it was nothing new at all. It was only too ordinary and therefore vulgar. The same was said of the messages later communicated through trance speaking, automatic writing, spirit drawing, spiritual telegraphs, partial and full-body manifestations, and all the other channels to eternity. The idea of spirits and the ideas said to come from spirits: all these were unexceptionable. The controversy was really over the modes of communication, which were so peculiar that they made ordinary words seem incredible, disturbing, and even sinister.

In this respect, spiritualism posed a threat to the dominant cultures in the United States, England, France, and elsewhere simply because its dramatic way with words, the way this movement appropriated language, made language in general appear as the subject of appropriation. Language then would seem more theatrical than instrumental, more creative than instructive, more potential than referential. If only by the comparisons they forced people to make, the practices of spiritualism highlighted language as practice, words as wording, and so discomposed the processes people generally took for granted in making sense to each other. The elaborate apologetics that developed with this movement also contributed to this effect, as did the exotic jargon it insinuated into mundane surroundings and conventional forms.

Spiritualist practices made the workings of language look like spontaneous ritual rather than systematic reason, symbolic exchange rather than progressive understanding, improvised gesture rather than indwelling essence—an emotional social drama rather than a disciplined and responsible means of identification. These practices made language appear to be anything but the neutral medium of communication. Literally and figuratively, spiritualism materialized language, pulling it down from the ghostly realm of ideality into the world of historical invention, physical objects, institutions, social power, and unpredictable personality. Hence the staginess of spiritualism: the impression it gave that all objects were props, all events drama or potential drama. As the opponents of the movement indirectly recognized when they protested too much that spiritualism could make no difference at all, language could not suffer such treatment without being disturbed to its very bottom. Stirred up from the depths of the dictionary, the most commonplace expressions imaginable, clichés of all sorts, might rise to the surface of language and disturb its every feature along the way.

The human medium, utterly passive and yet articulate, also provided an image of language taking on a life of its own. A reaction against this image appeared when spiritualism was associated with mesmerism and vampirism in popular fiction such as T. S. Arthur's *The Angel and the Demon*, Edward Bulwer-Lytton's *A Strange Story*, Hawthorne's *The House of the Seven Gables*, and Hamlin Garland's *The Tyranny of the Dark*. Through this association, the spiritualist idea of otherworldly knowledge, which came *through* instead of *from* individuals, was transmuted into an impression that some individuals (especially women) were vulnerable to the invisible power of others. When it communicated through magic, mesmerism, telepathy, or simply the force of personality, language appeared the means by which one might be helplessly controlled by others; but then it also might figure as a captivating otherness in and of itself. The fear of such a language was evident when critics mocked the spiritualist movement by describing it as propagating a reckless, unholy jargon by which susceptible individuals were possessed or even driven insane. Linguistic practices here overshadowed linguistic sense and the essence of the human subject to boot. Spiritualists, in relying on mediums, and their opponents, in criticizing the corrupting influence of mediums, both suggested that language might be socially unifying only at the cost of the integrity of individual identity. Although spiritualism was based on a conception of identity persisting even beyond death and its opposition on an appeal to a proper and respectable self in this life, both seemed to be driven toward an image of language that invaded, overpowered, and yet remained beyond individuals. Whatever side one was on, this controversy suggested that identity was an issue of wording. It appeared to be a matter of one's roles and acts within language and so ultimately nothing but an effect of language. As such, identity was liable to be dissolved at any moment into unconsciousness, utter alienation, or the vacant objectivity of "the ordinary." What if the spiritualist mediums were *exemplary* when they acted out their lack of autonomy, their absence of controlling will, to such a point that their very being seemed a confusion of tongues coming from before or beyond the boundaries defining individuals?

That the invention of a new human subject was in question is indicated by the way spiritualists fumbled for a name for their channels, drawing on mesmerist and other vocabularies, before most settled on "medium." "Automatist," "somnambulist," "sensitive," "*lucide*," "*extatique*," and "instrument" were among those canvassed. One might say that with these names spiritualists were groping after a subjectivity that was not prior to language but rather created and uncreated by language; and certainly this was the suggestion of many opponents of the movement, who characterized its productions as fraud or as illegitimate fiction. In the nineteenth century, these characterizations often amounted to saying that something was "sheer verbiage" or "merely a form of words." In the present context, however, it may be more precise to say that spiritualist practices, as they revolved around the figure of the medium, had the effect of leading people on all sides of this movement to confront the ways their world was at the mercy of its wording.

This effect came to the fore when spiritualism was associated with inflated and hence devaluing language. Its exotic jargon helped to furnish the grounds for this association, but this was not its only or even its most important basis. More significant was the link between modern spiritualism and the newspapers, which had become a new and powerful force by this time. (Nietzsche wrote of people reading "newspapers [in place of daily prayers].")[4] The proliferation of newspapers and their appeal to a broader, popularly educated audience turned them into institutions radically different from the journals that were their eighteenth-century counterparts, and spiritualism could not have gotten off the ground as a mass movement if it had not been for the publicity provided by these papers and by the house organs spiritualists added to the fray. From the very first, mediums and the mass media grew up together. Horace Greeley later became more skeptical toward the movement, but his *New York Weekly Tribune* gave invaluable notice to the Fox sisters in 1849. Geoffrey K. Nelson has noted, "While the press was often hostile, its reports gave great publicity to the movement, and the existence of a cheap and popular press throughout America at the time must be counted as one of the factors favouring the rapid spread of the movement."[5]

In fact, spiritualists often referred to the newspapers in such a way as to suggest that their own mediums were mimicking the role of the popular media. For instance, Robert Owen knew that his fortunes turned upon the wheel of publicity, as did his followers: an "Address of Congratulation to Robert Owen on His 86th Birthday, from his Friends and Disciples at Stockport," lauded him for "having aided in conquering for [them] the freedom of the 'fourth estate'" as the "medium" that enabled them to develop Owen's "system of mental and moral science." Similarly, in describing the "inconceivable rapidity with which news is disseminated, through the medium of this mass of print" in papers in the United States, Henry Spicer noted that the "never-ceasing agent" of the papers was "the electrical telegraph"—which, of course, was the popular image for spiritual communications. (And it was more than a metaphor—many found a more substantive resemblance between table-rappings and the clicking of the telegraph, between the great speed of electrical transmissions and the potential for instantaneously sending thought across the expanses of eternity.) Epes Sargent made the comparison between spiritualism and the publishing industry even closer when he said, "By ordinary persons, the supposed communications from the spirit-world will, we think, in this nineteenth century, be received as we receive communications through books, newspapers, and even weekly critical journals." Henry James was another who recognized this connection, in *The Bostonians*, in which Selah Tarrant, the father of a medium, is a publicity hound given to haunting newspaper offices and pestering everyone in them, right on down to the copyboys: "[H]is ideal of bliss was to be as regularly and indispensably a component part of the newspaper as the title and date, or the list of fires, or the column of Western jokes."[6]

Like the part played in this movement by tables and mediums, this association with newspapers highlighted the form in which language came to people and thus might seem to suggest that people's ideas were the sport of the institutional forms that happened to have grown up around them. Because it might seem to bear no determinate responsibility to identities or essences or distinct values, language then might be described as so much hot air or tempestuous "puffery." Thus, in writing as "Q. K. Philander Doesticks," Mortimer Thomson launched an invective against spiritualism ("which would be impious if it was not idiotic"); but in this criticism, he took the movement to exemplify a linguistic threat posed by modern society in general and, he joshed, even by his own writing:

> For at this time of triumphant and successful humbug — when indiscriminate puffery is freely used to boost into notice all kinds of shame, deception, and deceit, which thereupon grow fat and thrive — when vermin exterminators, lucifer matches, and patent blacking employ such high-flown language in commendation of their merits, that inventions of real merit and importance must resort to the basest bombast to keep pace with the foolery of their neighbors — when solid merit which *would* succeed, must vie in euphuistic phrase with brainless emptiness which *will* — when, in Literature, inane collections of stolen wit, diluted humor, and feeble fiction are spawned in scores from weak-brained fops and aspiring women, inflated by unsparing puffery into a transient notoriety, and palmed upon the public as works of sterling merit — when even these Doestick Letters are purchased and perused, it may easily be imagined that no impudent humbug, if properly managed, will turn the stomach of the enlightened Yankee Nation.[7]

This criticism is closely related to that which saw modern spiritualism as the latest in the line of systems, "-isms," or "-ologies" that seemed to be swamping the modern intellect and drowning out the voice of anyone who did not speak from within an all-devouring vortex of belief. It was also related to the popular idea that Americans were peculiarly susceptible to such influences because of their Protestant, dissenting, democratic, "New World" character, which at its most extreme might be seen as positively encouraging lunacy. This point is important, for instance, in Orestes Brownson's *The Spirit-Rapper: An Autobiography*. But while it may have seemed especially significant in the light of the history of America, this connection between newspapers and puffery was not confined to its shores and had more than a national significance. As Thomson's ironic use of the word "enlightened" indicates, spiritualism, in its relations with the devalued language of newspapers and other forms of modern communications, might be seen as laying bare a contradiction at the very heart of reason.

In his *History of Rationalism*, W. E. H. Lecky identified reason as a legacy of the Protestant Reformation, which he saw as making "the Word"

available to all and thus as encouraging the progressive spirit of free unprejudiced inquiry. As it was popularly understood in the nineteenth century,
the Enlightenment had a similar purpose. It proclaimed everyone an equal
participant in discourse (which would be characterized as rational precisely
insofar as it met this ideal) in the confidence that free discussion would
always sort out the better argument and so lead to the progressive revelation
of truth. John Stuart Mill's *On Liberty* is perhaps the purest expression of
this faith, but in its broad terms it was the common liberal understanding of
what the eighteenth century had wrought. It was not the only understanding,
for this period was also taken to represent atheistic materialism and rabid
political radicalism. But these tendencies generally seemed separable from
the liberating ideal of reason. In the words of Louisa Lowe, speaking to a
conference of spiritualists in 1877, this legacy taught one to "overthrow all
external authority in matters of thought; to free mankind from religious
dogma and the trammels of priestcraft—in a word, to teach the individual to
make his own reason an ultimate court of appeal in all matters of personal
concernment."[8] Whether the Enlightenment should really be traced back
to an earlier time and place, such as sixth-century Athens, or whether
eighteenth-century Europe and America actually maintained this ideal is not
the point here. What I have briefly described is the role of the interpreter
that seemed to be opened to the individual by the Reformation and the
Enlightenment, as they were popularly understood in the nineteenth century;
and from this understanding came disappointment, for it turned out that
this promised access to words was not all it was cracked up to be.

In the assumption that it was possible to blow the dust of priestcraft and
unthinking tradition off the pages of books, to speak one's mind freely and
openly, words were given a certain independence. One could deal with them
face to face, in the vernacular, divining their meaning without intermediar-
ies. To be sure, there were various obstacles to this new dispensation. As
Éliphas Lévi complained, reason could become "a bourgeois critique that
denies everything that it does not yet know how to explain."[9] Or one might
speak of free thought where in fact it was wanting. In *The Spiritual Telegraph*, S. B. Brittan compared the freedom of thought, as it was found in
many venues, to the story of the woman whose son asked if he might go
fishing: "Yes, John," responded his mother, "you may 'go a fishing' when
you please, but mind, my son, *don't you go near the water*."[10] Education or
miseducation, ambiguities in communication, and the financial difficulties
of publishing were among the other obstacles littering the path of reason.
But all these seemed simple problems relative to the threat that might leap
out from the very nature of words: that they might become so independent
as to take on a life of their own.

If in fact words cast off all impurities, presented themselves to men and
women without commentary or gloss, might one not be carried away by

words, transported out of one's own identity by their independent existence, shuttled about by the ungraspable forces of their differentiation and proliferation? Might not the spiraling growth of newspapers and other organs of opinion, like the multiplying numbers of spiritual mediums, show that human beings were liable to be overwhelmed by words? That they might not be their interpreters but rather the subjects of their interpretation, the nonsensical products of the babbling of history?

In writing of Martin Luther and the Reformation, Nietzsche touched upon this issue; and it was from a perspective such as this that Thomas Hardy's novels were to describe human beings as the creations of an idiotic, infantile, thoughtlessly cruel First Mover. They also suggested that the realization of this condition would lead to a new type of human subject. In discussing Little Father Time, the despairing child who has murdered his siblings and killed himself in *Jude the Obscure*, Jude Fawley reports to Sue Bridehead, "The doctor says there are [other children like him] springing up amongst us — boys of a sort unknown to the last generation — the outcome of new views of life."[11] The travesty that Jude found in nineteenth-century institutions and ideals may lead one to look differently on the travesty that critics of spiritualism found in the philosophical, religious, romantic, and artistic discourse of this cultural movement. John Hay provided a risible example in the trance-utterances of Bott, the hapless medium in *The Bread-winners* ("Let your earth-soul be lifted to meet our speerut-soul; let your earth-heart blend in sweet accordion with our heaven-heart");[12] but should one laugh at Bott's maundering or at the respectable clichés of nineteenth-century religiosity and sentimentality on which these utterances depend? Can it even be sensible to ask where the real travesty is?

This question might lead to Matthew Arnold's baleful descriptions of the dangers facing culture in his day, but Arnold's terms succeeded in describing the limits of nineteenth-century reason while failing to grasp the historical problem posed when such limits are indeed *de*scribed, or symbolically released from dogmatic authority. The problem was to determine what happens to the human subject that is given language: not the divine fiat, not dogmatic truth, not patristic interpretation, nothing of that sort, but just language on its own terms. By basing itself on modern miracles, spiritualism contradicted what Lecky saw as the definitive mark of rationalism, its rejection of such phenomena; but this reactionary appearance effectively dramatized a contradiction internal to the Enlightenment heritage. Simply put, the Enlightenment gift of language gave human beings both too little and too much. It gave too little in offering the Word, the spirit of language, without any given words and thus without a guiding history. It gave too much in offering words, expressions of every sort, without any given history and thus without a guiding spirit. It was an appreciation of this dilemma that led Hardy to adopt "The letter killeth" as his Pauline epigraph to *Jude the*

Obscure—an epigraph exquisite in its irony, since the novel went to great lengths to provide demonstrations that "the spirit" was also far from promoting good health.

What happens to the human subject that is given language? Both Hardy's novel and modern spiritualism suggested that it can experience its freedom and independence only in a manner of speaking (or rapping, writing, drawing . . .). Otherwise bound to debasing alternatives like the empty concepts without intuitions and blind intuitions without concepts of which Immanuel Kant had written, this subject can establish itself only in "wording." And the problem then is that one does not solve the contradiction of enlightenment but instead turns upon it, always startled at its reappearance in new forms, while what is *de*scribed is *re*inscribed, as with the violence of a Frankenstein monster that will not die: the monster of "nature," of "realism," of "society," of "truth." Nineteenth-century reason identified the human subject with rational discourse, which was supposed to transcend history and to demonstrate this transcendence through the progress to which it led; but then reason could neither find nor found its own history. Lecky's insistence on the incredibly unlikely emergence of reason from the contingencies of social life was an oblique recognition of this problem, as were the habitual references to divine power even in the works of thinkers who had explicitly dispensed with religion and yet could not help but see that reason was then somehow miraculous, a secular Providence.[13] It might seem an immense spiritual invention, refined over centuries, designed for the sole purpose of begging the question. Gerald Massey smirked at this situation when he played upon the common pronunciation of Daniel Home's name as "Hume": "we have one 'Hume' answered by the other."[14]

Since it was premised on the transcendence of history and thus of any particular events, persons, acts, or words, reason was forever driven to recognize that it existed only in a manner of speaking and yet was forbidden this recognition, which would have dethroned it as an effective measure of truth and guarantor of humanity. By refusing to define reason as the suppression of miracles, by dwelling on the miraculous nature of reason's own history, modern spiritualism exposed this contradiction. Although jarring in other respects, the connection with Nietzsche is relevant here. As a cultural movement, modern spiritualism showed that the gift of language opened the human subject to change, even to a completely new and superhuman form, and to this end proposed alternative ways of dealing with this gift while opposing those currently institutionalized. Rather than taking reason's miraculous transcendence of history to mean that history was under rational control, it took this transcendence to mean that history and human beings were open to any conceivable revelation and then sought to explore this openness through its inventive practices. Its description of the world was an undoing (which is also to say, a doing) of cultural conventions and associations. It saw reason as just this license to invent, or reinvent, the nature of humanity and human society. "Yahoo civilization is doomed," said Thomas Lake Harris, the eccentric spiritualist;[15] the connections between modern spiritualism and utopian communities such as those of the Owenites, Shakers, and Fourierists become very important in this regard, as one can see from Harris's own communal experiments. And if the freedom and independence that spiritualism assumed to be so readily available were pathetic (a characterization that does seem fair in relation to Harris's communities), the pathos belonged as well to the spirit of reason, which so unblushingly expressed confidence in its inexplicable history by appealing to an unforeseeable future. "We burn with the desire to find a firm position, and a final constant base on which to build a tower that rises to infinity," Blaise Pascal had written, "but our entire foundation cracks, and the earth opens unto abysses."[16]

To make this point more specific: one of the most important ways of speaking in modern spiritualism, and a way that exemplifies both the creativity and the limitations of this movement, was the giving of testimony. This was indeed a movement of the "modern" world—the world of reason inspired by Galileo and Newton and variously described by Locke and Hume, Kant and Hegel, Comte and Mill—and so it depended on the testimony of experience. David Hume had observed "that there is no species of reasoning more common, more useful, and even necessary to human life, than that which is derived from the testimony of men, and the reports of eye-witnesses and spectators";[17] and spiritualists did not demur. However, when Hume concluded that there could not be any testimony to a miracle that could establish its probability, much less its reality, spiritualists begged to differ. To some extent the difference stemmed from conflicts over the evaluation of evidence and testimony, but finally it represented an argument over what the giving of testimony *is*. In the end, what it meant to give one's word turned out to be the most important question and one that could not be solved by an appeal to reason or experience. Opponents of spiritualism generally assumed that giving one's word simply meant telling the truth, but the spiritualist assumption was very different.

Of course, Hume did not fail to note a crucial distinction between testimony and experience. In writing of miracles, which were his test-case in this regard, he recalled, "*I should not believe such a story were it told me by Cato*, was a proverbial saying in Rome, even during the lifetime of that philosophical patriot. The incredibility of a fact, it was allowed, might invalidate so great an authority."[18] The point seems basic enough, but it was given a very different twist in the opening sentences of Robert Bell's famous article about the prodigies manifested through the mediumship of Daniel Home. "Stranger than Fiction" begins as follows:

"I have seen what I would not have believed on your testimony, and what I cannot, therefore, expect you to believe upon mine," was the reply of Dr. Treviranus to inquiries put to him by Coleridge as to the reality of certain magnetic phenomena which that distinguished savant was reported to have witnessed. It appears to me that I cannot do better than adopt this answer as an introduction to the narrative of facts I am about to relate.[19]

A saying almost identical to the one Hume took to describe the superiority of experience to any testimony about miracles here takes on a very different purport, describing instead the inferiority of testimony to miraculous experience. The effect is not really to contradict Hume's words but rather to clarify how the divergence they leave between knowledge and belief also implies an ineradicable kinship between these two. This was emphasized in a footnote to the article by its editor, William Thackeray, in which he said, "I can vouch for the good faith and honourable character of our correspondent . . . [but] his readers are . . . free to give or withhold their belief."[20] It was further emphasized when Hermann Ulrici actually cited Hume's analysis of causality (and implicitly referred to Kant's) in his reply to Wilhelm Wundt's denunciation of spiritualism; Ulrici argued that since causality is a necessary law only for thought, not for nature, science cannot dismiss out of hand the possibility of the spiritualist hypothesis.[21]

In his *Enquiry Concerning Human Understanding*, Hume had argued that knowledge is based on relations, especially the relation of cause and effect, that are customary, not rationally grounded. But by giving knowledge the tests of "custom," "common life," and "enlightened" (as opposed to "vulgar") testimony, he made it seem that one could draw a clear distinction between lawful knowledge, based on rationally evaluated experience, and credulous belief, which lacks this foundation. With this support he could shove all supernatural belief off to the side as an error or at best a respectable tradition (in the case of Christianity), but the opening of "Stranger than Fiction" shows that the divergence between knowledge and belief cannot be so easily maintained. Instead of sanctioning knowledge and putting belief into quarantine, this divergence may be seen as so compromising both that their differing ways, ironically, make them inseparable. Rather than solving the problem of empirical reason, it may appear that custom, common life, and enlightened witnesses *are* the problem.

The same might be said of Kant's conception of pure reason, which sought to solve the problem of the limits of experience by invoking the regulative nature of the transcendental ego; for this ego amounted to the rule of communal unity in another form. "Our age is the age of criticism, to which everything must be subjected" (2n.), wrote Kant in his preface to the first edition of the *Critique of Pure Reason*, in which he sought to draw a stricter line between criticism and unfounded belief than Hume had been persuaded to trace.[22] In delineating "the boundaries of experience" (69), Kant assumed that we have — or at least that reason demands — forms of experience independent of and prior to cultural life. He argued that these are manifested in our perceptions of space and time, which necessarily include the concept of causality that had so troubled Hume; that causality, therefore, does not require empirical proof but rather is the very possibility of empiricism; and that this comprehension of a ground of experience holding priority over culture defines the scope of any knowledge worthy of the name. In criticizing Hume's vague notion of custom as providing an insufficient basis for the experienced regularities of nature, Kant took the understanding required by the modern sciences to be universal, incumbent upon all people in all times insofar as they would have a claim on truth. Thus, by identifying the boundaries of experience with the boundaries of what he considered to be the most enlightened European thinking of the late eighteenth century, he was able to portray experience as a tutor whose lessons could not possibly include a mental power "of intuiting the future by anticipation," or "a power of the mind to place itself in community of thought with other men, however distant they might be," or like phenomena. "But when we fashion to ourselves new conceptions of substances, forces, action and reaction, from the material presented to us by perception, without following the example of experience in their connection, we create mere chimeras, of the possibility of which we cannot discover any criterion, because we have not taken experience for our instructress, though we have borrowed the conceptions from her" (167–68). In other words, Kant identified experience with a way of being—with a wording of experience—and with unprecedented rigor and brilliance formulated the faculty of reason implicit in that wording. What he did not feel any need to do was to measure the way of being to which his philosophy is a monument against other wordings of experience, actual or possible.

Whether or not they had any specific awareness of Kant's writing, it was at this point that the spiritualists' critique of the line between criticism and belief took effect. With impressive dexterity, spiritualists responded to virtually every attack that reasoning from experience might launch against them. Let Hume put forward multiple arguments to show that miracles are rationally inconceivable, incoherent even in their conception: very well. These "miracles," replied the spiritualists, were never said to be supernatural in that sense. They appear to violate the laws of nature because we are only now beginning to understand the higher natural law they represent. And, they would add, do not think that such manifestations were something entirely unheard of before 1848. On the contrary, they allow us for the first time to come to a rational understanding of the reports of miracles that come down to us from ancient times and from all nations. We can now begin to understand what our ancestors failed to grasp in the phenomena of sorcery and possession, in Socrates' daimon and in the Seeress of Prevorst, in the Witch of Endor and in Scottish legends of second-sight, in mesmerism, and in all varieties of religious, mystical, and occult experience.

Say that spiritualism contradicts the general experience of humankind, and a similar riposte would be made. Spiritualism does not, as G. H. Lewes said, show the "want of a right appreciation of evidence which is common among mankind."[23] One can treat the spiritual manifestations scientifically. "I regard them," said Harriet Beecher Stowe, "simply as I do the phenomena of the Aurora Borealis, or Darwin's study on natural selection, as curious studies into nature."[24] You object that the movement does not proceed scientifically, despite its claims? The Count de Gasparin knows how to respond:

> What is, in effect, the general principle that governs the acceptance of scientific facts? We believe without seeing, when all those who have wanted to see have done so, and when we know that we could have seen in our turn.
>
> Reject this principle, and there remains only universal skepticism. Understand, then, that when I declare that one will see the movements [of the tables] if one goes to see them, I assume that one will fulfill the conditions of the experience. He who would try to go to America without climbing onto a boat would assuredly never arrive. I would say the same of he who would try to obtain the movements without following the path or means by which we have obtained them.[25]

Or perhaps you insist, with George M. Beard, that the "rejection of non-expert testimony is, and has ever been, the first step in the development of a science."[26] This may seem a strong position, a quintessentially modern and enlightened position; but does it really clarify matters? "It was not a churchman," Charles Massey remembered, "but a very learned professor, who refused to look through Galileo's telescope." And what of an acknowledged expert like Alfred Russel Wallace, who not only offered his own testimony but also pointed to the "cumulative evidence of disinterested and sensible men"? And why should "learned bodies" have such a monopoly on evidence anyway? In Emma Hardinge's words, "If the hundreds of intelligent persons, strangers to, and apart from each other, who have been closely observing such singular phenomena, all arrive at the conclusion that these supposed delusions are tangible facts, stern realities, — if all these, and thousands of others have been deceived, — of what use is evidence at all?" As Edward Cox put this matter, "On similar evidence a jury would instantly convict of murder and a judge would hang without hesitation."[27]

Although showing a rhetorical finesse that may be amusing, by themselves these examples scarcely constitute significant philosophical arguments. For this reason they might be dismissed as illustrating nothing more than how wide spiritualists could open their mouths to swallow absurd beliefs, but this conclusion would be unfounded. While they do lack philosophical cogency and illustrate a redoubtable capacity for a dizzyingly circular reasoning, the spiritualist arguments illustrate as well a vulnerability in the terms, procedures, and justifications of nineteenth-century reason. This vulnerability would haunt it right into the twentieth century, in which the difficulty of establishing a philosophical ground for scientific reason has become rather notorious since the researchers of many cultural anthropologists, the work of philosophers such as Ludwig Wittgenstein, and the studies by historians of science such as Thomas Kuhn, Michel Foucault, and Paul Feyerabend. In their specifics, the arguments of modern spiritualism do not hold up (unless one is a believer), but they are significant nonetheless for showing how the testimony of experience is always a giving of testimony: not a word, not a simple fact, but a wording.

Hume did not ignore this issue, either. "The reason why we place any credit in witnesses and historians," he wrote, "is not derived from any *connexion*, which we perceive *a priori*, between testimony and reality, but because we are accustomed to find a conformity between them." Furthermore, he argued that actions, not propositions or demonstrations, put a stop to epistemological quandaries and allow knowledge to arise from experience:

> The great subverter of *Pyrrhonism* or the excessive principles of scepticism is action, and employment, and the occupations of common life. These principles may flourish and triumph in the schools; where it is, indeed, difficult, if not impossible, to refute them. But as soon as they leave the shade, and by the presence of the real objects, which actuate our passions and sentiments, are put in opposition to the more powerful principles of our nature, they vanish like smoke, and leave the most determined sceptic in the same condition as other mortals.[28]

But then this was precisely the question of spiritualism: what is the nature of real objects? In other words: what constitutes the grounds of common life? Or more precisely yet: what may common life be?

The weak point in the notion of experience central to Enlightenment reason, to Kant's philosophy as to Hume's, was that it took the *sensus communis* and "common life" for granted even as it purported to put all of life to the test of experience. It assumed a common social world and a human nature shared by people in every place and historical era. This latter assumption, for instance, played a major role in Hume's refutation of miracles by enabling him to discredit credulous testimony even as it served to explain the existence of such credulity. The experience of which philosophers, scientists, and similar figures spoke was never experience pure and simple (even assuming there could be such a thing). Explicitly or not, it was always a common, uniform, law-abiding, educated, Western, male experience. As no one showed better than Hume, this was a modest and prudent experience well suited to scientific progress, middle-class trade and industry, and social conservatism. What it was not — as nothing showed better than modern spiritualism — was the only conceivable rational form of life. Other worlds were possible.

In one of his milder strictures, Hume had pointed out that if miraculous testimonies were considered as assertions, they could not be more conclusive than the testimonies arrayed against them. As a manner of speaking, though, these testimonies were something other than bare assertions, as far as the spiritualists were concerned. They were the evocation of another world, which in this respect was not a heavenly reality but the world called into being precisely by this practice of testimony and the other practices embraced along with it.

In the first place, testimonies were *self*-assertions: demands for a public recognition of the value of personal experience, no matter how extraordinary or idiosyncratic it might be. As such they were also challenges to the centrist definition of "the public" and "the public world," and included in this challenge were the opportunities for a social position and a remunerative occupation that mediumship offered to many women, who would otherwise have had nothing of the sort. (From the beginning, mediumship was a profession as open to women as to men—unlike the professions of law, medicine, divinity, and business.) The giving of testimony meant the subverting of established authority and leadership, since the very fact that testimony was called for implied that experience had not yet been sufficiently codified so that it could be handed down in the form of generalizations or generalized procedures. This aspect of spiritualism was nicely caught by the joke printed in the *Banner of Light*, an American spiritualist journal, that tells of a young man asked to explain the difference between spiritualist meetings and other sorts. "The prompt reply was, 'A Spiritualist meeting is where the speaker goes to sleep and the audience keeps awake; the other is where the audience goes to sleep and the speaker keeps awake.'"[29]

It might be objected that the giving of testimony carries these implications under any circumstances, but what is significant here is that spiritualists acted them out. They did not take them for granted as the ground of common life, and so they made the giving of testimony something radically other than what it seemed in common life. They made it an action that did not submit individuals to the homogenizing test of experience but instead raised them out of the common world into one that better satisfied their desires. It empowered them to challenge and reject authority that spoke against and never from their sense of experience. Through the act of giving testimony, one could experience language without feeling dispossessed by it and yet without feeling that one necessarily had to master it or dominate other people through it. Spiritualists then related their experience without appealing beyond it. They reached the other world by shrinking the boundaries and demands of this world. Hence the domesticity of spiritualism, its architectural and psychological interiority, and its femininity (as in the table that was its symbol and otherwise an object associated especially with womanly activities and domains). In testifying, spiritualists made the philosophical character of propositions bow to the emotional, social, and political images they might be taken to suggest.[30]

At the same time, the giving of testimony was an acknowledgment of insecurity. First, insecurity in identity: the testimonies typically emphasized the reputations of the deponents, their professions or respectability in the community, the skeptical or reluctant or accidental nature of their initial participation in the movement, and their sobriety or responsibility. These details all served to strengthen the value of their words but by the same token acknowledged that these words could not stand by themselves. Accordingly, the giving of testimony also showed a certain insecurity in social relations. In featuring descriptions of the conditions at seances (the brightness of the light, whether the tables involved were on casters, the number of sitters, their disposition about the room, and so on), the testimonies showed an anticipation of the possibility of fraud or at least of possible accusations of fraud. Furthermore, insecurity appeared in the relations between people and objects, for these descriptions showed that people were often uncertain what conditions were relevant or, in other words, what constituted evidence. In the account of Dr. Justinus Kerner, for instance, one can see this gentleman trying to determine if the size of the table is important, or the time waiting for manifestations, or the age of the participants, or their sex, or even the color of their hair. (He believed he had found that "children with blond, or even better, with red hair" were most effective in circles.)[31] Other accounts offer painstaking measurements of each part of the table, its weight, the temperature of the room, the mood of the company, whatever might come to mind as possibly being of interest even though presently seeming of no consequence whatsoever. This evocation of insecurity further appears in the way testimonies were connected with tests: names written and then concealed so the medium could try to divine them, messages one circle would mentally transmit to another ("the spiritual telegraph"), names or dates or information offered to mediums to see if they could flesh out the histories they represented, all sorts of techniques. (In the section of his Swedenborgian *Book of Human Nature* entitled "Pneumatology: Spirits, Possession, Inspiration," Laroy Sunderland included subsections on "Tests of Congeniality," "Tests of Knowledge," "Tests of Truthfulness," "Tests of Personal Identity," "Tests of Intelligence," "Tests of Grade," and "The Great Test of Use.") Here again the very multiplicity of the tests shows people floundering to define what was to be tested and what would constitute a meaningful test.

While some type of uncertainty might be said to be implied in the very notion of testimony, the specific insecurities marked out in the practices of spiritualism are what is important here. They evoke a world that is domestic, indeed, in its intellectual scale and physical surroundings, and yet very *unheimlich* in its every detail. As restricted as these surroundings are, there is no telling what they contain, much less which of their contents are to be honored with meaning. The common parlor, the domestic circle, here is as mysterious as the deeps of the universe; so too the people within it. This is the household interior as it might appear to persons who have lived so long with walls like these, this kind of furniture, and these curtains and windows that the objects have become more like independent beings than property. This is a logical conclusion for people inclined in any event (as Karl Marx

argued) to fetishize things by repressing from consciousness an understanding of property in terms of social relations and productive conditions. The
house comes alive, like the room of a daydreaming child; but as it comes
alive, its elements are so multiplied and disordered by the psychosocial in-
vestments let loose among them that one cannot tell what's what anymore.
This household was still manageable, but its manageability had become almost incredible, unthinkable, except as a miracle.[32]

The problem with the house that no longer exists as property is that the
Other Side to which it then opens cannot be owned. At least to some extent,
one must submit oneself to its investigation. Opening oneself to experience
in this way, giving testimony of one's experience, leaves an opening—dissolves the walls of the parlor—finds satisfaction, but surrenders the assurance of propriety. And this surrender, this disruption of the human subject,
may have been the point all the while, for it could be a way out of the mirage
of common life. The desire for such an exit is written everywhere in the
literature of modern spiritualism.

So testifying was also a risky act. Disbelief would be anticipated, and
ridicule, even diagnoses of madness. Many witnesses requested anonymity;
many professed to have been persecuted for their beliefs or complained of
the persecution of others. In this respect, testimony involved one in a community both public and occult. By testifying, one went public: one gave one's
words to the world at large. In doing so one identified that world and identified with it: one sublimated oneself. Nothing was more frustrating to spiritualists than what they saw as their opponents' shortsightedness, which could
not look beyond humble surroundings or the occasional fraud to the sublime
perspective onto the whole universe offered by their movement. In spiritualist testimony, one assumed this perspective of the universal community; and
yet, no matter how bravely one boasted of this movement's numbers, this
testimony also set one apart as a member of an embattled minority. The
riskiness of testifying lay in the conflict between the assumption of universality and the knowledge of deviance, for the exaltation of the former was
forever forcing spiritualists further into the frustration of the latter. The
more thoroughly one believed, the more extraordinary one's testimony was
likely to be; the more extraordinary the testimony, the more one was likely
to experience a sense of alienation from the very community whose existence
one was proclaiming.

Almost any group that claims a superior access to knowledge may face
this kind of risk; spiritualists were not slow to compare the persecutions they
claimed to suffer to those endured by the early Christians and by martyrs to
ignorance such as Galileo. What distinguishes this aspect of testifying in
modern spiritualism is that the risk was so completely centered in the presentation of character. On a very few occasions, spiritualists faced some physical
danger, and a few prosecutions were mounted, as of Dr. Slade in England,
on the grounds of fortune-telling or fraud; claims that one's livelihood was

threatened occasionally appeared, almost always without any substantiation. But spiritualists themselves agreed with their opponents that above all else it was the presentation of character that was risked when one testified for this movement. Giving one's word meant focusing attention on the truth of character even more than on the truth of the words. Testifying thus ministered to a personalized sense of authority, which was also encouraged by the fact that the spiritualist medium was neither tutor, technology, nor institution. It was a medium that seemed wholly personal, not logical; and so was character in the practice of testifying made to be a quality superior to any established conventions, irreducible to logic or tradition. That to which one testified was less significant than the way testifying made character, like the domestic circle, the medium for all the universe. Testifying was then the demand that character be seen as rational and as the basis for judging rationality. By giving this new ground to words, spiritualists could overcome the threat that language might overwhelm human beings.

In addition to being an assertion of one's self, an opening of the human being and the home, and a presentation of character, testifying could then be an offering of one's self to the world. With the reassurance that comes from making character rather than words speak truth, one might freely open oneself to words, be carried away by words in a way now overwhelmingly pleasurable. No wonder the spiritualist movement was often sexualized, as when Reuben Briggs Davenport smacked his lips over "the licentious tendencies and opportunities of private spiritualistic intercourse." Even a friendly witness like the Reverend Charles Maurice Davies could not forbear noticing that "dark séances . . . are admirable for a flirtation." Proponents and critics alike noted a voluptuousness in the atmosphere of seances and spiritual communications; Warren Chase's account of the reception of his speaking tours is one of many that tells of how the concern with immortality often seemed indistinguishable from immorality. This image was so prevalent that Arthur Symons, in a 1904 article on Dante Gabriel Rossetti that had nothing to do with spiritualism, would still invoke it: "In Rossetti's work, perhaps because it is not the greatest, there is an actually hypnotic quality which exerts itself on those who come within his circle at all; a quality like that of an unconscious medium, or like that of a woman against whose attraction one is without defense."[33]

In the doctrines of Thomas Lake Harris, one of those dogged by this accusation of immorality, the altered visions of the self that could attend this offering of oneself to the world were given particularly striking form, as in this passage about "fays," or tiny spirits, in his *Arcana of Christianity*:

> Those who inhabit the left feminine breast are called kings and queens, because they correspond to the truths of Divine Love, and live in a pure, ambrosial existence, in the midst of the sweet, blossoming affections of the inner life. Those in the right feminine breast are called priests and priestesses, because they are

preeminently in the good of Divine Truth. There are corresponding pairs in each
bosom. These are the little graces of the breast . . .[34]

Aesthetics entered into this aspect of testimony. Spiritualist poetry is uni-
formly horrible if one reads it with an eye accustomed to touchstones such
as Alfred Tennyson and Emily Dickinson, but the fact that it often made
spiritualists ecstatic may be less a measure of their differing judgment than
of the differing ways they gave themselves to these words in seances, lectures,
or readings at home. Just as the act of giving testimony could thrust one into
a world where tables spoke, walls opened, and deceased relatives became
comforting familiars, this act could be an offering of oneself to all of one's
surroundings, including words. It could be a submission that made even the
most familiar aspects of experience, even the most banal words, touch one
as physically as the hand of a living person. Those dreary accounts of seances
featuring raps and tunes and glimmering lights, all so much the same, and
those spiritualist writings endlessly featuring angels, tears, spheres, and the
like: they are quite another sort of thing if one does not look to them for
logical truth, empirical verification, or stylistic tact but instead identifies
them with the offering of a self to the world. Then it hardly matters what
they say, as long as their saying bespeaks one's desired community. No
further justification is needed; Logie Barrow has noted that many spirit
communications "were printed with little stronger editorial endorsement than
that they were 'interesting' or simply 'beautiful.'"[35] Or "facts" would be printed that had nothing to do with spiritualism save that they might be taken to
uphold the aesthetic sense of the movement: "A very curious phenomenon is
noticed in the Mexican papers as having been seen near the convent of San
Francisco. Water, it is said, springs from the earth in the same manner that
rain falls from the clouds."[36]

What distinguishes spiritualism from other mystic experience is just how
pedestrian it remained even in its most ecstatic moments. It was so in its
objects, of course—the slates, the tambourines, all that lot—and in its diction, which never rose far above the hapless rodomontade of Bott. It was
also resolutely pedestrian in its meetings, which cultivated mystery and yet
were thoroughly unceremonious in all but the singing of a hymn here and
there, and in its effects on believers, who would regularly occupy themselves
with an eternity and with messages from the great beyond that generally
seemed not to change in the least the other occupations of one's everyday
life. Even in its flashiest manifestations, spiritualism did not set itself apart
from the world; and the only objects it invented (if one does not count the
spiritually born "ectoplasm") were the planchette and the spirit cabinet, a
"little plank" and a box. In reaching to the ends of the universe, spiritualism
showed no curiosity that reached beyond the familiar. It was a minimalist
movement, one might say, and the offering of its testimony was a way of

illuminating experience simply by letting its banalities, its endless common-places, have their say — until this saying became wondrous.

These are at least some of the more important elements that appear in the giving of testimony if one analyzes what this practice meant in modern spiritualism. It is from this perspective that the seance, the spiritualist meet-ingplace, appears as a way of meeting. Instead of being a site of truth or error, it appears as a place to do things. It can be seen as a way of gathering persons together who might have no relation to each other, a way of giving them a grasp on objects like the table so they could feel them to be at once completely common and yet marvellous, a way of adding philosophical and aesthetic dignity to the sentimental value conventionally accorded the home, and a way of recreating oneself through participation with others in sur-roundings that were secure and yet opened to spontaneity and unpredictabil-ity. This place and the testifying and other practices associated with it then help to explain the spiritualist revision of the human subject, even at its most bizarre, as in Harris's doctrine of spirits, or as in the testimony before the London Dialectical Society of a certain Mr. Lowenthal:

> The words my mouth utters come involuntarily. I have seen people of standing in society, and most refined, act in as free and unrestrained a manner as wild Indians in the wood, imitating the camp life and the war dance, and speaking in strange languages. This was done, I believe, to take the starch out of them, so that they might receive spiritual knowledge. On one occasion I was with a man who fell on my lap and addressed me in the most endearing language; when he recovered, he explained that I had given him great gratification in personifying his dear sister, then in the spirit land. . . .[37]

What Mr. Lowenthal had to say hardly constitutes an orthodox philosophi-cal investigation, but then one could say that the ultimate purpose of spiritu-alism was to lead one to reconsider just what kind of game philosophy was. Thus, when he reflects on the mysterious rappings coming from his furniture, the narrator of Herman Melville's "The Apple-Tree Table" recalls that Cot-ton Mather, the author of the *Magnalia Christi Americana*, "was no roman-tic Mrs. Radcliffe" but rather "a practical, hard-working, earnest, upright man, a learned doctor, too, as well as a good Christian and orthodox clergy-man."[38] Although this story ends with a rationalized, Radcliffean explana-tion, the suggestion remains that skeptical philosophy (represented in this case by Democritus) may be at once correct and trivial, since it fails to explain human character and history. After all, what sense would it make to say that Lowenthal was *incorrect*? Although he spoke of knowledge, the knowledge of which he spoke was clearly developed by practices outside of those acknowledged by philosophical tradition and even systematically opposed to this tradition insofar as it relied upon logical rather than theatri-cal demonstrations, such as trance-speaking, inspired writing, seance rappings, and personal testimonies. Here spiritualism was indeed a different world, a world intersecting with but irreducible to the world of the skeptic. At the same time it was a world distinguished from that of traditional Christianity by being all phenomena and possibilities rather than dogma and responsibilities. It was a world no more and no less ritualized than the experiences yet to be developed by ordinary individuals day by day.

To take spiritualist words as wording, as I have done to this point, is to take a cultural view of this movement. This view is significant not only as a comparison but also as a challenge to what might otherwise purport to be the simply logical perspective. To leave the analysis at this point, however, could still be to condescend to the subject, though now in a romantic mode. To avoid this possibility, it is necessary to consider some crucial political aspects of the spiritualist way with words.

What I have called the pathos of spiritualism is not what its contemporary critics would have referred to under this name: the pitiful sentimentality, the ignorance as laughable as it was touching, the uncultured aspirations and desires, the vulgarity. Whereas its contemporary critics would think spiritualism pathetic because it fell abysmally short of the standards of middle-class propriety that were being codified in art, science, fashion, and other areas of social life, the pathos of which I have written is that spiritualism was only too middle-class even in many of its radical and plebeian elements. The medium, unfortunately, did recall the middling and the mediocre. As I have described it, the interrelationship of modern spiritualism with realism, empiricism, and rationalism shows it to be a meaningful and critical movement, one that haunted middle-class culture, displaying its contradictions, its baseless presumptions, the deathliness of its smug limitations. Yet this intimacy, which enabled spiritualism to investigate and challenge the culture of reason, also disabled spiritualism.

To say this is not to criticize the fact that from the very beginning, spiritualism relied on the same elements of culture to which it was opposed. This movement drew on Christian tradition, sentimental literature, the rhetoric of reason, and the reverence for modern technology, but the problem is not in this indebtedness as such. You work with what you have: in the medium of history, one cannot invent language, ritual, or truth with complete freedom, pulling it out of nowhere, like a rabbit out of a hat. The problem was the refusal of spiritualists to assert the newness they did have.

By insisting that their modern miracles, their revelations, were part of the rational order of nature even though they appeared beyond the ken of orthodox scientists, theologians, philosophers, artists, and other respectable figures of the day, spiritualists presented their movement as one that did not rebel and did not even seek rebellion. They adopted what is still the popular middle-class practice of applying revolutionary and eschatological language (the overturning of tradition, the advent of a new order, miracles, wonders, signs, and so on) to phenomena envisioned entirely in terms of technique, not at all in terms of cultural and social choice. In our day, this practice is most obvious in the way science is popularly understood to be driven by its own "discoveries," so that even opponents of programs such as space-based missile defenses often stress only the potential impracticalities of such programs, not thinking to challenge the grotesque political conception of the science that has been pushed toward this end. However, it is also shown in the way psychological, aesthetic, and other discourses are apt to speak of revolution in relation to modifications of their objects of study without any concern for the significance these changes have, or do not have, to any social life that extends beyond the narrowest of disciplinary and canonical boundaries. One need not read very far in the literature on modern art, say, or on psychoanalysis, deconstruction, or even MTV, to find this amazingly self-centered talk of crisis, radicalism, violence, worldly transformation, and so on and on. Formal, conceptual, or methodological change—technique— is taken immediately to signify significant social change. And in the second half of the nineteenth century, this practice of worshipping technique was represented most dramatically, if pathetically, in the passivity of the spiritualist movement before its own avowed ends.

Passivity was not only the attitude definitive of the medium: it was also the attitude enshrined in the spiritualists' insistence that they were not engaging in willful trickery but rather discovering truths of nature, learning more of reason, in one way or another opening themselves to the reception of a greater knowledge. If there is any one quality that can summarize the ideologies that developed with middle-class business and industry and education and art, it was the demand that truth be discovered in nature, not arbitrarily prescribed by man. This demand defined the difference between enlightened reason and dogma and might seem unexceptionable if nature were, indeed, simply given to us for investigation; but of course it is not. Our cultures, our economies, our institutions, the technologies we support and those we do not: all these elements of social life delimit what, where, when, how, and why nature is to be. While the quintessential Enlightenment distinction between reason and dogma could be (and in many respects certainly was) immensely liberating, it would also frustrate liberation by leading people to misrecognize the constructions of their desire, which would always be inextricable from their conceptions of nature and yet could be recognized only as messages communicated by nature or inscribed in nature for humanity to find and interpret.

The problem is not that spiritualists, with a bit more insight, might have recognized what desire truly is and so might have become the perfect rebels and revolutionaries they ought to have been. It should be clear that my argument is opposed to the idea that it is possible to distinguish desire from historical life in such a way that one could achieve this completely fulfilling self-consciousness. (Indeed, the possibility of doing so is another formulation of the reason of which I write.) The argument here is that the peculiar pathos of spiritualism stems from the representation of desire in the tradition of modern reason, and more particularly in the art and philosophy and science of the second half of the nineteenth century. The pathos lies in the equation of trickery and desire, on the one hand, and technique and the revelation of truth, on the other—the assumption being that technique differs from trickery in expressing no willfulness and thus in remaining essentially neutral in regard to the determination of truth. By subscribing to these identifications, spiritualists did not prevent themselves from questioning, challenging, and even opposing many aspects of the societies in which they lived; but their movement did set strict limits to its adventure, like a lady or gentleman preparing to explore an exotic locale but only during a month's holiday, on a careful budget, and in clothing that makes no concessions whatsoever to the differences that may exist between the foreign clime and the homeland.

The signs of this pathos are many, but perhaps the most excruciating is the way the Other World was generally seen as a higher sphere or series of higher spheres. The communication of truth, then, was a transmission to a lower consciousness from one that was more elevated. This formulation mirrored the common idealization of women as being (like divine nature) spiritual tutors to men, who were more "of the earth, earthy," as one would say then; and it also mirrored the most pernicious assumption in nineteenth-century educational theory and practice: that education is essentially a labor of condescension, not so much a process as a path, a one-way street, leading from simple ignorance to enlightenment. The spirits then were stand-ins for intellectuals, figures consulted for divine truths but also as people today consult *soi-disant* experts, therapists, psychologists, or Abigail Van Burens (whose homey, feminine advice is bolstered in crucial cases by the assistance of "specialists").

As familiar as they were, these spirits still composed a force as humbling as it was enlightening. This movement without dogma and dictators, this movement whose members were often drawn also to egalitarian, communitarian, and socialist themes,[39] nonetheless reproduced a sense of hierarchy to which everyone was meant to be submissive in the act of communication. A typical element in spiritualist discourse was the claim that mediums and believers came from all ranks of life and all sorts of occupations and represented various degrees of intellect and education, but this levelling was counterbalanced by the common teaching that the "Summerland" was segregated into levels of purer souls and of underachievers. Similarly, while the public and yet personal nature of the movement suggested a kind of democratic consciousness, a conservative elitism was implied in the way spiritualist testimonies paraded forth as support for their positions the names of those eminent and titled persons who had deigned to approve of them. In this aspect of the movement, its insistence on character holds no more possibility than an insistence on public reputation defined in the terms of the dominant culture from which spiritualism deviated but to which it was destined to return.

Pathetic, too, is that spiritualists felt they had to resort to unconsciousness in order to challenge received authorities. While this recourse had the advantage of symbolically suppressing the presence of authority and thus empowering individuals to see, hear, feel, and testify for themselves, it was limited from the very start by the defensiveness it showed. It displaced authority from any one individual in this life, just as the movement in general was characterized by a mediation of opinion through a multitude of mediums, spirits, and communications; and yet, no matter how vigorously or contentiously it was presented, this was an infinitely *polite* suppression of authority.

In this regard, the pride many believers expressed in their movement's genius for disorganization appears as an excuse for letting causes and ideas be nothing more than a trivial entertainment. Their words and wording alike then seem the ritual dress by which members of a community identified each other while excluding themselves from the very problems they claimed to be addressing. Some spiritualists did establish lyceums and other formal organizations, and Andrew Jackson Davis, for instance, created extremely elaborate plans for the construction of schools and parallel bodies on spiritualist principles; but for all their eccentricities, these works succeeded better in unconsciously mimicking than in rebelling against the disciplines enshrined in middle-class culture. After all, the spiritualist discourse of "progress" and "development" was lifted whole, as it were, from the vocabulary of middle-class ambition. It is significant, too, that spiritualists always complained of social opposition but most often did not conceive of theirs as an oppositional movement except in a moral or spiritual sense. From this came their tendency, when organized at all, to conceive of themselves as isolated, persecuted, upstanding witnesses to truth, students or patients or mediums or victims in the cause of truth, but never workers—never even so active as a trickster might be.

And then, of course, the very basis of spiritualism, its insistence on immortality during a time that Thomas Carlyle complained was turning "soul" into a mere figure of speech, was a pathetic gesture.

It was not necessarily so. While showing a fear of the implications of materialist science, these souls pressing forward to speak to the living also expressed dissatisfaction with traditional religion and with culture in general. And in some respects, one might even see spiritualism as an occasion that just happened to present itself to a kind of free-floating desire that was not grounded in particular or local frustrations. This description might be appropriate, for instance, to those persons who would speak of the "charm" or the "sweetness" of the movement, or to those moments among their other experiences that spiritualists would describe in terms like these. Spiritualism then might seem to have no shame and defensiveness about it, appearing rather as a movement designed to punctuate everyday words and experiences with a tranquil — as spiritualists would say, an "ethereal" — pleasure.

Still, the insistence on the soul in this movement was everywhere most dramatically related to a denial of desire. The soul was what spiritualists gave themselves instead of desire, as one can see from the common assumption among spiritualists that the materialism they opposed necessarily implied a reign of brute passions. The ironic fact that opponents of this movement thought it vulnerable to a criticism that associated immortality with immorality, and specifically with vampirish sexuality, conveys this same point. Spiritualism was a sentimental movement because of its domesticity but also because it generally portrayed desire, as any good sentimentalist would, as a dangerous and even murderous force that had to be sublimated into a higher form. It is because of this portrayal that spiritualists could take Charles Dickens's deathbed scenes to represent their beliefs.

Sublimation was not always so dramatically marked. Opposition to the institution of marriage, sometimes as a result of discoveries of "spiritual affinities" between persons saddled with other spouses, did play some part in this movement, and Victoria Woodhull is remarkable as one who rebelled against the sentimental tendency by arguing for what was called "free love." But it should be noted that even this rebellion was directed more against the legal institution of marriage than it was against the conception of desire as the root of dogma, ally of trickery, and enemy of reason. Moreover, even though she was elected president of the American Association of Spiritualists and ran for president of the United States in 1872 on the Cosmo-Political Party ticket, Woodhull was very unusual among spiritualists in her position on this issue. Her example provides some important nuance, but it does not alter the picture of spiritualists giving life to this figure of speech, the soul, so that they could put to death the figure of desire. This was the death they ritually, even obsessively demonstrated by the way they brought truth forth from practices characterized by stillness, receptivity, passivity, and unconsciousness.

It is in the nature of the case that it is difficult to pick out a representative participant in this movement, but Robert Owen's role as a spiritualist at least may indicate how, for individuals, the medium of reason was related to the issue of wording as the subject of spiritualism. Above all else, Owen was (as he never tired of proclaiming) a man of reason. His was a kind of kindergarten rationalism, to be sure, which threw its arms around one Enlightenment bromide — that human beings are creatures of circumstance — and never let go. His life and writings were a continuous reiteration of the Enlightenment ratio that made educational development, moral growth, economic profit, and social improvement practically indistinguishable from each other, so closely bound were they to each other in the lockstep logic of rational progress. The monomaniacal simplicity of Owen's vision, from his earlier days as a self-made man, industrialist, factory reformer, militant critic of religion, socialist, and leader in programs of cooperation to his latter days as a participant in modern spiritualism, can help to provide a final summary as to how central this eccentric movement was to the social history of the nineteenth century, why it had such appeal, and what exactly made it so pathetic in this appeal.

Before he became a spiritualist, Owen found that every aspect of social life had become a false and insane medium to human existence, so pernicious were the effects of the dominant assumption that human beings, rather than circumstances, are responsible for their own character. "I therefore viewed human nature in my fellow-creatures through a medium different from others, and with far more charity."[40] Money was a false and destructive medium, but then so was religion, the economic system, government, language, or any element in society one might care to name. All represented and exacerbated this fundamental error of blaming men and women, rather than their environment, for their nature.

In this conviction, Owen was obsessed with the image of spatiality. Harriet Martineau observed that in Owen's characteristic doctrine of the influence of circumstances, "circumstances" meant "literally *surroundings*."[41] Owen sometimes spoke of his work as the science of surroundings, and he would write of the need "to *replace* and *well* place all of the human race." An account he gave late in life of the response of some visitors to his model industrial community at New Lanark is unreliable as history but captures the wonderfully easy millenarianism that he could preach as a result of his definition of circumstances in spatial rather than temporal terms. (Not so incidentally, it closely resembles the formulations that David Hume and Robert Bell used in writing of miracles.) "Mr. Owen," one visitor is supposed to have said, "this is a new world to me, and a new human nature; and if my brothers, in whom I place all confidence, had described to me what I have seen in common practice here, I should not have believed them."[42]

History was forever a *tabula rasa* for Owen, horribly overlaid at present by insane systems but needing only the intervention of rational technique to be utterly transformed. So he thought already when he organized his factory, where he came up with his famous invention of silent monitors (which his workers called "telegraphs") as a way of turning shiftless laborers into reformed human beings:

But that which I found to be the most efficient check upon inferior conduct, was the contrivance of a silent monitor for each one employed in the establishment. This consisted of a four-sided piece of wood, about two inches long and one broad, each side coloured — one side black, another blue, the third yellow, and the fourth white, tapered at the top, and finished with wire eyes, to hang upon a hook with either side to the front. One of these was suspended in a conspicuous space near to each of the persons employed, and the colour at the front told the conduct of the individual during the preceding day, to four degrees of comparison. Bad, denoted by black and No. 4, —indifferent by blue, and No. 3, —good by yellow, and No. 2, —and excellent by white and No. 1. Then books of character were provided, for each department, in which the name of each one employed in it was inserted in the front of succeeding columns, which sufficed to mark by the number the daily conduct, day by day, for two months; and these books were changed six times a year, and were preserved; by which arrangement I had the conduct of each registered to four degrees of comparison during every day of the week, Sunday excepted, for every year they remained in my employment. The superintendent of each department had the placing daily of these silent monitors, and the master of the mill regulated those of the superintendents in each mill. If anyone thought the superintendent did not do justice, he or she had a right to complain to me, or, in my absence, to the master of the mill, before the number denoting the character was entered in the register. But such complaints rarely occurred. The act of setting down the number in the book of character, never to be blotted out, might be likened to the supposed recording angel marking the good and bad deeds of poor human nature.

Like the other systems used in conjunction with it (such as the patrols he sent through the village to take note of workers who got drunk at night), this invention was conceived with the idea that surroundings were as infinitely malleable as they were wholly spatial. Technique was all. It was the long-standing source of present misery and the way to virtually instantaneous change. Although invented well in advance of modern spiritualism, Owen's monitors—as his comparison with the "recording angel" tells us—may be fairly compared to the spiritualist table, planchette, and cabinet. Each was a simple device, so simple as to be less a device than an embodied technique, in effect nothing but the sign of a machine, and yet able to communicate a divine power to human nature. In Owen's nonspiritualist writings as in his spiritualism, a fascination with systems is closely related to the achievements of modern technology, as symbolized especially by the electrical telegraph; and in his monitors, as in a device such as the planchette, the machine was the medium of reason, pure and simple. (Owen noted that when he was young he was nicknamed "the reasoning machine.")[43] In other words, the simplicity of these inventions conveyed his refusal to recognize the way machines produced at the expense of the human imagination and labor that went into them. They were taken to embody unlabored desire, and thus they served symbolically to deny desire a place in human life.

Having been such an important figure in the labor history of Great Britain, Owen has sometimes been an embarrassment to historians of socialism, who want to distinguish his latter-day spiritualism from his role in factory reform and the cooperative movement. Yet one might say that spiritualism was little more than a change of name for Owen's earlier reformism and socialism. It did not alter any of his ideas on subjects other than life after death and in fact hardly changed his writing in any respect. It simply gave him a new way of turning space into history, words into wording, the forms of systems and objects into the exercise of purified desire. Thus, in his *Millenial Gazette*, he compared the present system of things to what one might look for in the future by saying, "The first makes religion to consist in words, forms and ceremonies, — the words and actions being generally in direct opposition to each other. The second makes religion to consist *not* in words, forms, or useless ceremonies, but in the heartfelt constant desire and practice to make all around them happy, making no distinction of colour, country, sex, or class."[44]

Like many spiritualist productions, Owen's writings before as well as after his conversion have an incantatory, boiler-plate quality, suggesting a sense of language that has more to do with social than with logical propositions (although he would have objected vehemently to such a characterization). The only difference spiritualism seemed to make to him was that it gave pleasure where his social and political engagements by this time were returning only disappointments. For bringing him such pleasure, he lauded the late Duke of Kent, with whom he had hobnobbed in his earlier days of success in industry, when he had also associated with the likes of William Godwin, Jeremy Bentham, James Mill, the archbishop of Canterbury, and, in America, John Adams, Thomas Jefferson, and James Madison:

> His whole spirit proceeding with me has been most beautiful; making his own appointments; meeting me on the day, hour, and minute he named; and never in one instance (and these appointments were numerous as long as I had mediums near me upon whom I could depend) has this spirit not been punctual to the minute he had named.
>
> The unwisely taught, and therefore strongly prejudiced against these new manifestations, cannot believe in their reality, and I greatly pity them. They know not the pleasure and the knowledge which they lose. Some of the most gratifying and satisfying moments of my existence have been when in direct communication with my departed relatives and friends since they left their earthly forms in their graves. These and congenial spirits are now actively engaged in preparing the population of the world for the greatest of all changes in the history of humanity while on earth in its visible form. And they smile at the puny efforts of the poor mistaught of the present generation to stay their progress in this heavenly work.[45]

Owen's life illustrates the most intractable problem resulting from the Enlightenment gift of words: that it gives one a faith in progress that is as uncomprehending toward others as it is challenging to one's self. This gift helped to invent the modern individual and to put that individual in the immediate presence of the world; but it did so only at the cost of distancing the world from history, which had nowhere else to go but into an "other world." This other world might be the past of "superstition" and "error" symbolically suppressed by the continuous renovation of "the modern," or — for those still not satisfied — it might be the heaven of utopian change or of chatty life-after-death. In this crucial respect, these conceptions were all of a piece, bespeaking wondrous possibilities to individuals while forcing them to be uncritical toward their way of wording things and therefore to ignore the ways of others. Owen's blockheaded refusal to countenance any ideas that did not fit his *idée fixe* was simply an illustration of the tendency of reason always to be deaf to its own discourse, techniques, systems, and machines, which, like Owen's "silent monitors," would be assumed to have no voice of their own, being rather the neutral medium of truth.

In spiritualism as in the world of reason generally, the same hand that gave language to everyone also stole desire away from language, leaving it a medium in which people could meet only by chance; for coincidence constitutes the only knowable structuring of experience for individuals who so identify with universality that they cannot comprehend the differences among people in historical life. For such individuals, experience is no more comprehended as labor than desire is comprehended as sociality. One always expects and yet is perpetually and ecstatically amazed to find others sharing one's experiences, for history appears always beyond reason.

Following their desires, the surrealists would try to bring this history beyond reason back into everyday life.

6

The Pathology of Beauty

Ugliness — a burning question and one that is a touchstone of our modern art and its criticism.

PAUL GAUGIN[1]

What is beautiful? What is ugly? What is grand, strong, weak? What is Carpentier, Renan, Foch? Don't know. What am I? Don't know, don't know, don't know.

GEORGES RIBEMONT-DESSAIGNES[2]

It isn't beauty that we love . . .

ROBERT DESNOS[3]

Immanuel Kant claimed that when we talk of beauty, we speak in a voice of subjective universality. Were it not so, language would be profoundly confused. Beauty would lose its distinctiveness. It would not be autonomous but heteronomous, answerable to no single definition, unresponsive to the demands of reason, and communicable, if communicable at all, only by chance. The very notion of aesthetics would be upset if this situation were to obtain, but its consequences would not be limited to aesthetics. Ripped out of their proper frames of consciousness and thrown to the earth to be trampled underfoot, connoisseurs, collectors, curators, and philosophers would find their distraught cries drowned in a riotous mob of voices that would leave no perception, pleasure, or article of taste undisturbed.

According to Kant, an aesthetic voice that grows inaudible before reaching the bounds of universality ought not to be speaking of beauty but of agreeableness. This term covers the tastes that cannot be disputed, the pleasures individuals find in their daily lives without expecting that others must share them. But even if one's aesthetic voice is universal, it still may be misspeaking. That which is universal and objective becomes a concept and so belongs to knowledge, not to aesthetics. It is vital, Kant argues, that we orchestrate this talk correctly. Properly speaking, beauty is purely a matter of form and so is not to be confused with sensations or cognitions. Beauty is distinguished by a disinterested judgment, which does not concern itself with the actual existence in our world of individual responses (the domain of empiricalness and agreeableness) or of rationally apprehended objects (the domain of lawfulness and goodness). The judgment of beauty follows "a subjective principle, which determines only by feeling rather than by concepts, though nonetheless with universal validity, what is liked or disliked." This principle can be called a "common sense (*sensus communis*)."[4]

Thus defined, beauty is systematically differentiated from truth and yet obeys Kant's assumption that language must either be articulated logically or incorrectly. Allow this assumption to be put into question, and Kant's notion of beauty comes to look more willed than compelling, more political than transcendental. It may seem at once an arbitrary assertion of symbolic order, a symptom of unconscious drives, a fluttering banner in a war of interpretations, an imperious demand for a unified culture and a hierarchical society, a sign of European ethnocentrism and racism, and a badge of social affiliation.

In these and other respects, Kant's beauty would later appear to be an ideological mystification, since its "logic" depended on and yet denied certain "anthropological" premises: matters of personal experience and of contingent historical or rhetorical power. No longer would aesthetics be able to rely on a *sensus communis*, and Kant's own writing might appear to be disrupted from within by the very statements meant to secure its meaning. Certain verbal flourishes — for example, "A figure could be embellished with all sorts of curlicues and light but regular lines, as the New Zealanders do with their tattoos, if only it were not the figure of a human being"[5] — would speak in a distasteful voice, a very different voice than the one the author apparently intended them to have. The *parerga*, or inessential ornament, would become an inescapable thesis. In place of Immanuel Kant, we would have cultural interpreters such as Karl Marx, Friedrich Nietzsche, Sigmund Freud, and Jacques Derrida, and we would have artworks such as Charles Baudelaire's "The Love of the Lie":

Isn't it enough, that you make an appearance,
To please a heart that flees veracity?
What does it matter, your dumbness or indifference?
Decor or mask, hail! I love your beauty.[6]

When Kant contrasted beauty with agreeableness by describing the latter as a pleasure that arises from "the pathological ground [*Grunde*],"[7] he was drawing on the etymological root through which *pathos* refers to feeling as physical sensibility. However, if his distinction between beauty and agree-ableness were not to hold, his aesthetics would be forced to turn toward pathology in the more modern sense of that word, which commonly refers to disease, abnormality, deformation, and deviation. These are all paths of figuration that are irrational or, one might say, *artistic* in a modern sense. When André Breton characterized artistic value in terms of the power "of certain *diversions*,"[8] it was this modern sense of things that he was support-ing. Baudelaire had pointed him toward this conclusion, as had Nietzsche, who had turned over the ground of Kant's aesthetics to find "a fat worm of error" in it:

> If our aestheticians never weary of asserting in Kant's favor that, under the spell of beauty, one can *even* view undraped female statues "without interest," one may laugh a little at their expense: the experiences of *artists* on this ticklish point are more "interesting," and Pygmalion was in any event *not* necessarily an "unaesthetic man." Let us think the more highly of the innocence of our aestheticians which is reflected in such arguments; let us, for example, credit it to the honor of Kant that he should expatiate on the peculiar properties of the sense of touch with the naiveté of a country parson![9]

Without specifically referring to *The Critique of Judgment*, Freud also investigated "the peculiar properties of the sense of touch" in a way that held disturbing implications for Kant's philosophy. "There is to my mind no doubt," he wrote in *Three Essays on a Theory of Sexuality*, "that the concept of [the] 'beautiful' has its roots in sexual excitement and that its original meaning was 'sexually stimulating.'" By drawing a conceptual boundary be-tween "perverse" and "normal" behavior, Freud did try to maintain some-thing like Kantian propriety; but even as he made this distinction, he was forced to admit, "In the sphere of sexual life we are brought up against peculiar and, indeed, insoluble difficulties as soon as we try to draw a sharp line to distinguish mere variations within the range of what is physiological from pathological symptoms." He could not help noticing that what he called perversions were at the very heart of normal life, and the writing inspired by his observations might even be said to represent a new kind of beauty, a strange beauty undreamed of in Kant's philosophy. Before surrealism had come into existence, Freud was offering the world passages of surrealist prose, as when he blandly remarked that kissing, which is a contact "between the mucous membrane of the lips of the two people concerned, is held in high sexual esteem among many nations (including the most highly civilized ones), in spite of the fact that the parts of the body involved do not form part of the sexual apparatus but constitute the entrance to the digestive tract."[10]

The title of a book mentioned in one of Leonora Carrington's stories — *The Vulgarity of Food* — carries this sense of diversion to an end that is at once logical and pathological. So, too, does Salvador Dali's argument that since beauty "is but the sum of consciousness of our perversions," the "Venus of 'bad taste'" is destined to displace "the Venus of logic." Dali's conclusion, a rewriting of Breton's motto that "beauty will be convulsive or will not be," also plays with the Kantian conception of taste and its supposed disinterestedness. He concludes, tastefully, "Beauty will be edible or will not be."[11]

The mere suspicion that sexuality might be at the origin of beauty is not the crucial point here, for Kant was perfectly willing to entertain such a possibility.[12] The vital question was when—or if—this coupling of beauty and sexuality was broken. For Kant, the achievement of reason meant the superseding of this origin, which in any event was knowable only as a "speculative beginning"; but once let the likes of Nietzsche and Freud into the picture, and pathological diversions might entirely displace logical conclusions. We arrive at a formulation that would sit well with any hard-boiled detective but that had to sound scandalous coming from a philosopher: "Truth," Nietzsche said curtly, "is ugly."[13]

Works such as Nietzsche's and Freud's would lead Breton to decry "the absurd distinction between beauty and ugliness, truth and falsity, good and evil."[14] In a more recent formulation of this disfiguring of idealist notions, Jean Baudrillard has argued that aesthetics, "in the modern sense of the term, has nothing more to do with the categories of the beautiful and the ugly."[15] These statements indicate how beauty in the modern world has tended to move beyond questions of identities into negotiations of arbitrary qualities. In this world beauty may indeed be entirely a matter of form, as Kant argued, but of form displaced from any logical ground and so turned into an issue of chance. Think of bodies and parts of bodies diverted from the possibility of organic unity, and then think of the fortuitous meeting of an umbrella and a sewing machine on an operating room table—and there you are.

The well-known intimacy between "modern" and "primitive" art makes perfect sense within this revision of beauty. Undo the distinctions of Kant's aesthetics, which make beauty a civilized ideal, and it might be more appropriate to look for beauty in what is supposed to be the most primitive figuration, as in the Homeric representation of Helen of Troy. Fated and fateful, unspiritualized by Platonic philosophy or Christian theology and romance, hers is a beauty that is stipulated, as it were, instead of being rationally conceived. In this respect it is like the appearance that African, Oceanic, and American Indian objects possessed for many artists of the early twentieth century, who did not see them primarily as examples of culture but rather as signposts directing one beyond cultural boundaries, to "primitive" human origins and essences. The same vision, begot by modernism out of romanticism, would make objects of art out of things made by children and the insane.[16]

Within the framework of Kantian reason, a "modern mythology" would have to seem a contradiction in terms; but it was this kind of mythology to which the surrealists of the 1920s and 1930s dedicated themselves, as did many other artists and intellectuals of the time. Specific paths differed, but the surrealists, at least, were eager to claim a kinship with individuals such as Pablo Picasso who were never formally allied with their movement and yet seemed to share their desire to make reality kneel before the power of myth. "Mythology," then, would not be (as it would for one such as Kant) a superstitious, unenlightened, or precritical grasp of the world. Instead, no matter how irrational it might appear when viewed from a philosophical perspective, it would body forth the truth of reason, a truth inseparable from bodies and body parts and bodily movements even at their most singular or ugly.

No longer a divine form, organic whole, or regulative idea, beauty in this mythology simply became the subject nominally framed by art: man, mannequin, machine, fetish, whatever. Art increasingly lent itself to the ad hoc, the available, what surrealists called the *disponible*, or whatever happened to be at one's disposal. The decorous subject of art disappeared, along with the notion of the artistic masterpiece, which, Tristan Tzara noted acerbically, was "within spitting distance" of "the principles of *beauty*, of static and unchangeable beauty." The traditional idealization of the great artist was also placed under attack: "I prefer an artist who's a fart in a steam engine."[17] Beauty then became entirely human at the same moment that it ceased to be humanist. Consequently, it raised disturbing questions about idiosyncrasy, monstrosity, conflict, and deliverance. These questions still furnish material for contemporary art and critical theory, as the work of Baudrillard and Derrida attests; but they had already set the stage for surrealism. While distinctively modern, this disturbance of beauty had long been threatened. It is legible even in Kant's writings, as Nietzsche pointed out, and in various other literary and philosophical works.

For instance, among the poems by Baudelaire that might be cited in this context there is one titled, with mocking reference to a traditional reverence, "Hymn to Beauty." This poem uses the terms of desire to frame Baudelaire's insight into the possible destruction of aesthetic frames. Confounding seeming opposites — "the good deed" and "the crime," "sunset" and "sunrise," "the black gulf" and "the stars," "joy" and "disasters" — the beauty addressed in this poem "governs all and pledges nothing." It appears decked out in some of its favorite jewelry, including "Horror" and "Murder," and is recognized as an attraction at once luxuriant and deathly. The question that opens the poem, whether beauty comes from heaven or the abyss, is finally dismissed as a meaningless or rhetorical question. What does it matter, the poet concludes, as long as beauty makes the universe less hideous, lightens passing time, opens the door to an infinity the poet loves but has yet to reach?

In this conception, which gives *Flowers of Evil* its disfiguring, deflowering title and reigns throughout all its assembled poems, beauty appears within perceptions that correspond to no rational ends. Accordingly, the origins of

beauty must appear by turns obscure, equivocal, contradictory, and dismissable. What remains of beauty in its traditional conception is the ideal, but
the ideal without justification, without philosophy. The ideal in "Hymn to
Beauty" has become a mistress whose attraction is the power to overcome
questions with desire, and this attraction is also her threat. A profoundly
unstable figure, sowing joys and disasters "haphazardly," this "queen" rules
as a despot, revealing herself only as an unaccountable alienation of desire
from human control, explanation, and form. (Hence the uncircumscribed
and yet intimately conjoined figures with which the poet identifies her: "fairy
with velvet eyes / Rhythm, perfume, gleam, O my only queen!")[18] In contrast to Kant's ideal of the beautiful, which "must be expected solely in the
human figure,"[19] Baudelaire's ideal consumes the figuration of the human in
the prospect of a lascivious, corrupting, infinite semiosis.

However, even in this despoiled and dispersed form, Baudelaire's beauty
does preserve its ideality. One might compare him on this point to one of his
admirers, Algernon Charles Swinburne, who wrote, "Beauty may be strange,
quaint, terrible, may play with pain as with pleasure, handle a horror till she
leave it a delight," but concluded, "No good art is unbeautiful."[20] Baudelaire's beauty preserves its ideality in uncertainty, confusion, punishment,
torment, and a driving dissatisfaction; it is beauty taking on teeth, escaping
from morality, refusing "to confuse ink with virtue";[21] but still the ideal is
there, in the thematic preoccupations of "Hymn to Beauty" as in its exqui-
sitely measured meter, rhyme, and stanzaic form. For all its boldness, this
poem might be said to evade the most troubling questions that would arise
when the conception of aesthetics championed by Kant was felt to be slipping
away. For what if beauty were not a form of deliverance? If it did not
conduct one to *any* infinity, whether good or bad? ("Like dogs," wrote the
Comte de Lautréamont, "I feel the need for the infinite . . . I cannot, I
cannot satisfy this need!")[22] What if there were no monstrosity in the world
because the distinction between the beautiful and the ugly had grown—not
confusing or vexing—but ridiculous? (A friend of Guillaume Apollinaire's
protagonist in *The Assassinated Poet* says that he has found the perfect
woman for him: "She is ugliness and beauty; she is like everything we love
these days.")[23] What if beauty were artifice without ideality, so that Baudelaire's "implacable Venus" became Joris-Karl Huysman's adorable machine?

And then, to examine accurately that which is considered to be the most exquisite
of [Nature's] works, the one among her creations whose beauty is, by universal
agreement, the most original and perfect—woman—has not man, for his part,
fabricated all on his own an animated and artificial creature that is worth just as
much, in terms of plastic beauty? Does there exist, on earth, a creature conceived
in the joys of a fornication and come forth from the sufferings of a womb whose
model, whose type, is more dazzling, more splendid, than that of the two locomotives adopted on the northern railroad line?[24]

With questions like these, we enter the culture of Villiers de l'Isle-Adam's *The Future Eve*, of Alfred Jarry's "supermale," and of Filippo Marinetti's steely futurist condescension toward the Winged Victory of Samothrace. What Theodor Adorno calls the "ominous generality in the concept of the beautiful" gets its comeuppance and is tossed aside by those who (in the surrealists' words) "recognise in the name of beauty nothing but a muzzle."[25]

In his criticism as in his poetry, Baudelaire generally resisted the possibility of this recognition. *"Beauty is always bizarre,"* he would write, but then he would carefully qualify his statement:

> I do not mean that it should be willfully, dispassionately bizarre, because in that case it would be a monster jumping off the tracks of life. I am saying that it always contains a bit of bizarreness, of naive, unplanned, unconscious bizarreness, and that it is this bizarreness in particular that makes it the Beautiful. It is its matriculation, its characteristic. Reverse the proposition, and try to conceive of a *banal beauty!*[26]

The last sentence is meant to be a *reductio ad absurdum*; but in the era of dada, when Marcel Duchamp began to make art out of things such as snow shovels, it could be taken as a prescription. At least for some, it was no longer banality but the pretension to ideality that was ridiculous.

"The basis of the word BEAUTY," wrote Francis Picabia in a dada manifesto, "is nothing but an automatic and visual convention. Life has nothing to do with what grammarians call the *Beautiful.* . . . We no more believe in *God* than we do in *Art* or its priests, bishops, and cardinals."[27] A century earlier, Hegel had announced that art, in its highest sense, was no longer possible in the modern world, but surely he had not foreseen its obsequies being presided over by a cultural movement characterized by execrations, hallucinations, and absurd demonstrations of a sense of irony cut loose from all ideals.

Or had he? After all, he did note that "if irony is taken as the keynote of representation, then the most inartistic of all principles is taken to be the principle of the work of art." Furthermore, in commenting that romantic art "intertwines its inner being with the contingency of the external world and gives unfettered play to the bald lines of the ugly,"[28] he marked the point where a revolutionary irony could insert itself into the tradition of romanticism and erase the formal difference between beauty and ugliness. Like Kant's, Hegel's writing has its confusions of desires and destinies; his voice, too, betrays itself. It is really not so surprising that the surrealists found much to appreciate in Hegel even as they drew inspiration from Marx and Freud.

The confrontation between aesthetics and history played out in fin-de-siècle symbolism and in the early-twentieth-century agitation of dada was dramatically reformulated by the surrealists, who saw no contradiction in paying homage at the same time to Hegel and Nietzsche, Baudelaire and dada, psychoanalysis and Marxism and pataphysics. Surrealism sought to live in contradiction, unreasonableness, and pathology. Even as they pronounced the end of beauty in its traditional conception, surrealists sought in art "the unconditional defense of a single cause, which is *the emancipation of man*" (Breton).[29] Only "external" boundaries divided Hegel's voice from the voices of dreams and dada, and the surrealists argued that emancipation required above all else the overthrow of exteriority. Depending on the context, this term had various meanings for their movement, signifying everything from cops and clothes and professors to consciousness, government, and God; but in terms of aesthetics, it referred especially to the image of an independent, objective, universal nature that was supposed to provide art with its materials and rules.

For the surrealists, this nature was not what one perceived: it was what enslaved our perceptions. It was not a guiding reality or an inspiring ideal but rather an imprisoning lie, a torturing social compromise, the kind of bargain that ever so rationally joins the torturers to the victims in the works of the Marquis de Sade. The categorical distinction between beauty and ugliness was not the mark of an organizing reason but the wound of a castrating repression.

Following this antagonistic approach to nature, Max Ernst would ask the question, "What is a forest?" and would frustrate it with his response, "Outside and inside, all at once. Free and imprisoned. Who can solve the enigma?" Or he would describe a forest becoming "geometrical, conscientious, needy, grammatical, juridical, pastoral, ecclesiastical, constructivist, and republican."[30] The trick of these descriptions is similar to the one Baudelaire used when he tried to capture an "incomparable beauty" by yoking together sublime extremes ("this sea so infinitely varied in its frightening simplicity, and which seems to represent by its games, its allures, its anger and its smiles, the moods, the agonies, and the ecstasies of all the spirits who have lived, do live, and will live!").[31] However, the surrealist passages occlude the very summary they pretend to be seeking. They are not synthetic but deliberately unbalanced. They do not aspire to transcendence; and if they find beauty, they find it to be "incomparable" in a very different sense than the one suggested by Baudelaire's prose poem. Incomparability here is not an aspect of nature in relation to art but a strategy of art employed against what is perceived to be the oppressive illusion of nature. And while the beauty that emerges in this matrix is opposed to the natural world, as in the writings of Huysmans or the paintings of Gustave Moreau (which both Breton and Huysmans loved), it is also opposed to any exaltation of artifice that would result in another code of law to replace what the surrealists disparagingly referred to as "Euclidean" space and "retinal" appearances. Although they honored Baudelaire's queen, Moreau's figures of neuraesthenic luxury, and the locomotives of Huysmans and Marinetti, the surrealists were after a different beauty. They wanted it to appear more as it does in Robert Desnos's *Mourning for Mourning*, which revises the traditional image of woman into a figure that travesties at one and the same time romantic iconography, utopian rationalism, patriotism, aestheticism, and grammar:

> The blinds were hung from invisible hinges and opened onto a window through which there appeared a dark beauty with clear eyes at the very instant when, nude and with bound breasts, she was triumphantly emerging from the crowd that was shouting cowardly condemnations without being able to place even the nail of a little finger on the white shoulder and the majestic cunt of she who, from the height of a window in the sky, contemplated their useless pantomime. She finally saw me and told me, "I am and you are and nevertheless I cannot say that we are. The ridiculous conjugal convention of the word separates and attracts us. I have marvellous eyes and jewels like all hell. Look at my arms and look at my neck. An unspeakable love is born in you even as and to the extent to which I speak. I am the dark Beauty and the fair Beauty. The triumphant beauty without beauty. I am You and You are I.[32]

Such a beauty, if we accept it as beauty, is not consciously wrought. Instead, it is found, it is met, it comes, as in the automatic writing that would be adopted as one of the definitive practices of surrealism soon after Desnos produced this passage. Thus, in writing of Picasso, Paul Eluard wished for thought that "would not regard itself only as a scrutinizing or reflecting element but (the connections among things being infinite) as a motivating element, as an element of panic, as a universal element." This is what Breton defined in *Nadja* and *Mad Love* as "convulsive beauty": "erotic-veiled, explosive-fixed, magic-circumstantial." There could be no doubt about it: "Beauty will be CONVULSIVE or will not be." As opposed to those sentimentalists who, in Aragon's words, "prefer paradise to poetry," the surrealists sought a beauty so unsettling that it would render nugatory the distinction between itself and ugliness.[33]

Such a beauty would have nothing to do with the funerary aspect of traditional art, which, as the saying goes, captures for posterity a vision of the past. Even when its images were drawn from contemporary life or from imagination, art could be said to have this funerary character insofar as it was designed to memorialize the passing appearance or thought. And if one reflects on this *faithful* design, what could be further from the surrealist desire for a "language without reserve"; for "a day when thought and imagination [would] become spontaneous and imperious, like the senses, having no further need of words but blossoming into sumptuous states of being"; for an enslavement by "the pure faculty of sight," by "unreal and virgin eyes, ignorant of the world and of themselves," which would lead to the experience of finding oneself "in a mirror without tain"?[34] Instead of looking to what was past or passing, surrealist art was to look to the coming apocalypse.

It is too simple to say that the surrealists sought the absolute unless one notes that the realization of this absolute was supposed to mean the end of any definable art. At the ultimate limit that was also the motivating ethic of this movement, art was nothing more or less than the experience of living. It was Gerard de Nerval taking his pet lobster for a promenade; it was Breton and Jacques Vaché taking their dinners with them into movie theaters and chatting companionably, seemingly oblivious to the other patrons, as they enjoyed their repast; it was Philippe Soupault knocking randomly on doors and asking those who answered if Philippe Soupault was at home; it was writing that "vanquished beauty, that pretext, with authentic poetry."[35] Adopting this attitude in praising Matthew Lewis's *The Monk*, Breton commented, "What is admirable in the fantastic is that there is no longer anything fantastic: there is only the real."[36] Maxime Alexandre emphasized the same point when saying of his days among the surrealists, "Nothing was more contemptible to our eyes than the wish to fabricate art, to fabricate literature."[37] Creativity had to be life itself, not a profession or, God forbid, a talent. In this modern mythology, beauty would be driven to the mad extreme of being all *and* nothing.

Despite the differences I have noted, it is certainly possible to argue that Baudelaire's writings also suggest this strategy of completely deranging nature and aesthetics. It was not for nothing that Baudelaire had been interested in mesmerism and in the writings of Emanuel Swedenborg; the surrealists did have good reason to adopt Baudelaire as one of their forerunners. Like the writings of Kant and Hegel, his are not all of a piece, and one might lift whole passages and use them, with nary a word of modification, to express what would come to be the aims of surrealism. (For instance, the passage in which Baudelaire offers "the entire formula of true aesthetics" in the following statement: "The entire visible universe is but a storehouse of images and signs to which the imagination will give a relative place and value; it is a pasture that the imagination must digest and transform.")[38] No matter what path one takes through Baudelaire's writings, though, there remains a difference in the nature of surrealism as a collective movement that so emphatically, systematically, and belligerently explored the possibility of conceiving of art in opposition to formal standards of any sort. "Above all else," wrote Michel Leiris,

> let no one speak of what is beautiful or ugly, "harmonious" or "dissonant," or of what is classic or romantic, ancient or modern, reactionary or advanced.
>
> More important than anything else is the battle that we are obliged to wage for all eternity against the exterior world, foiling its savage tricks with the help of even more savage tricks. Beneath the superficial variety of the different proceedings that for centuries have informed one of these tricks (that which not so very long ago we still called the "fine arts"), there is a single proceeding that today is putting itself on trial: reality.[39]

When nature is seen as history, as something no more solid than any other funereal monument of tradition, the object of art becomes a spirit that will be defined entirely by the struggles over its realization. As the surrealists saw it, this is the object suggested by both Hegel and Marx. It has no existence, objectively or transcendentally, beyond the historical, polemical, urgent conflicts in which it appears. Correspondingly, once beauty is seen as a power transgressing formal standards of reason, it turns from a question of pleasure and possession into a question of desire and imagination. Beauty changes from a formal aspect of things to a recognition of an illimitable potential for turning things into values and values into things. This is what Breton was getting at when he asked, rhetorically, "What holds me at its mercy as much as certain lines, certain colored spots?"[40] In its broad outlines, this is the dialectical framework of understanding that shaped the surrealist sense of art.

One of surrealism's heroes, the Comte de Lautréamont, had sneered at God as "the Great Exterior Object."[41] In battling exteriority, the surrealist object was meant always to be latent, resistant to the grasp of conventional reason. Honor was to be paid to images such as those Picabia had produced in the era of dada, which mimicked schematic drawings of machines in a way that made machinery enigmatic, impractical, functional only in generating unpredictable meanings. "We have decided that nothing may be defined," wrote Eluard, "save by the finger accidentally positioned through the commands of a broken apparatus."[42] The mock scientism in many of Ernst's dada productions, in which cross sections of landscapes and pseudozoological figures recall (and sometimes were taken from) textbook illustrations, was another early exploration of the accidental object that Eluard was to describe in his 1932 poem. Or one might instance Paul Klee's works of the 1920s, such as *Times of the Plants* (1927) or *Around the Fish* (1926), for the way they propose a non-Euclidean space in which any notation of ground, horizon, or perspective is nothing more than a disposable convenience, at the same time populating this space with figures that look representational while proving faithful in no particular to familiar rules of form and kinds of knowledge. Many other examples could be named; but in terms of acknowledged influences on surrealism, no one was more important in this regard than Giorgio de Chirico.

A characteristic early de Chirico, one that can help to illustrate the paths beauty was likely to take when its ground became pathological, is *The Song of Love* (1914). In this painting, which was much admired among the surrealists, the background is put into place by the flat outline of a locomotive with a puff of smoke suspended above the engine. The foreground is established by a street running beside a building that is stolidly geometrical and yet, it appears, oddly hollow. In the midst of the space thus demarcated, a huge wall or backdrop has obtruded itself. On its surface, it bears the frontal half of a plaster head of the Apollo Belvedere; an orange rubber glove, which is

Giorgio de Chirico, *The Song of Love* (1914)
Oil on canvas, 28¾″ × 23⅜″
New York, Collection of the Museum of Modern Art. Nelson A. Rockefeller Bequest
Copyright Estate of Giorgio de Chirico/VAGA New York 1990.

Photo courtesy of the Museum of Modern Art

affixed to the wall with a tack; and another tack, fixing nothing. On the street before this backdrop is a ball. Although the building, ball, glove, nail, and head are all starkly shadowed, as if from a sun off to the viewer's right, the overall disposition of their shadows is illogical, given the appearance of these objects in relation to each other. However, this inconsistency is thoroughly consistent with the incoherence in the perspectives organized by the shadows, building, backdrop, and train. (For instance, the bottom edge, top, and surface of the backdrop all seem to press out at different angles from the building.) This inconsistency also fits with the confusion a viewer is likely to encounter in trying to sort out the proportions of the objects in this picture. (Is that train dwarfed by distance or immediately behind the neighboring brick wall? Is that ball bigger than a man, or does it only seem so because it is so abruptly foregrounded? How can that glove be the height of the first story of the building?) Furthermore, the fact that the plaster head and the glove seem equally weighty, both thematically and physically, adds still greater force to these illogical connections.

To be sure, one can make sense of the objects thus arranged. They might even seem to lend themselves to allegory. The antique head and the building (whose arches vaguely allude to classical architecture) form a contrast with the modern glove and locomotive. If one reads the picture from left to right, the structure is repetitious and balanced, from the modern (train) to the traditional (bust) to the modern (glove) to the traditional (building). Moreover, the centered head and glove mark the form of the human within the scene, whereas the train and building on either side of them are pictorial frames and practical shelters (mobile and fixed, respectively) for this human form.

Yet even as it is suggested, the allegory is disturbed. After all, humanity is represented here by a fragment of a statue of a mythical god and by a glove that is single and empty: emblems of difference, loss, incompleteness, pastness, partiality, and absence. The train looks more like a toy (fit company for the ball) than a "real" train. There is a languor about the whole picture, symbolized especially by the cartoon-like puff of smoke, that makes the title of the painting seem hopelessly ironic or cryptic — in either case, arbitrary in relation to the allegory that this scene might have seemed to encourage. What can a song of love be in this landscape? How could a voice even be heard in this frozen moment?

Under the pressure of these illogical and yet compelling connections, the objects depicted here may come to seem more like wishes, signs, and symptoms than things. They might be dream objects, then, just as the surrealists considered them to be — objects of the kind that Freud analyzed and that Dali made his special province in the 1930s. Dali described his "symbolically functioning objects," which were inspired by Alberto Giacometti's *Suspended Ball* (1930), as representing the process of *"sexual perversion*, which resembles, in every aspect, the process of the poetic act."* When the surrealist object was fully developed, he confidently proclaimed, "the culture of the spirit will be the same as the culture of desire."[43] From similar premises, Hans Bellmer developed his outrageously responsive and polymorphous dolls, no less philosophical than they were pornographic, to receive his argument that the "self-identical object remains without reality" because objects are real only through their fashioning by desire, bottomless and endless desire.[44]

Yet it is by no means clear that surrealist objects in particular, and the surrealist sense of beauty in general, were ever what they were meant to be. Even if what they were meant to be was ambiguous from the very beginning, and recognized as being so by this movement that always drew attention to desire—the frustrated or diverted "meaning to be" in objects of all sorts, beautiful and ugly—such an ambiguity cannot bear all the questions that arise from the encounter of history and aesthetics over the surrealist abyss of reason.

The most obvious place to begin these questions is with the relation between the surrealist sense of beauty and objects taken from non-Western cultures to be turned into Western art. This is the most obvious place because of this movement's early and continuing attraction to what it saw as the non-Western world, which was taken to represent an alternative to the world of reason, an alternative visible in its statuary, masks, and other constructions; this is also the obvious starting point in the sense that the question to be raised here is already familiar in intellectual circles today. I certainly say nothing new when I state that while the modern treatment of such "primitive" objects might seem more sympathetic than what could be expected from Kant and the civilization that he represented, this treatment had certain racist aspects of its own when it assumed that Melanesians, Africans, and other groups were more natural or more spiritually free than white Europeans. Like the use of African objects in the exhibitions at the dada Cabaret Voltaire in 1916, surrealist appropriations of such things were more than a little presumptuous and self-indulgent, revealing the ethnocentrism that thrives, ironically, where the exotic is praised and fetishized. This aspect of surrealism deserves to be measured in relation to the group's public protests of the French war in Morocco against Abd-el-Krim in 1925, of the 1931 Colonial Exhibition, and of other instances of racist and colonial designs; as it is the most obvious, so this may be the least significant of the aspects in which surrealist aesthetics betray their professed intentions. But we would be doing no favor to surrealist desires by discarding this issue under a rubric such as "culture" or "history," as in statements to the effect that the surrealists were "creatures of their time." It was this kind of imprisoning, degrading banality that they always fought to overcome.

Just as Kant's aesthetics is an overdetermined articulation of certain historical, cultural, and personal forces, so, too, must modern approaches to art be seen to be implicated in the very world they mean to interpret. This point would be made clear in the 1930s when a split arose between Dali and other

Hans Bellmer, *The Doll* (1935)
Paris, Galerie Français Petit

Photo courtesy of Giraudon/Art Resource

surrealists that was attributable, in large part, to Dali's fascist sympathies; but long before this time, when Baudelaire was revising the sense of beauty in a way that would be crucial for the surrealists, it was already becoming clear that the implications of this revision were far from being self-evidently emancipatory.

One place where the connection between Baudelaire's aesthetics and a revolutionary sense of politics is suggested is in a poem titled "The Mirror," in which a man, asked why he looks at his reflection when he cannot do so without displeasure, explains that it is his right to do so "after the immortal principles of '89."[45] Of course, the reference is mocking, but it is serious as well. When the decorum of classical aesthetics is broken and the frame of art admits subjects hitherto condemned as vulgar, diseased, peculiar, mad, childish, offensive—in a word, ugly—there might well seem to be a parallel to the way the revolutions of the late eighteenth and mid-nineteenth centuries extended greater political recognition to the masses of common human subjects. (George Eliot recognized this parallel when she had *Middlemarch*'s Dorothea Causaubon meditate critically on the traditions of art, concluding, "I am not at all sure that the majority of the human race have not been ugly.")[46] But this is not to say that revolutionary art necessarily implies revolutionary ethics and politics, as the example of Baudelaire should make clear. Despite his friendship with Gustave Courbet, who did labor mightily to establish this line of implication for art, and despite his support of the republicans in the 1848 uprising, Baudelaire was no democrat, at least in any simple sense of the word. Like the surrealists who were to follow him, he tried to make a new thing of beauty by forcing it to confront democratic perceptions and experiences, no matter how low or illogical they might be; but he did so in revulsion against a different sort of commonness, which was created by the combined forces of an ossified aristocratic tradition and of the anxious, moralizing, bourgeois emulation of the traditional standards. Like Hegel, Baudelaire saw an incompatibility between art and modernizing societies characterized by legality, bureaucracy, and (in the broad sense) democratic rights; unlike Hegel, he was not prepared to subordinate art to the presumptively higher aims of philosophy and religion. Therefore, like Nietzsche and the surrealists after him, he exploited the opportunity for democratic perceptions, in his revolutionary treatment of the subject of art, so that he might oppose democratic identifications that would degrade the figure of the artist before images of common humanity. By taking this path, he helped to define the revolutionary terms of modern art, in which a disdain for the values of the bourgeoisie accompanies a recognition that aristocratic ideals may be aesthetically attractive precisely to the extent that they are historically moribund. The characteristic result is a conception of beauty that unites metaphysical longing with cynical self-laceration, as in Baudelaire's praise of vicious queens, Nietzsche's proclaimed and yet disavowed nihilism, or surrealism's mixture of sentimentality and sadism.

What might otherwise be seen as a divergence in surrealist works between the innocent and evil romanticisms of Ann Radcliffe and Matthew Lewis, both of whom Breton admired—the divergence between Joan Miró and Dali, say, or between Eluard and Bellmer—is really the coherent expression of this sense of beauty, which must tread the fine line between naiveté and cruelty if it is to maintain its apocalyptic ambitions. To what end it arrives on this path is not a simple question; but the ethnocentric presuppositions in the modernist appropriation of primitive art, the way Dali turned to Francisco Franco and other surrealists to Joseph Stalin, and artworks such as Bellmer's grotesquely manipulated and disarticulated dolls, which invite us to take sadism as the definitive motive of art—all these may lead us to wonder whether the surrealist sense of beauty truly goes beyond tradition. Could it be that this sense of beauty actually recapitulates everything the surrealists thought they hated in that tradition and therefore travesties all they claimed to love, from "primitive" creativity to Picasso? Nietzsche, for one, suggested that art might find itself coming to such an end:

Yes, we have thrown off the "unreasonable" shackles of Franco-Hellenist art, but without knowing it, we have gotten used to finding all shackles, all limitation unreasonable. And so art moves toward its dissolution, and touches in the process (which is to be sure highly instructive) all phases of its beginnings, its childhood, its imperfection, its former risks and extravagances.[47]

Nietzsche's diagnosis at least suggests that the conception of the end of art is a problematic one. After all, the idea of beauty and compelling impressions of beauty do not evaporate simply because modern aestheticians may find that a universal aesthetic rule is untenable. Grant that Kant's *sensus communis* is a kind of mythical construction, a figure that speaks against the very logic and universality it is supposed to represent, and one still has the problem of coming to terms with the real power that this construction enjoyed and may continue to enjoy. The emphasis on aesthetic theory to this point in this essay will be misspent if it leads anywhere but to a recognition that "theory," insofar as it bears discussion at all, cannot simply be talked in or out of existence. As the surrealists recognized, logic is only one kind of power, and hardly the greatest one around; so Nietzsche had remarked that God might die and yet still live on in all sorts of forms, including philosophy, grammar, and yes, beauty.

Kant was most certainly revised by modern aesthetics, but rejecting him was no simple task. If it did not express a compelling truth, Kant's description of the subjective universality of beauty could still describe a compelling aspect of the desire implicated in beauty: its impulse toward rationalization, totality, and an ultimate violence that would obliterate objective impediments to its realization. When the worm in Kant's ground was unearthed, when the rational presuppositions of his philosophy were felt to be slipping away, beauty might lose the integrity it had seemed to have for that fantastic creature, the disinterested spectator; but it would survive as the necessity of articulating values in a world that might seem to lack any ground beyond abyssal desire. Similarly, although Friedrich Schiller's argument that "it is through Beauty that we arrive at Freedom"[48] might fall apart *qua* argument, it could survive as a polemical program, an assertion in a manifesto, a characteristic expression of desire. His argument is not as far as it might seem from Tzara's words, first published in 1919, "*Liberty, liberty*: not being a vegetarian, I don't give out recipes."[49] Nor is it that far from works of art such as Wassily Kandinsky's *Black Lines* (1913), in which a surface that is dense, alive, scribbled with the suggestion of form nonetheless burns with an energy that resists all form as if it were a terrible insult to the imagination.[50]

In fact, Kant's voice telling of beauty, this voice of subjective universality, might not seem so different from the unconscious that the surrealists figured as the ground of their art (an unconscious in this respect significantly different from Freud's). To say so is not to accuse the surrealists of being, despite themselves, contemptible aesthetes. When this accusation was made by their contemporaries, they responded, with considerable justification, that no one was more opposed than they were to the notion of art as an end in itself. Nor am I speaking here of a *philosophical* failure—for instance, a failure to recognize the extent to which surrealist figuration was captivated by a cluster of traditional metaphysical oppositions between presence and absence, interiority and exteriority, essence and accident, and so on. (Such a critique might be made, but it would have to treat surrealism as a thing of arguments and books while disregarding its existence as a radical kind of poetic activity, an emancipatory *movement*, a "meaning to be" that rejected what Walter Benjamin termed "the penny-in-the-slot called meaning.")[51] The more interesting question does not concern taste or logic but pathology. It concerns a certain way of feeling: a logic, pathos, or pathology traced out by desire.

As I have noted, surrealist desires were preoccupied by apocalypse, took their course from apocalyptic figures. The surrealists felt their way through the world on a path defined by the end of things. Most generally, this appeared in the desire for a complete aesthetic, social, and (by the late 1920s) political revolution, a call for complete change by which they defined themselves as a group and as a movement. The echoes of Pieter Breughel and Hieronymous Bosch in some of Ernst's works, such as *The Joy of Living* (1936) and *The Temptation of Saint Anthony* (1945), are only some of the more obvious visual signs of this turn toward the end of things. Others include Dali's lurid, hallucinatory landscapes and the delirious calligraphy of André Masson's drawings. And in language as in art, the assault on exteriority—in automatic writing, the trance-speaking of the *temps des sommeils*, or the deliberate chaos of surrealist demonstrations and disruptions—was meant to exhibit the characteristics and foster the advent of this apocalypse.

Surrealism meant the end of things in their ordinary acceptation: such was the import of Duchamp's ready-mades and of the surrealist objects devised by Dali, Meret Oppenheim, and others. In whatever occupied the members of this movement, this apocalyptic preoccupation showed itself in the conviction that every gesture ought to be complete, total, pure, uncompromising. It showed itself also in the readiness to use the most vicious terms imaginable to scourge anyone or anything that was perceived to fall even the slightest bit short of the lengths to which the group aspired; in the confidence that the past ought to be rejected *in toto* (which was accompanied by the assurance that inspiring figures such as the Marquis de Sade and Baudelaire were really not of their own time and so could be treated as contemporaries and honorary members of the movement); in a contempt for ordinary work and mundane ambitions; in a love of monstrosity, insanity, outrageous crime, contrived detective stories, and eccentricity in general; and even in the especially poisoned vituperation reserved for the Catholic Church, which the surrealists saw as having institutionalized a particularly galling betrayal of the apocalypse they were heralding.

The question I am raising is whether this apocalyptic preoccupation was not, in fact, a very limited way of feeling and thus of living. Limited not because it was so extreme (as one can imagine an outraged bourgeois complaining) but because it was so comprehensive, so all-encompassing, and thus so *un*extreme.

As a way of feeling, this apocalyptic turn was indiscriminate and self-absolving. It was characterized by a blindness to its own possible banality and a callousness toward possible differences in the circumstances of others. In its indiscriminate demands, it did have special affinities with conditions of being in which distinctions between beauty and ugliness disappear; but it recognized only those that inflated the sense of self, such as terror and ecstasy, while overlooking those that did not, such as boredom, hunger, shame, humility, and courage.

If this apocalyptic path, or pathology, was finally very narrow, it is because the universal end of things is predicated upon the figure of a privileged individual who can witness this end. Without that individual, there can be no vision of totality; it is only before the unchanging one that everything can be changed. And there surely is a reason, a haunting reason, why the surrealists chose as one of their slogans the motto from Lautréamont, "Poetry must be made by all. Not by one."[52] It is notable that in a 1925 article on the surrealists that is otherwise extremely sympathetic, Victor Crastre offered an objection on this score. In writing of the "rough work of criticism and of demolition" that his *Clarté* group was attempting, he struck a cautionary note: "[W]e do not have enough pride to think that it can create these great transports that the surrealists think are still possible."[53]

The surrealists would not have accepted my description of their way of feeling. At least they would not have accepted it while they remained "orthodox" surrealists; but many accounts of the differences that eventually emerged among members of the group can be taken to support this account, and it is always important to keep in mind that the definition of the group was never self-evident. If it was generally assumed, as I generally assume here, that "the surrealists" were those who at any point in time were clustered around the ultimate arbiter, Breton, it nevertheless remains the case that "surrealism" was a term whose possession was contested from the very beginning of this movement. Although those who left or were excluded from Breton's circle would follow the general practice of referring to the current members of this circle as "the surrealists," they did not necessarily cede all rights to "surrealism," or even to "orthodox surrealism," to this reconstituted group. The movement of surrealism was never contained within itself; it was composed of these disruptions and crosscurrents, too.

Even when one takes this qualification into account, however, it remains true that one of the founding principles of the surrealist movement stated that individuality was comparable to the state or the church and that unconscious powers could be liberated only if this sense of individuality were obliterated. "Art has truly ceased to be individual," proclaimed Aragon, and Ernst gave a detailed explanation of this idea in describing his use of *frottage*:

> The process of frottage, based on nothing but the intensification of the irritability of the spiritual faculties by appropriate technical means, excluding all conscious mental conduction (of reason, of taste, of morality), reducing to the utmost the active part of that which up to now was called "the author" of the work, this process subsequently reveals itself as the true equivalent of that which was already known under the term of *automatic writing*. It is as a spectator that the author assists, whether indifferently or passionately, at the birth of his work and observes the phases of its development. Just as the role of the poet, since the famous *letter of the seer* [of Rimbaud], consists in writing under the dictation of that which thinks itself (articulates itself) in him, the role of the painter is to discern and to *project that which sees itself in him*. In devoting myself more and more to this activity (passivity), which later was called "paranoiac criticism" [by Dali] . . . and in always trying to restrain further my own active participation in the development of the picture so as to enlarge the active part of the hallucinatory faculties of the spirit, I have come to assist *as a spectator* at the birth of all my works ever since August 10, 1925, the memorable day of the discovery of "frottage." A man of "ordinary constitution" (I employ here the terms of Rimbaud), I have done everything to *render my spirit monstrous*.[54]

If the virtue of surrealist art was that it tried to revolutionize the distinctions petrifying the art and aesthetics that came before it, its most fundamental weakness may have been that it failed to appreciate how thoroughly the end of art, its contemplated dissolution, had traditionally defined the end of art in the sense of its *telos*. Here, perhaps, was Kant's revenge on those who thought to do away with his logic of the beautiful. Art was traditionally funerary, but it was also suicidal, self-abasing, abyssal in its desired monumentality. Insofar as the idea of representation had entailed the self-effacement of the particular material work before its own ideal—the situation that, from the viewer's viewpoint, led to Kant's demand for the disinterested spectator—Ernst's spectator, with his monstrous spirit, may come to look quite normal. The acknowledged resemblance between his process of *frottage* and Leonardo's anecdote about looking at a stained wall to see what forms he could see in it may then lead one to ask whether the modern does differ essentially from the classical. As is indicated all too well—to the point of becoming a critical cliché—by the current holdings of surrealist works in the contemporary temples of commerce and culture that are our art museums, appropriation can be a two-way street. The Ernst who thought he was claiming Leonardo for surrealism, who believed he was allowing a force beyond himself to think through him, may have been unconsciously claimed by a past the surrealist program could not begin to comprehend.

Is not the figure of chance always the figure of a privileged individual: one who can afford to imagine total freedom? And is it not then both self-contradictory (since it assumes the secure foundation it claims to deny) and yet, in this contradiction, a coherent representation of a way of feeling that inclines one to idolize selected individuals as heroes and leaders while viewing this abject devotion as a revolutionary action? Is not the very emphasis on the distinction between consciousness and unconsciousness, which is so definitive of modernism, one that serves to glorify the figure of the individual by insisting that this figure is fundamentally mysterious and impervious to analysis? The divided individual, the individual who is spectator to himself, the consciousness that gives way to unconsciousness: is not this way of figuring the overthrow of logic, convention, and tradition still presumptuous in its abasement, elitist in its presumed universality, terribly—even, at times, ridiculously—shortsighted in its apocalyptic ends?

And since these are not, strictly speaking, philosophical questions, but rather questions about a pathology, a way of feeling and living, could one summarize them all by asking whether surrealism would have been more emancipatory if it had not felt itself to be so free? One might remember at this point the issue of how the surrealists made free with objects from Africa and other exotic places. In this context, the issue is no longer so obvious or so easily settled. It turns into the paths of questions—from Karl Marx and Martin Heidegger, among others—about the way things may be using people who think they are using things. In many respects, "beauty" is a word that resembles "dignity"; and just as many spiritualists compromised themselves in their attempts to revise the prevailing notions of the practices, circumstances, objects, and feelings befitting those holding commerce with the dead, so did the surrealists often run into trouble in their would-be revolt against the prevailing commerce in art.

Of course, the questions I have raised here run the risk of themselves being presumptuous. I write of fine matters of feeling, matters that could be described, following Nietzsche's and Freud's revisions of Kant, as involving a cultural sense of touch; and whatever else the surrealists may not have known, they certainly were aware that the intellectual issues of the modern world would turn on an elusive sense of being in or out of touch. Even at their most apocalyptic, they were concerned with things that always turned and returned through ways of feeling of the sort dizzily set forth by Nietzsche in *Beyond Good and Evil*:

> There are occurrences of so delicate a description that one does well to bury them and make them unrecognizable with a piece of coarseness; there are acts of love and extravagant magnanimity after which nothing is more advisable than to take a stick and give the eyewitness a thrashing and so confuse his memory. Some know how to confuse their own memory, so as to take revenge at least on this sole confidant — shame is inventive.[55]

The problem was in preventing delicate feelings from taking on the coarsened forms of identity, property, and tyrannical rule. Breton did recognize this problem, and specifically in relation to aesthetics. Comparing the influence of commerce on contemporary art to the context he imagined for the prehistoric paintings in the caves of Altamira, he wrote the following passage:

> Doubtless, here again, it is necessary to admit that the fault lies with the first who, having enclosed a landscape or a figure within the limits of a canvas, decided to say, "This is mine" (or "is part of me"), and found people simple or corrupt enough to let him get away with it. There are still men who care to talk only for themselves alone; but the buffaloes, the marvellous reindeer of the caverns carry us back, at a single bound, to the prehistoric.[56]

Here the prehistoric is the nostalgic counterpart to the posthistoric or apocalyptic. We have some idea where these conceptions lead, if not from the questions I have raised above, then at least from some of the fatuities that currently parade themselves under the name of "postmodernism." But if the weakness of surrealism was in its feeling that art could transport us out of history, its strength was still to have encouraged historical questions. Consistently, surrealists insisted on these questions when they simply refused to believe that beauty could ever have emancipated anyone by turning its back on the ugliness of the things of this world. In its apocalyptic turn, this refusal unquestionably led to certain misrecognitions, to certain stupidities and brutalities; but we must not forget how many did not even get as far as this refusal, do not even get that far today.

7

Dream Work

The sexual street comes alive . . .

ANTONIN ARTAUD, "The Street"[1]

A city street, tilted toward us, dominated on either side by the impassive arcades of anonymous buildings. Nothing happens, nothing much. A shadowed girl rolls her hoop past a wooden cart, also in shadow. Like the girl, it is turned away from us, the open doors in back permitting us to glimpse an interior that is perfectly empty, at least as far as our vision can reach. By their attitudes, the running girl and the undistinguished cart draw us toward another shadow: a silhouette fallen across the street. This figure elongated by the sun seems to be waiting for, or heading toward, the girl, the cart, and us.

Giorgio de Chirico painted this scene in 1914, and in 1928 André Breton reproduced it near the beginning of his *Surrealism and Painting*. By that time de Chirico had been dropped by the surrealists, who were appalled by his decision to trade in his earlier style for an earnest neoclassicism; but they saw no reason to disavow their attachment to those early works that helped to show them their way. In de Chirico's dispassionate rendering of *Melancholy and Mystery of a Street*, in which there seems no obvious reason for this girl, these forms, these shadows, or any other elements of the composition to meet each other as they do, the surrealists of the twenties and thirties could still see an encounter with the street that was crucial to their movement.[2]

Nothing much ever happens, really, in surrealist encounters, including that signature scene (borrowed from the Comte de Lautréamont's *Songs of Maldoror*) in which beauty is born from the mating of an umbrella and a sewing machine on an operating room table. In terms of anecdotal interest,

Giorgio de Chirico, *Melancholy and Mystery of a Street* (1914)
Private collection, Europe
Copyright Estate of Giorgio de Chirico/VAGA New York 1990

Melancholy and Mystery of a Street could not be more unlike the historical, classical, and scriptural scenes traditionally favored in Salon art, in which the subject, even when so obscure as to demand an elaborate gloss, would be meant to capture a moment of elevated drama. The remaining alternative might seem to be a scene of common life, but no one would confuse de Chirico's work with realist, impressionist, or postimpressionist painting or with the modern visions of the everyday world in cubist still lifes and futurist paeans to metal, motors, and motion. De Chirico's street seems—or seemed to Breton and company—a scene that comes from nowhere, breaking with all tradition, including the recent traditions of the real and the modern. Nothing much happens in it—and yet wondrous drama may yet arise if this is a scene of dreams in which images "genteelly dress their hair and burn up the road, / Their bared breasts uniting the street with eternity," or if it is a street in which (to quote Paul Eluard again) "we shut our eyes / Only so we may know better what we shall see."[3] On this street one may wander in search of the unpredictable encounters (with artists, authors, machines, breasts, shadows . . .) that give a cultural movement its identity.

Of course, like other movements, surrealism took on many identities and could not hope to unite them all anywhere short of eternity. Even as they collaborated on discussions, demonstrations, magazines, paintings, poems, *cadavres exquises*,[4] and various other projects, the surrealists were never all of one mind; and from the very first their movement met with appropriations of its identity that the surrealists judged to be unauthorized and flagitious.[5] Definition becomes still more difficult if one moves from an overview of the early days of the movement, when it was little more than the friendship shared by Breton, Eluard, Louis Aragon, and Philipe Soupault, and plunges into its troubled history of ostracisms, recruitments of new members, and attempted rapprochements with other groups, such as the French Communist Party (PCF) or the circle around Georges Bataille.[6] These considerations suggest that if one looks for the identity of surrealism in persons—even in that grand panjandrum, André Breton himself—one is likely to go wrong. To approach surrealism as a movement, as opposed to a theory, aesthetic, art, doctrine, or dictator, the better way is to identify it as a meeting-place or, in one of its own terms, a street.

Like other cultural movements, surrealism acquired definition through a critical mass of representations, a certain density or accumulated gravity of cross-references, through which one could sense its shape, features, impulsions, and likely density. To say so is not to deny other factors: the political circumstances of France between the wars, the heritage (if this is not a contradiction in terms) of dada, the influence of Freud, the leadership of Breton, and so on. To regard surrealism as a swarm of representations that came alive in a movement is simply to say that all the conditions vital to its existence were publicly recognized, interpreted, and reinterpreted through this rhetoric. This was not "simply" rhetoric but rather the life of surrealism insofar as this movement existed at all, *moved* at all. Quarrels might erupt over the real or true or authentic surrealism, but any perspective had to begin with an identifiable movement, which existed through a power of rhetorical implication that could seem to unite the diverse images, emblems, names, allusions, quotations, books, acts, and other sorts of signifiers through which surrealism communicated. Here is where interpretation had to start, with this desire for or suggestion of a movement. Drawing together (for instance) Paolo Uccello, Gerard de Nerval, pornographic postcards, the Café Certà, Melmoth the Wanderer, a fur-covered tea setting, an eye sliced by a razor, the habit of kissing ladies' hands, and the metaphysical painting of de Chirico, this work of implication became this word, "surrealism"; and nowhere in this movement were the implications denser, the excursions and recursions and transformations more intense, than in the street.

In fact, the street may be taken as a summary figure through which all the turnings of this movement can be approached. Taken in this way, it is finally an arbitrary figure (for where but in dreams or hallucinations does totality yield its image?). Nevertheless, the figure of the street can still have critical value if it will remind us that any approach must face the implications of arbitrariness; in this way it will lead us to confront precisely what the surrealists argued to be the source of their challenge. In allowing criticism to take up this challenge, the figure of the street will let us explore what happens when history is experienced as a polemical and variable state of things, a movement, as opposed to a unified and finished past. In other words, foregrounding the surrealist street can be a way to evaluate how power and possibilities create each other in the dreamlike encounters through which culture is constructed.

Clearly, the passage to so much of the rhetoric of a movement can have no single entrance, exit, or end. De Chirico's painting provides one opening, but it is one of many. As an alternative, one might mention Jean Arp's *Infinite Amphora* (1929), in which the titular vessel, a rather small and unassuming form centered in a wood relief, is displayed against a blue background. A white stream, gently undulating, broadening at the top of the relief, generously flows into — or from — each end of the amphora, as if to illustrate Nerval's line about "the overflowing of the dream into real life."[7] Here, too, is an exemplary surrealist meeting-place, composed of exceedingly simple elements and yet, to the surrealist eye, having the power to call forth Georges Braque's collages, Breton's wanderings in *Nadja*, de Chirico's urban perspectives, Lautréamont's definition of beauty, or the moving liquid essence of every seminal moment that chance might shape into a form of eternity.

One who thinks this way, who turns and moves this way, may begin to understand how surrealists could hope, perhaps even believe, that their movement would be revolutionary in the most complete sense of that word.

Jean Arp, *Infinite Amphora* (1929)
Private collection
Copyright 1990 ARS N.Y./COSMOPRESS

Through this work of implication, this passionate movement, any person, place, or thing, no matter how mundane, could become a marvellous avenue of transfiguration.

Things could truly work this way, according to the testimony of the surrealists and their admirers; but even if one believes in the transfiguring power of the street, a question still remains. It is a question as nagging as it is simple: how can the street possibly work this way? If the street can figure as the site of arbitrary meetings, how can this arbitrariness be chosen, found, liberated, or allowed to happen in the ways recounted by the surrealists? After all, the simplest reflection will show that this movement never worked with elements taken entirely at random, despite its devotion to the power of chance; and it seems clear enough that its achievements do not include world revolution. Even its fans must recognize that if one wants to see how surrealism came to life in history and in the street, heaven must wait; one must turn elsewhere.

So let us first consider what this street was not. For surrealism, the street was most emphatically not the space of the bourgeoisie. It passed by domesticity, psychological interiority, and repressed passion—features considered definitive of the bourgeois home and the classic novel—and, in passing them by, sought to show how insupportable they were. "We do not strive to change men's manners," the surrealists said in their "Declaration of January 27, 1925," "but we certainly intend to demonstrate to them the fragility of their thinking and the shifting foundations, the caves, over which they have placed their trembling houses."[8] Unlike these homes, the street was not private, but then again it was not public, at least not in the sense suggested by places of assembly officially consecrated to rituals of social pride. It was as if the surrealists were trying to overcome the distinction made by Remy de Gourmont when he wrote, "Successes are made in the streets; glory emerges from cenacles."[9] This conflation of receptivity and occultation figured in Breton's promise to the readers of his first "Manifesto of Surrealism" that the future would see public assemblies "and *movements* in which you had not expected to take part."[10] As desire, suggestion, or dream, the street of this movement was open and yet difficult of access. Just as the mannequin (with a good nudge from de Chirico) became the exemplary surrealist figure because it seemed a profoundly enigmatic representation of the human, this unpredictable street became the surrealist landscape *par excellence*. Opposed alike to the respectably ordered forms of home, plaza, school, and place of business, the surrealist street was more a passage than a place, more an opportunity than a location. As in the title of a journal associated with Berlin dada, it was *Die Freie Strasse*, "the open road."

This street still conveyed some of its nineteenth-century associations with barricades, revolutionary mobs, marches, uprisings, and democratic sympathies. In this respect, Eluard's fervent images, whose bared breasts unite the street with eternity, may seem a twentieth-century version of Eugène

Delacroix's famous *Liberty Leading the People* (1830). To quote Eluard again:

> It has been more than a hundred years since the poets descended from the summits on which they believed themselves to be. They've gone into the streets, they've insulted their masters, they've had nothing more to do with gods, they've dared to kiss beauty and love on the lips, they've learned the songs of revolt of the unhappy crowd and, without rejecting it, have tried to teach it their own.[11]

However, as the uneasy qualification in the last clause may indicate, the popular tradition summed up in these associations was a rather vague inspiration, to say the least. As distant as surrealism was from the bourgeois home, it was just as far from the fury of Georg Grosz's *The Street* (1915), a painting one might expect to wither the fingers of any burgher with the temerity to hang it as an adornment on his wall. The surrealist street was open, and it did suggest the popular, the quotidian, the common way, and rebellion against any higher authorities that might seek to control that way; but this was not a street filled with crowds or limned with popular anger. If crowds of people existed in this context, they were in the background. They neither caused nor explained what happened there.

Yet this was an urban street. In this respect it recalled Charles Baudelaire's Paris ("Are there any oddities one *does not* find in a great city when one knows how to go for a walk and look around?");[12] the uncanny road in which Stéphane Mallarmé found himself in "The Demon of Analogy"; the Cairo told of in Nerval's "Journey to the Orient," in which he deliberately lost himself in the hope that he could find its truth in the unpredictable turnings of its passageways; and especially the magical city streets through which Nerval wandered, in his visionary trances, in "Aurélia." The urban scene was as much an impetus to surrealism as it was to futurism, as the intersections of these two movements by way of de Chirico and Vladimir Mayakovsky, among others, might indicate. It is not going too far to say that even scenes of nature in surrealist works should be read as urban scenes, and not just in the sense in which critics find pastoral poetry to be generically urbane and nature in any given case a trope articulated through the figuration of civilization. More specifically, this nature was always urban because the modern city was implicated within this cultural movement as the scene that defined the ultimate possibilities of experience through its random juxtapositions, unpredictable events, unclassifiable comings and goings, and unfathomable labyrinthine turnings. The street was a nervous urban stimulus, something like the Hermetic *vis imaginativa*; it suggested at once a visionary power of mind, a critical perspective for redescribing things, and a stylistic capacity for marking out new worlds and alternative ontologies. "The street," wrote Breton, "which I believed capable of lending its surprising detours to my life, the street with its uneasiness and attentiveness, this was my true element: there as nowhere else I caught the scent of possibility."[13] Wherever forms unexpectedly met—in Kurt Schwitters's *Merzbau* (the architectural collage on which he worked from 1923 until its destruction in 1943),[14] in André Masson's drawing of the *City of the Skull* (1939), in Aragon's description of the Passage de l'Opéra in *The Peasant of Paris*, in Eluard's love poetry, in the frequent surrealist evocations of the story of Ariadne, or in the *frottages* Max Ernst lifted from the surfaces of leaves, tree bark, and other objects—this street appeared in the movement of surrealism. Surrealist representations were always inflected, as it were, with the impression of city streets.

Since it could start and stop virtually anywhere, there was no *locus classicus* to the surrealist street. Many participants in this movement loved to let themselves go on long walks, in no particular direction, searching only for the moment that their passionate companionship might render vertiginous or instinct with brilliant discoveries. They wandered in the Paris through which Breton is led, like an extremely earnest child through a fairy-tale forest, by the titular figure in *Nadja*. A young woman living on the edge of poverty and well beyond the borders of respectability, Nadja becomes an inspiration to him because of her irregular, floating, haphazard, and, therefore, alluring life. This is also the city of Soupault's narrative, *The Last Nights of Paris*, which is largely composed of wanderings through darkened streets in which the narrator becomes fascinated by a woman who is the very image of the city: a place in which "death alone is strong enough to extinguish" the "pointless passion" moving the narrator, this being the logically impossible determination "to complete a promenade without end."[15]

As epitomized by the Passage de l'Opéra, the street defines modern perceptions even as it is threatened (just as Nerval's Cairo was) by an impending modernization of urban space. Even as Aragon describes it, his peculiar old street is about to be destroyed by an extension of the Boulevard Haussmann, which is named after the official of the Second Empire who directed the construction of Paris's grand avenues (which not only eased traffic but also served to make it easier for the army to quell popular uprisings). In the meantime, this street can still serve to illustrate how "our cities are . . . peopled with unrecognized sphinxes." Unlike their classical forbears, these sphinxes "do not bring the dreamer to a standstill if he does not turn his meditative abstraction toward them"; but "if he knows how to divine them . . . then, although he interrogates them, it will still be into his own abysses that he will plunge, thanks to these shapeless monsters. The modern light of the unusual, that is what will control him henceforth."[16]

As these examples should show, even when surrealists referred to concrete streets and to the modern reality of the urban scene, their concern was unconfined by particular places, specific images, or historical developments. Even though Paris, especially at night, was where one seemed most likely to find it, the surrealist street was not the manifest city.[17] Above all else, this street was a demanding, provoking, dreamlike, and—perhaps—revolution-ary sense of things. It was not where things happened: it was what happened.

What happened, that is, if one approached it with the right attitude, in a condition of perfect *disponibilité*. Difficult to translate in its surrealist usage, this cherished term defined the attitude one sought in the street. "Availabil-ity" is the most obvious translation, but one has to squint at the connotations of this word to get at the meaning of *disponibilité* in surrealist discourse. It suggested openness and an unguarded vulnerability to chance but at the same time a quality of freedom, liberty, readiness, and autonomy. If its negative connotations could be erased, "opportunism" might be the best translation. *Disponibilité* could mean an erasure of individual will (for instance, as it was used to describe the condition in which one produced automatic writing), and yet it also would describe one's irreducible singularity. It signified drift-ing and maintaining a state of attention at the same time. Most simply, it was the antithesis of feelings structured by a conventional sense of responsi-bility. With a nod toward Heidegger, one might say that *disponibilité* was Being-at-loose-ends or Being-at-large.

In his *Treatise on Style* Aragon mocked the American "foundling concept, the man-in-the-street," as a symbol of all the common cant that unthinkingly parades itself as thought;[18] and in the terms of common cant, *disponibilité* might be described as an attitude that holds nothing sacred. This was not a wholly negative attitude, however, nor one meant to suggest ease and uncomplicated pleasure. The surrealist was not the American man-in-the-street, but neither was he the flaneur of Baudelaire's Paris. To say he was at large, at loose ends, is not to say he had no conception of an end. In its rigorous demands, the surrealist quest to live in the street in a state of *disponibilité* is comparable to the search for an unprejudiced account of experience that was being carried out by Edmund Husserl around this same time. Like Husserl, the surrealists insisted on the need for a certain purity of attitude, and for some of the same reasons, including a deep dissatisfaction with positivism as the dominant model of knowledge. Husserl and Breton may as well have lived in different worlds as far as any historical relationship between them is concerned, and the resemblance between phenomenology and surrealism is by no means close; but neither is it negligible. When Husserl wrote that the phenomenological attitude and method were "destined to effect, at first, a complete personal transformation, comparable in the begin-ning to a religious conversion, which then, however, over and above this, bears within itself the significance of the greatest existential transformation which is assigned as a task to mankind as such," he might have been describ-ing an initiation into surrealism.[19]

"Surprise must be sought out for itself, unconditionally," Breton pro-claimed in *Mad Love*, reprising a theme that had been advanced by Arthur Rimbaud, Guillaume Apollinaire, and Tristan Tzara, among many others whom the surrealists took to be their progenitors; but the rest of *Mad Love* makes clear that it was not just any old surprise that Breton was after.[20] Here a comparison of surrealism to Russian formalism becomes appropriate, for the surprise sought by Breton and his friends bears a strong resemblance to the "poetic language" investigated by Viktor Shklovsky and the other critics who developed their thought immediately before and after the Russian Revolution. Particularly relevant to surrealism is the formalists' concept of defamiliarization (*ostranenie*) as the passage to living poetry and literary development, for both groups defined their concerns in opposition to what they saw as the routinized, pragmatic, deadened prose of ordinary life. Even the difference between the formalists' aspiration to a scientific poetics and the surrealist desire to create a revolutionary movement might not be as significant as it seems, since one might well argue that the "poetic" in formalist works conveyed an ethical and political as well as stylistic judgment. One should also think here of Mallarmé's search for the pure Word or Book, in contradistinction to language as merchandise, means of exchange, mode of production, or routine practice.

Yet these comparisons should not be allowed to blur the distinctiveness of the surrealist movement. It was a definite kind of chance encounter that the creature of *disponibilité* hoped to find in the street, as one might gather simply from the fact that this figure was defined as part of a group and as such had to roam within boundaries that were no less real for being invisible and indeterminate. In fact, the surrealists recognized quite early on that they could not count on the discretion of chance; if it was not guided and helped out by the concerted movement of the group, one would find that "chance does not always show the same talent," as Robert Bréchon remarks, or that "even a wonderland can be monotonous," as Clifford Browder has noted.[21] He who was *disponible* was available and opportunistic, yes, but he was not ready for just anything, and he could not be diverted just anywhere. Always there was the implicit orientation, the movement, constituted by the elective affinities of the group. This guidance of chance in surrealism was sometimes defined formally (by manifestos, essays, or rituals of membership) but was also evident rhetorically, in the attitudes surrealists figuratively assumed in relation to the power of chance.[22]

This orientation is evident in *Mad Love*, for instance, where Breton compares himself to navigators who discover new worlds and to scientists who come upon unknown phenomena, remarking, "Today I still expect nothing from my own *disponibilité* except the thirst to wander so as to *happen upon* everything, with the assurance that it will keep me in a mysterious communication with others who are *disponible*, as if we were called suddenly to reunite ourselves."[23] Like the Paris of Baudelaire's *Flowers of Evil*, the city of the surrealists was an image for all of life; but unlike Baudelaire's Paris, which exhibited the workings of "evil chance" and rhymed with life in an afflicting way ("Horrible vie! Horrible ville!"),[24] the surrealist city was a place of enchantment even at its most dark and disturbing. Thus, in writing of Nadja, "the creature, always inspired and inspiring, who longed only to be in the street, for her the only field of valuable experience," Breton was led to comment that he hoped the record of his encounters with her "would precipitate some men into the street after having made them conscious, if not of the nothingness, at least of the grave insufficiency of all so-called rigorous examination of themselves, of all action that allows premeditation and demands continued application. These are carried away by the wind of the least thing that takes place, if it is truly unforeseen."[25] The street was the architecture of life turned inside out and so permitted to display the powers usually visible only through stingy windows and eyes.

In relation to someone in a condition of perfect *disponibilité*, the street was an offering that entailed no sacrifice. It was a find, a *trouvaille*, a perversely pure gift, having nothing to do with capitalist buying and selling or with the compromised give and take of everyday encounters. In a contemporary logic adumbrated in the paintings of de Chirico and Picasso, in Aragon's *The Peasant of Paris*, and in Freud's works, among other places, it was thought that the most modern discoveries might find an adequate image only in the most ancient art and myth; and so it was in this case. The perverse purity of this gift could suggest this originative state of things. In the communication Breton described as secretly drawing together those who were *disponible*, in this working of "objective chance" (to use the phrase he borrowed from Hegel), one might even see some resemblance to the mysteriously unifying role of the circulating system of exchange that Marcel Mauss described in his *Essay on the Gift*. Mauss's concern was to show that there was a social logic, an accountability, in rituals that otherwise might seem to represent an unreasoning expenditure; similarly, the surrealist sense of the primitive argued for a reason beyond reason, a surrationalism, as Gaston Bachelard called it.[26]

Yet this phenomenon, a thing to be apprehended scientifically, was at the same time a thing of dreams to be interpreted. It existed beyond the structures of Mauss's anthropology. The street was the domain of the *absolutely* primitive gift, the find, which would seem to come out of nowhere. This object was simply given and therefore was not possession, property, or commodity, not even an object of social circulation, but rather the object of unforeseeable and continuing poetic adventure. Such was the domain of Marcel Duchamp's ready-mades, including the *Bottlerack* (1914) that he took for a modern work of art merely by turning it into something found, a thing seemingly given without a giver. And, again, as unlikely as the comparison with Duchamp may seem, this was a domain that Husserl helped to map:

In any case, anything built by activity necessarily presupposes, as the lowest level, a passivity that gives something beforehand; and, when we trace anything built actively, we run into constitution by passive generation. The "ready-made" object that confronts us in life as an existent mere physical thing (when we disregard all the "spiritual" or "cultural" characteristics that make it knowable as, for example, a hammer, a table, an aesthetic creation) is given, with the originality of the "it itself," in the synthesis of a passive experience. As such a thing, it is given beforehand to "spiritual" activities, which begin with active grasping.

Like Husserl, the surrealists wanted to get beyond (or behind) the cultural presuppositions that shaped the objects of experience; like Husserl, again, they thought traditional philosophical reasoning to be one of the worst culprits in the repression of primary experience. The difference, of course, was that Husserl was still committed to the possibility of philosophical demonstration. He wrote that "phenomenology's purely intuitive, concrete, and also apodictic mode of demonstration excludes all 'metaphysical adventure,' all speculative excesses," and he said he wanted "to turn all romanticism into responsible work."[27] No aim could have been more sinister to the surrealists, who believed that in the modern world things had come to such a pass that one could get at the absolute only through pure perversity. Hence their fondness for gimmicky techniques that took the brush out of the artist's hand so that it could be waved by chance. In addition to automatic writing, collage, and the practice of using rubbings that Max Ernst called *frottage*, these included the trance-seeking initiated by René Crevel during the so-called *temps des sommeils* of 1922, which were further inspired by Robert Desnos's talent for hypnotic suggestibility; the cameraless technique of Man Ray's rayogrammes; Wolfgang Paalen's *fumage*, in which the marks left on a canvas by candle smoke became the inspiration for an artwork; Oscar Dominguez's spontaneous decalcomania (a kind of automatic painting made by pooling colors on a sheet of paper and then pressing another sheet on top of it); and a variety of word games more or less resembling the *cadavre exquis*, such as question-and-answer forms in which responses were given in ignorance of the question.

In the context of surrealist practices, Duchamp's ready-mades, even though they were generally left physically unchanged by the artist, were not essentially different from Ray's *Gift* (1921): an iron with nails sticking out from the surface ordinarily used to press clothes. In both cases, the object's utilitarian origins and ends were symbolically overcome even as the object was precluded from appearing as art according to recognized formulas. What was given, then, were objects that in a sense overcame themselves, objects that had become an uncompromising site of adventure, and thus objects that represented the movement offered by the surrealist street. What double entendres or parapraxes are to logical communication, these objects were to the things of classical physics. Instead of the table, that immemorial example for philosophy and science, one came upon Victor Brauner's *Wolf-Table* (1939–47), a piece of furniture diverted from its ordinary condition by the erect and snarling wolf's head that rises at one end of it to match the tail and

Man Ray, *Gift* (c. 1958; replica of 1921 original)
Painted flatiron with row of thirteen tacks; heads glued to the bottom,
  6⅛″ × 3⅝″ × 4½″
New York, Collection of the Museum of Modern Art. James Thrall Soby Fund
Copyright 1990 ARS N.Y./ADAGP.

Victor Brauner, *Wolf-Table* (1939)
Paris, Musée National d'art moderne, Centre Georges Pompidou
Copyright 1990 ARS N.Y./SPADEM

hindquarters at the other. Since the legs of this piece of furniture do not "logically" fit with the wolf's belly-up position, the table does not seem a combination of animal and object or a metamorphosis of one into the other. Instead, it seems a sexual coupling of the two, in which their separate identities are at once merged and maintained in their independence. A thing, Brauner proposed, is in reality a fierce act of coition, a dialectical fuck. His table is as far from the furniture of the spiritualists as it is from the classical objects of physics and philosophy, but it, too, speaks to a ghostliness in even the most material and vulgar things; it, too, is an argument that communication in reality takes paths inconceivable to reason. Dali's "paranoiac-critical" method of producing double images (so as to see, for instance, a profiled head in a scene of people gathered around an African hut) participated in this argument, as did the surrealist conception of the "woman-child" and the game of "One in the Other" (in which the trick is to discern an object described through the attributes of another thing).

"To think of an object," wrote Paul Nougé, the Belgian surrealist, "is to act upon it."[28] The physical thing is then a virtual point of fixation at which unconscious processes of objectification are played out in all their irrational mobility and heterogeneity. A gift thus defined, bereft alike of origin, end, and structured relations with any class of things around it, could come to signify something like "life," "necessity," "chance," or "fate"; could seem at once gratuitous and inescapable; and so, like the street, might seem to keep on giving itself inexhaustibly or (in de Chirico's language) enigmatically.[29] (Here one might make a comparison to the elbow of plumbing pipe that Morton Schamberg turned into a sculpture entitled *God* [c. 1918] or to the photo of an eggbeater that Ray labelled *Man* [1918].) In the early days of surrealism, as Breton nostalgically remembered them in his *Conversations*, "No one tried to keep anything for himself, each awaited the fructification of the *gift* to everyone, of the sharing with everyone."[30] The later days of surrealism (and the subsequent *embourgeoisement* of Duchamp and Ray in galleries, museums, and auction houses) might well lead one to a classical suspicion of this modern gift; but still it is not easy to dismiss. Ours is a world in which many of the forces the surrealists meant to oppose—nationalism, militarism, racism, and dogmatic rationalism in all its forms, including professional cynicism—are still very much alive. Suspicion is necessary, but it may come too soon if it refuses to follow the turnings of the surrealist street for a certain distance—if not to the impossible end to which Soupault aspired, then at least through some of the more striking passages, or pathologies, of this way through things.

For instance, this street that might figure as a found object might also figure as the intersection of objects in a collage. Arp's pioneering *papiers déchirés* often carry the subtitle, "Arranged According to the Laws of Chance"; and in "Painting Defied" Aragon proclaimed "the morals of the collage," reasoning that "a pair of scissors and some paper" form "the only palette that does not bring us back to the benches of the school."[31] Along with related techniques (such as photomontage and automatic writing), collage seemed a way of finding art without founding it on the traditional principles that surrealism, following the lead of dada, was determined to combat. In addition to the discipline of the schools, these included every aspect of aesthetic tradition that either subjected art to the world (as commodity, object of taste, or entertaining diversion) or elevated it above the world (as an expression of individual genius or as art for art's sake). Precisely because this technique called attention to the material composition of the work, collage seemed a perfect way to dematerialize everyday reality, showing its apparent objectivity to be illusory. Because of Braque and his *papiers collés*, wrote Breton, the wallpaper of rooms in the modern world had come to suggest "a tuft of grass at the edge of a precipice."[32] Whether its elements were literally thrown together or arranged more deliberately, the collage seemed the model of art as event or as movement. In the lines where its juxtapositions took form were the schematics of a machine, a boogie-woogie map of city streets, the intersecting patterns of artworks arranged on the walls of an exhibition, the warp and weft of a canvas, the lineaments of a body stripped of its confining skin, and finally all the images in which "the most elevated degree of arbitrariness" could prove conducive to the beauty whose advent Breton proclaimed in his "Manifesto of Surrealism."[33]

In his *Aesthetics*, which was greatly admired by Breton, Hegel said poetry involved "reaching a totality [*das Erringen einer Totalität*]" but noted, "To define the poetic as such or to give a description of what is poetic horrifies nearly all who have written about poetry."[34] In terms of surrealism, this seeming conflict might be read positively as an account of the perverse purity of the street, the found object, the collage. In these forms totality was not turned against itself, as in the romantic irony that twists into a vortex of self-consuming despair, but *upon* itself, as in the moving implications given to the elements comprising a text when a dream frees them from the grammar of routine consciousness so that "words make love." From this perspective, poetry could be described as the discovery that totality is an unavoidable but critically upsetting violation of definition, *ostranenie* with a vengeance, a movement with an aggressive and perverse purity of purpose.

Perhaps some such recognition accounts for Freud's admission, near the end of his "Constructions in Analysis," that he is nagged by "the enticement [*der Verlockung*] of an analogy," which leads him to see delusions as "the equivalents of the constructions which [psychoanalysts] build up in the course of an analytic treatment."[35] Here the implication of totality logically borne by any rational interpretation becomes a bond between scientific analysis and hallucinatory conviction. Unable to disavow this implication (for to do so would mean surrendering the possibility of reason) and yet unable to accept it (and thus to claim a certainty for his argument that Husserl might describe as intuitive but that a psychoanalyst must find psychotic), Freud was led to describe totality as "enticement," a term which suggests the promise of a pleasure shadowed by deception or betrayal. In surrealist terms, one might call this a poetic moment in Freud's text.

For the surrealists, this was precisely the poetic adventure of reason: to discover identity in the alien, even to the point where madness proves a mirror to reason. The sleep of reason breeds monsters, yes, but *desirable* monsters, monsters even *necessary*, as far as the surrealists were concerned. From a dogmatic slumber, one awakes — into a dream. Thus it is at the end of Ray's film, *Emak-Bakia* (1927). A woman (Kiki de Montparnasse), who first appears to be looking out at the world, is seen actually to have eyes painted on her eyelids; she then opens her eyes. Only someone unworldly enough to think that Sancho Panza represents a reality distinct from the Don's "madness" could believe that we see the real eyes, the real vision, in that last movement. We do not see a final reality or the finality of reality; we see the enticement of surrealism.

In arguing that the works of Joan Miró illustrate the need to plunge into absurdity, to seize the unforeseeable and impossible aspect of things, Tzara sought to capture this ultimate table-turning, in which totality turns upon itself:

> But the ambition to encompass Totality is destined to failure. Only by a kind of humility before the limits of certain phenomena can one attain to the universal. There is no intermediary state: either reason makes itself so penetrating that its painful point touches upon an initial substance of unreason and thus emerges into complete clarity, or it marries itself to the sentimentality of superficial movements and so contents itself with being nothing more than a joke. I am speaking of intensity.[36]

Here the surrealist street turns into a kind of text. This was most famously represented in the automatic writings inaugurated by Breton and Soupault's *The Magnetic Fields* and in the sentences composed by the method of the *cadavre exquis*. However, insofar as it took on the insatiable urgency of totality, in which seductive poetic assemblage disrupts rational classification and narrative, any surrealist representation could become this kind of text. Paintings like Paul Klee's, manifestations like the one Breton organized to protest the opening of a club on the Boulevard Edgar-Quinet that someone had had the effrontery to name *Maldoror*,[37] and other sorts of actions, such as Soupault's gesture of entering paint stores to inquire about the purchase of birds, could all be seen as dream texts in which the workings of the dream uprooted the conventional definitions of signs. As Breton said in "Ideas of a Painter," in a comment he went on to apply to the traditional language of painting, "The sight of a page of characters in a book is extremely troubling: think of what that sets in motion."[38] One might think especially of Yves Tanguy's art, which, after some early casting about, came to concentrate on

quasi-abstract figures that were generally amoeboid, squiggly, and ectoplas-
mic, reminiscent by turns of clouds, driftwood, bones, clay, jelly, rocks,
candy, and entrails, among other things. These fantastic figures may seem to
carry all the conviction of an alphabet developed and revised through years
of work, but this is a system of representation that from its beginning puzzles
over the mystery that a sign could ever be representational. "Until Tanguy,"
wrote Breton, "the object, despite the several outward assaults to which it
was submitted, remained in the last analysis distinct and prisoner to its own
identity. With him we enter for the first time into a world of total latency."[39]

To the student of literature and art today, who has plunged into (or at
least peeked over) the abysses of deconstruction, this challenge may seem
unremarkable. Even in the twenties it had ample precedents, as the surrealists
themselves acknowledged, in dada, cubism, and the work of figures stretch-
ing back from Paul Valéry to Heraclitus. (The worldly Francis Picabia, a
sometime fellow traveller with this movement, is reported to have shrugged
off the surrealists' enthusiasm for the Comte de Lautréamont by saying that
he, too, was once a young man.) However, it is easy to overestimate the
familiarity of this textual challenge and thus to flee from the monsters we
think we are facing head on. After all, can one really cozy up to an abyss?
This temptation toward a *comforting* radicalism is one reason Breton resisted
attempts to identify the surrealists too closely with the *poètes maudites* of
the last century: because their representation of evil might not be vital
enough for his day, in which evil had also to be enchantment if it would
signify the convulsive beauty of arbitrariness, the totality that turns upon
itself, the eternity that burns up the road.

Language thus understood was increasingly monstrous the further it was
penetrated, in accordance with the example of Maldoror: "[S]ee before you
only a monster, whose form I am happy you cannot perceive — even though
it is less horrible than his soul."[40] This monstrous language did not inhere in
the forms of signs ("Letters are my ignorance," wrote Eluard) but in the
moving totality of their possible implications, whose textual form could only
be a deformation of the lines along which identities were usually assigned.
(So Eluard continued, "You go from one concrete thing to another / By the
shortest path: that of monsters.")[41] This is the language asserted in the *cadavre exquis* (such as the one that says, "The endless sex sleeps with the
orthodox tongue");[42] in the aphorism, "Words make love," with which
Breton concluded one of his essays;[43] in the adventurous iconography of
Miró's paintings, which can suggest a thread of identity uniting (for example)
eyes, the sun, the foliage of trees, and the female genitalia; and, implicitly,
in all surrealist representations. Like city streets, language might seem intended to be a grid systematically organized by principles of classification
and combination; but when language or a street is grasped as an event, not
assumed to be a fixed ground to events, then this logical grid turns into a
text with "hidden virtues" and "secret ramifications that propagate them-

selves across the entire language, channelled by the associations of sounds, forms, and ideas. Then language transforms itself into an oracle, and there we have (however tenuous it may be) a thread to guide us through the Babel of our spirit."[44]

In this description by Michel Leiris, as in the other representations to which I have referred, the surrealist conception of the text is likely to appear idealist, captivated by the dream of godlike totality no matter how demonically turned back upon itself this totality may be. Indeed, this was a criticism made at the time by Bataille and by members of the PCF, despite persistent attempts by Breton and others, from the mid-twenties onward, to align their movement with the doctrine of historical materialism developed by the heirs of Lenin. Critics like these dubbed Breton the pope of surrealism, and the nickname stuck; it did seem to fit. But just as there may be a premature sophistication in our rush to embrace the abyss, so may a postmodernism that preens itself on having surpassed idealism find that what it has left behind may not be so easy to shake from its tail, may in fact be lurking ominously before it. At least it is important to see that if this is idealism, it is idealism in extremis, founded on compulsion rather than reason and willing, if not achieving, its own dissolution.

In this regard, consider how the surrealist street figured as the meeting-place of people who had few or no connections with each other outside this movement. In this street Arthur Rimbaud might run into the Douanier Rousseau, the divine Charlot (Chaplin) shake hands with the divine Marquis (de Sade), or Lautréamont meet with Gustave Moreau, Hegel, Picasso, Monk Lewis, Fantomâs (the criminal hero of a popular mystery), *le facteur* Cheval (a postman who built a fantastic palace in his yard out of rocks and shells and whatever else he could get his hands on), and others still more unexpected, such as Gisèle Prassinos, the child whose writings captivated some of the surrealists for a time. Although a collection this eclectic may still suggest a canon, a pantheon, a coercive (and notably male) assertion of culture — in short, the stink of the ideal — it may have a very different import if one looks at it for what it could mean as it was being made, when the disparate figures coupled by surrealist enthusiasms could be as shocking as, say, Dali's combination of crystalline technique with warm Camembert form.

Thus, in the *Short Dictionary of Surrealism*, when the entry on "dialectic" offered citations from Hegel, Meister Eckhart, Friedrich Engels, Lenin, and Freud, this definition was fashioned to violate any form of dialectics one could name, whether it came from philosophical idealism or Stalinist academicism. In the manner of the surrealist object and in a winking homage to Hegel's *Aufhebung*, this definition was meant to surpass itself. In the same way, surrealist idols, whether persons or things, might be better described as fetishes that were meant to suggest universality only as the impossible end to an errant chain of substitutions.[45] (The surrealists, as it happens, took an early interest in the writings of Jacques Lacan, and he in them.) In naming things that assert an impossible totality or, in Freud's terms, that deny castration, fetishism might also name the general condition of objectivity in the world of surrealism. Hence the signature objects in the works of many surrealists: Dali's crutches, Ernst's birds, René Magritte's harness bells, Tanguy's squiggles, and so on. The displacement here described by fetishism belonged to the general desire for displacement in this movement, which signified an obligation on the part of individuals to descend into the street and thus to try to get out of their own skins and into the plastic conditions of truth.

The fetishized object cooperates with the anthropological metaphor forever resurfacing in surrealist works, preoccupied as they are with deracinations, explorations, strange lands, marvels, discoveries, and cryptic events. If the recourse to the primitive is a (or perhaps *the*) definitive gesture of metaphysical idealism, the surrealists' preference for interpretive wandering over systematic explanation may yet make this gesture a different sort of thing. With the exception of Tzara and Leiris, the participants in surrealism who collected "primitive" objects from Oceania and elsewhere were as unconcerned with their native conception or use as artists such as Picasso and André Derain were when they went shopping for such things. The second issue of *Minotaure*, the journal with which the surrealists were closely associated in the 1930s, was entirely devoted to the French Dakar-Djibouti expedition and to the Museum of Ethnography in Paris, both of which were concerned to promote a more scientific, historically contextualized approach to artifacts; but it was not cultural origins that were primitive for the surrealists but desires and dreams, which they took to transgress all symbolic boundaries. When Oceanic objects were shown with Ray's work and American Indian pieces with Tanguy's in 1926 shows at the Surrealist Gallery in the Rue Jacques-Callot, the juxtaposition was much more likely to suggest a war against all culture than a new cultural trend or a reconciliation of traditions.

From the standpoint of Oceanic as well as French culture, this juxtaposition was likely to seem a crime; and, indeed, crime is still another name for the kind of thing that happens in the surrealist street. Breton's most notorious statement defined the simplest surrealist act as a descent "into the street, revolvers in hand, to fire at random, as much as one can, into the crowd";[46] and crime scenes play a distinctive role in surrealist representations as images of revolt and as mocking allusions to the characterization that this movement could expect from the established powers of society. (So Breton joked that the surrealists' crime was "*lèse-réalité*.")[47] This role played by crime had been well rehearsed in the era of dada, as in Aragon's "Program," which begins at "the rendezvous of the assassins" with "blood and fresh paint" and concludes, "I place anarchy into competition / in all the libraries and stations."[48] Like dada, surrealism was fond of crime scenes that were murky, melodramatic, fundamentally indecipherable, and so rather smirkingly comic. The enthusiasm for Gothic novels that Breton shared with other participants in this movement (Breton even had a dog named Melmoth) also demonstrates their interest in crime, which is further suggested by works such as Magritte's *The Threatened Assassin* (1926), Tanguy's *Fantomâs* (1925–26), and Ernst's *Two Infants are Threatened by a Nightingale* (1924).

The important point again is that the figure of crime carried a power of implication that could seem to articulate virtually all of surrealism, not just those paintings or passages where it was explicitly represented. In this metaphysical sense, even de Chirico's *Melancholy and Mystery of a Street* was a scene of crime, or actually of several crimes. In addition to the suggestion of menace it might seem to draw around the running girl (who was borrowed for one of the figures in Ernst's *Two Infants*),[49] this painting could represent a crime against reason (in its oneiric atmosphere), against art (in the violations of traditional rules of perspective that help to create its dreaminess), against fixed structures and stable forms (in the power it assigns to shadows), and ultimately against any philosophical pretension that would rise above the level of the flotsam and jetsam of a city street.

If one wants a single name for this sense of crime, it has to be the Marquis de Sade. In relentlessly developing the line of Enlightenment reasoning that displaced Providence by referring all things to natural law, Sade's writings represented the law of nature as a crime best served by crimes. Because it did not recognize morality, which Sade argued to be a purely social business, nature itself was "unnatural" and therefore could not possibly recognize any contravention of itself. In this abyssal universe, bottomless in transgression, in which all notions of divinity and rationality were driven beyond any identity that was not ceaselessly and excruciatingly violated, nature was nothing because it was everything. Ultimately, there was no "nature itself." Thus did Richardson's Pamela become Sade's Justine.

This vision held great appeal for a movement that considered its world not only shot through with hypocrisy but actually founded on a logic to which the inevitable conclusion was the carnage of the First World War. One cannot begin to understand what surrealism was doing when it courted public outrage, in actions that ranged from its innovative art to Breton's praise for random murder to Benjamin Péret's habit of insulting priests he happened to run into on the street, unless one considers how this movement always bore reference to a society that permitted this war to happen and then seemed actually to encourage the ways of living that had sanctioned this impossibly outrageous experience. Sadism meant the sacrifice of the object, the sacrifice of nature and objective reality, so as to reveal the desiring imagination that forms them and that also must deform them, through its incessant vitality, even to the point of taking pleasure in its own destruction. In this respect Sade was taken to be an illustrious precursor, but he was also a response and a weapon created out of the urgency of doing battle with the shameless crimes of reason. It is in light of these circumstances that Aragon was able

to bring Sade into alignment with Marx, Engels, and Isidore Ducasse (Lautréamont) even though he recognized the dangers of such homologies:

> When Engels and Marx, pursuing the historical dissolution of Hegelianism, over-
> came the system of absolute idealism with the notion of becoming from which it
> issued and thus ruined once and for all the spirit of system in the name of dyna-
> mism, denying the Hegelian moral conclusion necessitated by the fixity of the
> system at any given moment of the world, they employed evil as Sade and, indeed,
> Isidore Ducasse had.
>
> . . . Sexual contradiction in Sade, social contradiction in Engels and Marx, and
> purely ethical contradiction in Ducasse are the fault-lines along which these three
> ways of thought pursue their work; on their basis the conception of good and evil
> and their role as historical motivation (of the individual, of society, of facts in
> themselves) are put into question.[50]

In Sade's world, in which a stable system of reference is unthinkable and the
only law is the law of crime, the imagination is sovereign and yet prisoner to its
own sovereignty. Each exercise of power also defines its limits, as one sees in
the continual elaboration of enclosures, physical and tactical, around his
actors. Therefore, every novelty is already repetition, sameness, and an irritat-
ing compulsion toward an infinitely frustrating excess. At the center of things,
nature ordains nothing but an endless dispersion of differences and transformation of forces, and there is no other motivation for representation than these
provide. In proliferating differences and in metamorphic forces there can be no
social law that is not ultimately incoherent, indistinguishable from—or known
only through—its violation. Therefore, in this world in which all forms are
hallucinatory, crime is a means of questioning the mystifying objectivity of
appearances in the most provocative way imaginable and thus the best way to
think through the world of human creation, community, and communication.
Crime can enable us to see how certain signifiers get under our skin, into our
very blood and flesh, where they continue to work in and through us unless we
can find a way of figuratively getting outside of ourselves and beyond the world
of customary perceptions. Crime is then a way of recognizing the falsity of the
subject-object distinction that Breton represented in the notion of "communicating vases," which would allow a free exchange between their interiority and
exteriority; but the figure of crime especially emphasizes how viscerally upsetting this dialectical moment must be.[51]

Or so at least it could appear to the surrealists, who generally showed little
interest in a close textual exegesis of Sade's writings, which served them more
as instruments of semiotic stimulation and political provocation. Along with
the writings of Horace Walpole, Monk Lewis, Ann Radcliffe, and Charles
Robert Maturin, Sade's Gothic was taken to represent a necessary displacement, an adventure of necessity. "It could be," Breton wrote,

> that life demands to be deciphered like a cryptogram. Secret stairways, frames
> from which pictures rapidly glide and disappear to give way to an archangel

carrying a sword or to make way for those who must move forward forever, buttons on which a very indirect pressure provokes a displacement in the height and depth of an entire room along with an immediate transformation in its decor: it is possible to conceive the greatest adventure of the spirit as a voyage of this kind to a paradise of traps.[52]

There may be no better image for the assault of this paradise than that given in Ernst's *Oedipus Rex* (1922). Like Sade's writing, this painting may seem less violent in its images than in the deliberation with which it coolly proposes the execution of these symbolic crimes. This deliberation is emphasized by the almost naive or anti-artistic modeling and coloring of the forms in the painting. Here reason finds its limit, not in logical axioms or constructions, but in disturbing suggestions and poetic transformations.

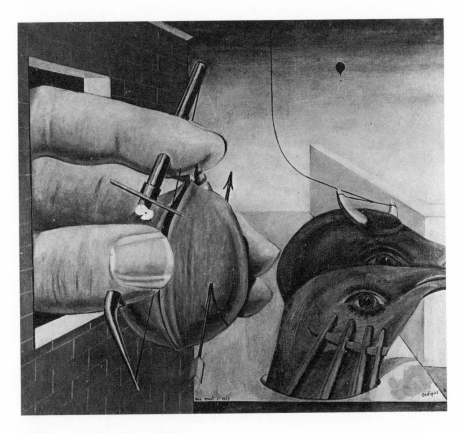

Max Ernst, *Oedipus Rex* (1922)
Private collection
Copyright 1990 ARS N.Y./SPADEM/ADAGP

One motif is penetration: a hand thrust through a window, with fingers pierced by a metal instrument, holds a seashell behind a larger nutshell, which is transfixed by an arrow, over a roof that collars two strange birds' heads. One of the birds has horns, which are tied together by a line that ascends into the sky, where it is held by a force beyond the frame of the picture. This line and the other elements tie the penetrations into a series of distortions: the hand is large enough to fill the window completely, and the birds' heads, of normal size in comparison to the outstretched fingers, seem huge in the context of the roof from which they emerge. The palings that hem in the bird in the foreground emphasize this disproportion; other distortions include the absence of any sign of blood or pain in the hand; and these elements and others also make this a scene of frustration. This aspect is emphasized in the sky, where, diminished by distance, like an exclamation point, there appears the lyrical interjection of a balloon. This marvel of the last century here seems a vestigial reference to a more innocent art and time, perhaps recalling the balloon in Rousseau's 1890 *Portrait-Landscape*.

If the window, the fingers, the two eyes visible in the profiled birds, the birds themselves, the nut and shell, and the needlelike instrument all symbolically suggest genitalia, then the juxtaposition of these multiple penetrations, distortions, and frustrations can be related, via Freud, to the literary title of the painting. It is notable in this respect that even in its early days surrealist art was sometimes alleged to be too literary or anecdotal, still basing itself on image and theme when the art supposed to be more progressive was moving toward abstraction. *Oedipus Rex* does lend itself to a Freudian interpretation just as easily as it does to a reading in terms of dada motifs (the interpenetration of human and mechanomorphic forms, the fragmentation of bodies, the emphasis on brute physicality and animality, the determined lack of sentimentality, and so on); but it lends itself in a peculiarly charmless and uninviting way. It suggests that one can throw many different kinds of readings at it and find them all equally plausible and equally beside the point. The Freudian analogy is an enticement, which, if accepted, leads to a repulsive totality. The crudely violated hand, which does not suffer, is itself as insufferable as the nut (which surely holds no kernel of truth), the birds (which, if vaguely hieratic, suggest a strangulated sacredness), or the line that disappears into the air like a cheap fakir's rope. From the distant balloon, perhaps, the scene would be a simple crime, easy to classify as violence or madness or childish play; but from the foregrounded viewpoint that we are given, the scene is as precise as a mathematical formula and, like a formula, dreamily indifferent to any conclusions that may be drawn from it. It is a place where ideas, in Artaud's words, are "simple assemblages of objects."[53] It is the surrealist street that creates thought by repelling it, forcing it to skid from one image to another until it recognizes itself as nothing more or less than this movement — or so this painting may appear to one who regards it with the proper *disponibilité*.

Corresponding to the street that is a scene of crime is the pedestrian whose *disponibilité* has encouraged a systematic disordering of the senses, in accordance with the recipe for poetic sensibility that the surrealists adopted from Rimbaud.[54] Given this perspective, Ernst's painting does not *represent* but instead *enacts* a scrambling of the forms of perception. The birds staring out at the viewers then suggest the eyes of those very viewers, who, if they are ready for the opportunity to experience the affinity, will not find this scene strange or even exterior to themselves. Traditional painting, which stops at the retina,[55] then is turned into something like the hashish pipe of Baudelaire's *Artificial Paradises*, which the smoker finds to be smoking him. Or it comes to resemble the thought Rimbaud found to be thinking him, leading him to the motto, "I is an other"; the crocodiles mentioned in *The Magnetic Fields*, which "recaptured the valise made with their hide";[56] or the comical door designed by Duchamp that could be open and closed at the same time (contradicting the French proverb to the opposite effect) because it swung from a corner of his apartment and fit frames in both of the convergent walls. One might also think of the "soluble fish," which gave the title to one of Breton's manifestos, or of Dali's "paranoiac-critical" interest in Giuseppe Arcimboldo's trick paintings, which show, for example, a face composed of fruit and vegetables. In looking for works that could become this kind of event, the surrealists were looking to catch representation in the act of transfiguration, which was the primal scene of poetry as they conceived it. The desire was to bring out the scandalous activity of perception in its engagement with things and by this revelation to break out of the abstractions (flesh, blood, humanity, walls, gravity . . .) that structured the bourgeois home and eye.

Had not the challenge been thrown down by Baudelaire, in the last lines of "The Voyage"? "To plunge to the depths of the gulf, Hell or Heaven, who cares? / In the depths of the Unknown to discover something *new*!"[57] The early writings of Artaud are particularly interesting for the way they pick up this challenge, this "love of the lie," even though his involvement with surrealism was relatively brief. (He got the boot when he refused to accept the political direction it took toward the end of the twenties.) Artaud described himself as "a complete abyss"; and if this identification smacks of melodrama, he made this melodrama seem something convincingly given, like a physical constitution or an abstract fate—something that simply demanded exploration. In the febrile, meticulous, scary style of his *Fragments of a Journal from Hell*, the consequent disordering of the senses is not so much explained (a ridiculous word in this context) as it is manifested, like a drive or a compulsion:

In the space of a minute in which a lie's illumination remains, I construct for myself an evasive thought, I throw myself on a false trial indicated by my blood. I close the eyes of my intelligence, and I give myself the illusion of a system whose

terms escape me. But from this moment of error I retain the feeling of having
kidnapped from the unknown something of reality. I believe in these spontaneous
conjurations. On the roads where my blood leads me, there must come a day
when I will discover a truth.[58]

In a way interrogated by writers as different as George Eliot, Friedrich
Nietzsche, and Franz Kafka, the rejection of the ontology traditionally provided by religion offered the possibility that the definitive and unsurpassable
model of modern existence might be the physical experiment. The systematic
derangement of the senses counseled by Rimbaud and given a modern motto
in Breton and Eluard's "Notes on Poetry" — "A poem should be a debacle of
the intellect"[59] — was the plunge into the abyss through which one accepted
the infinite parameters of this experiment, which, like all surrealist travels,
could never be finished — could only be taken further. ("Street-singer," wrote
Breton and Soupault in their inaugural exercise in automatic writing, "the
world is big and you will never arrive.")[60] Weirdly but logically, this experi-
mentation was influenced by the model of empiricism, as the surrealists
pointed out by establishing a "Bureau of Researches" and in fashioning their
first periodical after an established scientific journal, *Nature*. However,
as with the nineteenth-century spiritualists' appropriation of scientific language and claims, the surrealist program was just as critical of orthodox
science as it was of every conventional form of knowledge. Rather than
appealing to judgments of fact, this modern trial would contribute only to
demonstrating the possibilities of transfiguration. Such is wandering, writing, or painting in the absence of fixed objects and ground, or such is the
journey that is its own object because it cannot be satisfied with anything
short of everything.

As observers were quick to notice, there is an irony in this emphasis on a
systematic disordering of the senses. It might be taken to suggest that Breton
and the other boys did not really distance themselves very far from the
schoolyard, and surrealism did produce absurdities that are more patent than
profound. For instance, in *The Magnetic Fields* and many other examples of
automatic writing, it is notable that the unconscious generally took care to
compose its prose in complete sentences. The surrealists themselves quickly
became aware of the difficulty in gauging the extent of conscious intervention in supposedly unconscious performances, and automatic writing became
notably less prominent in the affairs of the group after a couple of years; the
same is true of the accounts of dreams that initially filled many columns in
The Surrealist Revolution. And whether or not the writing was automatic, it
is not difficult to find a formula for many yards of surrealist verse and
prose: confuse the attributes conventionally assigned to animate and inanimate bodies ("the sighs of the window"), put the resulting images into phrases
in which abrupt juxtapositions of times, places, and identities disrupt the
sense that grammar suggests ought to be there ("the sighs of the window eat

the bankrupt moon"), continue until weariness sets in, *et voilà*. While some were scribbling in this fashion, the other works of this movement could be just as dubious. Many paintings by Ernst, Klee, Miró, and others associated with surrealism do not threaten anything but cuteness or silliness; and in their memoirs the surrealists themselves have admitted that many of their "manifestations," such as the seances held in the early days of the movement, could be simply boring. One might think here of the less-than-stimulating farce that ensued when Dali had to be rescued from the deep-sea diving suit he had decided to wear for his presentation at a surrealist exhibition in London in 1936.

Yet noting this weakness, like making the accusation of idealism, can be too easy. After all, there was a deliberate irony in the notion that automatic writing could help to break the automatized routines of social behavior, poetic and otherwise.[61] Surrealism turned away from romanticism and symbolism in thus setting itself up as an experiment in transgression rather than a search for transcendence or escape. It would make totality turn upon itself so that it would either be found in the street or nowhere; and if the resulting works often fell into a routine, this was an eventuality that the surrealists themselves addressed in their demand for a practice of unceasing innovation directed to, if not totally controlled by, the exigencies of contemporary social events. To criticize surrealism simply as a fixed style, practice, or product is to refuse to consider it as a movement that was polemical and topical and therefore, in intention, mobile and self-critical, as in fact it showed itself to be in moving on from automatism to other concerns. It may be convenient to avoid this consideration and to drag surrealism, squalling and kicking, into the history of art while turning its rebellious motivation into a matter incidental to its literature, paintings, and other works; but then it is this type of critical performance, not surrealism, that only slouches around the block instead of actually daring to run away from home.

A more challenging criticism must return to the issue of chance, since in all things the surrealist movement took this to be its motivation. The street, remember, was where one went to take one's chances. And here I need to return to my earlier question as to how this chance could possibly work. Although I have tried to give an account of some turnings through which chance could gain a certain power, the question of how this power could be possible still remains. By this I do not mean the primitive origins of this power, which was finally imaginary, a rhetorical supposition not necessarily communicated to anyone in particular. In addressing the power of chance in this way, I mean what had to be taken to be true if one was to have a chance of getting it.

If surrealism was ever to have any power, what had to be true was that people did not work in the street. This street, *disponibilité*, the gift, the collage, the monstrous text, the fetish, Sadean crime, the poetic transfiguration of the senses, the experiment: none of this could be where work was.

This incompatibility does not simply translate the difference between id and ego, although some of the surrealists and their admirers have been inclined to see it in this way. What was at stake was not conflict but what the surrealists imagined conflict to be.

Those who were *disponible* went beyond art by letting chance work for them, creating a truth surpassing the possibilities of rational calculation. This is the irony more extensively implicated in surrealism than the ironies of canon and system: that it opposed tradition of all sorts by identifying with the ideal of artlessness that had long been the end of art and that could even be said to define Christian ontology, in which totality forever exists without ever laboring to be and grace can be won but never earned. While the other ironies might be excused in terms of the need for a political identity, which the surrealists recognized but held open to revision, this one is more significant because it has the effect of denying politics and thus led the surrealists to serious misrecognitions of the conflicts in which they were engaged. This is where idealism truly had its revenge — where it pinned this movement down. Work in surrealism was always dream work, work that comes, happens, is given, or takes place, but never work that one labors to do; and this dreaminess carries implications that turned the street of surrealism into something considerably less than the meeting-place of ultimate possibilities. It could even turn out to be, *horribile dictu*, a *picturesque* street.

Consider the most obvious consequence of this irony: the surrealists' disdain for ordinary labor. In "Factory," Breton wrote, "The accidents of work, nobody will contradict me, are more beautiful than the marriages of reason"; and this aesthetic was also an everyday ethic among the surrealists.[62] Routine work was to be anathematized in every instance but especially in those cases (journalism being among the most prominent) in which it might seem to claim an intellectual spirit. In this regard, the emblematic story among the surrealists came from Breton's first attempt to join the PCF, which proved abortive when he was assigned to a cell of gas workers that promptly gave him the humiliating task of preparing a report on social and economic conditions in contemporary Italy. With a few exceptions, such as Eluard, the surrealists had to work hard to scratch out a living in the twenties and thirties, so they were not ignorant of the exigencies of making a living: they simply despised them. Utilitarianism, which they saw as the deathly motivation of modern rationality, science, and statecraft, defined ordinary work for them as a profanation of creativity. When surrealists turned to communism, their Marx did not preach the dignity of labor; he dreamed of a revolution in all productive relations that would transform the nature of work. As Breton put it in *Nadja*, "The event from which everyone has a right to expect a revelation of the sense of his own life, this event that I go toward in seeking myself even though I may not yet have found it, *is not the reward of work.*"[63] For the surrealists, work was the way of the coward, weakling, fool, or victim. It meant taking what was given by the world, not as an opportunity for liberating revelation, but as onerous duty. It meant suffering the tyranny of objects instead of entering the transfiguring events between subjectivity and objectivity that the man of *disponibilité* could find when wandering in the street.

To oppose utilitarianism and its attendant moralism was to reject the conviction that *"laborare est orare"* preached by Goethe, Thomas Carlyle, and George Eliot; illustrated in Ford Madox Brown's famous painting, *Work* (1852–68); and, more to the point, taken up as a way of praising the working class in the French communist and socialist press between the wars. In rejecting this conviction the surrealists also opposed the Hegelian theme that saw work as history-in-the-making and thus as the way to art and transcendent spirit. However, in seeking to reject the popular and philosophical ideals, what they did not see was work as the demanding materiality, at once biological and cultural, through which historical possibilities are lived, fought, and even dreamed.[64] In seeing work as alienation and profanation, they turned away from work as exertion and communication and passion. In this sense, work is the irrecoverable experience of sociality. It is experience that does not lend itself to science or metaphysics, to logical origins or to universal ends, and yet is not given up to chance. Although formally unpredictable and rationally irresoluble, this sociality is articulated as forms of life that are not transfigured arbitrarily and that cannot stand around and wait for chance to change them. Dreams, too, have their histories; dreams, too, labor to be.

Nietzsche, who helped to suggest the surrealist pleasure in chance ("[N]ow and then chance guides our hand, and the wisest providence could not think up a more beautiful music than that which our foolish hand produces then"), also suggested the problem with this pleasure: "No victor believes in chance."[65] Believe what you will about chance, says the victor; do what you will with it; chance alone will never displace me. This voice the surrealists did not always hear.

For all its aggressiveness, the movement of surrealism was drawn by the implications of its own rhetoric toward an acquiescence to society, which was supposed to be repulsed and yet finally was favored by the figure of chance. This acquiescence was not total and to some extent must be seen as inevitable, unless one believes (as the surrealists often did) in an apocalyptic resolution to change; but still this acquiescence need not have taken the form it did, which made the surrealist movement peculiarly deceptive precisely because it seemed so open to every passing breeze. When this openness turned out to be acquiescence, surrealism could come to look fatally reasonable as well as horribly picturesque and cryptically Christian.

A conclusion something like this was drawn by Roger Vailland in the pamphlet, *Surrealism Against the Revolution*, in which he disdainfully rejected the title of the movement's journal of the early 1930s, *Surrealism in the Service of the Revolution*. In criticizing the surrealists from a position of communist orthodoxy, Vailland was surely wrong in claiming that "in order to like Max Ernst, it is still necessary to have had the time to like and then to reject Cézanne and Braque"; but his general point, which concerned the bourgeois education and privilege presupposed by those who entertained surrealist positions, does have some force.[66] At once a figuration of privilege, resentment, rebellion, and passivity, the surrealist's chance simply was not adequate to the task of overcoming work — no, not even in dreams.

The surrealists dreamed of making the world work for them. Nothing much happens in *Melancholy and Mystery of a Street*, and in other surrealist meeting-places, because the one tradition of art that the surrealists could not root out of their practices was that which defined things of pleasure through the invisibility of labor. The sewing machine does not whir, the umbrella is at rest, and their mating is accomplished without any shudderings, sighs, groans, moans, and sweat. In wanting to take their chances in the street, the surrealists did not care to recognize that everyone does not always have the same chance for transfiguration. Chance overcomes work only in visions that some are privileged to enjoy while to others they offer, if anything, only the enigmatic shadow of pleasure. Chance is finally the name of this privilege; chance is the enticement proffered, paradoxically, by the ideal of total mastery. If Freud recognized this point, the surrealists wanted to go farther than he did, or they did not want to go as far — the image at this point becomes impossible to pin down, lost in dreams.

The participants in the surrealist movement might play with definitions all they wanted, but still they were bound by definitions that were more than a matter of chance, more pressing than they ever dreamed, even if these definitions were not a matter of providential destiny. In the swarm of representations that was this movement, in its gravity and inertia, there was a historical implicature of possibilities that the surrealists lived but sought to deny in their experiments. It appears in them nonetheless as a life that is irrecoverable, because totality is impossible to grasp, and yet determinate, because partiality leaves its mark in definite forms of life, such as "men" and "women," even as these things are given to us unreasonably, like figures in a dream.

A mark one may hate to see:

Who is the true Nadja . . . the creature, always inspired and inspiring, who loved only to be in the street, for her the only valuable field of experience; in the street, within reach of the question posed by every human being launched toward a great chimera — or (why not admit it?) the one who would *fall* sometimes, because in the end there were others who believed themselves authorized to address her, having been able to see in her only the poorest and worst protected of women? I came to react with a frightful violence against the excessively detailed story that she made for me from certain scenes of her past, from which I judged, no doubt very superficially, that her dignity could not have emerged completely redeemed. A history of a punch right in the face that made blood gush out one day in a room in the Zimmer restaurant, a punch received from a man to whom she had refused herself, with malicious pleasure, simply because he was short—and several times she had cried for help, not without taking the time, before disappearing, to bloody the man's clothes—at the beginning of the afternoon of October 13, when she recounted it to me for no good reason, this had to distance me from her forever. I do not know what sentiment of absolute irremediability I was made to feel by a story as mocking as that horrible adventure, but I cried after having heard it, in a way I had believed myself no longer capable of crying.[67]

As Breton recognized, the irremediability that hit him in this story was unthinkable in the surrealist street. This irremediability was the effect of historical circumstances, which are likely to be at once banal and demanding, as they are in this case, and which are bound to be embarrassing to desire, especially desire that dreams of turning the irrationality of social life into satisfying figures and turns. Of course, as told by Breton, this story *is* a story, an account of experience; but I have not quoted it here to claim it as historical fact and evidence. The point is that Breton represents himself as one who can acknowledge but cannot understand his own distress when he learns that the pleasure in turning away from work may entail conflict, humiliation, and loss. If they had followed a slightly different path through their heroes' writings than the ones they usually took, this is the lesson the surrealists might have gained from Sade, Hegel, and Freud: that it is impossible to have pleasure as one thing and the repetitions, routines, and structures of work as something completely other.

Chance may give pleasure, but it does not give liberation, which is what the surrealists wanted to believe pleasure must be. In this situation, therefore, what they wanted to believe was bound to show up in the form of a mystifying subjection, for which "woman" is the most obvious name.[68] And this mystifying subjection was bound to reappear, over and over again, in the writings of surrealist fans. "It does not matter whether this be a serving-girl or a queen; it is a woman free from any bonds who appears for a second, at the moment of wakening": yes, this statement by Michel Carrouges is supposed to describe Nadja.[69] In this situation it is necessary to speak of a brutal idealization or of a glamorized brutality; in any case, of a vision willfully divorced from any responsibility for the sacrifices on which its existence depends. I am not referring to Nadja as such a sacrifice; to do so now could only be a stupid adventure in sentimentality and naive reading. What is more, as the passage I have quoted indicates, Breton was not blind to his possible implication in Nadja's troubling fate. The sacrifices to which I refer do not involve this particular character or historical personage; they involve the attitudes that make this turn that Breton describes in Nadja, this wavering between desirability and offensiveness, appear as a characteristic turn of the surrealist movement.

In describing the surrealist interest in wandering adventures through language, streets, and dreams, Breton said, "The unforeseen encounter, which always tends, explicitly or not, to take on the features of a woman, marks the culmination of this quest."[70] He was right, and he was wrong. Everywhere in surrealist writings and art the figure of the street becomes the figure of a woman, but this culmination is also a diversion into turnings dividing women and work, women and men, passive objects and active subjects — all the drearily familiar forms of the everyday world that prove refractory to transfiguration even in this movement that was supposed to be given over to dreams. In this respect, one might return to Ray's *Gift* and note that this transfiguration is also a sexual allegory in which masculine nails turn the feminine iron away from work and toward an eroticism as equivocal as it is traditional, with its suggestion of romantic violence. Transgression is not always the call of the wild, just as nature is not necessarily distant from the city. As in this instance, the call of the wild may be the dreamy voice of patriarchal tradition.

In an interesting passage of fantasy and burlesque near the end of *What Is to be Done?* Lenin exclaims, "That is what we ought to be dreaming about!" and then imagines himself confronted by accusers from a rival, social-democratic group. "I ask," demands one, "has a Marxist any right at all to dream, knowing that according to Marx man always sets himself achievable tasks and that tactics is a process of growth of tasks, which grow together with the Party?"[71] The voice, with its stupid, smug, hectoring narrowness, might be that of Vailland attacking the surrealists; and Lenin, like Breton, portrays himself as arguing in favor of the need for more dreaming, especially in the (to him) threatening context of pragmatic, untheoretical, uncentralized, reformist attitudes. Breton, who on occasion liked to look past Stalin and Stalinists to quote Lenin (for instance, on the importance of free expression), might have taken strength from this passage, had he noticed it; but of course the similarity of Lenin's prescription to his is not altogether a flattering sign. Dreams, too, can be dogmatic.

Rather than overestimating the power of dreams, as the accusation of idealism might initially suggest, the surrealists underestimated this power. Because their rejection of tradition was an incorrigibly artistic gesture, they failed to recognize how it is the pleasure of dreams to demand labor. In other words, they went beyond or stopped short of seeing that their movement was not fighting "reality" or "work" but the workings of other dreams, other possibilities of representation, other interpretive movements, other pleasures; and as a result they often believed they were surpassing tradition when in fact they were simply exhibiting one of its most characteristic turnings. Meanwhile, they continued along the street, blissfully unaware of the other dreams that their own were laboring to censor, even though their experiences should have alerted them to this unsettling, abrasive work within dreams. At the very outset of the surrealist adventure, during the *temps des sommeils*, this disturbance had become evident. The stirring last words of Aragon's memoir of this period, *A Wave of Dreams*, are "Let the infinite enter"; but in this trumpeting command he seemed to forget what he himself had reported, how his friends had abandoned their early experiments with hypnotic and quasi-hypnotic trances when these walking dreamers ended up quarrelling with each other and even threatening each other with death. Yet this early turn in the history of surrealism indicated that the conflict between dreams and work, as far-reaching as it was and is, might finally be less significant than the conflicts within dreams.

To say so is not to throw blood on the clothes of this movement. The conclusion I am coming to here was given by the surrealists themselves, even if the rhetoric that set them loose on their wanderings also drew them into passages from which they could not exit with their *disponibilité* intact. In Ernst's *Oedipus Rex*, for example, this is the lesson to which our attention is drawn precisely, sadistically, by the absence of any sign of suffering: the lesson that dreams bleed, draw blood, really work.

8

Thinking Things

Amazingly, de Chirico has managed to paint new *landscapes. We know all their elements and organization, these places are* externally *similar to existent places, and yet we have* never *seen them. These banal mannequins did not exist before him. We are in a world previously unthought, unthinkable.*

PAUL ELUARD, "Ancient First Views"[1]

Imagine that Descartes's evil genius showed up as one of the students in a literature class. (Although I cannot speak for all teachers, I doubt that even the most good-humored will find this event very difficult to picture.) And let us say that the evil of this student first manifests itself during a discussion of a passage from Shakespeare. The teacher, who speaks of the interrelation of natural, social, and metaphysical hierarchies, is nonplussed when the student insists that a speech about "degree" must be concerned with levels of temperature. As far as this student is concerned, the teacher's reading makes no sense. Like Ozzie in Philip Roth's "The Conversion of the Jews," he just does not get it; and the relentless persistence with which he asserts his own reading utterly confounds the teacher.

The teacher would like to say that this student's reading is absurd. The teacher would like to call the student a fool and then, when the student asks why he is foolish, tell him what Thersites tells Patroclus: "Make that demand of the Creator; it suffices me thou art" (2.3.66–67).[2] But remember, this is not just any student, not the ordinary evildoer. This student is a genius. He is at once an intangible spirit and a masterly presence because he maintains his comportment as a student and yet refuses to enter into the axioms of the classroom. Because he cannot be addressed within the established terms of the teacher's authority, his absurdity appears as a reflection on that authority. Descartes warned of this danger when he advised that a man "who makes it his aim to raise his knowledge above the common should be ashamed to derive the occasion for doubting from the forms of speech invented by the vulgar."[3] A teacher who gets mixed up with a student such as this one is in for big trouble.

The teacher may insist, again and again, that this student's reading is obviously wrong, but with every reiteration the teacher's own reading will appear less obvious. Authority depends on what Roland Barthes called "a certain speed of delivery."[4] It depends on an implicit economy of discourse, and anyone who breaks with this economy raises the threat that all discourse will appear as logorrhea. Paradoxically, the more the teacher does in trying to convince the student of the need to accept some basic assumptions, the more baseless those assumptions may appear. Even if the class were reading a contemporary text, the situation would be no different. As Ludwig Wittgenstein put it, "And here the strange thing is that when I am quite certain of how words are used, have no doubt about it, I still can give no *grounds* for my way of going on. If I tried I could give a thousand, but none as certain as the very thing they were supposed to be grounds for."[5]

Question degree, Shakespeare's Ulysses says, and before you know it, everything imaginable, "what is or is not," will serve as "stuff . . . to make paradoxes" (1.3.183–84). If what is said meddles too much with what goes unsaid, with that which is taken for granted, nothing can be taken for granted any longer. Precisely to the extent that we claim that our assumptions are legitimate, discourse in favor of them is likely to appear suspicious: unmotivated, excessive, redundant, and, in general, meaningless. In Wittgenstein's words, "The queer thing is that even though I find it quite correct for someone to say 'Nonsense!' [*Unsinn*] and so brush aside the attempt to confuse him with doubts at bedrock, — nevertheless, I hold it to be incorrect if he seeks to defend himself (using, e.g., the words 'I know')" (*OC*, 65e).

Thought that ventures too far into itself seems bound to lose itself. To convey any authority, it must restrain itself from itself. Hence the nice rhetorical problem that Wittgenstein's forerunner confronted in his *Meditations*: to prove the existence of God, he had to doubt this existence and yet to insist that he was not doubting it at all. One of the exclamations in *Troilus and Cressida* seems designed for the fix in which Descartes found himself: "O madness of discourse / That cause sets up with and against itself: / Bifold authority, where reason can revolt / Without perdition, and loss assume all reason / Without revolt" (5.2.140–44).

Descartes had to establish doubt in order to produce a reasoned discourse, and yet he had to confine this doubt within this discourse if he were not to be accused of fomenting the very unbelief he was setting out to counter. In this maddening situation, his strategy for maintaining his sanity was to distinguish knowledge from social practices: "For I am assured that there can be neither peril nor error in this course, and that I cannot at present yield too much to distrust, since I am not considering the question of action, but only of knowledge" (*MFP*, 148). He created this distinction by representing himself, at the beginning of the *Meditations*, as a lone mind sequestered from all the world: "To-day . . . very opportunely for the plan I have in view I have delivered my mind from every care . . . and . . . I have procured for myself an assured leisure in a peaceable retirement" (*MFP*, 144).

Thus, as with his examples of dreams, madness, supernatural malignity, and perceptual ambiguity, Descartes suggested that authority is sure only in imagination. In isolated consciousness as in the visions of sleep, the actions of passion, or the behavior of people who believe their heads are pumpkins and their bodies are made of glass, knowledge is certain but imaginary; utterly convincing but impossible to articulate with any universality; true for the individual subject, meaningless for the world.

Of course, Descartes tried to differentiate consciousness from the possibilities of disagreement and error canvassed in his analysis. The whole purpose of the *Meditations* was to establish "the just limits of truth" (*MFP*, 154). However, to do so he had to separate not only himself but also his writings from the world. The first and last sentences of the *Meditations* remind us that the necessity of acting in the world does not leave us time for the sure understanding he has sought. And then, as his reference to vulgarity indicates, language itself is a problem: "[F]or although without giving expression to my thoughts I consider this in my own mind, words often impede me and I am almost deceived by the terms of ordinary language" (*MFP*, 155). It may seem that the only place where authority can be sure is beyond discourse . . . if such a place is imaginable.

Even as Descartes tried to bring authority within discourse by proving the existence of God, his dedication of this work to the "Deans and Doctors of the Sacred Faculty of Theology in Paris" admitted that words are not necessarily an accurate index to the truth they are meant to represent; and this admission was not as formulaic as it might seem. Descartes, too, was troubled by the malignant students that he could imagine on the other end of his discourse. In fact, his *genium malignum* could be said to represent the countertutelage of language itself, which Descartes feared would transform him from its master to its servant as a result of the conflicts inherent in social relations. In such conflicts language could get carried away with itself, sweeping individual subjects off their feet and leaving even existence in doubt. In raising this monstrous possibility, however unwillingly, Descartes set the stage for the writings of Hegel, Marx, and other favorites of the surrealists, such as the Marquis de Sade and the Comte de Lautréamont. "Without doubt," wrote René Crevel,

> when it is a question of speech or writing, affirmation proves itself less a certitude than a desire for certitude born of some fundamental doubt. Our most sure and

most secret condition is that which is sufficient unto itself, which does not ask to express itself. On the other hand, what is unstable, unsettled, demands a proclamation; thought in motion does not desire anything more than to fix itself in a form, because this stop sign gives birth to the illusion of definitiveness, which, to our perpetual torment, we are pursuing.[6]

Although Descartes sought to avoid this conclusion through the analysis that led to his famous proposition of identity, he recognized that this philosophical labor served only to displace the problem of language. This recognition is evident in the way he worried over the problem of converting infidels, the many who cannot reason with enough concentration to appreciate philosophical authority on its own grounds, and then the many among students of philosophy who are spurred on by egoism and so will dispute even the most important truths. Having admitted to this worry in the dedication to his work, Descartes doubted that his writing would have its desired effect unless it was aided by the "patronage" of the Sacred Faculty ("*nisi me patrocinio vestro adjuvetis*"). Because "the name of SORBONNE" had "so much authority" ("*tantaeque sit auctoritatus SORBONAE nomen*"), he concluded that the "public testimony" of its members might give his work the support it could not bear within itself.

Along with this conclusion, Descartes did say that *veritas* alone was sufficient to bring wise men to agree with his writing, thereby suggesting that discourse can be transparent to truth. However, even in this case Descartes gave rhetorical priority to the support of institutions. Wise men, he said, would "subscribe" to the judgment of the deans and doctors (*MFP*, 48) and so ratify a foregone conclusion. Here, too, it seems that philosophical agreement would not be forthcoming if it were not for the worldly force that this text at once rejects and requests.

Of course, this dedication to the *Meditations* may be judged to be a pragmatic gesture. Descartes had before him the example of Galileo's condemnation by the Inquisition, and despite his cautions his own work was controversial and eventually was placed on the Index. However, this consideration simply reinforces the point that certainty exists only in imagination. This reading of the *Meditations* and its historical fate teach us the same lesson: that the difference between *veritas* and *auctoritas* disturbs the rational argument of this text, murmuring that the world is irreducible to consciousness, discourse irreducible to logical truth, social reality irreducible to philosophical rhetoric. Consequently, like Ionesco's distraught professor in *The Lesson*, who is told that "philology leads to abomination,"[7] Descartes in the *Meditations* finds that linguistic vulgarity is not as easily shunned as one might wish. His words seem to revolt against him. The demand for the exile of philosophy is contradicted by the worldly aid, the institutional supports of the *gentilhomme*, necessary to satisfy this demand. The result, once again in Wittgenstein's words: "At the end of reasons comes *persuasion*. (Think what happens when missionaries convert natives)" (*OC*, 81e). Or, as he suggests elsewhere, think what happens when teachers convey knowledge to students.

It is more than logical, then, that the beginning of *The Peasant of Paris* finds Louis Aragon invoking "the famous Cartesian doctrine of evidence" and criticizing "the ravages of that illusion." Who can fail to realize, Aragon asks, that error "is accompanied by certitude. Error imposes itself through evidence. And everything we say of truth, we may as well say of error: we will not be fooling ourselves any more."[8] Although Aragon's style in this work is very different from Edmund Husserl's in his *Crisis of European Sciences and Transcendental Phenomenology*, his criticism resembles Husserl's argument that the very ideas "which were supposed to ground [Descartes's] rationalism as *aeterna veritas* bear within themselves a *deeply hidden sense*, which, once brought to the surface, completely uproots it." According to Husserl, Descartes was undone, "as if following a hidden teleology of history," by his own words—by the "hidden absurdity" of his own rationalism.[9] While not going to Aragon's length of denying the possibility of any absolute philosophical conviction, Husserl did recognize a quality of hallucinatory doubleness in Descartes's writing, a quality that might well be called surreal, in accordance with Salvador Dali's paranoiac-critical approach to things.

Given this perspective, it may not seem so strange to use Descartes's characterization of man as a thinking thing, *res cogitans*, to describe the surrealist mannequin. Although the one was conceived to be a spirit of rationality, a creature of God, and the other an image of irrationality and thus a revolutionary figure, the motivation for the surrealist thing was already at work in the disturbances of Descartes's text. The difference is a slight (and yet tremendous) matter of emphasis or force.[10] Whereas Descartes's man was a *thinking* thing, the surrealists' mannequin was a thinking *thing*. Or one might say (with a tip of the mannequin's hat to Martin Heidegger) that the surrealist figure was a *thinging thing*: a representation of thought as the being of things (letters, images, objects, bodies of any sort) leading on to other things. "What will the aim of future painting be?" asked Giorgio de Chirico in a manuscript written in the era of his "metaphysical" painting. "The same as that of poetry, music and philosophy," he answered, " . . . to see everything, even man, in its quality as *thing*. This is the Nietzschean method."[11]

The surrealists could and did still speak of the human spirit, and they could even use images reminiscent of Descartes's, in which spirit struggles to emerge from the weltering confusion of the world, yearns to exhibit its absolute truth, and frequently is frustrated by the vulgar crowd; but with this slight difference in emphasis, from man to mannequin, the spirit could no longer enjoy its exile. No longer could man be flattered to show off his obedience "when he is only a mannequin," as Nietzsche had put it.[12] The human spirit had to face the necessity, even the attraction, of the evil genius that contraverted its dignity.

If the surrealist desire for a dialectical overcoming of contradictions could often seem facile — "Everything leads us to believe that there exists a certain point of the spirit where life and death, the real and the imaginary, the past and the future, the communicable and the incommunicable, the high and the low cease to be perceived contradictorily" (Breton)[13] — it could also be a forceful way of bringing into relief the desires, worries, anxieties, compromises, and contradictions in things that would otherwise be silenced by the historical stratagems of reason. As opposed to Descartes in his statement, "I must be careful to see that I do not imprudently take some other object in place of myself" (*MFP*, 150), the surrealists deliberately sought to confuse themselves with objects, hoping thereby to force subjectivity to illuminate its hidden connections with the things of this world. "This object is not an image but the supreme game of truth," said Georges Hugnet in an article on the art of Oscar Dominguez.[14]

The focus on the object within the surrealist movement became especially evident in the 1930s, influenced in part by Dali's contributions and by a better acquaintance among the surrealists with the writings of Sigmund Freud. André Breton summarized this direction in a 1935 address to a conference in Prague, "The Surrealist Situation of the Object"; but this marked more of a clarification than a new direction in surrealism. From the beginning, those involved in this movement had understood that the modern world could be defined in terms of a crisis of the object. Perhaps this had been most dramatically played out in cubism, which often was seen as exemplifying this crisis in the early years of this century; but a host of other movements and quasi-movements, including constructivism, futurism, dada, phenomenology, psychoanalysis, and Einsteinian relativity, struggled for their own definition in terms of a new conception of objects. The distinctiveness of surrealism does not lie in this "point of interest," as Breton termed it,[15] but in the determination to use it as a point of revolt against the ensemble of forces (logic, morality, aesthetics, patriotism, militarism, and so on) that it saw as the nightmarish delusions of awakened reason. The surrealist thing was meant to differ not only from commodities and the things of classical physics, but also from all things collected by that immense gravitational pull toward repetition, toward the *recognizable*, that forms cultural classifications in general; it was against this that the movement of surrealism strove to develop its own gravitational pull. If only reason could be put to sleep, as in the seances of the surrealists' *temps des sommeils*, so that humanity could return from its anxiety-ridden, duplicitous, embattled exile from the true world, what then?

As Eluard's description of Giorgio de Chirico's work indicates, an early and continuing figure for the exploration of this question was furnished by the mannequin. A mannequin dangled from the ceiling of the surrealists' "Bureau of Researches"; André Masson's *Mannequin* stood out among the figures decorated by various hands in a corridor at the 1938 International

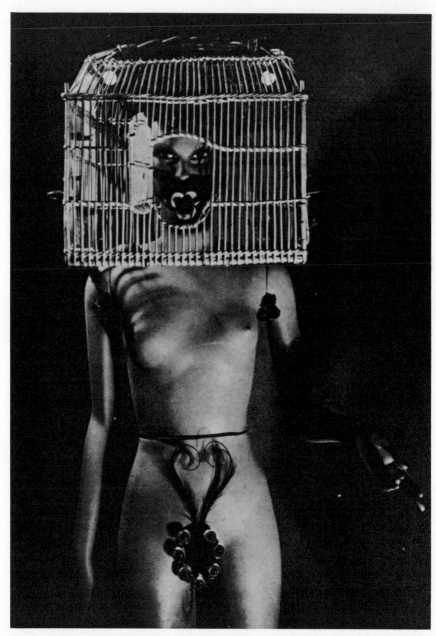

André Masson, *Mannequin* (1938; no longer in existence)
Copyright 1990 ARS N.Y./SPADEM

Exhibition of Surrealism at the Galerie Beaux-Arts, each with a street sign above it (which sometimes had the names of "real" and sometimes of "imaginary" streets); Clovis Trouille, a painter of anti-clerical eroticisms admired by the group, had worked during the 1920s for a company that made mannequins; among the surrealists, these figures seemed to pop up everywhere. (Even Husserl, as if magically participating in the movement, invoked a mannequin in an example of the perceptual confusion that he wanted to explain.)[16] Here I am referring to a literal use of mannequins and similar figures (mummies, scarecrows, dolls), but I will also, and more importantly, be referring to the thinking of these things. The surrealist mannequin in some respects had nothing to do with the usual denotation of this word; rather than being a sculptural image of the human form, it was a verbal structure, an "object" in the philosophical sense, a condition of being, or something still more remote from common definition. Yet to say this is not to search out the *meaning* of the mannequin: as should become clear, the notion of meaning in logical, symbolic, or some other form was just what was mocked by this surrealist figure. In refusing to separate consciousness from action or knowledge from the world, the surrealists had to think— and allow themselves to be thought by—things. To analyze the surrealist mannequin is then to figure out what the mannequin *proposed*.

As with my treatment of the surrealist street, this approach runs the risk of being too broad or too reverent, offering too much latitude to the figure of the mannequin or to the ideological pretensions of the surrealists. This is not an extraordinary risk, for no cultural criticism can evade it, in one form or another; but still it becomes especially evident when one is dealing with a movement premised upon a rebellion against what is supposed to be the proper meaning of words and things. (Professors, objects of fervent mockery among the surrealists, must be very doltish indeed if they sense no risk in addressing this movement.) It can hardly be presumptuous, and in fact may now be trite, to argue that Descartes could not truly separate consciousness from the world, but it does not follow that any and all challenges to the authority of consciousness are valuable. Some choices are called for; and yet when criticism follows a movement like surrealism in seeing culture as more closely resembling a tumultuous storm than a system of ideas, one consequence is that research, description, interpretation, and evaluation cannot be distinguished from each other as if they were separate activities, with those that are fundamental lending support to those that are more elaborated until, in the end, one reaches the cross atop the cathedral. Criticism that refuses to reify culture encounters the same problem that rebellious movements such as surrealism are bound to face: the problem of formulating unorthodox standards of judgment that can carry some weight even in the world they oppose. It is easy to be a recalcitrant or obnoxious student, but to be a truly upsetting pupil—or by the same token, a truly convincing teacher—that does call for something like genius.

The surrealists believed in and aspired to such genius. A critic may want to be more modest, as I do, suspecting that this quality may be harder to come by than the surrealists wanted to believe; but still the communicability of critical work can never be taken for granted unless its author is satisfied to be the ghoulish soul of propriety. The risk of too generous an identification with surrealism is serious enough, but only as a comparatively trivial concomitant to a more immediate danger. This is the possibility that criticism might not even try to come close to what it addresses, fearing it to be less a patient object than a monstrous genius, a thing alive with questions and demands that might turn the critical enterprise topsy-turvy, reducing the entire institution of education to a ruin of scattered bricks and smashed icons.

The mannequin can be the focal point for considerations such as these because it served, in effect, as the surrealists' response to established authority. It was the classroom of a critical confrontation. Even as its appearance was evidence of rebellion, it retained a humanlike form and so acknowledged the need to communicate with a world still largely under the sway of this authority. It spoke of reason, humanism, and associated things, but turned away from them even as it spoke. It referred to the past while advocating its destruction; it sought the force of rational persuasion.

The mannequin was perfect for surrealist purposes because it approached the condition of abstract universality, in which it could figure as the simplest and most flexible unit of representation imaginable, and yet in its specificity lent itself to some of the concerns the surrealists found most important for articulating their rebellion in the specific historical circumstances of the 1920s and 1930s: themes of oppression, death, mechanicity, and erotic redemption. Although it proposed nothing definitive or conclusive, the mannequin did convey a general disposition of thought in relation to its worldly supports that can still offer a powerful challenge.

At its most abstract, the mannequin represented eviscerated reason, which is to say, reason without a soul or the letter without the spirit. Generally speaking, it makes no sense to ask what a mannequin is "inside" or what it "truly" is; and if the surrealists were correct in seeing reason as a masquerade of reality, then the mannequin's featureless exteriority could suggest the appearance of the world stripped of the logical disguise of consciousness. It would be what remained of the human being after humanism was emptied from its insides and so cleansed from its surface, and it would also begin to look like the figure of meaning in general. As the simplest imaginable element of any composition, it would be the key to unlock whatever was constructed around it: in pictorial terms, a dynamic element to take the place of the logical vanishing point of Renaissance perspective. It would be the signifying body (of a living creature, object, word, anything) that scatters thought in all directions, from the origins of civilization to the depths of the individual mind, with stops of varying lengths at all points in between, because it cannot be satisfied by any rhetorical restraints. This is the signifier that owes its being to unstoppable imagination, as in the line that opens one of Lautréamont's *Songs of Maldoror*: "[I]t is a man or a stone or a tree that is about to begin the fourth song."[17] This is the mannequin as an *unsettling* perspective. In sleep, wrote Breton, man is "in the very womb of that over-populated night in which all things, living beings and objects alike, are *him*, compelled to partake of his eternal being, falling with the stone, flying with the bird."[18]

In this respect, the mannequin played a role in surrealism also performed by other totemic forms, such as the harness bells that figure in many of René Magritte's paintings. With a virtuosity as stubborn as it was undramatic, this kind of form could play virtually any rhetorical part in a work: background, detail, substance, modifier, accent, verb. It could become a kind of all-purpose thing and thus, rhetorically, might seem to reveal the elemental structure of signification. ("There just had to be a face," wrote Eluard in a love poem, "that answered to all the names of the world.")[19] Such a thing then fulfilled the anti-psychologistic thrust of surrealism, demonstrating that the mind seemingly isolated by reason is actually right out there in the world, no more or less certain than its objects. The supports of Descartes's retirement become Dali's crutches: underlings moved to center stage, metonyms of an impossible transcendence of things. These objects illustrate Freud's dictum, "Thought is after all nothing but a substitute for a hallucinatory wish," by confessing their overweening ambition to be manifest and original truth.[20] In a painting such as Dali's *Javanese Mannequin* (1933–34), in which the deformed legs of the titular figure are partially supported by a crutch and in their turn support an abstracted spine, rib cage, and breastbone, this drama of supporting parts in search of an overreaching authority is spelled out with particular clarity.

When the veil of rational discourse is whisked away and naked reason shows itself as an imaginary construction, a veil in its own right, truth can no longer be the mystic form, perilous to approach, that Friedrich Schiller's "The Veiled Image at Sais" made it out to be. "And as for our future," wrote Nietzsche in allusion to this poem, "one will hardly find us again on the paths of those Egyptian youths who endanger temples by night, embrace statues, and want by all means to unveil, uncover, and put into a bright light whatever is kept concealed for good reasons." The mannequin conceals nothing, offers no hidden power, because it represents truth without holding it aside, away from the active practices and supporting institutions of the world. The mannequin is not a statue; one may decorate it with veils or other things, but the decoration does not hide its true form. "We no longer believe," wrote Nietzsche, "that truth remains truth when the veils are withdrawn."[21]

As the simplest imaginable unit of representation, the mannequin is the body that is its own veil and so is mysterious without being otherworldly. It is a body among others, a veil in a world of veils. In its impassivity and banality, the mannequin is the spectator of otherness within the spectacle of the self. It murmurs of irrational authorities that hold sway over our representations of ourselves and our world; it describes an impersonal structuring of the most intimate, individual, human things. Inanimate, it is nonetheless a stormy vortex of meaning, a snapshot of the dialectic in the moment of its transfiguration, a transcription of frozen panic or convulsive beauty, a sign of vital imagination. In the modern world, in which God is no longer seen as lending support to institutions that must themselves support the word of truthful consciousness, the veiled and motionless statue gives way to the brash and pushy mannequin, as in Antonin Artaud's "Correspondence of the Mummy":

> Have you seen the mummy fixed at the intersection of phenomena, that ignorant, that living mummy, which ignores all the frontiers of its emptiness, which scares itself with the pulsations of death?
> The voluntary mummy has arisen, and all of reality moves around it. And consciousness, like a brand of discord, crosses the entire field of its constrained virtuality.
> There is a loss of flesh in that mummy. . . .
> . . . But all this flesh is only beginnings and absences, and absences, and absences. . . . [22]

This mannequin is the imaginary resting place of an insupportable and unending show of representations. It is the word that would be obvious if such a thing as an obvious word could be salvaged from the linguistic errancy broadly described as metaphor. ("Man is a mobile tree," wrote Michel Leiris, "as much as the tree is a rooted man.")[23] This is the fantastic word or object of thought that Eluard saw as being isolated by surrealist heroes, such as de Chirico, Sade, and Lautréamont: "By their violence, Sade and Lautréamont rid solitude of everything with which it decorates itself. In this solitude, each object, each being, each awareness, each image thinks of returning to a changeless reality; of no longer having a secret to reveal; of being tranquilly, uselessly brooded over by the atmosphere that it creates."[24] If one could isolate a wine glass from the overlapping and intersecting planes of a cubist still life, this might be the wine glass that it would be; or more to the point, if one could isolate a word from the flow of automatic writing, this would be it.

Allow degree to be put into question, Ulysses warns, and "right and wrong— / Between whose endless jar justice resides, — / Should lose their names, and so should justice too" (1.3.116–18). This at least seems the inevitable consequence to those who idealize authority, as Ulysses craftily recognizes; but the surrealists came to a different conclusion. If objects, images, and even isolated words were given their head, as it were, the ensuing revolution might be the best way to learn what justice is and is not. When considering the world that subscribed to reason in the aftermath of the First World War, the concern to maintain order and hierarchy seemed laughable at best. "The crocodiles of the present day are no longer crocodiles," Eluard and Max Ernst lamented, playing the part of nostalgic senior citizens. "Where are those good old adventurers who snagged you in the nostrils of minuscule bicycles and pretty glass earrings?" Like the mannequin, their poem mimicked the appearance of humanity, of "meaning," even as it forced this figure out of its imaginary retirement so that it had to reveal that it secreted no truth: that its structure was that of a signifying body among others, to be called upon for a joke, a laugh, why not? "There are no more true watercycles, microscopics, bacteriology. My word, the crocodiles of the present day are no longer crocodiles."[25] For all its fancifulness, the humor is really quite unforgiving, quite vicious.

Yet the mannequin had more than one expression to display. In conveying the effect of bodies in a world of swirling social activity, the mannequin was bound to play multiple and ambivalent roles, depending on one's imaginary position in relation to it. When it was addressed from the position of a frustrated rebellion against reason—the viewpoint of a disillusioned pupil—it would carry a sense of oppressiveness. It would be a *cadavre* not at all *exquis*, a reduction of the human to undistinguished form and pointless function, a vision of humanity displaying its alienation much as convicts in striped suits wore the image of their imprisonment. Then it showed reason to be in truth "cold and hostile unreason, the same ceremonial exterior under which there suddenly appears the survival of the sign beyond the thing signified." When writing from this position of disillusionment, in which one attacks a thing with the weapon of its own ideal, Breton could sound virtually identical to the Ulysses of *Troilus and Cressida*: "All intellectual values are harried, all moral ideas routed, all the benefits of life stricken with corruption, indiscernible. . . . What is designated by the word 'homeland,' or the word 'justice,' or the word 'duty' has become foreign to us."[26] This position yielded the most conventional and, one might say, the most adolescent of surrealist worlds. In this world God was "the Great Exterior Object" (Lautréamont), and even forces that might be liberating, such as psychoanalysis, were so swayed by authority that they threatened to turn their discoveries into "a uniform for an abstract mannequin."[27] A pioneering version of the mannequin appropriate to this vision of the world was the dummy designated to represent the accused, Maurice Barrès, in a trial organized in 1921 by Breton and a number of other dadaists. (Barrès was a writer who metamorphosed into a propagandist of French chauvinism after a seemingly rebellious beginning, during which he had greatly influenced Breton and Aragon, among others.)

When viewed in this way, the mannequin at its most extreme was a figure of death. In this form it allowed the surrealists to use their perception of oppression to try to get beyond the dead weight of the ideal. A surrealist then might take a position that would force teachers to show their hand or missionaries to admit their violence, thereby destroying their own credibility. This confrontation might still have an adolescent tone, something like the snickering atmosphere around Dean Stockwell when he frustrates the dignified professor of law in Orson Welles's *Compulsion*; but this viewpoint could lead to a more open-ended, thinking rebellion.

In the last line of *Artine*, René Char announced, "The poet has killed his model";[28] and when regarded from this position of extreme alienation, the mannequin could signal the obsequies of the very notion of the model. As the surrealists saw it, this notion always returned to a humanism that put the world into a condition of rigor mortis, petrifying its movement in the name of forms that pretended to represent the appearance of things while actually revealing nothing but the bourgeoisie's deathly self-image. This judgment was their version of Hegel's conclusion that in the modern world of reflection, rationality, and civil law, "art, considered in its highest vocation, is and remains for us a thing of the past."[29] In such a world, they would see the human body of the mannequin as the sarcophagus of objectivity, as in Magritte's *At the Beautiful End of an Afternoon* (1964), in which two coffins sit companionably on a stone wall overlooking a saccharine vista of mountains and fluffy clouds. Or as in Breton's favorite image for the false fronts of consciousness, the mannequin would be a scarecrow: an entirely defensive form and, therefore, an empty threat against the world. This scarecrow was prominent, for instance, on the cover of the second issue of *The Surrealist Revolution*.

By representing death, the mannequin would show how authority could insinuate itself into forms far beyond the obvious figures of the teacher or master. What seemed most personal to individuals, their bodies, could carry this death, as could the most abstract figures of speech. In fact, this deathly mannequin could even be metaphor itself, insofar as the conception of metaphor still hearkened to the categorical distinction between interiority and exteriority and so honored the model of humanism. So Crevel boasted that surrealist objects, like surrealist film, had "reanimated, *concretely*, without metaphor, the cadavers of things."[30]

If this revitalization were imaginable, then the mannequin could appear liberating where it had seemed the very image of oppression. It could signify the enigmatic origin of all objects in the perceptions of the human body and, more specifically, in the body of the individual subject, which Freud described as the first object of libidinal attachment. Imagine autoeroticism turning into symbolic identification, allowing subjectivity to be articulated against objectivity and vice versa, and the human body could appear as the site on which the labor of negativity etched culture from formless being. In creating all things, starting from and including the form of the body, this negativity would go unrecognized in the resultant culture insofar as the culture valued established perceptions or models over the polymorphous possibilities of bodies; but one did not necessarily have to accept these coffins. When Aragon ended *The Peasant of Paris* by ordering, "Push the idea of the destruction of persons to its extreme limit, and go beyond that,"[31] what he called "destruction" signified this potential for creativity. If art was dead for those who subscribed to the authority of the deans and directors of the bourgeois world, it could still be alive for others; and so the mannequin, as a lifeless, cadaverous, or coffin-like form, could also figure in surrealism as an exuberant revolt against the lifelessness of institutionalized cultural signs. This is the situation figured in Aragon's conclusion to "Leaden Sleep," in which he recounts an adventure in "the subterranean country of the dream":

My body I call your name that mouths have lost since the creation
of the world
My body my body it's a red dance it's a mausoleum a pigeon shoot a
geyser
Nevermore will I drag this young man from the arms of the
forests.[32]

And the mannequin could draw still other things into its vortex of ideation. If the body-as-mannequin resembled a dead letter, a coffin, or a corpse, it also resembled (and here is perhaps its most precise modern description) a machine. In its featureless, mindless, passive utility, the mannequin could easily become an image of mechanicity, and the oppressiveness of this image could also be liberating. Rather than being opposed to the spirit of humanism, in accordance with conventional wisdom, this mechanicity might represent it only too well. It might be a persuasive image of the absurd and hallucinatory certainty that made this spirit work in an automatic way. In its mechanical aspect, the mannequin would then appear as description, criticism, rebellion, and outrageous release all at once.

In writing of the films of Charlie Chaplin ("Charlot" to French fans), Aragon captured this potential of the mannequin: "With the discovery of mechanicity and its laws, which haunt the heroes to such a point that an inversion of values turns every inanimate object into a living creature, every human person into a mannequin whose crank we must seek, decor is the very vision of the world for Charlot."[33] Here the mannequin is Descartes's man translated into the world of things, of "decor," which the effects of industrialization dramatically brought to the attention of a resistant consciousness that had wanted to think itself essentially independent of such things. Industrialization, of course, was just a catalyst in this drama; as Breton suggested, it was not industrialization as such that was the concern so much as it was the "mania for control" that it represented, with all the attendant values that the surrealists saw as logically culminating in war.[34]

Yet the surrealists did not conclude, as did Filippo Marinetti, that war must perforce be the modern beauty. They did not stop thinking at this point of potential fixation. For them the mannequin was beautiful but also disturbing. In Breton's famous phrase, it was "convulsive beauty."[35] In de Chirico's works and elsewhere, it marked the point at which human and mechanical images coincided, but it did so without adopting the emotions of romantic despair, bourgeois equanimity, or futurist celebration. Instead, it insisted on the enigmatic quality of this conjuncture and thus marked recognition, resistance, and revolt at the same time. In other words, the mannequin served as a tactic, the dreamlike tactic of a formal denial of understanding to insistently familiar images. Placed in situations where one would ordinarily expect to find living people or images of people, the mannequin was imperturbable, acting as if nothing was wrong, nothing out of place. It took for granted that a revolt had already occurred, was already in place, and that it was only stupid resistance — the resistance of reason to perception — that could keep one from appreciating this surreality.

In this respect, the mannequin was akin to the surrealists themselves in their role as machines, or "recording apparatuses," when they engaged in automatic dictation, writing, or drawing.[36] Even as it bore the disturbing face of an anonymous, dehumanized compulsion, the very admission of the image of mechanicity would signal a lifting of repression. This conclusion might seem paradoxical, given the romantic tradition that associated freedom with nature and alienation with machines; but Friedrich Nietzsche, as well as Freud, had helped to clear up this point. "We like to be out in nature so much," Nietzsche noted with acerbity, "because it has no opinion about us."[37] In this respect, nature is a comforting image of transcendence; in contrast, the mechanical aspect of the mannequin proclaimed the power of creative values (or veil use) over any such stopping point. Here, again, the very ambivalence of the mannequin could become a positive value for the surrealists, because it enacted as well as described the derangement of reason.

This positive connotation was further strengthened by Freud's argument that complicated machinery and apparatuses in dreams represent the genitals, especially of the male.[38] By embodying a sense of mechanicity, the mannequin could also suggest sexuality (as opposed to sentimental romance) just as it suggested death (as opposed to humanist spirit). (Nietzsche had given a hint on this point, too, when he wondered if the name of truth was not the name of the female genitals.)[39] Precisely because it was so unmoving and so alien to human emotions, the mannequin could speak of unconscious instinct in a way that disturbed the image of conscious decision and vocation. It would suggest the living organic body *because* it was so mechanical, so clearly a physical thing. De Chirico, Breton said, "does not suppose that a ghost could introduce itself otherwise than through the door";[40] and the mechanical nature of the mannequin, like the otherworldly nature of the ghost, emphasized human vitality by its contradiction, as in the grammar of the dreams Freud analyzed. Because it was disturbed and disturbing, the mannequin would insist on its definition, unlike the humanism "that takes a vague thought for a free thought" (Crevel).[41]

In this sexual aspect, the surrealist mannequin recalled the characters in Sade's writings, who are equally featureless (even with his standard notation of age, hair, color, and form) and equally open to any imaginable manipulation. This is the mannequin as La Mettrie's "man-machine," which finds no contradiction between vitality and mechanicity, discovering instead that the image of the machine brings out a fantastic power in humanity before which the traditional image of the spirit seems a very pallid thing. It was not La Mettrie's materialist philosophy that was at issue in the mannequin but rather the way this philosopher thought with things or, perhaps, was thought by things, led on by signifying bodies, of which the most prominent was the machine. La Mettrie not only influenced Sade, who influenced the surrealists, but also came up with sentences that these latter might well have envied:

To be a machine, to sense, to think, to know how to distinguish good from evil, as blue from red—in a word, to be born with the intelligence and the certain instinct for morality, yet to be only an animal—are things that are no more contradictory than to be a monkey or a parrot and know how to enjoy oneself. Because (as long as the occasion presents itself for saying it) who would ever have divined *a priori* that a drop of the fluid that shoots out during mating should have the effect of such divine pleasures and that from it should be born a tiny creature, who would be able one day, given certain laws, to enjoy the same delights?

As a sexual figure, as in its abstract, oppressive, deathly, and mechanical aspects, the mannequin opens a perspective within reason that no element of reason can endure unchanged. With its eyelessness (as in de Chirico's tailor's dummies) or with its blank stare, it bespeaks a vision of things inaccessible to and yet comprised within the classical surface of reason. Try to imagine that gaze, and reason comes to strange conclusions, as in the troubled perspectives of de Chirico's paintings, or as in the way La Mettrie, in a work of enlightened reason originally published in 1748, could anticipate the irrational drift of a surrealist such as Leiris: "Here are the hairs that cover the summit of our heads, there are leaves and flowers; throughout all shines the same luxury of Nature. . . . Perhaps there are even animal-plants."[42]

If simple oppressiveness was at one end of the mannequin's roles—or one might say, of its thinking—at the other end was redemption. For the surrealists, the difference did not measure a Hegelian trajectory so much as it did an expanse of representational possibility or an arc of creative potential. Hegel was an important influence on their movement, but they read him as a poet of transformative attitudes and actions, not as a logician or (perish the thought) a Christian theologian. For surrealism, redemption was not the end of the dialectic. It was not the end of anything. It was available, immediate, at hand, in the eros of the mannequin.

In surrealist works, woman under any other name is this redemptive mannequin. The identification is clear enough in the dolls that Hans Bellmer
made in the 1930s, which posed for a series of photographs that displayed
their capacity for an unhinged, polymorphic, sadomasochistic perversity; but
it was also evident where the image and label of the mannequin as such went
unsaid, as in Eluard's prose poem, "Sleep":

> This girl that I discover in going to sleep, like a black star in the oblivion of the
> day, knows of herself only what I miss in myself. Her extremely gentle flesh
> responds to the pleasure she takes in my caresses but responds only from the
> height of her virtue. Neither wins, nor loses, nor is risked, nor is certain. No
> longer is the will a mask one lifts or eyes that open. She neither asks me to abdicate
> nor to maintain my place. I am delivered, truly delivered over to the reality of a
> mirror that does not reflect my appearance. Delivered over to her desires. I imag-
> ine myself the prey. Without yesterday or tomorrow. The pure visage is renewed.[43]

In this work as elsewhere in surrealism, the mannequin is a dream girl. It is
then the antithesis or the deliverance of the alienated mannequin that serves
as a fashion model. As Eluard's syntax and images suggest, this figure is
conceived in negativity and passivity and yet is powerfully active and fulfilling. It is muse to its own creation, as if consciousness no longer suffered the
slightest exile from the world. It is the surrealists' version of philosophy in
the boudoir: the erotic veil, the erotic thrill, which captures the transformative vitality of the dialectic. It is humanity as pure creativity, bound by
no established appearance. A dream girl, a magic glass, an overpowering
mannequin.

Or, often, a prostitute. The surrealists evinced a fascination for prostitutes
(as in Breton's *Nadja* or Philippe Soupault's *The Last Nights of Paris*) because, like the mannequin, they seemed at once completely artificial and
profoundly human. It is no accident, perhaps, that the Café Cyrano, a
favorite meeting-place on the Rue Fontaine, also numbered among its regu-
lars a goodly contingent of streetwalkers. Mechanical in her banal routine,
the prostitute was creative in her vivid opposition to the behavior normally
expected of women. She was faceless, since she could always be equated to
the abstract figure of a sum of money, but all the more touchingly individual
when one approached her on some other basis. From the perspective of
society, she was violated, but from the upsetting vantage point that she took
up in relation to respectable appearances, she was revolutionary. She was
"cheap," as mannequins of plaster or wood seemed cheap in comparison to
the human body; and yet, like these mannequins, she might prove to have a
value off the scale of humanity. At least the prostitute was all these things
for the surrealists, to whom this figure seemed ready-made to convey their
thinking. "Old whores," wrote Aragon in his description of the Passage de
l'Opéra, "centerpieces, mechanical mummies, I am so glad that you figure in

the habitual decor, because you are still living gleams of light in comparison to those housewives that one meets in public walkways."[44]

Although Aragon's whores, parading along an obscure street, may seem as distant as they could possibly be from the delicate creature of Eluard's narcissistic dreams, this apparent difference is swept away when one recognizes them both as mannequins. The surrealist mannequin was designed to do away with just such differences, as no one recognized better than Crevel when he wrote "The Great Mannequin Seeks and Finds Its Skin." This essay appeared in *Minotaure*, the journal that became a home to the surrealists after 1933, when *Surrealism in the Service of the Revolution* foundered.[45] (*Minotaure* also published photographs of Bellmer's dolls, among other things; it was through this publication that they came to the surrealists' attention.) The orgasmic "Great Mannequin" that Crevel exalted is a ubiquitous, godlike figure, hermaphroditic but markedly feminine, distinguished by her fantastic actions and transfigurations. Her antennae and dreams, according to Crevel, "are going to conduct her to the very secret of man." Her body is so perfect "that she does not always bother to carry with her, in her peregrinations, a head, arms, legs." This passage is characteristic:

She leaps over the traps and ferocities of irony. As if for a sinister carnival, they have made a travesty of her, imprisoned her in old hand-me-downs. And here she is nonetheless, free, at once witness and mistress of a time: mirror whose reflections will illuminate days to come, cluster of gleams already opening into tragic, decisive, exacting thoughts. Thus, always, from the most quotidian opacities, she shoots herself forth, bouquet of specifications, geyser of anger, flames of futurity, sun whose sulphurous fist lacerates, strangles, the lepers of sentimental dawns. But in violence she is still gentle, the Great Mannequin. . . . [46]

As the surrealists would have it, the mannequin is not a representation, in the ordinary sense of the word, not a tool or vehicle or expression of thought, but a thinking thing (which is also to say, a thinking of things). It is an action and an event. To use one of the words that the surrealists carried over from the idiom of dada, it is not a representation but a manifestation: the acting out of the polymorphous, spasmodic, uncertain truth of things, human and otherwise. It tells of a world in which there are masters and slaves, victimizers and victims, uncountable experiences, from the most tender to the unimaginably violent — but no teachers, no pupils. Just thinking, things.

Of course, the surrealists did not pull this figure of the mannequin out of thin air. To a great extent, it was an interrogation or reworking of various sources, of which dada was the most proximate. Surrealist mannequins, such as those that lined the entranceway to the Paris exhibition of 1938, recalled ancestors in the dada manifestations in Zurich some twenty years earlier. Mannequins make repeated appearances in Tristan Tzara's *Mister Aa the Antiphilosopher* and in other writings by participants in this movement whence surrealism came. For instance, in Aragon's "The Young Lady of

Principle," the protagonist makes use of a doll to clarify the absurdity of the young lady's world. Surrealist mannequins are also related to the mechano-morphic figures in Francis Picabia's work during the period of dada. Elements of Marcel Duchamp's art, especially the abstracted figures in *The Bride Laid Bare by Her Bachelors, Even* (1915–1923), were important in this regard; and it is not going too far to see another influence in the skeletal grill or armature typical of the surfaces of analytical cubism, which was so stimulating to writers like Guillaume Apollinaire and Breton a decade or so before surrealism got off the ground.

Beyond dada were still other precedents. How far back should one go? After all, the figure of the mannequin led surrealism back into the entire history of figuration, for it mocked (in both the older and newer senses of that word) humanity, the very image and concept of the human in distinction from the rest of creation. Anticipations of the surrealist mannequin, then, are everywhere. For example, I have no reason to believe that any of the surrealists were aware of the seventeenth-century philosopher, Giovanni Pietro Bellori; and yet his argument about art and history could be taken to prefigure the surrealist treatment of the mannequin. Bellori argued that Homer was deceptive in his portrayal of the Trojan war; no real live woman, Bellori was confident, could possibly inspire an event of this magnitude. He concluded that the true cause of the hostilities must have been the theft of a beautiful statue, since art alone could have such power; and if this historical revision was not surrealist, what is?[47]

More immediately, Apollinaire, Raymond Roussel, and Alfred Jarry were among the avant-garde figures in whom Breton and others took an early interest, and each produced works that might well have helped to stimulate the surrealist interest in the mannequin. In Apollinaire's "The House of the Dead," the revenants who walk the streets of Munich are described as mannequins. Roussel's *Impressions of Africa*, replete with artistic contraptions that seem born of an unthinkable mating of Franz Kafka and Rube Goldberg, also suggests the effects of death-in-life and life-in-art that were explored through the surrealist figure. The distortion of the Pygmalion theme in Jarry's tale of an outrageously virile, superlatively mechanical "supermale," who could not fall in love with a woman until she appeared to be a corpse killed by his lovemaking, was also a precedent. Comparisons can also be made to Villiers de l'Isle-Adam's *The Future Eve*, in which Thomas Edison goes his invention of the phonograph one better by constructing a woman with a perfect mechanical body and the soul of an angel; to Wilhelm Jensen's *Gradiva*, to which Freud devoted a study; to the paintings of skeletons and masks that James Ensor produced in the 1880s and 1890s; and to E. T. A. Hoffmann's "The Sandman."

This last work (to which Freud also turned his attention, in his essay, "The Uncanny") is especially close to the preoccupations that the surrealists embodied in their mannequins. Hoffman's tale features human beings transformed into disarticulated wooden dolls along with a doll that successfully passes for an adorable human being, inspiring love in a young student named Nathanael. The general issue of representation is never far from the surface of the story, which toys with the consideration that all living people, like all characters in literature and art, are perhaps at best quasi-human. Perhaps, says the narrator to the reader, "you will come to believe that real life is more singular and more fantastic than anything else, and that all a writer can really do is present it 'in a glass, darkly.'"[48]

And of course the twists and turns of the surrealist mannequin also had sources outside of literature and art, as these domains are usually defined. Insofar as it suggested a certain impersonality, alienation, and weird stiffening in the human form, it might recall the symptoms of hysteria, in which the surrealists, influenced by Freud and others, took a great interest. (Philippe Soupault has noted the influence of Pierre Janet's *Psychological Automatism* on the beginnings of surrealism,[49] and in *The Immaculate Conception* Breton and Eluard sought to mimic aberrant behavior as it was classified by contemporary psychologists.) Through all the foregoing allusions, one could also see the surrealist mannequin as implicitly equating children's dolls and tribal objects with all other objects of human creativity, from vulgar Punch and Judies to the highest works of art, including that most fantastic invention, humanity itself, which in a sense is the bewitching model of all models. A model, this humanity, whose impressiveness is revealed in the same mannequin that shows the need to surpass it: "To escape, as far as possible, this type of humanity from which we all arise, that is all that seems worth the least bit of trouble to me" (Breton).[50]

Oskar Kokoschka was also, at least indirectly, indebted to Hoffmann. Together with Jacques Offenbach's *Tales of Hoffmann* and Max Reinhardt's Berlin production of *The Sandman*, Kokoschka's work influenced what Bellmer did with dolls in the 1930s and had been recognized during the 1920s, at least in passing, as being worthy of surrealist attention.[51] In terms of the surrealist mannequin, however, Kokoschka's tenuous connection to the movement and the inspiration he gave to Bellmer are less important than the comparison yielded by the drama he created for himself with his notorious project for the construction of a doll that would be his "fantasy princess" (247), "idol" (251), "goddess," "fetish," and "beloved" (252).[52] A well-known dollmaker, Hermine Moos, created this thing for him by following the directions he sent her in a series of letters; and although I know of no evidence or likelihood that the surrealists ever had access to this correspondence, what remains of it, as preserved in Paul Westheim's *Confessions of Artists*, raises crucial questions for thinking of the surrealist movement.

What Kokoschka had in mind was a life-sized figure of a woman such as the world had never before seen — and perhaps something still more ambitious, something like the figuration of an entire society:

If you solve this problem happily, mimic for me such a witchcraft that I'll believe, from the appearance and touch of the woman, that my idea has been brought to life, dear Miss M[oos], then I'll thank your inventiveness and your womanly nerves for what you'll have been able to capture from our vague discussions.

I believe that there will yet be a need for you to make a whole series of figures to keep my heroine company. (244)

If not absolutely annoying, Kokoschka's instructions were extremely demanding, although his demands were often couched in the form of solicitation and flattery. He writes of "this wish-creature," which Moos "will certainly make so that it will swindle all the senses" in order that he may reach his goal "of being deluded" (245). He tells the dollmaker "to turn all [her] patience and sensuality into reality" (245), and he does not neglect to tell her how to work this witchcraft:

I'm concerned with an experience that I must embrace! If you're unclear about the directions here and there, as to how a muscle, a tension, or a bone fits in, it's better not to examine an atlas but instead, with your hand on your own body, to investigate the place that you must move until you are clear about the warm and living feeling of it. Often hands and fingertips see more than eyes. (246)

As the correspondence continues, accompanied by sketches and pictures, Kokoschka's letters come to mix poetic with practical concerns in a way that must be quoted at length to convey the effect:

As far as the head is concerned, the expression is very, very noteworthy and above all should not be strengthened, but as far as possible all traces of design and of artisanship should disappear! Is the mouth to be capable of opening? And will there be teeth and a tongue inside? I would be glad.

. . . It would be nice if one could also close the lids over the eyes.

In general, again, [the doll should be] as sinewy as in the oil sketch, with the greatest [attention] to the details!

I would like to ask you to put still more detail into the bust! The nipples not to be elevated, but more uneven and raised only through their convexity. The perfect model is Helene Fourment in the small Rubens book, where she holds the little boy in her lap while the other stands. This shows all the fine aspects of the bust that make it so graceful and swelling. As for the covering, make sure that the chest has no unintended wrinkles and seams that come only from the unwelcome human hand! How you will do it, I don't know, but I leave myself in your hands. (248–49)

. . . Do not embroider the hairy places but instead put in real hair, for otherwise, if I wish to paint a naked figure based upon it, it won't have the effect of life but of arts and crafts. Please!

Finally, the skin should be peachlike to the touch, with no sewing permitted in places where you think that it would grieve me and remind me that the fetish is a poor rag doll, only there where I can't look in and where the contour or the natural flow of the lines and limbs won't be disturbed. Is it not true, dear Miss M[oos], that you are refusing to permit anyone to disturb me for [these] many years of my life while you are permitting the malicious real objects – padding, stuffing, thread, chiffon, or whatever else the horrible things may be called – to intrude upon all your earthly simplicity, even while I intend to embrace with my eyes an ambiguous creature, dead and living spirit! (249-50)

. . . Even though I feel ashamed, I must write of this, but it remains our secret (and you are my confidante): it must also have its *parties honteuses* made perfect and voluptuous, with hair affixed; otherwise it will not be a woman but a monster. And I can be inspired to works of art by a woman only if she also lives in my imagination. (251)

I imagine that most readers, given even this abbreviated familiarity with the correspondence, will not have too much difficulty in guessing its conclusion:

Dear Miss M[oos], what shall we do now? Even though I have long been prepared for a certain loss in its realization, I am honestly shocked to find that in so many points my doll contradicts what I desired from it and hoped from you. The outer covering is a polar bear pelt that would be suitable for an imitation of a bedside rug but not for the softness and suppleness of a woman's skin. . . . (352-54)

As these letters so vividly show, a "doll" for Kokoschka was not a "thing" in the ordinary sense of that word. (The "usual dollmakers," he angrily noted at one point, "never bother to avoid" the mistake of allowing their sewing to be visible, "because they think it is so traditional and they have no boldness and no feel for the rhythms of the living form, which should not be disturbed because of a poor seam or a casual, mechanical old woman" [249].) Within these letters, a doll is a discourse that will allow a certain world to be possible, a certain complex of relations to be entertained. For instance, it will allow Kokoschka to touch Miss Moos's body, her womanly emotions, and that which is "woman" in general without having to be concerned with the actual "malicious" stuff that goes into the making of such things. It will enable him to be passive, ministered to by Miss Moos's hands and by the doll's inspiring form, and also to be active, one who poses and paints models. It will make the senses of sight and touch unalloyed pleasures. It will give him beauty of a kind best represented in art and at the same time will take this beauty from life that one can touch, address, and entertain. This doll will have its secrets, to be sure; but as in Nietzsche's revision of Schiller, they will be secrets one does not seek to uncover. It will permit variations or manipulation (with eyes that open and close, an overall form that can be turned into art) and yet will be unmistakable as anything other than itself, right down to the smallest bump, swelling, and hair. This doll, this discourse, will allow Kokoschka to have an absolute control over its appearance and yet will have an utterly distinct appearance and so be a completely independent thing. It will take Kokoschka away from ordinary reality, bringing him into a domain of witchcraft, fairy tales, dreams, and transcendent abstractions; but as it does so it will bring him face to face with ordinary reality, carrying this before his eyes with a microscopically focused precision on this thing of hair, protuberances, and skeletal tensions.

The end of the object made by Miss Moos is merely sad. Kokoschka is said to have been ridiculed by his friends when they saw the thing he had so eagerly anticipated; as the last letter I quoted indicates, he was furious, despairing. He did produce an unremarkable painting of the doll; it is said that he took his fetish out with him on several occasions, to the opera and to other public places. Finally, he destroyed it.

This ending is merely sad, scarcely interesting, because it traces the banal course of a pattern of romantic love. (Freud would speak of "object choice," but it would still be an old story of idealization and disillusionment, as he would be the first to admit.) If all we knew of Kokoschka's doll was this dénouement, the doll might be an object lesson in the mystification and misogyny of romantic desire, or in the aesthetic and philosophical problem of mimesis, or in the psychology and psychopathology of artistic creativity; but would there not be far more interesting things to look to for such lessons? The doll would not amount to much.

In comparison to the nude figure of classical art, which can be modelled with so many signs of healthy, undegenerate control, Kokoschka's fetish, like Bellmer's dolls of the 1930s, is bound to seem a degraded and degrading image of a woman. It would be pretty to think so. But just as the health of the classical nude becomes suspect when examined with instruments designed to detect sexism, racism, class oppression, and logocentric dogmatisms of various other kinds, so the diagnosis of degeneracy in the works of Kokoschka and Bellmer may be misleading. In Bellori's version of the Trojan war, it was neoclassical aesthetics that was proud to establish the vitality of art by assuming that real live women were inferior objects of desire; and it is relevant to note that in the 1930s, it was the Nazis who classified Kokoschka's work as "degenerate art."

What is distinctive about the dolls made by these two artists is that in them a sadistic control fundamentally at work in all art (if we are following Freud's account of sadism) is willed but failed; it is this failure, this breakdown in the articulation of power as absolute barriers and compelling logic, that makes these dolls unhealthy by classical standards. Kokoschka's doll turns out to be a vulgar mess, and Bellmer's multiplication of universal joints in his dolls can lead only to further sockets, contortions, and exhibitionisms — to an endless, rabid attack on the misleading presence of an object, which is not the desired object but rather a frustrating alien or usurper. One may even be too quick in sexing these things, Kokoschka's and Bellmer's dolls, since their supposed femininity often seems more to suggest a denial or refusal of sexual difference; the sadistic trauma of these works is then directed back at their maker at least as much as it is focused on an image of woman. The dolls fashioned for Kokoschka and Bellmer display a sense of repugnance, a bad attitude, violence, and misogyny, certainly; but the criticism that wants to stop here to assert a moral judgment, never to go further, is bound to be oppressive. No matter what the surrealists did not know, no matter what criticisms they deserve—and certainly I am not alone in being repelled by their homophobic and patriarchal attitudes, as well as by other aspects of their movement—they did know enough to ridicule this kind of stopping place, this *comforting* morality. Robert Desnos was speaking to this point when he referred to "that category of imbeciles, denounced by Baudelaire, who like to mix up honesty in matters of love."[53]

Yes, if one considers only its end, Kokoschka's doll did not amount to much. Given a knowledge of Kokoschka's letters, however, it is quite another thing. Then the doll is not an object upon which a pathetic, bizarre, and fitfully brilliant artist focused his obsessions. In these letters the doll is nothing more or less than the discourse about it, which, in taking form, traces the outlines of the possible world that would enable this doll to be. Of course, this description would have to be different if we had Miss Moos's side of the correspondence—a consideration to which I will return. But in these letters, as Kokoschka certainly knew (as his nervous and escalating demands make clear) and yet did not know (or he could never have been so disappointed), a "doll" is a rational hallucination, a shared desire, a common culture. What this doll may teach us is that these last two terms, which are banal, may really be as novel as the first, which is an oxymoron. By definition and by Cartesian tradition, a rational hallucination is unthinkable—and yet what else (this doll asks) are things of love, beauty, appearances? As the history of modern spiritualism suggested, and as psychoanalysis suggests in the phenomenon of transference and language in the name of metaphor, communication is always a matter of semiotic contagion and manipulation and thus, in effect, a rational hallucination. In this thinking (of the dead, of the doll, of Freud, of surrealism), all things become mobile relations, theaters of conscious and unconscious discourse, supports in an insupportable world.

If one suppresses the dissonance in Descartes's *Meditations*, the murmuring that tells of the unsettling difference between *veritas* and *auctoritas*, then a support, as Descartes would conceive of it, is something auxiliary to a real or true object. It is a thing only in respect to its function: a support without an intended object is nonsense. In the form of institutions, country homes, and the like, a support is incidental to rational thought, which accepts it with the negligence of a lord acknowledging the obeisance of a peasant. For a support to act otherwise, to seek independence, to desire to venture out on its own, is unthinkable.

However, if one pays attention to the rhetorical confusion in Descartes's writings, a different support may emerge. This support stands on its own and yet is not isolated from other things, as the meditative philosopher is. It does not bear any necessary reference to any other thing, and yet it cannot be detached from other things as if it were an independent subject or object in relation to which these other things were accidental and inessential. This support is, as if by definition, incomplete in some fundamental sense and so oriented to movement, attraction, explosiveness; and yet completion, in its world, is literally unthinkable.

This question of support describes the mannequins that de Chirico divined and that the surrealists appropriated. In de Chirco's paintings, the mannequins or dummies are nothing but supports. In some works, such as *The Grand Metaphysician* (1917), this description is suggested by the way the bust of a mannequin is poised atop an odd assemblage of things that serves at once as socle and body. Drafting instruments are often featured among the seemingly unrelated and haphazardly fitted scraps in these collage-like assemblages, which in some paintings entirely displace the mannequin, as if to suggest that this humanlike figure was never anything other than a supportive scaffolding. The relation between "support" and "art" suggested by these instruments is reinforced in works, such as the *Evangelical Still Life* (1916), in which these constructions are immediately juxtaposed to framed paintings. The support is then revealed as a picture's frame as well as an artist's tool, and it is also an easel, as in *The Jewish Angel* (1916). Through these associations, combinations, and identifications, which define mannequins as armature, scaffolding, tool, easel, frame—in short, as support—de Chirico may seem to withdraw us from reality while organizing the problem of an irrational subjectivity. As the surrealists liked to imagine, something big had to be afoot when the same experience could happen to Breton and Yves Tanguy before they even met each other: seeing an amazing painting in a dealer's window as they rode past on a bus, rushing off at the very next stop, and returning to the window to read the hitherto unfamiliar legend, "de Chirico."

Traditionally, instruments, easels, and frames organize a painting but are not themselves considered to be part of the painting. They go into it without being absorbed by it, aid it without proving necessary to it. So Hegel argued that what the spirit wants in the work of art is a "sensuous presence which indeed should remain sensuous, but liberated from the scaffolding of its purely material nature." Similarly, in writing of artistic creation, he argued that general rules must turn out to be "wholly inadequate" because at best they can apply only to that which is "mechanical" and "external," not to the true work.[54] However, if the surrounding frame can migrate into the picture, supports take the place of independent presence, then the picture can no longer be formally set apart from an environing world. However recognizable its images may seem, they are unsupported by the world to which, traditionally, art was thought to bear reference. When supports *are* the work, the formal elements of the work are not framed or defined so much as they are proposed by a judgment that cannot be appealed because there is nothing beyond the work to which one can advance an appeal. In Kantian terms, this is the situation that obtains when legitimate ornaments and meretricious finery become indistinguishable, leaving no way to frame what is presumed to be intrinsic, so that there remains only exteriority, drapery thrown over drapery, the values of veil use.[55] Or this situation could be described by saying that the Dalian prosthesis replaces the Cartesian thesis; in place of irrefutable intuition and axiom and the procedures of logical deduction, this world provides only for unjustifiable supports, substitutes, or, in a word, fetishes.

Among the artists associated with surrealism, none carried out this line of thinking more exactly than Magritte, who also showed his affinity with de Chirico in the deadpan style of his painting. One of the favorite devices in his work, as in de Chirico's, is the painting-within-a-painting. Through *trompe-l'oeil* effects or in other ways, this serves to interrogate the integrity of objects in general and of the artwork in particular. A related questioning is carried out through manipulations of mirrors (which speak of reflection, transparency, and mimesis), windows and doorways (which are kinds of frames and liminal passageways between exteriority and interiority), curtains (which are both frame and veil), and objects that in general are fragmented, doubled, or otherwise distorted from realist expectations. Sometimes two or more of these devices are combined, as in *The Magic Mirror* (1928–1929), in which the frame of a mirror leans against a wall, facing the viewer of the painting, with the words "human body" occupying the place of the silvered glass.

In terms of supports, however, perhaps Magritte's most interesting work is *Representation* (1937). This is a nude, more or less classically conceived, but with a few notable differences. As with most of Magritte's nudes, the pudenda are peculiarly smooth and sexless, in a fashion that may refer to the coyness of classical decorum but that seems more closely related, visually, to the pornographic photos of this time, in which the erasure of pubic hair was meant to forestall criminal prosecution. The nude is also remarkable for showing only part of the body. Although nudes disposed in a classical scheme might be partially obscured by veils or other sorts of objects, the veiling here is extreme, limiting what we can see to a torso that starts at mid-thigh and ends at the breastbone. (There is a joke here, based on a prosthetic aesthetics, involving classical sculptures that have lost arms, heads, or other parts to the ravages of time—a joke all the more telling because this body "looks like" living flesh, not stone.) Perhaps most notable of all is the shape of this picture, which follows the curves of the body, hugging it from thighs to breastbone, so as to leave nothing in the way of background to "frame" it.

If one takes into account this last aspect of the painting, then this semiclas-

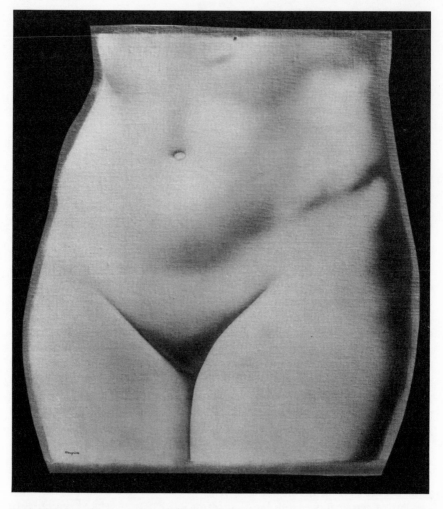

René Magritte, *Representation* (1932)
Private collection
Copyright 1990 C. Herscovici/ARS N.Y.
                    Photo courtesy of Penrose Film Productions Ltd.

sical body, by turns sensuous, pornographic, sadistic, and risible, is effectively no longer a body at all. It suggests, perhaps, a landscape, with its
rounded forms (and here, too, there may be a joke, on the familiar trope
that represents natural landscape as a feminine, naked, nurturing body); but
at best this remains a suggestion. There is no trickery or *trompe-l'oeil* here,
as there is in some of Magritte's other works; the hint of a landscape drifts
away. This body is pressed so far forward that it is forced into a virtually

depthless abstraction from which we cannot deduce a proper perspective. The body, so distinctly female, so sensuously and classically rounded, becomes completely artificial. It becomes the utterly solid (not to say stolid) wisp of an anecdote, caught in passing, which may draw our attention by saying something we do not quite catch about the illusions of commonplace reality. One might compare the effect to that of Baudelaire's sly poem, "The Frame," which relates the enchantment added by a painting's frame to the "jewels, furnishings, metals, [and] gilt" surrounding a beautiful woman, who "voluptuously" drowns her nudity in these things and whose every movement, the poet concludes, shows "the childish grace of a monkey."[56] Or (to move from symbolist bile to surrealist passion) one might compare Magritte's painting to one of Aragon's descriptions of the alarming nature of ordinary things:

Men live with their eyes closed in the midst of magical precipices. They play innocently with dark symbols, their ignorant lips unknowingly repeat terrible incantations, formulas akin to revolvers. There is cause for trembling in the sight of a bourgeois family that has its *café au lait* of a morning without noticing the incomprehensibility that shows up in the red and white squares of the tablecloth.[57]

The other side of Magritte's picture might be Picabia's project for a *Portrait of Cezanne* (1920), which perhaps was also, in a less ironic sense, a homage to Baudelaire. It was to consist of a frame affixed to a floor and strung with threads, with a living monkey chained to it. Although it could not be realized in accordance with its original conception (a stuffed monkey had to substitute for the living one), this project mocks the real model as Magritte's does the modelled image. As these and like works show the crisis of the object culminating in the image of the support, they shuttle us into the world of the mannequin, which knows no radical distinction between inside and outside, form and essence, or thinking and things. The word "frame" often crops up in surrealist writings as a pejorative term for any sort of enclosure, limit, border, or form, and the consequences of this denigration are spelled out in the mannequin and its relatives.

However, if this conception of support effectively responded to the disturbances in Descartes's *Meditations*, it was not without its own upsets. If exile is a problem for Descartes's man, castration is a problem for the mannequin. Where subjectivity and objectivity were troublesome, partiality becomes the modern source of difficulty. Isolation, which Descartes found as necessary as it was elusive, becomes the surrealists' "purity," which would prove to be a seemingly indispensable but radically unreliable watchword. (In this respect, Descartes's problem with communication would become the surrealists' controversy over excommunications.) While finessing the philosopher's problem with establishing certainty, the surrealists would find that in its stead they had to struggle to establish a sense of adherence among themselves and other things. Whereas the definition of form was a crux for Cartesian rationalism, organization was a vexing issue for a world of supporting parts. Identity was a ground that would prove shaky for Descartes, but association would prove an equally dubious ground in surrealism.

If only in a rough form, this comparison summarizes the difference between Descartes's man, who poses the problem of reason, and the surrealist mannequin, which poses the problem of the group. As it resolves the crisis of the object into a question of what "support" is, the surrealists' mannequin solves one problem only to create another. Logic may have been surpassed, but persuasion then shows itself to be a tricky thing; if the desire for truth can be ignored, the desire for desire cannot. All of which is to say that where *veritas* is no longer at issue, *auctoritas* may yet persist and prove all the more efficacious for being castrated, incomplete, and contentious. As Magritte wittily reminds us, even where there is only the fragment of a body, and that fragment partially obscured, we still are likely to envision it in terms of a completed form, with the legs, genitals, arms, and head that allegorize what we take to be natural, social, and metaphysical hierarchies.

So where consciousness found it had a problem in uncovering itself, the comparable problem for the surrealist group was that of managing its appearance. This showed itself most obviously in the surrealists' penchant for advertising themselves, in forms ranging from ordinary publicity seeking to various individual and collective stunts. This activity can be related to the suspicion, which some contemporary artists and critics share with a goodly number of civilians, that creativity in the modern world is driven by nothing but a transient desire for publicity—a lust for one's fifteen minutes in the sun. Taken as more than a *bon mot*, this suspicion is a great oversimplification; but at least it indicates the atmosphere that accumulates around values when man gives way before the mannequin, which has no need to prove its own existence but which does have to prove the influence of a group.

What if Kokoschka's friends had not laughed? This is one way of putting the question of the group: to ask how we take pleasure in things or, more generally, respond to things. Or what if Hermine Moos had participated in the discourse of the doll as something other than a paid employee, a role in which she could not possibly give Kokoschka the understanding he sought (as he recognized in his eagerness to address her as a woman, a confidante, an artist, anything other than a worker)? This is another way of putting the question of the group: to ask how we take power over things. Or what if a teacher and a student, locked in an irresoluble battle—or more likely, in an all-too-tolerable system—begin to study the likes of Descartes, Shakespeare, Marx, Freud, Kokoschka, and Magritte without assuming that truth should be the guide and goal of this activity? This is another way of putting the question of the group: to ask what we take things for. Freud is in these questions along with Lautréamont, Marx, Nietzsche, and, arguably, Husserl and Heidegger; and perhaps there is yet another figure in this questioning, a figure that threatens to stop it short, if the surrealists, too, had their evil genius.

Unlike its illustrious ancestor, this figure could not be at all provoking, unsettling, or deceiving without playing right into the surrealists' hands. Its evil would have to be as unthinkable in Descartes's world as it would be unwelcome in the surrealists'. It would not ask after the grounds of truth, then, and it would not question anything. Instead, this infinitely malicious power would be that of an utterance for which there is a completely satisfactory response, an utterance that would require no thinking at all. When this genius spoke, it could be answered all too easily and so would deny the revolutionary conception of the group, returning it to reason. This genius would be *comforting*.

The surrealists played a game in which figures from the past or present were imagined as showing up at one's door, the point of the game being to decide whether to open the door to them; the evil genius who could disrupt this game would do so by showing up and being instantly made to feel right at home. Its malice would lie precisely in its lack of provocation, in its immensely attractive banality.

Just imagine an evil genius showing up before the supporting members of the revolutionary group, asking to be taken to their leader, and finding them all pointing *without hesitation* to a rational hallucination—what is it?—a cadaver or a head or a fetish or Breton?

9

Purity

Once an artist imagined how he would look if he plucked out an offending eye. He painted a self-portrait in which the orbit on the right side of his face was gaping, dolorous. Seven years passed, and then there came a day when the artist tried to break up a fight among his friends. In the ensuing melee, a bottle was thrown, and the artist lost his left eye—the one he must have painted out all those years before, when working on the self-portrait, if he based his image on the sight of himself in a mirror. Mirrors, of course, reverse the images before them.

If we could forget niggling qualifications, epistemological hedges, all the huffing and puffing of the sense of responsibility that distinguishes intellectuals from assassins, then this story might be frightening, uncanny. As it is, I suspect most of my readers would find it terrible only in the derogatory sense. Although it has a certain primitive simplicity, it seems facile, as if it might have served for one of the weaker episodes in Walter Scott's Waverley Novels or Rod Serling's "Twilight Zone." Even if it were presented by a master of simple plots, I can imagine it succeeding only as an occasion for metaphysical conjectures, glistening thorns and blossoms of irony, and the like. (Play around with the comparison to *The Picture of Dorian Gray*, sure, and throw in a reference to E. T. A. Hoffmann, do a turn on Lewis Carroll, or tell us one more time about the sly ruses of representation, if you must— none of this will make the story *moving*.) And even if I were to say that this is a true story, that Victor Brauner painted this *Self-Portrait* in 1931 and suffered this injury in 1938, it seems unlikely that it would be more affecting. How could such a corny plot raise a shiver from anyone past the age of reason? If this story is true, so much the worse for truth. It ought to know better than to seek us out with such shopworn devices.

But perhaps this very perception can be turned into a story. It will open

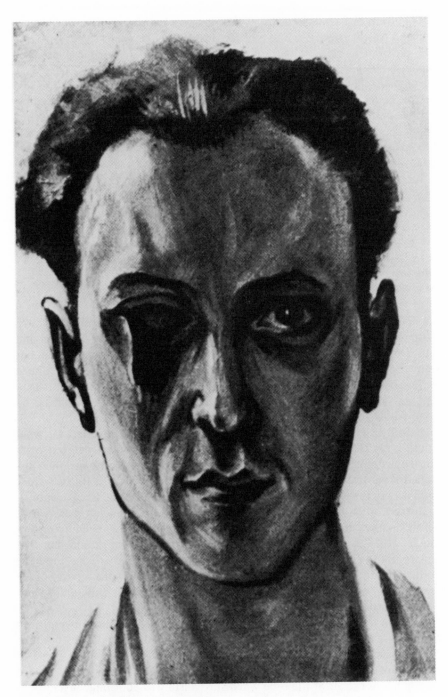

Victor Brauner, *Self-Portrait* (1931)
Paris, Musée National d'art moderne, Centre Georges Pompidou
Copyright 1990 ARS N.Y./SPADEM

with a group of friends in a room. (Other openings are possible, but friends gathered together make a fine lure for drawing readers into a narrative: we take pleasure in being wise enough to know that matters cannot possibly remain as they are.) The friends see each other often, and they pass their evenings in playing games, many of which they have invented themselves. On this night, they are engaged in a desultory "game of truth." In the course of the entertainment, one of the company says that another, who is present, will be the first among them to commit suicide. Immediately, the friends are discomfited; a deep silence overcomes them. Within a decade, the prophecy is fulfilled.

René Crevel killed himself on June 22, 1935, and Jacques Baron would later comment:

> I carry the burden of that stupefying, inexcusable piece of bravado, and the specter of René comes to visit me every time that I would speak of him. And my hand trembles. "The true atrocities are even more criminal in youth than in maturity." I cite Jean-Jacques neither to console myself nor to make good, but to try, despite everything, to carry on with René Crevel.[1]

I do not know if this story is any more successful than the first. It seems more frightening to me because it brings the issue of truth into the open and thus denies it any significance. If the story of Brauner's eye cannot help but seem too neat, too practiced a truth, like a stage gesture brought into a parlor, Baron's story shows that truth is beside the point. It does not matter that his horribly bumptious prediction came true; the story would be no more reassuring if it ended with the notation that Crevel lived to be an old man and died of natural causes in a bed with a downy coverlet. Or what would it matter if we knew more: that Crevel was chronically ill but resolutely uncomplaining, a homosexual in an avant-garde company that disdained homosexuality, a talented writer, somebody's son? In Baron's story truth is only the terrible formality of a plot that can never be terrible enough to distract attention from the image of one friend pronouncing these words before another. (And is this what does finally drive Brauner's life into uncanniness? Not that he lost his eye, as he seemed to predict he would, but that he lost it at the hands of friends? Oscar Dominguez, the artist who threw the bottle, died by his own hand on New Year's Eve in 1957 while a party of his friends was waiting for him to join their revelries: does this addition to Brauner's story clarify anything for us?)[2]

Both stories involve figures actively engaged in the surrealist movement in the 1920s and 1930s, and together they can be taken to indicate the most crucial issue for this movement, which was that of establishing a sense of purity. Not that "purity" was anything new in French culture—it was a word very much in the air at the time when surrealism was aborning. It had been important to writers such as Stéphane Mallarmé and Pierre Reverdy, whose works (carefully culled to extract only the purest efforts) were among those admired by the surrealists; and it was also a focus of theorizing among avant-grade artists. So while trying to establish their new sense of purity, the surrealists were really trying to steal the sense of this word away from others or at least to place a special stress on their own use of it. In fact, their possessiveness toward this term was so notable that it was quickly singled out for criticism. Getting their backs up, Louis Aragon and André Breton categorized this claim that they overemphasized purity as one of the four stereotypes that outsiders held of surrealism;[3] nevertheless, this term continued to be crucial to the movement and even today finds a welcome in much of the literature on surrealism, where it is usually entertained in an entirely uncritical way, as if speaking of purity were sufficient to establish its presence and value. Yet as the surrealists themselves sometimes recognized, it is not such a simple matter.

Surrealist purity was supposed to be a new sense, a modern way of being, which would radically alter the faculties of sight, touch, taste, smell, and hearing. It was to be a sense of confidence, which would make possible presentiments of things to come by giving individuals the multiplied strength of a group, in accordance with the motto from the Comte de Lautréamont: "Poetry must be made by all. Not by one."[4] Purity then would upset the customary perception of truth, and so a new mode of statement would be necessary, as when Breton recounted his experiences with Nadja, the woman of the Parisian streets whom he took to embody the absolute liberty he was seeking. On one occasion, when they were dining outdoors, she drew his attention to a window in a neighboring house and told him that in a minute it would be illuminated by a red light; in a minute, it was. Breton commented, "While unable to do anything about it, I regret that this may pass the limits of credibility. Nevertheless, with such subjects, I should like to take a stand: I limit myself to *acknowledging* that this window, which was black, then became red, that is all."[5]

As distinct from truth, a concern of cops, judges, priests, and intellectuals, purity was the concern of a cultural movement that sought to extend its influence without losing its identity to the absorbing viscosity of the world. For surrealism, purity was not defined by reason but by antagonism, organization, affection, and association; and so its enemy was not error but slackness, an absence of discipline that could take many forms, including the overfamiliarity that would spoil Baron's memory and, perhaps, the tale foretold of Brauner's wound.

As Baron unhappily learned, purity did not ask one to speak the truth even in a game of truth. What it asked was that one speak effectively, movingly, for the cause. "Truth" was insufficient to describe this movement, to which one might adhere for no logical reason at all. One's membership might be at once "an acquiescence and a misunderstanding . . . from the beginning—from its foundation."[6] It was much later that André Masson thus

described his participation in the surrealist movement, and so his characterization might be judged to have been affected by the intervening years,
not to mention the effects one would expect from his experience of being
excommunicated from his erstwhile group of friends within a few years after
he joined them; but whatever its motivation may have been, his characterization provides an apt image for the incapacities the surrealists always found
in truth and sought to reverse with their sense of purity. As Victor Crastre
has put it, "The liberty of everyone in the group depended entirely on the
one condition that certain clumsy or ill-intentioned doings not oppose themselves to the realization of the common ideal."[7] A tacit understanding, a
sense of purity as unformalizable as it was imperative, held together the
participants in this movement, who could not be held to the word of truth.

On the other hand, as the stories of Brauner and Baron make clear, the
fact that this movement refused to take its marching orders from truth did
not mean that it had to forge an alliance with lies. To the surrealists, the
opposition was senseless; purity was something else entirely. After all, purity
would never have become an issue in the first place if truth had not been
found to be a grotesque formality incapable of meeting the simplest needs of
the modern world and yet still claiming to reign over it. Purity sought that
something else:

> But behold the advent of pure men, unforeseen acts, words in the air, illusions,
> ecstasies, blasphemies, dreamy love, behold the fire and the blood rediscovering
> their original splendor, behold the sufferings and the delights, at their ease, haunt-
> ing the soul and the body, and the thought that has no more doors to open. . . .
> (Eluard)[8]

One of the most important tasks of purity was provocation. Where truth
might seek to fix and define things, purity would set out to delineate an
inflammatory movement. It was concerned with order but even more obsessed with desirability. It would blow the chaff away from the wheat, incessantly stimulating those within the movement while repulsing those on the
outside who could not be proselytized. It concerned separation, classification, and cleansing, as in Mary Douglas's anthropological analysis of pollution and taboos, but also excitation, propagation, contagion, destruction,
revolution, the body disfigured and transfigured — all that Douglas showed
lurking around her borders.[9] As the surrealists conceived it, purity was the
disorder of order. "Truth," wrote Crevel, "that's fatigue, lassitude," which
the surrealists would throw over in favor of a motivation that acknowledged
the world only as an object of possible transformations.[10] Rimbaud's conclusion about the end to which "creative impulsion" should lead provided the
surrealists with one of their favorite slogans: "In any case, have done with
actual appearances."[11]

Already in the era of dada the problem of revolutionary organization had been posed, in terms that differed from contemporary Leninist dictates as much as they did from the structuralist strictures yet to come. However, this articulation was never easy. As Breton complained, a movement generally blamed for its flouting of logic would also be accused of an excessive attachment to it, because critics would "willfully insist on the words 'group,' 'leader,' 'discipline.'" What they failed to see was that the dada agitators were connected by "differences above all else."[12] Yet the Breton who voiced this complaint was also the man who agreed with Charles Doury's admiring characterization of Alfred Jarry: a man "carrying, if I may say so, even in his derangements, a discipline and principles."[13]

The problem was to say "purity" without appealing to truth or risking facile and self-defeating paradox (such as my "disorder of order"). And then Breton's defensiveness in itself was questionable, for it revealed a will to subsume differences so as to present a common front against the world. Is not a dadaist who objects to being misunderstood as ludicrous as a surrealist who wants to put "a sort of stamp or seal" on objects and thus "to establish a precise line of demarcation between that which is surrealist in its essence and that which seeks, for public relations or other ends, to pass itself off as such"?[14] In envisioning a surrealist trademark, Breton was protesting ripoffs; but he might have been foretelling the fate of his movement in the last quarter of the twentieth century, when surrealism might look to be little more than a fashion statement. In this and in other ways, the possessiveness of the surrealist sense of purity could lead to dispossession.

The absence of this kind of defensiveness from the early writings of Tristan Tzara offers a clue as to why Paris proved not to be big enough for both Tzara and Breton in the early 1920s. More than personalities was at issue in the clashes between these two (and in the eventual reversal of their positions that took Tzara toward, and Breton away from, orthodox communism). Theirs was a story of purity and friendship; their difficulties in coming to terms with each other speak beyond their individual fates to the general problem of articulating a revolutionary organization. In his *Memoirs*, Philippe Soupault nicely captured this problem when he described a dada game as it was played in the Café Certà around 1920:

> For most of the dadaist friends, what was most aggravating was the obligation André Breton imposed on us of giving marks, from −20 to +20, to writers, philosophers, scientists, or politicians. On other days it would be necessary to give, in addition, marks to feelings, abstractions, attitudes . . . Breton alone did not give marks. He figured the "averages," which were falsified because Tzara always marked −20 and [Georges] Ribemont-Dessaignes gave random responses. But Breton was not discouraged. We continued, night after night. It was tedious.[15]

Having been one of the first to be read out of the ranks of surrealism, Soupault had good reason to remember this game as a tedious exercise; but still it may have had a point. If the game the surrealists were trying to capture was a provocative movement, not a truth, then falsification was impossible. All that mattered was whether this tedium was aggravating in a sufficiently creative way. As with a game Breton and Louis Aragon used to play around this time, in which they tried to write sonnets as rapidly as possible, the object would be to create a "hunting tableau," not a table of systematically measured values. The game in which one participated was the game one was trying to catch: there was no object distinct from this play, this agitation, this hocus-pocus of cultural movement. That the effects of the game described by Soupault were equivocal might even have made it especially successful in capturing what Aragon called the "hitherto unknown" prizes that dada was chasing.[16]

In any case, Soupault's memory is of a kind with the stories of Brauner and Baron. In complaining of aggravating differences in the game of evaluation, it points to the troubling issue of purity, which would become even more pressing when surrealism sought to turn the lessons of dada into an unabashedly collective and political enterprise.

As the surrealists conceived it, purity is something like truth and may well be confused with this other if it loses its avant-garde edge and becomes saddening, tedious, or automatically predictable. When truth reigns, purity is singularity, essence, simplicity, ineluctability; whereas the purity surrealism sought out, aside from truth, was the moving plurality imagined by Breton when he was hunting for a rapprochement with Leninism and the French Communist Party (PCF): "the plurality in which, so to speak, I must at once lose and rediscover myself."[17] As in the popular movies that the surrealists liked, identity was to be a flickering light and a constantly shifting image, an "I" that shivered and jumped in unpredictable sympathy with the other pure souls it chanced to meet. In this respect, the demand for purity could mean, paradoxically, the elevation of impurity into an ideal, as when Salvador Dali praised the mixture of contradictory styles from the past that was to be found in modern architecture, writing of "this horrid impurity that has no equivalent or equal except in the immaculate purity of oneiric intertwinings."[18] This moving plurality was exemplified institutionally in the "Bureau of Researches," which was founded on October 11, 1924 at 15, Rue de Grenelle. Initially under the direction of Francis Gérard, the Bureau was meant to serve as a central clearinghouse, open to the public six days a week, for receiving all sorts of surrealist communications and initiatives from wherever they might come. And yet (Breton's announcement said) there was no question of incoherence: "We continue . . . to insist on the purely revolutionary character of our enterprise, in whose service we will always be found at the sides of those who are ready to give their lives for liberty." The Bureau was to isolate the "mental substance common to all men, that substance hitherto soiled by reason," and thus to help "establish a disturbing machine at the center of the world" that would "supplement intellectual power as others do physical power."[19]

Like Crevel, the Bureau died young. In January of 1925, it no longer seemed possible to keep it open to the public, and so it was turned into a more secluded workplace under the direction of Antonin Artaud; not long thereafter, Artaud was expelled from the group and the Bureau was defunct. The surrealist machine went on with the aid of other apparatuses (its journals and other publications, a short-lived gallery, exhibitions, films, demonstrations); but the story of the Bureau of Researches is fateful. That it came to an end is insignificant (since permanent institutions were never high on the surrealist scorecard), but that it could not remain open to all comers may tell us much about the revolutionary purity of its conception.

Like the door Marcel Duchamp once made for his apartment in New York, which could be open and closed at the same time because it hung from a corner and fit frames in both adjoining walls, the public of a cultural movement is an equivocal thing at best. The very word, "public," suggests people considered as a whole and yet is always used to mark a division between an inside and an outside, and so a nominal universality turns out to be wounded by forces of differentiation, solicitation, desire, and aggression. The door that opens onto the public is also the door that closes it off from whatever is referring to it, whether it be a government, a publicity-seeker, or a cultural movement. And while Duchamp's door had a jokey air about it, there was something haunting about the public of surrealism.[20]

It is difficult to say whether Jacques Baron was in private or in public when he predicted René Crevel's suicide in the presence of Crevel and a group of friends. And what are we to make of the way Crevel showed his concern to fulfill the prediction? Was this a public or a private gesture or (as most accounts hedge their bets) a combination of the two? Crevel killed himself shortly before the opening of the International Congress for the Defense of Culture, which was an anti-fascist assembly that he had unsuccessfully lobbied on behalf of the surrealists. Having closed its doors to the public a decade earlier, surrealism now found doors shut in its face; but who had shut them, the communist organizers of the congress or the organizers of surrealism, who wanted to participate but did not wish to surrender their movement's identity in doing so? Eluard's praise of purity in terms of "thought that has no more doors to open" recognized the threatening nature of doors, and the surrealists were well aware that the public could open and close in disconcerting ways: one of the demands the congress would not discuss was the surrealists' "refusal to judge the quality of a work by the actual extent of its public."[21] Indeed, one of the reasons for Breton's abandonment of dada may well have been his suspicion that it had to be growing too acceptable to the public if Jacques Rivière could write sympathetically about it in *La Nouvelle Revue Française*.[22] From the very beginning, as Masson said in speaking of his own history, surrealism was to be composed of contradictory motivations, militating against the kind of acceptance that pacifies uncanny events into familiar truths.

Yes, from the very beginning it seems as if surrealism was fated to live

out, repeatedly, an experience of confounding inclusion and exclusion for
which there was no name but "purity"—or "the public"—or, perhaps, "suicide." (Does this act signify the opening of a door, as Crevel once thought,
or a closing, or something too uncanny for words?)[23] Perhaps this is how we
should understand one of the first questions officially raised by surrealism,
which was distributed in the form of an "Inquiry," with the responses to be
printed in the second issue of *The Surrealist Revolution*. The inquiry read:
"One lives, one dies. What is the part of the will in all this? It seems that one
kills oneself as one dreams. It is not a moral question that we pose: Suicide,
is it a solution?"

At least one member of the public was certain how he should respond.
Francis Jammes advised his questioners to go to confession and then concluded, "Not only do I authorize you to publish this letter *in extenso*, but
also to forward it to your mother." Such responses could be laughed off,
but others had the potential to be genuinely upsetting. (Crevel's began, "A
solution? . . . yes.") Just how violent this articulation of purity could be is
suggested by Maxime Alexandre's account of Breton's state of mind after the
disruptions within surrealist ranks that were occasioned by the attempt to
connect surrealism with the PCF. According to Alexandre, "Breton, in 1930,
abandoned by a great number of his best friends, talked to us for months
about *collective suicide* as the most worthy outcome of the surrealist experience."[24] Breton as Jim Jones and surrealism as the People's Temple *avant la
lettre*: stories of despots and cults are always popular. But even though it
might be supported by adversaries such as Georges Bataille, who portrayed
Breton as the pope of surrealism, the comparison is too tempting. Among
other things, it would obscure the differences between surrealism and fascism, which it opposed early and insistently, and between surrealism and
Stalinism, with which it broke long before many more sober organizations
and thinkers could see anything to criticize in Uncle Joe. Alexandre's recol-
lection is more interesting for what it says of the feelings of risk that purity
could demand. The exemplary figure in this regard is Friedrich Nietzsche,
who was an admired figure among the surrealists despite his contempt for
socialism—or, tellingly, because of it. He wrote,

> [O]ne could conceive of such a pleasure and power of self-determination, of such
> a *freedom* of the will that the spirit would take leave of all faith and every wish
> for certainty, being practiced in maintaining itself on insubstantial ropes and
> possibilities and dancing even near abysses. Such a spirit would be the *free spirit*
> par excellence.[25]

So Breton would write of "surrealism, *this extremely narrow footbridge
above the abyss*."[26] If this description, like the talk of collective suicide,
appears melodramatic, purity would demand to know whether this judgment
is not a noxious form of truth. Or more specifically, purity would ask

whether it is not a form of aesthetics that represses possibilities of perception vitally necessary to human life (and, incidentally, makes it all but impossible for us to tell when a story is truly uncanny and when it is merely corny). This issue of melodrama is comparable to what William Rubin has called "a problem of credibility that pervades all the images of monsters produced by the Surrealists,"[27] and it might also be related to the tendency to verge on cuteness that often shows up in surrealist art (as with Max Ernst's birds, Joan Miró's giggly beasties, or René Magritte's lesser paradoxes and enigmas-by-the-numbers). Where criticism might be inclined to speak of "weaknesses," "excesses," or (in the totem that unites these contraries) "fail-ures," it might be important to entertain the possibility that where we find aesthetic failure is where we fear being disturbed by an irrational feeling.

If they knew nothing else, the surrealists knew that feeling was always an important movement of the will. As one might gather from their fondness for broadsides, manifestos, disruptive "manifestations," and other kinds of publicity stunts, the surrealists' was an entrepreneurial disaffection, always looking forward, unwilling to languish in misery, anomie, alienation, or despair. ("Pure eyes in the woods," wrote René Char, "search, weeping, for a habitable head.")[28] In place of morality, which they saw as the abject poetry of bourgeois subjectivity, the surrealists needed a political motivation that would appeal to desire over truth, including even that form of truth traditionally addressed as art. Yet this motivation was bound to be pro-foundly divisive inside as well as outside the movement, a door that opened in as it swung out, producing emancipation and abasement in the same movement, as nothing showed more clearly than the waves of bitter ink that were spilled when Breton came to believe that purity demanded an allegiance to the PCF. Surrealism then found itself losing some of its earliest devotees even as it struggled, with little success, to persuade the PCF that surrealism was a legitimate revolutionary movement in its own right. Discipline clashed with discipline until 1935, when the issue of Trotsky led the main body of surrealists to a definitive break with the PCF and a general repudiation of Stalinism; but in the meantime Breton argued that there was nothing extraordinary in the fact that surrealism should have stormy relations with the Communists:

It is normal that surrealism should appear in the middle and perhaps *at the price* of an uninterrupted series of failures, zigzags, and defections that demand at each instant the reconsideration of its original grounds, which is to say, a recall to the initial principle of this activity joined to an interrogation of the *dicey tomorrow* that would wish hearts to be finding and losing each other.[29]

At this point purity seemed identifiable with the party, as if both implied the same discipline. And why not? The quotation from Ferdinand Lasalle that Lenin had chosen for his epigraph in *What is to Be Done?* might have lent support to the course surrealism would follow: "Party struggles give a party strength and life . . . the best proof of the weakness of a party is its diffuseness and the blurring of clearly defined borders . . . a party becomes stronger by purging itself." However, even as Breton wrote his "Second Manifesto of Surrealism," there were signs, for eyes that could see them, indicating that purity could not be drawn within the party line.

When Lenin described "the tendency of unbounded opportunism, which passively adapts itself to spontaneity,"[30] he was scourging reformist compromises and terrorist excesses that he considered to be irresponsible to an organized revolutionary movement; but he might have been uncannily anticipating the doctrine of surrealism, which renounced consciousness in favor of passive "automatism" while simultaneously elevating the idea of spontaneous activity into the imperative rule of *disponibilité*, which named a readiness to abandon oneself to the vagaries of street life. The PCF may have been stupid, but it was not blind; and it may have been insensitive to the uncanny, but it could still read. Breton could quote Lenin for his purposes,[31] but then so could Satan quote scripture. If the purity the surrealists sought was more than an inchoate intuition, it was something other than a party line, program, or law, as one can see even in the "Second Manifesto," in which the accord Breton seeks with the PCF is couched in decidedly nervous terms. Purity would indeed thrive on struggles and zigzags, but it would also suffer in taking this course and, at last, peter out into travesty and regret, with individuals on all sides feeling that they had been betrayed.

This history can give pause even to the staunchest supporters of the movement, such as Patrick Waldberg,[32] and in at least one case the betrayal was a matter of life and death. In 1950 Breton urged Eluard to exert whatever influence he might have to save their former comrade, Závis Kalandra, from the sentence of death given him by the governing regime in Czechoslovakia; Eluard declined to interfere, and the sentence was duly carried out. This is, to be sure, an exceptional case, one that occurred years after the period between the wars of which I write and long after Eluard, like Aragon and Tzara, had opted for Stalinism over surrealism; but an event can be exceptional and yet exemplary. People did and would have died, with or without the surrealist movement; betrayal we must always expect; but the execution of Závis Kalandra, like the mutilation of Victor Brauner's eye and the suicide of René Crevel, must be taken into account if we wish to evaluate the implications of the surrealist sense of purity, which always promised a certain mercilessness even as it promised collective movement and power.

In a remembrance that he wrote on the occasion of Breton's death, Ernst described that "strange exercise," the surrealist game of truth, in which friends were also not-friends. They were at once public and private figures, and not even the thought of failure could allow them to escape this afflicting position:

A born confessor, André Breton passionately loved *the game of truth*, with everything that this strange exercise implied as to admissions, concealments, indulgences, and penances. For him, the game of truth belonged to the domain of the sacred. He accepted the rules voluntarily, even rigorously. To Paul Eluard's question, "Do you have any friends?", his response was "No, dear friend." Undoubtedly, he realized that his response implied a terrible demand: to be admitted as a friend, it was necessary tacitly to accept a contract of non-reciprocity. . . .

Thus, for André Breton, friendship was lost in *the game of friendship*, the tragic exercise to which he devoted himself uncompromisingly until the end of his life. He took all the risks, including that of the absolute failure of his friendships.[33]

Like Soupault, Ernst wrote from what popular journalism calls "bitter experience." Was it worth the effort and the pain, as Breton argued at the time of the "Second Manifesto"? If we look at the hard feelings occasioned by surrealism's political controversies with the hindsight that tells how the relationship with the PCF was destined to end in failure, we may find his argument both self-serving and self-deluding. Perhaps it was; but then what have we observed in this judgment if not the problem with which I began, the problem of a rending purity, to which there seems no other alternative than truth in its dismal popular expression? "What was the secret of the surrealists?" asked Paul Nougé in 1941. "One can only suggest here that they felt more than any other the terrible interior rending that undoubtedly will characterize in the future the beings that we all are."[34] This wounding division, I would add, is "interior" only insofar as it marks the differentiation of interior and exterior, the private and the public, or those incorporated into the body of the group and those it vomits out of itself.

What the demand for openness was to spiritualism, the demand for purity was to surrealism: a motive initially creative and finally desperate or frustrating. No contrast could be more stark than that between the spiritualists' zealous bonhomie and the surrealists' determined uncharitableness. As a cultural movement, modern spiritualism showed nothing like the surrealist obsession with group definition; it is even ironic that orthodoxy should have been such a terribly pressing issue for the twentieth-century movement, influenced by the likes of Nietzsche and Freud, whereas identity for these Victorians was easily and even cheerfully accepted to be disintegrated, dispersed, or out of control. The irony goes only so far; many spiritualists, too, sought a certain control over their image in the form of social respectability; but purity, in anything like the surrealist sense of the word, was not their concern. The difference lies in the spiritualists' assumption that the revelations and revolutions they desired were not to be made but to be recognized and accepted. Such an attitude is likely to seem much less destructive than the surrealists', but once again matters are not so simple. This attitude, too, could be profoundly damaging. Even though it was not really a complacent attitude, as one can see from the many believers in spiritualism who found that it gave them strength to fight for causes such as women's rights, it was premised upon a *desire* for complacency, which at its worst finds its contemporary avatars in figures such as Werner Erhard and Shirley MacLaine.

A movement that seeks not to be demanding can ruin as many lives, or blissfully overlook the ruin of as many lives, as can a movement that demands an irrational purity. Robert Desnos, the star of the *temps des sommeils*, died of typhus in a Nazi concentration camp shortly after it was liberated in 1945; before dying, he spoke fondly of the surrealist movement to a student of avant-garde literature who had chanced to recognize his name on the rolls of the camp. We know that Desnos had felt extremely hurt by his expulsion from the surrealist group, and we know that those responsible for his death had claimed to be moved by a certain ideal of purity; but Desnos knew that theirs was not the surrealist ideal. It is vital to tell the difference even as we see how examples like those of Brauner and Crevel and Kalandra and Desnos call this difference into question; it is important not to be too sure of ourselves here. "Is the solution of a sage the pollution of a page?" asked Desnos in his trancelike persona (borrowed from Duchamp) of Rrose Selavy.[35]

If we are not to be too wise and thus too undemanding, like readers who can predict what is to come because they cannot perceive anything outside of established formulas, it is important to sense the attraction and the difficulty of the surrealist sense of purity. It is important to invite the possibility that the lives of Brauner, Crevel, and other surrealist figures do touch us even when their stories leave us cold or inspire us only to laughter and contempt. In other words, we must ask whether purity could ever have been finer and friendship ever more true — or whether Nietzsche was right when he said that "one can achieve the domination of virtue only by the same means as those by which one can achieve domination of any kind, in any case not by means of virtue."[36] It may be important to note that even in Kant's philosophy, praise is offered to rending motivations of the sort the surrealists found in purity. "[T]hanks be to nature for the incompatibility, for the distasteful, competitive vanity, for the insatiable desire to possess and also to rule. Without them, all of humanity's excellent natural capacities would have been eternally dormant."[37] In praising the social value of antagonisms among men, Kant differed from Nietzsche in assuming an ultimately redemptive pattern in history; but the resemblance between his comments, on the one hand, and Nietzsche's or even Sade's remarks on social affections, on the other, may serve to indicate how the logic of enlightenment's subversion lay within Enlightenment reason, just waiting to provoke receptive individuals. Kant's notion of aesthetic purity, which distinguished the formal judgments of taste from empirical judgments of sensibility, could not have been farther from the surrealist sense of purity . . . as long as one fails to see the polemical assumption of a privileged group identity within it. The surrealists at least wore their hearts on their sleeves; they at least knew that their reasoning and their power, however far they might or might not go, would always remain an issue of the group.

Although it bears some relation to the discipline at work in any social grouping, surrealist purity was not the anthropological and sociological banality that this comparison might make it out to be. The need for a pragmatic and referential order is comprised within but cannot account for the surrealist demand for purity as it was worked out in relation to schools of philosophy and art, religious institutions, orthodox communism and psychoanalysis, popular patriotism, and other social forces. Nor can this purity be accurately described as an ideal, if by this term one means a metaphysical postulate comparable to the appellation of truth in any group's ideology. Purity is one of those words whose "truly magical power" controlled groups, as Freud saw them; he described how "groups have never thirsted after truth" and how "the notion of impossibility disappears from the individual in a group."[38] But Freud himself was still seeking truth in his analysis of groups, which is to say, still seeking a truth beyond groups, whereas the surrealists sought to open themselves to the magical virtues of collective action. They sought to compose their group's desires without any regard for truth. Like Nietzsche's Zarathustra, they would still toss around the words or "the gestures of truth" when it suited their purposes to do so, but they did not seek to transcend "the game of truth," beyond which reason (and the institutionalized discourse of psychoanalysis) takes on a reassuring form.[39] Instead they appropriated ideals from truth for their determinedly unreasonable purposes, or at least tried to do so — how successfully is the question to which I will continue to return.

Certainly there was good reason for Breton to be guyed as the pope of surrealism and for the movement as a whole to be seen as a caricature of the Catholic Church it had meant to subvert. Certainly Breton was overbearing, the George Steinbrenner of surrealism. He and his cohorts were often no less vicious to their friends than they were to their opponents, as readers of *Nadja* should know even if they are unaware of the history of the movement; and where the surrealists were not petty, foolish, or mean, they were likely to be ridiculous, as in their precious, elitist, patriarchal egoism. They produced some excitement and a fair amount of interesting work along the way, but it is difficult to imagine the sense in which they would appear pure.

Yet the issue of purity does not disappear even in such mockery. If anything, it becomes more urgent; for it is what informs us that this movement defaulted on its commitment. Truth could never yield this insight: it could claim only that surrealism was mistaken or lacking in knowledge. It cannot speak of uncanny risks and betrayals, but purity can, in the same way that it can explain how we may find a story to be at once true and trivial. There is a question of fitness here that has little to do with logic but everything to do with the fate of our feelings.

Purity is the question of irrational order. As the provocative basis of surrealism, purity was a goal only insofar as it was a tactic. It was a call for incessant agitation and as such a definitively dissatisfied conception of representation. This movement tried to secure its identity before the wisdom of the world, its "actual appearances." In this as in other respects, surrealism owed a great deal to the experience of dada, which had so strongly identified volatility with creativity, as in Tzara's *Mister Aa the Antiphilosopher*:

> As soon as they are pronounced, words become antagonistic conclusions, take on an existence that acts directly on the cell and the speculation of the blood. Outside of their ineffaceable sonority, established as the base of a logic of bargaining and compromise, nothing can testify to their real virtue except the pleasure that I have in making them move. And again. Reality is only an explicit conclusion.[40]

Given that words were so suspicious, it might seem contradictory that one of the most distinctive characteristics of surrealism was its visual and verbal sloganeering. A penchant for oracular pronouncements was virtually everywhere in this movement, even in the most fluid examples of automatic writing, such as Breton's "Soluble Fish."[41] The explanation is that the slogan opposed the proposition just as image making opposed ratiocination—all the better to show up the pitiful pretense that reason could transcend icons, mottos, popular symbols, the weird materiality of its representation. Maurice Blanchot wrote that with surrealism we arrive at "rhetoric become matter."[42] As Breton would comment in his *Conversations*, slogans were a call to order, a way of maintaining a "posture of aggression" that would brook no delay or temporizing.[43] They were not conceived in truth but in purity, and the surrealists even had the slogan to explain this imperious sloganeering: "All the water in the ocean will not be enough to wash away one stain of intellectual blood."[44] If the precise import of this phrase remained unclear (*intellectual*, for instance, might be taken in a praiseworthy or utterly negative sense), the point of the surrealists' appropriation was not to establish a precise meaning but rather to signify a collective sense of urgency and disgust. The motivation was similar to the attitude Breton and Aragon shared in the time of dada when, Aragon would remember, "We would say of a poem: would this poem make its mark if one made a poster of it, would people in the street stop to read it?"[45]

Isidore Ducasse, who prompted the surrealists with the line about "intellectual blood," was also the pseudonymous Comte de Lautréamont from whom they took their most famous catchphrase, in which beauty was described as "the fortuitous meeting of a sewing machine and an umbrella on an operating table."[46] The work of visual artists could also be of service: for all their iconoclasm, surrealists would refer to certain pictures as if the mere mention of a genuinely inspired de Chirico, an early Giacometti, or a pre-Francoist Dali would specify a necessary response. "The light here is the supernatural fire that directs pure men," wrote Roger Vitrac of de Chirico's paintings.[47] And when events so conspired as to turn artists like these into dissenting or reprehensible figures, the sense of purity enabled the movement to come to terms with the unfortunate change. A painting de Chirico signed in 1917 and one he signed in 1925 might both be true de Chiricos, but only the former was pure. Surrealism could claim it with a clear conscience while offering nothing but execration to the other work. As Breton said of de Chirico's post-1917 productions, "So much the worse for him if he came to believe himself the master of his dreams!"[48] In February of 1928, to counter an exhibition of de Chirico's recent work at Léonce Rosenberg's gallery, the surrealists went so far as to put on an exhibition of "pure" de Chiricos, gathered from their own collections, at the Galérie Surréaliste in the Rue Jacques-Callot. The exhibition was accompanied by a catalogue insulting de Chirico and by a mock grave entombing his genius.[49] And when the surrealists faced one of their first internal disputes, over the involvement of Ernst and Miró in a production of Serge Diaghilev's ballet company (which was looked upon by the others as a decadent aristocratic business), Eluard was able to calm the troubled waters with his conclusion, "The purest remain with us."[50]

With the small posters (or "butterflies") that the surrealists printed and distributed from the Bureau of Researches, their slogans came as close to being conventional advertising as they would ever be; with the "152 Proverbs" that Eluard composed in collaboration with Benjamin Péret, their sloganeering may have found its most complete expression.[51] Some of these are wittily disorienting, in the common surrealist mode that turned appearances back upon themselves: "7 Like an oyster that has found a pearl." (Compare, for instance, the reference in one of Péret's poems to "the cloak of rainshowers indispensable to eternal voyagers"; the passage from Rimbaud's letters, beloved by the surrealists, in which he proclaimed that "I is an other"; and the scene in Thomas De Quincey's *Confessions of an English Opium-Eater* in which he concludes, in recounting a childhood horror, "It appears, then, that I had been reading a legend concerning myself in the *Arabian Nights*.")[52] The rest of the proverbs in this collection offer mock psychology ("17 A crab under any other name will never forget the sea"), philosophical banality ("27 The sun shines for no one"), programmatic nonsense ("32 The further from the urn, the longer the beard"), simple silliness ("113 I came, I sat, I left"), irony piled upon irony ("54 Grandeur does not consist of tricks but of mistakes"), and a kind of banter that could be turned to a darker effect, as in Brauner's story ("46 Seize the eye by the monocle").[53] As if in illustration of Tzara's complaint about words, the general impression is of a serious purpose that cannot be pinned down in any particular expression or (to swing the door the other way) of laughter from a mouth that clams up as soon as one tries to identify it. But this is not your run-of-the-mill satire, ambiguity, indeterminacy, or *différance*: the provocation is more specific.

We may be free to do as we wish, as far as the crippled freedom of reason will carry us, but the sense of purity would say that if we cannot get this specific provocation, then it is our tough luck. "If you cannot comprehend the gesture that he is making, a sign, something less than a sign, a silence, shame on you!" said Aragon of Breton in a 1925 article.[54] As far as surrealism was concerned, there was a world of difference between words meant to be judged and words that moved, and woe to those who could not see the latter for the former. The surrealist slogan was meant to act on this difference, to be nothing more or less than this seething alchemy of difference, which would identify adherents by the same marks that would disorient the unconverted. Surrealism took language to be the power of a group, not an instrument of consciousness, individual subjectivity, reason, or structural logic. Its words were all performatives: watchwords, passwords, maledictions,[55] tocsins, "springboards for the spirit" (Breton),[56] open sesames. If they tested anything, it was not meaning or truth but friendship.

The proposition, this movement suggested, is really a rare and peculiarly baseless form of utterance, which, to our misfortune, has enjoyed a history entirely out of proportion to its deserts. Surrealists advised that those who would know their history and their feelings should look to the laugh, the image, the slogan, and the verbal assault. If one considers how both Freud and J. L. Austin were interested in demonstrating that a certain magic is at work in even the most banal performatives of rational life (such as "I pronounce you man and wife"), then the surrealist sense of purity can be described as a technique for setting this power free so that it could show its hidden workings in every aspect of worldly affairs.

Like sympathetic magic or the thoughts of children and madmen (as these were understood in the anthropology and psychology of the early twentieth century), the sense of purity relied on association in place of the distinctions that reason would demand. Like the savages who were said to believe that a man and woman coupling beside a field would make it fertile, the children said to be ignorant of the difference between their mental reach and their physical grasp, and the psychotics who seemed to venture beyond the reality principle to find hallucinatory satisfactions, the surrealists believed that reason told only half the story of human life: the waking, sunlit, inferior half. If there were indeed any logic in the world, then by the same logic that enabled a priest to make two persons "man and wife," an artist could feel free to identify the image of a bowler hat with the word "snow," as in Magritte's *The Key of Dreams* (1930); and a foolish cultural movement might expect to change the world by persisting in its folly. "Until there is a new order," wrote Breton in his early days, "everything that can delay the classification of beings and ideas — in a word, that can maintain ambiguity — has my approval."[57]

Even as it led the surrealists to distrust all appearances, purity led them to

privilege certain artistic forms, in which they found a revolutionary potential, over others, like the scholastic proposition and the usual wedding ceremony, that seemed a debasement of magic. Novels in particular and realist
works in general were held to be despicable. Thus, Breton remembered Paul
Valéry assuring him that he would never write a sentence like "The Marquise
went out at five o'clock" — and then he asserted his greater purity by wondering if Valéry had managed to keep this promise.[58] This establishment of a
generic hierarchy might seem unjustified by surrealism's own principles,
which declared a suspicion of all forms and a concomitant readiness to
discover surreality even in appearances that seemed sober and down to earth
(as Salvador Dali would in Jean François Millet's *The Angelus*);[59] but of
course this attitude was never meant to be reasonable. So what if school-
teachers got indigestion at the slightest hint of an unresolved contradiction?
The will to privilege certain forms was a motive force in the propagation of
the movement; as long as it served this end, it had no need to answer to any
gripes that would restrain its hallucinatory purity and practical inconsistency.

A more troubling equivoque involved precisely this question of forwarding
the movement. Elements in the political left and in the artistic avant-garde
accused surrealism of being outmoded, even reactionary, almost as soon as
it announced itself as a movement; and at the very least this criticism suggested that the sense of purity as the surrealists construed it could conceiv-
ably evolve in other, arguably better ways. To the political left, surrealism
was likely to appear as dilettantism, and to those in the artistic avant-garde
who were moving toward a doctrine of abstraction, surrealism could even
look quaint in its attachment to a representational art, no matter how fantastic its subject might be. The situation was almost a Hegelian squeeze, with
surrealism caught between the communists, whom they found too rigidly
bound to the particulars of this world, and the cutting edge of art, which, in
the advancing form of abstraction, seemed too ideal and free of conflict, as
if prematurely anticipating the revolution. On the one hand, then, there was
Breton's initial attempt to join the PCF in 1927, which proved abortive when
he was assigned to a cell of gas workers that promptly ordered him to prepare
a report on conditions in contemporary Italy — needless to say, not at all
what he had in mind when he signed up for the revolution; on the other
hand, there was the fact that even conservative critics could find surrealist
art to be retrograde because of its alleged reliance on literary rather than
properly pictorial concerns.[60] What is to become of a cultural movement that
radically questions the actual appearance of objects when another movement
comes along that relies only on point, line, mass, and color, making a concern with objects of any kind seem provincial?

Given this perspective, it is no wonder that the surrealists could find common cause with Nietzsche even after they were oriented to proletarian concerns that would seem to represent everything that philosopher had despised.

As it contended with these other vanguards, which had their own powerful images and games of truth, surrealism seemed compelled to move closer to Zarathustra's theme of select friendships even as it continued to profess a sympathetic identity with the masses. Like Charles Baudelaire, when he was facing prosecution for his *Flowers of Evil* and so was led to write to his lawyer, "I do not address myself at all to the crowd," the surrealists who felt themselves pinched between overparticularity and overgenerality could find themselves moved to measure their virtue in terms of their evasive insularity.[61] "In the failed salon," wrote Char, "on the great hostile floortiles, the sleeper and the beloved, too unpopular not to be real, interminably unite mouths dripping with saliva." More prosaically, in the first issue of *The Surrealist Revolution*, Soupault wrote, "On any given day, in a city with several million inhabitants, there are no more than ten, fifteen, or let us say thirty individuals who live in opposition to good sense, which is to say, who live according to reality, who live purely and simply." This statement antedated surrealism's involvement with the PCF, but Char's poem came after, as did Breton's "Second Manifesto," in which he wrote that "unswerving fidelity to the actions of surrealism requires a disinterestedness, a contempt for risk, a refusal of accommodation of which very few men reveal themselves capable over the long run."[62]

Contending with the pullulating agitation of other movements while facing a public that it feels it must at once address and ward off, the group tends to become its own privileged form; and so all questions of purity also become questions of friendship. The notion of friendship in modern culture in general can be profitably pursued, with attention to writers as various as Nietzsche, D. H. Lawrence, Virginia Woolf, James Joyce, and Ernest Hemingway; but here I am able to speak only to the surrealist example, which has the distinction of combining political, emotional, and aesthetic questions in particularly striking ways. Breton once claimed that the world had never known a human association as "ambitious" and as "*passionate*" as surrealism, at least since the time of Saint Simon[63] — an impossibly grandiose statement and also one that should have been cautionary, given the transformation of the Saint-Simonian movement after 1829 into a formal religion with Prosper Enfantin as its "Pope" and with all sorts of defections and apostasies due to break out shortly thereafter. Yet Breton's claim remains interesting, as does surrealism itself, precisely because of its outrageous ambition.

In surrealism as in dada (one thinks of Ernst's painting, *At the Rendezvous of the Friends* [1922]), all the pother about friendship was a way of trying to think of social collectivities without relying on the faculty of reason or the practical reasons of state, logic, and law, all of which were felt to have deserved their burial in the vile trenches of the First World War. (When they first met, Ernst and Eluard were pleased to be able to figure out that during one period, at Verdun, their German and French companies had been directly opposite each other's lines, shooting at each other.) At the same time,

Max Ernst, *At the Rendezvous of the Friends* (1922)
Cologne, Museen der Stadt Köln
Copyright 1990 ARS N.Y./SPADEM/ADAGP.
                              Photo courtesy of Rheinische Bildarchiv, Cologne

this friendship was a notably and even determinedly masculine affair. Like
Baudelaire, Nietzsche, Lawrence, and Hemingway, the surrealists were no
less opposed to domestic sentimentality, which they saw as the officially
sanctioned feminine alternative to the public life of the state, than they were
to the state itself.

Naturally, some qualifications are called for. Some women, such as Meret
Oppenheim and Leonora Carrington, participated in the art and the other
activities of surrealism,[64] and many surrealist works set out to upset current
conceptions of gender and to cultivate qualities that were commonly termed
feminine. Nevertheless, this movement generally composed itself as in the
widely reproduced 1925 photograph that shows a group of surrealists bending over a typewriter while the only woman in their company, Simone
Breton, is seated at the keyboard. The grammar is significant when Breton
tells his daughter, in the last line of *Mad Love*, "I wish that you may be
madly loved."[65] As Nadja recognized when she predicted that Breton would
write a book about her, women were to be addressed, adored, desired, and,
as it were, written on; but a woman in any of these roles was never far from
her oppressive role in Ernst's painting, *The Blessed Virgin Chastises the
Infant Jesus Before Three Witnesses: A. B., P. E., and the Artist* (1926),

Man Ray, *La Centrale surréaliste* (1927)
Copyright 1990 ARS N.Y./ADAGP
Left to right: Max Morise, Roger Vitrac, Jacques Boiffard, André Breton, Paul Eluard, Pierre Naville, Giorgio de Chirico; *first row:* Simone Breton and Robert Desnos

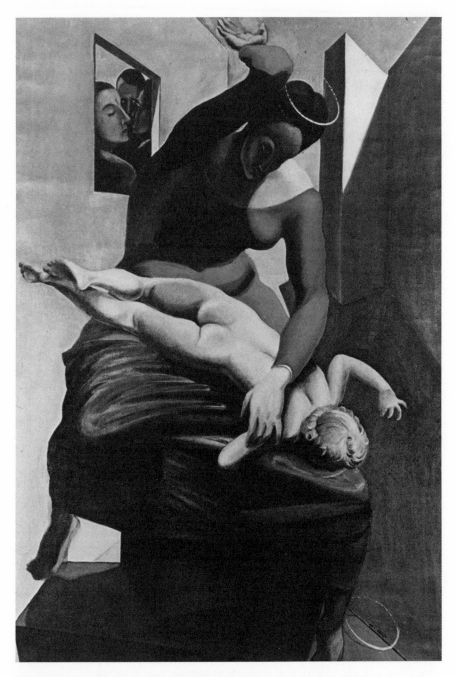

Max Ernst, *The Blessed Virgin Chastizes the Infant Jesus Before Three Witnesses, A.B., P.E., and the Artist* (1926)
Cologne, Museum Ludwig
Copyright 1990 ARS N.Y./SPADEM/ADAGP.

which shows the Savior's mother heartily paddling his bare butt, knocking his halo onto the floor, while Breton, Eluard, and Ernst look on through a window, full of disdain for the sight before them. It is no surprise to learn that late in her life, in speaking of her few visits with the surrealists, Gisèle Prassinos commented, "I would have liked them to have explained a lot of things to me, but they kept me from reading so that I might remain ignorant and virginal. Breton, fearing that I was losing my innocence and stopping myself from writing, very quickly excommunicated me."[66]

Of course, this attitude toward women was not at all extraordinary. Its significance for the conception of the group lies precisely in the fact that it is only too predictable, like a story whose effect is ruined by overfamiliarity. That the surrealist group could be so conventional in this instance may lead one to wonder in what other respects its purity fell into tiresome truth, and of course there were many. As I have previously noted, there was a generally communicated disapproval of homosexuality.[67] Although Robert Desnos and some others used drugs, the surrealists also had a surprisingly negative attitude toward them, despite the comparisons that the "Manifesto of Surrealism" drew between surrealist experiences and drug-induced reveries, such as those described in Baudelaire's *Artificial Paradises*. And there were also all the minor expectations of the group that some have remembered as coercive: the kowtowing of newcomers before the likes of Aragon, Eluard, and Breton; the regular attendance at meetings in cafés; the signing of petitions; even the agreement on mandarin curaçao as the quasi-official drink of the movement. No matter how informal or deliberately peculiar they were (and the frequent ingestion of mandarin curaçao would indeed seem to require some sort of purity), rules such as these show this movement mistaking individual pride and trivial opinion for political provocation.

Even more important (and closely related to surrealist attitudes toward the public and toward women) was the conventional artistic ambition that this movement could never entirely pluck out of itself. Immediately after the First World War, Aragon, Soupault, and Breton assiduously sought the acquaintance of literary lights such as Valéry, Apollinaire, Pierre Reverdy, and André Gide; and the sense of young men on the make was often confused with the sense of purity in the surrealist movement, as those who fell out with Breton were quick to point out. To a significant extent, and despite the fulminations against conventional art and aesthetics, surrealism was an attempt to claim a place in the cultural world for a new generation of artists and writers. This aspect of the movement was bound to affect its treatment of women if only because virtually all the major players the dadaists and surrealists tried to court, convert, or push out of the way happened to be men, for reasons that had little to do with chance. Similarly, it is hardly a matter of coincidence that the youthful Breton had a series of friendships with men who held themselves superior to him in one way or another (Tzara,

Apollinaire, Jacques Vaché, Francis Picabia) while he himself began to assume this dominating role with his associates and acolytes. Nor is it insignificant that these idolized acquaintances were paralleled by a list of cultural lights, almost always male (Rimbaud, Lautréamont, Freud, Lenin), who were invariably addressed as heroes and leaders. In this respect, what might otherwise appear as provocative tergiversation in the surrealist movement may appear instead as an all-too-common oscillation between a self-important arrogance and a cringing humility before authority.

That surrealist purity was compromised should not be surprising. However, as Lenin knew, "There are compromises and compromises."[68] Like all of us, the surrealists were making it up as they went along; unlike many of us, they tried not to seek refuge in truth. Through the sense of purity, surrealism searched for history as movement, collectivity, polemic, passion, and irrational form. They were well aware that what they were about could neither be isolated from nor completely identified with history, since either case would presuppose a logical conclusion to desire. As Aragon commented in *The Surrealist Revolution*, "The irregularity in the appearance of this review translates an entire intellectual life manifested at intervals of an apparently arbitrary length, gives us the notion of a series of ideological crises and graphic divergences. Each issue summarizes what has been able to reunite several men at the date that it marks, it has a value in consequence."[69]

History was a complex problem of perception, the problem of the sense of purity. It was evident in surrealism's equivocal relation to the public, in René Crevel's suicide, and in Jacques Baron's memory of Crevel. It showed up in the irony that nihilistic dada could appear as an authoritarian daddy against which surrealism rebelled, and it was multiplied in the many movements with which surrealism had to come to terms in one way or another: positivism, postimpressionism, expressionism, communism, cubism, futurism, orphism, fascism, all the rest. History was the sway of truth that could not be easily discarded even when truth was taken to be a game; it was the personal past of young men emerging from World War I and quickly involving themselves in public movements, thereby creating influences for themselves that would tend to prescribe the possibilities offered by the future; it was all that ordered a movement to be "a platform sufficiently mobile to confront the changing aspect of the problem of life even as it is stable enough to attest to the *unbrokenness* of a certain number of mutual — and public — engagements" among its participants (Breton);[70] and it was all that undermined this platform. It has been said that the theory of surrealism outruns its productions, which too frequently fail to match its claims for monstrosity, beauty, wonder, or whatnot; but as with Victor Brauner's life, the story of this movement is not simply a matter of matching works to expectations and seeing how they measure up. How to evaluate the relation between our perceptions and our expectations is precisely what was at issue in the surrealist movement. There are compromises and compromises.

In the last section of "The 'Uncanny,'" the essay in which Freud set out to show "in what circumstances the familiar can become uncanny and frightening" (220),[71] he chanced upon this issue of evaluation. The difference he found in the uncanny that appeared in art rather than life was what focused his attention on this issue. Referring to aesthetics, he said, "We have drifted into this field of research half involuntarily, through the temptation to explain certain instances which contradicted our theory of the causes of the uncanny" (251–52). But despite whatever foresight he may have been lacking, Freud came to a definite conclusion:

> The uncanny of fictional invention — of phantasy, of poetic works [der Fiktion — der Phantasie, der Dichtung] — merits in truth a separate discussion. Above all, it is much richer [reichhaltiger] than the uncanny in experience [des Erlebens], for it contains the whole of the latter and something more besides, which is not to be found in the conditions of experience [was unter den Bedingungen des Erlebens nicht vorkommt]. The contrast between what has been repressed and what has been surmounted cannot be transposed on to the uncanny in poetic works [Dichtung] without profound modification; for the releasing of its content from reality-testing is just what the realm of phantasy has as the presupposition of its value [denn des Reich der Phantasie hat ja zur Vorassetzung seiner Geltung, dass sein Inhalt von der Realitätsprüfung enthoben ist]. The seemingly paradoxical result [Das paradox klingende Ergebnis] is that in the first place a great deal that is not uncanny in poetic works [Dichtung] could be so if it happened in life [im Leben]; and in the second place that there are many means of creating uncanny effects in poetic works that are lost in life [in der Dichtung viele Möglichkeiten bestehen, unheimliche Wirkungen zu erzielen, die fürs Leben wegfallen]. (249)

Purity would tell a different story. From the beginning to the end of his work, Freud argued that reason and its servants, including aesthetics, were finally an elaborate way of naming frustration and failure. His aesthetics of the uncanny was designed to reinforce this lesson through its division between constricted life and the riches of poetry, whereas the surrealists — claiming devotion to Freud all the while — set out to reject the oppressive coziness of this distinction. Formal aesthetics, in effect, is a way of distinguishing a legitimate public and a proper order of the senses; and it is to Freud's credit (purity would say) that he felt uneasy about entering into this conclusion, especially since his own words say that the only obstacle standing between poetry and life is a "presupposition." Still, Freud did come to this conclusion, in his desire to eliminate the threat of contradictions to his theory. In this way he could evaluate stories with some assurance.

Although Freud's work can be taken to suggest that all the forms we perceive have a poetic, creative, performative life, it also suggests that we are bound to repress and misrecognize this life. The distinction of the surrealists' sense of purity lies in its attempt to reject the presuppositions of experience, with the institution of aesthetics and every other social order that catered to them; and it is possible to argue that in developing this sense the surrealists were more true to the implications of Freud's work than was Freud himself. In any event, Freud simply concluded that groups were effectively beyond any question of judgment. They worked by magic, by occult influence, as if by hypnosis, and fine distinctions were the last things from their mind. Collectivities, he said, were inevitably more stupid than individuals; groups could "only be excited by an excessive stimulus."[72] By the same token, once groups were set in motion they were as irresponsible as children, psychotics, and the id itself. Writing near the end of the First World War, Freud might have been reflecting on its armies and anticipating other parades soon to come. The group, as he portrayed it, is a terrible thing.

In their concern with purity, the surrealists deliberately courted this terror. Although F. Scott Fitzgerald's Paris was very different from the surrealists', something of the scenes remembered in "Babylon Revisited" was in this movement. Energies, gestures, lives were recklessly expended. There was a prophetic sense in the eulogy Breton pronounced on dada, in which he looked forward hopefully to the future, saying, "It would not be bad if we reestablished, for the spirit, the laws of the Terror."[73] Even as he and his remaining friends broke with Stalinism, Breton was capable of saying that "a perfume of deliverance rose from the blood" that was shed at the time of the First International.[74] In these instances and others, if the taste for sadism in surrealism generally seemed rhetorical, a matter of representational tactics that did not extend to physical violence, this characterization becomes dubious when one considers how the surrealists' own principles—their "DIABOLICAL MATERIALISM," in Brauner's words—would demand that one try to grasp the image as reality.[75] There may be a sense in which Brauner's painting of his *Self-Portrait was* directly connected to his disfigurement seven years later. When the surrealists were enchanted to see that de Chirico's 1914 *Portrait of Guillaume Apollinaire* could be taken to foretell the trepanation the poet underwent in 1916 for treatment of a war wound (a white circle on the poet's brow seemed to mark the spot), what were they asking for if not the right to have the world hold them accountable for their dreams? The "delirious images of surrealism," wrote Dali, "tend desperately toward their desperate tangibility, toward their objective and physical existence in reality."[76] Would we not be trivializing surrealism's potential influence, as well as its doctrines, if we did not entertain the possibility that works such as Alberto Giacometti's *Point to the Eye* (1932), in which a phallic tusk threatens a figure topped with the applelike organ, had something to do with Brauner's fate, Crevel's death, and Baron's grief?

Certainly questions such as these took on a real force when Aragon was threatened with prosecution for "Red Front," a poem in which he called

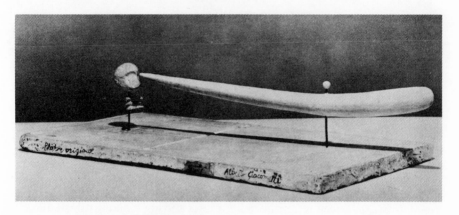

Alberto Giacometti, *Point to the Eye* (1931)
Plaster and metal, 12 × 59 × 30 cm.
Zurich, Alberto Giacometti Foundation, Kunsthaus Zürich
Copyright 1990 ARS N.Y./ADAGP

on his readers to shoot various enemies of the revolution, including Social
Democrats who would not toe the party line. Although he and Aragon were
already estranged, Breton circulated a petition to prominent artists and intellectuals that protested this government action on the grounds that Aragon's
words were a matter of poetic license; and as some noted at the time, this
attitude could seem hypocritical and contemptible in terms of the rules
of the surrealists' own game. He did not really mean it, Breton seemed
to be saying: so much for the books that metamorphose into revolvers in *Un
Chien Andalou*. In rejecting this attitude, members of the Belgian surrealist
group (René Magritte, E. L. T. Mesens, Paul Nougé, and André Souris)
actually welcomed the legal attack on "Red Front" as the sign of a breakdown
in the bourgeois aesthetic doctrines used to isolate poetry from social life.[77]
To add to the irony, Aragon himself disavowed Breton's justification for his
poem.

The case of "Red Front" was thus an embarrassing one for surrealism, as
was the case of Dali once he began to proclaim his fascination with things
Hitlerian, justifying his interest in the name of Sade, Lautréamont, and
surrealism itself.[78] These vexing situations may lead one to ask whether the
easy way with violent rhetoric among the surrealists, far from indicating
their desire to make their words really matter, instead showed their profound
undervaluation of language. For the contradictory impulses that confused
both cases seem to indicate a blindness, by turns amusing and frightening,
toward the powers with which the members of this group were conjuring.
Through their sense of purity, the surrealists were always driving themselves
toward a point at which imagination would become real, where the difference

between figurative and literal language would vanish; and then these situations arose to make their rhetoric indeed seem very easy, very rhetorical, and very cheap. There are consequences to treating Hitler as so much dream-stuff; and who but a creature compounded of shit, of something worse than shit, is not repulsed by Dali's pleasant accommodations with Franco or by Eluard's disgraceful complicity in the execution of Závis Kalandra?

Yet to be repulsed by such behavior is only too easy; to feel we have not made a mistake as bad as Oscar Dominguez's, when he threw that bottle, or Jacques Baron's, when he said those words, is only too easy. We betray ourselves with such judgments, which show such respect for the power of language and such confidence in our ability to distinguish its temporary flowers from its necessary roots. We do not escape violence so easily.

With few exceptions, surrealist violence was cool, intellectual, and meant to shock and dismay, not to draw blood. Germaine Berton, famed as an anarchist and murderer, was pictured in *The Surrealist Revolution*, but the surrealists themselves did not participate in assassinations; the first "Manifesto" described random murder as an exemplary surrealist activity, but no one tried to substantiate the claim;[79] the Marquis de Sade was a cherished precursor, but the surrealists seem never to have practiced kidnapping, rape, torture, and murder outside of the realms of sculpture, painting, and writing. When the self-induced trances of the early *temps des sommeils* got out of hand, leading to threats of mass suicide and, on one occasion, to Eluard being chased by an enchanted, knife-wielding Robert Desnos (as if he could tell what would happen to Kalandra), the surrealists called a halt to the experiences. Breton even noted this aspect of the movement in *Nadja*, where he contrasted his heroine's extreme liberty, which refused to bow even to the risk of self-destruction, to the way he and his friends always knew how to take care of themselves. "I dream of a War," Rimbaud had written, "of right or of might, of truly unforeseen logic";[80] but the surrealists' war was designed to burn the public with vitriol of its own manufacture, to throw back in the face of the public its crimes of civil and international violence, not to expose the participants in this movement to personal danger. In this respect, the stories of Brauner and Crevel may seem exceptional, more like failed poetic works than exemplary lives. A more representative case would be Aragon, who wriggled out of the "Red Front" controversy, remained loyal to Stalinism when Breton and other friends broke away from it, and lived a long, full life.

But maybe Aragon was bound to live out a certain story, much as Brauner and Crevel found themselves fulfilling uncanny predictions. "When It's All Over," a wonderful narrative Aragon wrote not long before the formal beginning of the surrealist movement, described a gang of youths who go on a rampage of criminal activity. They are inspired by a stew of romantic, anti-positivist, nihilist, Nietzschean ideas, and the narrator, Clément Grindor, characterizes their attitude as a "kind of terrorist sincerity" (71).[81]

(Their leader's slogan is "During my time, the deluge" [74].) Eventually, we learn that the narrator betrayed his friends to the police, reducing their enterprise to "nothing but a miserable comedy of revolt" (78). Subsequently, Grindor became an international philosophical agent provocateur, making a successful career of searching out the human weakness that would lead people into being traitors to each other and to themselves. One might say that he became the deathly individual who is the antagonist of the collective and liberating "disturbing machine" that the Bureau of Researches was meant to be. His account even intimates that his acts extended to a significant involvement in the First World War, and it ends with the savage suggestion that the narrator's good looks are simply the face of all the betrayals that brought Europe to its contemporary state.

If this story does have the effect I have claimed for it, it may stem from its satirical and yet darkly moving insistence that community is so complicit with revolt that it is profoundly impervious to any violence, its own being so great. Then it would be a story about the fatality of any feeling, something like the story Freud told in *Beyond the Pleasure Principle*. Or one might compare it to Ernst's visual parable, also composed just before the birth of surrealism, *Pietà or Revolution by Night* (1923). In this painting, the dead Christ is transformed into a living young man with Ernst's features, dressed in nightclothes and cradled in the arms of a homburg-topped, mustachioed, bronzed burgher with downcast eyes (a figure quoted from de Chirico's *The Child's Brain* [1915]). Held like a small child, a dreamer dreaming the imprisoning kindness of the arms of the bourgeois father, the young man looks coolly and skeptically at this protector. The hands of this complacent figure are ghostly outlines, clearly insufficient to restrain the more vibrantly painted youth they hold; and yet they do hold this figure, in a way that might suggest that the older man is his future identity as well as his present antagonist.[82]

If it works, Aragon's story may also owe its effect to the revision of a popular genre, the criminal mystery, into a vehicle for philosophical farce that manages to be funny and dead serious at the same time. Then it would be a story about the confounding of expectations, distinctions, and judgments. Its power would lie in the suggestion that *every* stimulus is excessive, as the word "betrayal" may seem excessive in its power to signify both violation and revelation, and as even the most familiar tale may seem magical when it calls forth divisive understandings and so looks to be less an object than an unformalizable desire.

And then interest may arise from the way this story may seem to foretell poetically the historical experience of surrealism, which found in its revolt such an overwhelming host of betrayals. At least Aragon seemed to be haunted by some such premonition when he went on, in *The Peasant of Paris*, to proclaim the birth of surrealism. Even as he had "Imagination" herald this movement, he also had this character describe surrealism as a "battle lost in advance."[83]

Max Ernst, *Piéta or Revolution by Night* (1923)
Collection Tate Gallery
Copyright 1990 ARS N.Y./SPADEM/ADAGP.

To be lost in advance is to be in a state of desire, is it not? To be embattled, moving forward into the past? When posed in this way, such questions may seem familiar enough, as may surrealism itself if it can be regarded, contrary to its own claims, as a form of art. But in the familiar aesthetic question that has occupied this chapter and this entire book, the question that asks how we tell whether a story works, a terrible purity is born.

Notes

CHAPTER 1

1. Friedrich Nietzsche, *Beyond Good and Evil: Prelude to a Philosophy of the Future*, trans. R. J. Hollingdale (London: Penguin Books, 1973), p. 84.

2. André Breton, *Manifeste du surréalisme, Manifestes du surréalisme* (Paris: Éditions Jean-Jacques Pauvert, 1972), p. 17. (Here and elsewhere, translations not otherwise noted are my own; I have given the original language within brackets where I have modified others' translations.)

3. William Howitt, *The History of the Supernatural in All Ages and Nations and in All Churches Christian and Pagan Demonstrating a Universal Faith*, 2 vols. (Philadelphia: J. B. Lippincott and Company, 1863), 2:244.

4. "Editor's Drawer," *Harper's New Monthly Magazine* 6 (May 1853): 850–51. In "The Fox Sisters and American Spiritualism," *The Occult in America: New Historical Perspectives*, ed. Howard Kerr and Charles L. Crow (Urbana: University of Illinois Press, 1983), p. 95, Ernest Isaacs estimates the number of Americans at least "giving credence to the phenomena" in 1855 at one million (out of a population of 28 million).

5. But see, for instance, Hanifa Kapidzic-Osmanagic, *Le Surréalisme serbe et ses rapports avec le surréalisme français* (Paris: Société les Belles Lettres, 1968); Paul C. Ray, *The Surrealist Movement in England* (Ithaca: Cornell University Press, 1971); and C. B. Morris, *Surrealism and Spain: 1920–1936* (Cambridge: Cambridge University Press, 1972).

6. See "Present Aspect of the World," *The Spiritual Telegraph*, vol. 4 (n.s.), ed. S. B. Brittan (New York: Partridge and Brittan, 1854), p. 360; and Karl Marx, *The Eighteenth Brumaire of Louis Bonaparte*, ed. C. P. Dutt (New York: International Publishers, n.d.), pp. 13–18.

7. Victor Crastre, *Le Drame du surréalisme* (Paris: Les Éditions du Temps, 1963), p. 102.

8. Roger Callois, "Monde d'images," *Cahiers du 20e siècle* 4 (1975): 15.

9. Breton, "La Perle est gâtée à mes yeux . . . ", *Le Surréalisme et la peinture* (Paris: Éditions Gallimard, 1965), p. 187.

10. See Breton, "Introduction au discours sur le peu de réalité," *Point du jour* (Paris: Éditions Gallimard, 1970), p. 22.

11. Some opponents of spiritualism would also give it a long pedigree, but to an opposite effect, as indicating a lineage of evil. See, for instance, Parsons Cooke, *Necromancy: Or, A Rap for the Rappers* (Boston: Congregational Board of Publications, 1857).

12. [Louis] Aragon, *Le Paysan de Paris* (Paris: Éditions Gallimard, 1948), p. 217; and Roger Vitrac, *Les Mystères de l'amour* (Paris: Éditions de la Nouvelle Revue Française, 1924), p. 47.

13. It is unclear whether Jarry, in making this dedication, knew of Crooke's spiritualism; in any event, the fact that Crookes could combine science and spirits as he did would seem to make him an apt figure for Jarry's "pataphysics," the science that supplements and burlesques conventional metaphysics and empiricism.

14. Walter Benjamin, "Surrealism: The Last Snapshot of the European Intelligentsia," *Reflections: Essays, Aphorisms, Autobiographical Writings*, ed. Peter Demetz, trans. Edmund Jephcott (New York: Harcourt Brace Jovanovich, 1978), p. 180. On the relationship between surrealism and spiritualism, with special reference to Breton's concern to maintain the distinctiveness of his movement, see Michel Thévoz's valuable essay, "L'Art du ruisseau," in *Regards sur Minotaure: La Revue à tête de bête* (Geneva: Musée d'art et d'histoire, 1987), pp. 187–99. Also, on the admixture of literature, occultism, spiritualism, and philosophy in the early years of this century, see Léon Somville, *Les Groups d'avant-garde et le mouvement poétique 1912–1925* (Geneva: Librarie Droz, 1971).

15. Sigmund Freud, "The 'Uncanny,'" *The Standard Edition of the Complete Psychological Works of Sigmund Freud*, trans. and ed. James Strachey et al., 24 vols. (London: The Hogarth Press and the Institute for Psycho-Analysis, 1959), 17: 242. See also Freud's writings on the occult: "Some Additional Notes on Dream Interpretation as a Whole," "Psychoanalysis and Telepathy," "Dreams and Telepathy," and the chapter on "Dreams and the Occult" in the *New Introductory Lectures on Psychoanalysis*.

16. Breton, "Manifeste du surréalisme," *Manifestes*, p. 17. See also "Entrée des médiums," *Les Pas perdus* (Paris: Éditions Gallimard, 1969), p. 127, where he discusses how René Crevel introduced the early members of the surrealist group to mediumistic activities; and for the later comments, see Breton, *Entretiens (1913–1952)*, rev. ed. (Paris: Éditions Gallimard, 1969), pp. 80–81. In the latter work, Breton describes the surrealists' criticism as concerning primarily "the crazy metaphysical implications" of the spiritualists' belief in communication between the living and the dead; he describes surrealism as resolving the apparent contradiction between the attitudes toward spiritualism of Victor Hugo, the enthusiastic practitioner, and Robert Browning, the skeptic.

17. Breton, "Lettre aux voyantes," *Manifestes*, p. 204.

18. Breton, "Le Message automatique," *Point du jour*, p. 179.

19. Martin Heidegger, *What Is a Thing?*, trans. W. B. Barton, Jr. and Vera Deutsch (Chicago: Henry Regnery, 1967), p. 44.

20. Paul Feyerabend, *Against Method: Outline of an Anarchistic Theory of Knowledge* (London: Verso, 1978), p. 25. Feyerabend's entire argument in this book, especially as he criticizes the identification of science with reason (and the parallel notion that unreason can be excluded from science), is relevant to my introduction.

21. Nietzsche, *Human, All Too Human: A Book for Free Spirits*, trans. Marion Faber and Stephen Lehmann (Lincoln: University of Nebraska Press, 1984), p. 19.

22. See Daniel Cottom, *Text and Culture: The Politics of Interpretation*, Theory and History of Literature, no. 62 (Minneapolis: University of Minnesota Press, 1989).

23. W. V. Quine and J. S. Ullian, *The Web of Belief*, 2nd ed. (New York: Random House, 1978), p. 5.

24. René Crevel, "Dali ou l'anti-obscurantisme," *L'Esprit contre la raison* (Paris: Tchou, 1969), pp. 62–63.

25. Max Ernst, quoted in J. H. Matthews, *The Imagery of Surrealism* (Syracuse: Syracuse University Press, 1977), p. 84n.

26. Hippolyte Léon Denizard Rivail, *Spiritualist Philosophy: The Spirits' Book*, trans. Anna Blackwell (Boston: Colby and Rich, 1875; rep. New York: Arno Press, 1976), p. xxiii; L. Alph[onse] Cahagnet, *The Celestial Telegraph: Or, Secrets of the Life to Come, Revealed through Magnetism, etc.*, 2 vols. in 1 (New York: Partridge and Brittan, 1855), 1: 127; and Breton, "Crise de l'objet," *Le Surréalisme et la peinture*, p. 276. (Rivail wrote under the pseudonym of "Allan Kardec.")

27. See Ann Braude, *Radical Spirits: Spiritualism and Women's Rights in Nineteenth-Century America* (Boston: Beacon Press, 1989), pp. 158–60.

28. Tristan Tzara, "Conférence sur dada," *Oeuvres complètes*, ed. Henri Béhar, 4 vols. (Paris: Éditions Flammarion, 1980), 1:424.

29. Paul Eluard, "Bonnes et mauvaises langues," *Oeuvres complètes*, ed. Marcelle Dumas and Lucien Scheler, 2 vols. (Paris: Éditions Gallimard, 1968), 1:432. ("Paul Eluard" was an adopted name; originally, the author was named Eugène Grindel.)

30. J. B. Ferguson, *Spirit Communion: A Record of Communications from the Spirit-Spheres, with Incontestable Evidence of Personal Identity, Presented to the Public, with Explanatory Observations* (Nashville: Union and American Steam Press, 1854), pp. 8–9; Ralph Waldo Emerson, "Demonology," *The North American Review* 124 (March–April 1877): 185.

CHAPTER 2

1. "Editor's Easy Chair," *Harper's New Monthly Magazine* 6 (December 1852): 129.

2. C. D. [Mrs. Sophia Elizabeth de Morgan], *From Matter to Spirit: The Result of Ten Years' Experience in Spirit Manifestations* (London: Longman, Green, Longman, Roberts, and Green, 1863), p. 27.

3. Henry Spicer, *Sights and Sounds: The Mystery of the Day* (London: Thomas Bosworth, 1853), p. 9.

4. A. B. [Augustus De Morgan], "Preface," *From Matter to Spirit*, p. xi. (The husband of Sophia Elizabeth De Morgan, Professor De Morgan was one of the more eminent mathematicians of this time.)

5. T. W. Adorno, *Aesthetic Theory*, ed. Gretel Adorno and Rolf Tiedemann, trans. C. Lenhardt (London: Routledge and Kegan Paul, 1984), p. 92.

6. Quoted in Robert Bernard Martin, *Tennyson: The Unquiet Heart* (New York: Oxford University Press, 1980), p. 563.

7. Comte Agenor de Gasparin, *Les Tables tournantes*, 4th ed. (Paris: Michel Lévy Frères, 1889), p. 129.

8. Anthony Trollope, *The Letters of Anthony Trollope*, ed. N. John Hall and Nina Burgis, 2 vols. (Stanford: Stanford University Press, 1983), 1:432. A "plan-

chette" was a small triangular device with wheels at the back and a pencil stuck in the tip, with which spirits would write when one or more persons placed their hands upon it; it was the ancestor of the pointers used with "ouija boards" today.

9. Henry David Thoreau, *Familiar Letters of Henry David Thoreau*, ed. F. B. Sanborn (Boston: Houghton Mifflin Company, 1894), p. 233; Nathaniel Hawthorne, *The Blithedale Romance, The Centenary Edition of the Works of Nathaniel Hawthorne*, ed. William Charvat et al., 14 vols. (Columbus: Ohio State University Press, 1964), 3:199; Ralph Waldo Emerson, "Demonology," *The North American Review* 124 (March–April 1877): 190. For comments that generally agree with Coverdale's, though in a more temperate style, see also Hawthorne, *The French and Italian Notebooks*, ed. Thomas Woodson, *Centenary Edition*, 14:398–99, 400–401, and 417.

10. Marie Corelli [Mary MacKay], *A Romance of Two Worlds* (Chicago: Donohue, Henneberry and Company, 1895), p. 142.

11. Harriet Martineau, *Autobiography*, ed. Gaby Weiner, 2 vols. (London: Virago Press, 1983), p. 250n.

12. Q. K. Philander Doesticks, P. B. [Mortimer Thomson], "An Evening with the Spiritualists – Rampant Ghostology," *Doesticks: What He Says* (New York: Edward Livermore, 1855), pp. 253–54.

13. The coinage is the Reverend C. B. Boynton's, as quoted in Spicer, *Sights and Sounds*, p. 167.

14. John Tyndall, "Miracles and Special Providences," *Fragments of Science: A Series of Detached Essays, Addresses, and Reviews*, 2 vols. (New York: D. Appleton and Company, 1897), 2:15.

15. William R. Gordon, *A Three-Fold Test of Modern Spiritualism* (New York: Charles Scribner, 1856), p. 369.

16. Allan Pinkerton, *The Spiritualists and the Detectives*, Allan Pinkerton's Detective Stories, no. 5 (New York: G. W. Carleton, 1877), pp. 220–21.

17. Robert Owen, *Robert Owen's Millenial Gazette*, 3 vols. (London: Published by the Author, 1856–58; rep. in one vol., New York: AMS Press, 1972), 2:30–32.

18. George Eliot, *The George Eliot Letters*, ed. Gordon S. Haight, 9 vols. (New Haven: Yale University Press, 1954–78), 5:49.

19. Reuben Briggs Davenport, *The Death-Blow to Spiritualism* (New York: G. W. Dillingham, 1888; rep. New York: Arno Press, 1976), p. 60.

20. [Henry Morley], "The Ghost of the Cock Lane Ghost," *Household Words* 6 (November 20, 1852): 222.

21. Bayard Taylor, "The Confessions of a Medium," *Prose Writings of Bayard Taylor*, rev. ed. (New York: G. P. Putnam, 1862), p. 460.

22. Quoted in "Professor Faraday on Table-Moving," *The Athenaeum* no. 1340 (July 2, 1853): 801.

23. Quoted in Robert Hare, *Experimental Investigation of the Spirit Manifestations, Demonstrating the Existence of Spirits and their Communion with Mortals, etc.*, 4th ed. (New York: Partridge and Brittan, 1856), p. 79. (The author identifies Bonjean as a "member of the Royal Academy of Savoy.") Cf. the conclusion of the Harvard committee organized to investigate spiritualism in 1857, quoted in Emma Hardinge, *Modern American Spiritualism: A Twenty Years' Record of the Communion Between Earth and the World of Spirits* (New Hyde Park, NY: University Books, 1970), p. 187:

It is the opinion of the committee, derived from observation, that any connection with spiritualistic circles, so called, corrupts the morals and degrades the intellect. They therefore deem it their solemn duty to warn the community against this contaminating influence, which surely tends to lessen the truth of man and the purity of woman.

Also, for a report on this investigation, see [George Lunt?], *Boston Courier Report of the Proceedings of Professed Spiritual Agents and Mediums, in the Presence of Professors Peirce, Agassiz, Horsford, Dr. B. A. Gould, Committee, and Others*, 2nd ed. (Boston: Office of the Boston Courier, 1859).

24. Spiritualists did distinguish between private sittings (held in domestic circles and by personal invitation only) and public sittings or exhibitions; the former were generally held to be more respectable. (A related distinction was often made between unpaid and paid mediums.) However, I use *public* here to describe two important aspects of spiritualist practices. First, the general public was always encouraged to witness the phenomena and make its own decisions about them. Second, spiritualists were convinced that even private seances were essentially public, in supposedly providing an opportunity for unmanipulated observation and thus the basis for credible public testimony about the phenomena.

25. Listed in the bibliography of the *Report on Spiritualism of the Committee of the London Dialectical Society, Together with the Evidence, Oral and Written, and a Selection from the Correspondence* (London: Longmans, Green, Reader and Dyer, 1871; rep. New York: Arno Press, 1976), p. 404.

26. Florence Marryat, *The Dead Man's Message: An Occult Romance* (New York: Charles B. Reed, 1894; rep. New York: Arno Press, 1976), p. 171.

27. W. E. Gunnig, quoted in Epes Sargent, *Planchette; Or, the Despair of Science*, Handy-Volume Series, no. 3 (Boston: Roberts Brothers, 1869), p. 124.

28. Quoted in Logie Barrow, *Independent Spirits: Spiritualism and English Plebeians, 1850–1910* (London: Routledge and Kegan Paul, 1986), p. 172. See also Barrow, p. 50 *et passim*, on the "democratic epistemology" involved in spiritualism.

29. Hawthorne, *The French and Italian Notebooks*, p. 399.

30. Laurence Moore, *In Search of White Crows: Spiritualism, Parapsychology, and American Culture* (New York: Oxford University Press, 1977), p. 23. Moore's is an excellent historical and sociological study; equally good are Janet Oppenheim's *The Other World: Spiritualism and Psychical Research in England, 1850–1914* (Cambridge: Cambridge University Press, 1985) and Ann Braude's *Radical Spirits: Spiritualism and Women's Rights in Nineteenth Century America* (Boston: Beacon Press, 1989). Although it did not appear in time for me to profit from it for my own study, I should also note Alex Owen's *The Darkened Room: Women, Power, and Spiritualism in Late Victorian England* (Philadelphia: University of Pennsylvania Press, 1990). Barrow's *Independent Spirits* is also important, as is Alan Gauld's *The Founders of Psychical Research* (London: Routledge and Kegan Paul, 1968). A useful early study is Frank Podmore's *Mediums of the 19th Century*, 2 vols. (New Hyde Park, NY: University Books, 1963). More specifically concerned with the literary treatments of spiritualism are Howard Kerr, *Mediums, and Spirit-Rappers, and Roaring Radicals: Spiritualism in American Literature, 1850–1900* (Urbana: University of Illinois Press, 1972) and Russell M. Goldfarb and Clare R. Goldfarb, *Spiritualism and Nineteenth-Century Letters* (Rutherford, NJ: Farleigh Dickinson University Press, 1978). See also Geoffrey K. Nelson, *Spiritualism and Society* (New York: Schocken Books, 1969); Jean Vartier, *Allan Kardec: La naissance du spiritisme*

(Paris: Librarie Hachette, 1971); Ronald Pearsall, *The Table-Rappers* (London: Michael Joseph, 1972); Brian Inglis, *Natural and Supernatural: A History of the Paranormal from Earliest Times to 1914* (London: Hodder and Stoughton, 1977); and Ruth Brandon, *The Spiritualists: The Passion for the Occult in the Nineteenth and Twentieth Centuries* (London: Weidenfeld and Nicolson, 1983).

31. Epes Sargent, *The Proof Palpable of Immortality; Being an Account of the Materialization Phenomena of Modern Spiritualism, etc.* (Boston: Colby and Rich, 1876), p. 223.

32. Quoted in Viscount Adare, *Experiences in Spiritualism with Mr. D. D. Home* (London: 1871; rep. New York: Arno Press, 1976), p. 32.

33. William Howitt, *The History of the Supernatural in All Ages and Nations and in All Churches Christian and Pagan Demonstrating a Universal Faith*, 2 vols. (Philadelphia: J. B. Lippincott and Company, 1863), 2:212–13. "The Kentucky Jerks" is not, as I would wish it to be, the name of a rock band, but rather the contemporary term for an outbreak of "spiritual" seizures among people in Kentucky's churches, hotels, and camp meetings earlier in the nineteenth century.

34. From the testimony of Dr. Joseph Leidy, quoted in *Preliminary Report of the Commission Appointed by the University of Pennsylvania to Investigate Modern Spiritualism in Accordance with the Request of the Late Henry Seybert* (Philadelphia: J. B. Lippincott, 1887), p. 104.

35. Quoted in Thomas Adolphus Trollope, *What I Remember*, 2 vols. (London: Richard Bentley and Son, 1887), 1:337. (Trollope goes on to note politely, "It may be observed, however, that he *did* appear to be much exhausted.")

36. See A[lfred] P[ercival] Sinnett, *Incidents in the Life of Madame Blavatsky* (London: George Redway, 1886; rep. New York: Arno Press, 1976), pp. 84–85.

37. From an article in *The Nation*, quoted in Sargent, *Planchette*, p. 288.

38. Robert Browning, "Mr. Sludge, 'The Medium,'" *Poetical Works 1833–1864*, ed. Ian Jack (London: Oxford University Press, 1970), p. 882. Daniel Dunglas Home (or Hume, as he was sometimes called, apparently because of his Scottish pronunciation in saying his name) was generally considered to be the original of Mr. Sludge. However, he appears never to have been detected in the sort of imposture Browning dramatized and, in fact, was widely regarded as the most impressive medium of the age.

39. Adin Ballou, *An Exposition of Views Respecting the Principal Facts, Causes and Peculiarities Involved in Spirit Manifestations: Together with Interesting Phenomenal Statements and Communications* (Boston: Bela Marsh, 1852), pp. 45–46.

40. George M. Beard, "The Psychology of Spiritism," *The North American Review* 129 (July 1879): 78.

41. William B. Yeats, *A Vision* (New York: Macmillan, 1961), pp. 24, 277.

42. On this point see R. Laurence Moore, "The Occult Connection? Mormonism, Christian Science, and Spiritualism," *The Occult in America: New Historical Perspectives*, ed. Howard Kerr and Charles L. Crow (Urbana: University of Illinois Press, 1983), pp. 150–51.

43. See, for instance, Frederic W. H. Meyers, a well-known psychologist at the turn of the century and a believer in spiritualism who helped to found the Society for Psychical Research: "All the objective is symbolic; our daily bread is as symbolic as the furniture of Swedenborg's heavens and hells." *Human Personality and its Survival of Bodily Death*, 2 vols. (New York: Longmans, Green and Company, 1903), 2:261.

44. Emerson, "Demonology," p. 190.

45. John Jones, *The Natural and Supernatural: Or, Man Physical, Apparitional, and Spiritual* (London: H. Baillière, 1861), p. 41; William Gregory, *Letters to a Candid Inquirer on Animal Magnetism* (Philadelphia: Blanchard and Lea, 1851), p. 209. The snail telegraph of which Gregory wrote was supposed to work when two snails, brought close to each other for a sufficient length of time, would establish a "sympathy" such that the movements of one would be mirrored by those of the other; as a result, someone could put a snail on an alphabet board, spell out a message, and have it reproduced at a great distance by the companion snail, if it were placed on a similar board.

46. Elizabeth Barrett Browning, "To Miss E. F. Haworth (June 16, 1860)," *The Letters of Elizabeth Barrett Browning*, ed. Frederic G. Kenyon, 2 vols. (London: Smith, Elder, and Company, 1897), 2:395.

47. Brian Wynne, "Physics and Psychics: Science, Symbolic Action, and Social Control in Late Victorian England," *Natural Order: Historical Studies of Scientific Culture*, ed. Barry Barnes and Steven Shapin (Beverly Hills, CA: Sage Publications, 1979), p. 177.

48. Artemus Ward [Charles Farrar Browne], "Among the Free Lovers," *The Complete Works of Artemus Ward*, ed. Melville D. Landon (New York: G. W. Dillingham, 1887), p. 57.

49. Cf. Oppenheim, *The Other World*, p. 227: "Phrenology, mesmerism, and spiritualism were thoroughly domesticated pursuits. They could be readily practiced in the home, apart from laboratory or hospital—those restricted preserves of the trained scientist and physician." On this subject of professionalism and spiritualism, see also Jon Palfreman, "Between Scepticism and Credulity: A Study of Victorian Scientific Attitudes to Modern Spiritualism," *On the Margins of Science: The Social Construction of Rejected Knowledge*, ed. Roy Wallis, Sociological Review Monograph no. 27 (Keele, Staffordshire: University of Keele, 1979), pp. 201–36.

50. "Professor Faraday on Table-Moving," p. 801; Leo Tolstoy, *Anna Karenina*, ed. Leonard J. Kent and Nina Berberova, trans. Constance Garnett (New York: Random House, 1965), p. 57.

51. Alfred Russel Wallace, *Miracles and Modern Spiritualism* (London: G. Redway, 1896; rep. New York: Arno Press, 1975), pp. 159–60.

52. Emerson, "Demonology," p. 185.

53. Braude, *Radical Spirits*, p. 45.

54. Eliot, *The George Eliot Letters*, 5:388.

55. [William E. Aytoun], "Modern Demonology," *Blackwood's Edinburgh Magazine* 97 (January 1865): 193.

56. J. B. Ferguson, *Spirit Communion: A Record of Communications from the Spirit-Spheres, with Incontestable Evidence of Personal Identity, Presented to the Public, with Explanatory Observations* (Nashville: Union and American Steam Press, 1854), p. 10.

57. Fred. Folio [pseud.], *Lucy Boston; Or, Woman's Rights and Spiritualism: Illustrating Follies and Delusions of the Nineteenth Century* (New York: J. C. Derby, 1855), p. viii.

58. Immanuel Kant, *Critique of Pure Reason*, trans. J. M. D. Meiklejohn (London: J. M. Dent and Sons, 1934), pp. 286–87.

59. Friedrich Nietzsche, *Human, All Too Human: A Book for Free Spirits*, trans.

Marion Faber with Stephan Lehmann, ed. Marion Faber (Lincoln: University of Nebraska Press, 1984), pp. 205–6.

60. "Scientistic Spiritualism," *The Medium and Daybreak* 3 (February 2, 1872): 37. Cf. Jean Burton's comment in *Heyday of a Wizard: Daniel Home, The Medium* (New York: Alfred A. Knopf, 1944), p. 164: "One of the functions Home quite unwittingly helped to perform, in fact, was to clear the ground for the anthropological study of world religions." One might add that spiritualism and its attendant controversies also could have served the purpose (although this challenge has rarely been accepted) of preparing science, philosophy, and Western culture in general, including the discipline of anthropology, to be "anthropologized."

61. Wilhelm Wundt, "Spiritualism as a Scientific Question. An Open Letter to Professor Hermann Ulrici, of Halle," trans. Edwin D. Mead, *The Popular Science Monthly* 15 (September 1879): 580.

62. Katherine H. Porter, *Through a Glass Darkly: Spiritualism in the Browning Circle* (Lawrence: University of Kansas Press, 1958), p. 43.

63. Alfred Cridge, "Tradition, Science, Marriage. Spiritualism a Destroyer of Enforced Marriage—Sexual Relations, Etc.," *Woodhull and Claflin's Weekly* (October 1, 1870): 7. See also Nelson's account of James Burns's speech against the emphasis on respectability, delivered at a convention of "progressive spiritualists," *Spiritualism and Society*, p. 100.

64. James Russell Lowell, "The Unhappy Lot of Mr. Knott," *The Poetical Works*, 5 vols. (New York: AMS Press, 1966), 3:108.

65. Emma Hardinge Britten, *Nineteenth Century Miracles, Or Spirits and Their Work in Every Country of the Earth* (New York: W. Britten, 1884; rep. New York: AMS Press, 1976), p. 192; Andrew Jackson Davis, *The Principles of Nature, Her Divine Revelations, and a Voice to Mankind*, 35th ed. (Boston: Colby and Rich, Banner Publishing House, 1847), pp. 694–71; C[harles] Hammond, *Light from the Spirit World. Comprising a Series of Articles on the Conditions of Spirits and the Development of Mind in the Rudimental and Second Spheres, etc.* (Rochester, NY: W. Heughes, 1852), p. 158; John Ashburner, *Notes and Studies in the Philosophy of Animal Magnetism and Spiritualism, with Observations upon Catarrh, Bronchitis, Rheumatism, Gout, Scrofula, and Cognate Diseases* (London: H. Baillière, 1867), pp. 14, 19; and L. Alphonse Cahagnet, *Arcanes de la vie future dévoilés*, 2 vols., 3rd ed. (Paris: Librarie Vigot Frères, 1896), 2:189. Davis actually set himself up as a seer and began publishing before the Rochester knockings, but he quickly affiliated himself with the subsequent movement, although he tended to prefer the "higher" manifestations of trance-speaking to material manifestations.

66. Dr. H. Ulrici, *Der sogennante Spiritismus: eine wissenschaftliche Frage* (Halle: C. I. M. Pfeffer, 1879), pp. 1, 2.

67. G. H. Lewes, "Seeing is Believing," *Blackwood's Edinburgh Magazine* 88 (October 1860): 391–95.

68. G. H. Lewes, "The Rappites Exposed," *The Leader* 4 (1853): 261–63; Newton Crosland, *Apparitions: An Essay, Explanatory of Old Facts and a New Theory* (London: Trübner and Company, 1873), p. 98. In his article, Lewes wrote of exposing Mrs. Hayden by figuring out her tricks and so leading her, in her spelling out of spirit communications, to spell out a confession that she was a fraud.

69. One might compare spiritualism on this point to the interest the surrealists took in vulgar language. See, for instance, Stuart Liebman's intricate and fascinating

analysis of the babble of vulgar wordplay in *Un Chien andalou*, "*Un Chien andalou*: The Talking Cure," *Dada/Surrealism* 15 (1986): 143–58.

70. John Nevil Maskelyne, *Modern Spiritualism: A Short Account of Its Rise and Progress, with Some Exposures of So-Called Spirit Media*, in *The Mediums and the Conjurors*, ed. James Webb (London: F. Warne, 1876; rep. New York: Arno Press, 1976), p. 71. This joke started even earlier than the one repeated by Martineau. J. F. C. Harrison reports a clergyman who told a follower of Joanna Southcott (the early nineteenth-century millenarian) "that he had no opinion of a Holy Spirit that could not write grammar." *The Second Coming: Popular Millenarianism 1780–1850* (New Brunswick, NJ: Rutgers University Press, 1979), p. 92.

71. G. W. F. Hegel, *The Phenomenology of Mind*, trans. and ed. J. B. Baillie (New York: Harper and Row, 1967), pp. 159–60, 371; and for his comments on mesmerism and allied phenomena, see Hegel, *Encyclopädie der Philosophischen Wissenschaften im Grundrisse*, 2nd ed. (Heidelberg: August Oswald, 1827), pp. 383–88.

72. Quoted in Sargent, *Planchette*, p. 305.

73. Charles Beecher, *Spiritual Manifestations* (Boston: Lee and Shepard, 1879), p. 13.

74. Gasparin, *Les Tables tournantes*, p. 166.

75. See Yeats, *A Vision*, p. 249; Thomas Mann, "An Experience in the Occult," *Three Essays*, trans. H. T. Lowe-Porter (New York: Alfred A. Knopf, 1929), p. 258; and Isaac Bashevis Singer, "The Séance," *The Collected Short Stories of Isaac Bashevis Singer* (New York: Farrar, Straus, Giroux, 1982), pp. 198–206. Mann's essay is especially notable for arguing that spiritualistic phenomena are indeed horribly undignified and yet not dismissable for that reason; Singer's story might be read as making a similar point.

76. Browning, *Letters*, 2:356.

77. Howitt, *The History of the Supernatural*, p. iv.

78. Charles Maurice Davies, *Mystic London: Or, Phases of Occult Life in the Metropolis* (London: Tinsley Brothers, 1875), p. 346; Browning, *Letters*, 2:158; D. D. Home, *Incidents in My Life* (New York: G. W. Carleton, 1863), p. 276; Ballou, *An Exposition of Views*, p. 79; Hippolyte Léon Denizard Rivail (Allan Kardec), *Spiritualist Philosophy: The Spirits' Book*, trans. Anna Blackwell (Boston: Colby and Rich, 1875; rep. New York: Arno Press, 1976), p. vii; Hare, *Spirit Manifestations*, pp. 21–22. (*Incidents in My Life* was ghostwritten by William M. Wilkinson.) For Browning's attitude toward spiritualism, see also the related comments in *Letters of the Brownings to George Barrett*, ed. Paul Landis and Ronald E. Freeman (Urbana: University of Illinois Press, 1958), p. 190; and in *Elizabeth Barrett Browning's Letters to Mrs. David Ogilvy 1847–1861*, ed. Peter N. Heydon and Philip Kelley (New York: Quadrangle/The New York Times Book Company and the Browning Institute, 1973), p. 97.

79. Virginia Woolf, *To the Lighthouse* (New York: Harcourt, Brace and World, 1955), p. 38.

80. Karl Marx, *Capital: A Critique of Political Economy*, ed. Frederick Engels, trans. Samuel Moore and Edward Aveling, rev. Ernest Untermann (New York: The Modern Library, 1906), p. 82.

81. Martin Heidegger, *What Is a Thing?*, trans. W. B. Barton, Jr. and Vera Deutsch (Chicago: Henry Regnery, 1967), p. 13.

82. Heidegger, "The Thing," *Poetry, Language, Thought*, trans. and ed. Albert

Hofstadter (New York: Harper and Row, 1971). Page numbers are given within the text.

83. Miss [Georgiana] Houghton, *Chronicles of the Photographs of Spiritual Beings and Phenomena, Invisible to the Material Eye. Interblended with Personal Narrative* (London: E. W. Allen, 1882), p. 74.

84. See, for instance, Herbert W. Schneider and George Lawton, *A Prophet and a Pilgrim* (New York: Columbia University Press, 1942). This is a biographical study of two spiritualists, Laurence Oliphant and Thomas Lake Harris.

85. Gauld, *The Founders of Psychical Research*, p. 30.

86. Emerson, "Swedenborg," *Representative Men: Seven Lectures, Emerson's Complete Works*, 12 vols. (Boston: Houghton, Mifflin and Company, 1893), 4:134.

87. On this point see Ronald Bruzina, "Heidegger on the Metaphor and Philosophy," *Heidegger and Modern Philosophy: Critical Essays*, ed. Michael Murray (New Haven: Yale University Press, 1978), pp. 184–200; and Jacques Derrida, "La Mythologie blanche; la métaphore dans le text philosophique," *Marges de la philosophie* (Paris: Les Éditions de Minuit, 1972), especially pp. 267–70.

CHAPTER 3

1. Laurence Oliphant, *Masollam; A Problem of the Period*, 3 vols. (Edinburgh: William Blackwood and Sons, 1886), 2:58–9.

2. J. B. Ferguson, *Spirit Communion: A Record of Communications from the Spirit-Spheres, with Incontestable Evidence of Personal Identity, etc.* (Nashville: Union and American Steam Press, 1854), p. 273.

3. Hippolyte Taine, *De l'Intelligence*, 12th ed., 2 vols. (Paris: Librarie Hachette, 1911), 1:16.

4. Sir William Crookes, "Some Further Experiments on Psychic Force," *Crookes and the Spirit World: A Collection of Writings by or Concerning the Work of Sir William Crookes, O. M., F. R. S., in the Field of Psychical Research*, coll. by R. G. Medhurst, with a general introduction by K. M. Goldney, and ed. with an introduction by M. R. Barrington (London: Souvenir Press, 1972), p. 36n.

5. Taine, *De l'Intelligence*, 1:69, 2:231.

6. *Preliminary Report of the Commission Appointed by the University of Pennsylvania to Investigate Modern Spiritualism in Accordance with the Request of the Late Henry Seybert* (Philadelphia: J. B. Lippincott, 1887), p. 15.

7. Count Agénor de Gasparin, *Science vs. Modern Spiritualism: A Treatise on Turning Tables, the Supernatural in General, and Spirits*, trans. E. W. Robert, 2 vols. (New York: Kiggens and Kellogg, 1857), 1:87. It may be noted that Gasparin rejected the spirit hypothesis in favor of a conception of a hitherto unrecognized natural force; in this attitude he was like many spiritualists who professed themselves unwilling to quibble over the difference between natural and supernatural agencies so long as one granted them the phenomena.

8. William H. Harrison, *Spirit People: A Scientifically Accurate Description of Manifestations Recently Produced by Spirits, and Simultaneously Witnessed by the Author and Other Observers in London* (London: W. H. Harrison, 1875), p. 36.

9. For this anecdote and other material relevant to this study, see Earl Wesley Fornell, *The Unhappy Medium: Spiritualism and the Life of Margaret Fox* (Austin: University of Texas Press, 1964), p. 23.

10. Charles Maurice Davies, *Mystic London: Or, Phases of Occult Life in the Metropolis* (London: Tinsley Brothers, 1875), p. 289. See also Dr. Sexton's address, "Spirit-Mediums and Jugglers," *The Medium and Daybreak* 4 (June 20, 1873): 261–65.

11. Robert Browning, "Mr. Sludge, 'The Medium,'" *Poetical Works 1833–1864*, ed. Ian Jack (London: Oxford University Press, 1970), p. 887. Cf. Logie Barrow, *Independent Spirits: Spiritualism and English Plebeians, 1850–1910* (London: Routledge and Kegan Paul, 1986), p. 58: "One of the preconditions for spiritualist belief to become and remain stable, was that it should offer logical procedures for relativizing — whenever one wished — any particular 'spiritual' revelation without undermining itself."

12. Oliphant, *Masollam*, 2:52. Another wonderful defense of mediums' failures was John Jones's argument — "The great proof of Mediumship is the total inability of the person to produce phenomena *at will*" — in *The Natural and Supernatural: Man Physical, Apparitional, and Spiritual* (London: H. Baillière, 1861), p. 269.

13. W. D. Howells, *The Undiscovered Country* (Boston: Houghton, Mifflin and Company, 1880), pp. 52–53.

14. John Tyndall, "Science and the 'Spirits,'" *Fragments of Science: A Series of Detached Essays, Addresses, and Reviews*, 2 vols. (New York: D. Appleton and Company, 1907), 1:451.

15. [G. H. Lewes], "Seeing is Believing," *Blackwood's Edinburgh Magazine* 88 (October 1860): 383.

16. Alfred Russel Wallace, "Preface to the First Edition" [1874], *Miracles and Modern Spiritualism* (London: G. Redway, 1896; rep. New York: Arno Press, 1975), p. vii.

17. See A. Leah Underhill, *The Missing Link in Modern Spiritualism* (New York: Thomas R. Knox and Company, 1885; rep. New York: Arno Press, 1976); and William Stainton Moses, *Spirit Teachings* (London: London Spiritualist Alliance, 1924; rep. New York: Arno Press, 1976). (*Spirit Teachings* was written, according to Moses, between 1873 and 1880; he died in 1892.) See also the exemplary "history of a convert to the spirit-theory" offered by Henry Spicer in *Sights and Sounds: The Mystery of the Day* (London: Thomas Bosworth, 1853), p. 474.

18. Thomas Adolphus Trollope, *What I Remember*, 2 vols. (London: Richard Bentley and Son, 1887), 1:379. (Trollope makes this remark in a discussion of Daniel Home; his own position is characterized as one of interest but not belief in spiritualism.)

19. J. W. Edmonds (in a letter), *The Spiritual Telegraph*, ed. S. B. Brittan, (n.s.) (New York: Partridge and Brittan, 1854), 4:538.

20. Gasparin, *Science vs. Spiritualism*, p. 141.

21. Emma Hardinge, *Modern American Spiritualism: A Twenty Years' Record of the Communion Between Earth and the World of Spirits* (New Hyde Park, NY: University Books, 1970), p. 59.

22. Quoted in Leonard Huxley, *Life and Letters of Thomas Henry Huxley*, 2 vols. (New York: D. Appleton and Company, 1900), 1:452. Huxley may have had Mrs. Hayden in mind in this passage; she was the first spiritualist to visit England from America, and she charged the price he mentions for a sitting.

23. Artemus Ward [Charles Farrar Browne], "Among the Spirits," *The Complete Works of Artemus Ward* (New York: G. W. Dillingham, 1887), p. 40.

24. P. T. Barnum, *The Humbugs of the World: An Account of Humbugs, Delusions, Impositions, Quackeries, Deceits and Deceivers Generally, in All Ages* (New York: G. W. Carleton, 1866), p. 101.

25. Clara Sherwood, *The Medium and Daybreak* 1 (October 14, 1870): 218; and Jones, *The Natural and Supernatural*, p. 314.

26. William Wetmore Story, *Conversations in a Studio*, 2 vols. (Boston: Houghton, Mifflin and Company, 1890), 1:295.

27. Hippolyte Léon Denizard Rivail (Allan Kardec, pseud.), *Spiritualist Philosophy: The Spirits' Book*, trans. Anna Blackwell (Boston: Colby and Rich, 1875; rep. New York: Arno Press, 1976), p. xxxv.

28. Moses, *Spirit Teachings*, p. 46.

29. Anna Mary Howitt Watts, *The Pioneers of the Spiritual Reformation* [*Life and Works of Dr. Justinus Kerner* and *William Howitt and His Work for Spiritualism*] (London: The Psychological Press Association, 1883), pp. 241–42n.

30. Charles Beecher, *Spiritual Manifestations* (Boston: Lee and Shepard, 1879), p. 59.

31. Nathaniel Hawthorne, "The Birth-mark," *Mosses from an Old Manse*, ed. William Charvat et al., *The Centenary Edition of the Works of Nathaniel Hawthorne*, 14 vols. (Athens: Ohio State University Press, 1974), 10:36.

32. References to telegraphy were very frequent; one of the main American spiritualist newspapers was *The Spiritual Telegraph*; and Leah [Fox] Underhill even claimed that at the time of the Rochester knockings "the same signal had been given to all mediums." She concluded, "Thus we see that God's Telegraphy ante-dated that of Samuel F. B. Morse" (*The Missing Link in Modern Spiritualism*, p. 49).

33. Dion Boucicault, quoted in T. L. Nichols, *A Biography of the Brothers Davenport* (London: Saunders, Otley and Company, 1864; rep. New York: Arno Press, 1976), p. 269.

34. Carl du Prel, *The Philosophy of Mysticism*, trans. C. C. Massey, 2 vols. in 1 (London: George Redway, 1889; rep. New York: Arno Press, 1976), 2:151. It is notable that in *The Interpretation of Dreams*, Sigmund Freud repeatedly referred to this author as "that brilliant mystic Du Prel." See *The Standard Edition of the Complete Psychological Works of Sigmund Freud*, trans. James Strachey et al., 24 vols. (London: The Hogarth Press and the Institute for Psycho-Analysis, 1953), 4: 63n.

35. Robert Owen, *Robert Owen's Millenial Gazette*, 3 vols. in 1 (London: Published by the Author, 1856–58; rep. New York: AMS Press, 1972), 2:9.

36. A[lfred] P[ercival] Sinnett, *Incidents in the Life of Madame Blavatsky* (London: George Redway, 1886; rep. New York: Arno Press, 1976), p. vi.

37. Friedrich Nietzsche, *Human, All Too Human: A Book for Free Spirits*, trans. Marion Faber and Stephen Lehmann, ed. Marion Faber (Lincoln: University of Nebraska Press, 1984), p. 281.

38. R. Laurence Moore, *In Search of White Crows: Spiritualism, Parapsychology, and American Culture* (New York: Oxford University Press, 1977), p. 26.

39. Quoted in [Epes Sargent], *Planchette: Or, The Despair of Science*, Handy-Volume Series, no. 3 (Boston: Roberts Brothers, 1869), p. 121.

40. Robert Dale Owen, *The Debatable Land Between this World and the Next* (New York: G. W. Carleton and Company, 1872), p. x.

41. Margaret Fuller Ossoli, "The New Science, or the Philosophy of Mesmerism

or Animal Magnetism," *Life Without and Life Within: Or, Reviews, Narratives, Essays, and Poems*, ed. Arthur B. Fuller (Boston: Roberts Brothers, 1874), p. 171. Cf. Levin's speech in Leo Tolstoy's *Anna Karenina*, ed. Leonard J. Kent and Nina Berberova, trans. Constance Garnett (New York: Random House, 1965), p. 57:

> "When electricity was discovered," Levin interrupted hurriedly, "it was only the phenomenon that was discovered, and it was unknown from what it proceeded and what were its effects, and ages passed before its applications were conceived. But the spiritualists have begun with tables writing for them, and spirits appearing to them, and have only later started saying that it is an unknown force."

42. Hawthorne, *The House of the Seven Gables, Works*, 2:263–84.

43. Quoted in Wallace, *Miracles and Modern Spiritualism*, p. 81.

44. John Ashburner, *Notes and Studies in the Philosophy of Animal Magnetism and Spiritualism, with Observations upon Catarrh, Bronchitis, Rheumatism, Gout, Scrofula, and Cognate Diseases* (London: H. Baillière, 1867), pp. xii–xiii; Robert Hare, *Experimental Investigation of the Spirit Manifestations, Demonstrating the Existence of Spirits and their Communion with Mortals, etc.*, 4th ed. (New York: Partridge and Brittan, 1856), Plates I–IV; and Crookes, "Spiritualism Viewed by the Light of Modern Science," *Crookes and the Spirit World*, p. 17.

45. E. W. Capron, *Modern Spiritualism: Its Facts and Fanaticisms, Its Consistencies and Contradictions* (Boston: Bela Marsh, 1855), p. 224. (Capron's account is taken from the June 29, 1854 issue of a Boston newspaper, the *New Era*, which was sympathetic to spiritualism.)

46. Hardinge, *Modern American Spiritualism*, p. 220. The circle at a seance was often described as a battery or magnetic chain, especially during the first few years of modern spiritualism. For instance, see Baron Ludwig von Guldenstubbé's understanding of American spiritual circles as involving twelve people, six who are positive or magnetic in nature (generally male) and six who are negative or electric (generally female) in *Pneumatologie positive et expérimentale: La Réalité des esprits et le phénomène merveilleux de leur écriture directe* (Paris: Librarie A. Franck, 1857), p. 65. This description, of course, is another example of the way scientific language would be borrowed and explored. Here and in other aspects of spiritualism, the question of sexual difference was part of this exploration.

47. Villiers de l'Isle-Adam, *L'Eve future, Oeuvres complètes*, ed. Alan Raitt et al., 2 vols. (Paris: Éditions Gallimard, 1986), 1:874.

48. Barnum, *The Humbugs of the World*, pp. 141, 143.

49. Hardinge, *Modern American Spiritualism*, p. 221.

50. Quoted in Hardinge, *Modern American Spiritualism*, p. 223.

51. See Paul K. Feyerabend, *Realism, Rationalism, and Scientific Method*, in *Philosophical Papers*, vol. 1 (Cambridge: Cambridge University Press, 1981), p. 199.

52. For Charles Beecher's theory of figurative language and its relation to Biblical interpretation and language reform, see *Spiritual Manifestations*, pp. 59–64; for Robert Owen's ideas, see the articles throughout *Robert Owen's Millenial Gazette*; for Victoria Woodhull's theories, see the series of articles on language and related topics published in *Woodhull and Claflin's Weekly* in the early 1870s.

53. Ralph Waldo Emerson, "Swedenborg; Or, the Mystic," *Representative Men, Emerson's Complete Works*, 12 vols. (Boston: Houghton, Mifflin and Company, 1893), 4:128.

54. Arthur Conan Doyle, *The History of Spiritualism*, 2 vols. in 1 (New York: G. H. Doran, 1926; rep. New York: AMS Press, 1975), 1:47.

55. Hawthorne, *The French and Italian Notebooks*, ed. Thomas Woodson, *Works*, 14:398.

56. William Gregory, *Letters to a Candid Inquirer on Animal Magnetism* (Philadelphia: Blanchard and Lea, 1851), p. 94; C[harles] Hammond, *Light from the Spirit World* (Rochester, NY: W. Heughes, 1852), p. 248; Ferguson, *Spirit Communion*, p. 5; and Moses, *Spirit Teachings*, p. 64. It is relevant to this point that on the title page of his work Hammond notes that it was "written wholly by the control of Spirits, without any volition or will by the Medium or any thought or care in regard to the matter presented by his hand."

57. Moses, *Spirit Teachings*, p. 40.

58. Frederic W. H. Myers, *Human Personality and its Survival of Bodily Death*, 2 vols. (New York: Longmans, Green and Company, 1903), 2:218.

59. Rivail, *Spiritualist Philosophy*, p. xxxiv; Sargent, *Planchette*, p. 290; and Hammond, *Light from the Spirit World*, p. 182. This argument was paralleled by the popular idea that spirits belong to different heavens or spheres (of which there were usually seven), according to their nature or "affections"; consequently, since they might be unaware of other heavenly realities, they might speak incorrectly in relation to the communications of other spirits.

60. Laroy Sunderland, *Book of Human Nature: Illustrating the Philosophy (New Theory) of Instinct, Nutrition, Life; with their Correlative and Abnormal Phenomena, Physiological, Mental, Spiritual* (New York: Stearns and Company, 1853), p. 270.

61. Pierre Janet, *Les Névroses* (Paris: Ernest Flammarion, 1909), p. 13.

62. Henry James, Sr., "Spiritual Rappings," *Lectures and Miscellanies* (New York: Redfield, 1852), p. 408. See also his similar opinions in "Spiritualism New and Old," *The Atlantic Monthly* 29 (March 1872): 358–62.

63. E. W. Capron, *Modern Spiritualism*, p. 117n. Cf. William Butler Yeats's description of the spirits he called "Frustrators" in *A Vision* (New York: Macmillan, 1961), pp. 12–13.

64. Underhill, *The Missing Link in Modern Spiritualism*, p. 110n.

65. See Mrs. Alving's speech in Henrik Ibsen's *Ghosts*, ed. and trans. James Walter McFarlane, *The Oxford Ibsen*, 8 vols. (London: Oxford University Press, 1961), 5: 384:

> "But then I'm inclined to think that we are all ghosts, Pastor Manders, every one of us. It's not just what we inherit from our mothers and fathers that haunts us. It's all kinds of old defunct theories, all sorts of old defunct beliefs, and things like that. It's not that they actually *live* on in us; they are simply lodged there, and we cannot get rid of them. I've only to pick up a newspaper and I seem to see ghosts gliding between the lines. Over the whole country there must be ghosts, as numerous as the sands of the sea. And here we are, all of us, abysmally afraid of the light."

66. Immanuel Hermann von Fichte, *Der neuere Spiritualismus, sein Werth und seine Täuschungen* (Leipzig: F. A. Brockhaus, 1878), p. 91.

67. George Eliot, *The George Eliot Letters*, ed. Gordon S. Haight, 9 vols. (New Haven: Yale University Press, 1954–78), 5:280–81.

68. Brittan, ed., *The Spiritual Telegraph*, 4:234. Cf. Elizabeth Barrett Browning's

adaptation of this term to poetry: " . . . is love's true thing / So much best to us [women], that what personates love / Is next best?" In "Aurora Leigh," *The Complete Poetical Works of Elizabeth Barrett Browning*, ed. Harriet Waters Preston (Boston: Houghton Mifflin Company, 1900), p. 277.

69. *Report on Spiritualism of the Committee of the London Dialectical Society, Together with the Evidence, Oral and Written, and a Selection from the Correspondence* (London: Longmans, Green, Reader and Dyer, 1871; rep. New York: Arno Press, 1976), p. 204.

70. Quoted in Katherine H. Porter, *Through a Glass Darkly: Spiritualism in the Browning Circle* (Lawrence: University of Kansas Press, 1958), p. 55.

71. See Théophile Gautier, *Spirite: Nouvelle fantastique, Oeuvres complètes*, 9 vols. (Paris: Charpentier, 1882; rep. Geneva: Slatkine Reprints, 1978), 4:173.

72. Taine, *De l'Intelligence*, 2:216.

73. Alfred Binet, *Alterations of Personality*, trans. Helen Green Galdwin, *Significant Contributions to the History of Psychiatry 1750–1920*, Series C: Medical Psychology, no. 5, ed. Daniel N. Robinson (Washington, DC: University Publications of America, 1977), p. 336.

74. Moses, *Spirit Teachings*, p. 65.

75. Rivail, *Spiritualist Philosophy*, p. xxxii. Cf. Robert Dale Owen's suggestion that a name may be assumed "by some spirit favoring the school of the sage whose name he gives" in *The Debatable Land*, p. 294; Warren Chase's argument that names "are only given to represent conditions and times" in *The Life-line of the Lone One; Or, Autobiography of the World's Child* (Boston: Bela Marsh, 1857), pp. 278–79; and Viscount Amberley's wry criticism of this "common but most inconvenient habit in the spirit-world" in "Experiences in Spiritualism," *The Fortnightly Review* 15 (n.s.) (1874): 84.

76. "Introduction," *"Rifts in the Veil": A Collection of Inspirational Poems and Essays Given through Various Forms of Mediumship; Also of Poems and Essays by Spiritualists* (London: W. H. Harrison, 1878), p. 10.

77. G. H. Lewes, *The Study of Psychology: Problems of Life and Mind*, 3rd series, *Significant Contributions to the History of Psychology 1750–1920*, Series A: Orientations, ed. Daniel N. Robinson (Boston: Houghton, Osgood and Company, 1879; rep. Washington, DC: University Publications of America, 1977), pp. 166–67, 168.

78. Cf. Gilles Deleuze and Félix Guattari, *A Thousand Plateaus: Capitalism and Schizophrenia*, trans. Brian Massumi (Minneapolis: University of Minnesota Press, 1987), p. 84:

> Language in its entirety is indirect discourse. Indirect discourse in no way supposes direct discourse; rather, the latter is extracted from the former, to the extent that the operations of signifiance and proceedings of subjectification in the assemblage are distributed, attributed, and assigned, or that the variables of the assemblage enter into constant relations, however temporarily. Direct discourse is a detached fragment of a mass and is born of the dismemberment of the collective assemblage; but the collective assemblage is always like the murmur from which I take my proper name, the constellation of voices, concordant or not, from which I draw my voice. . . . To write is perhaps to bring this assemblage of the unconscious to the light of day, to select the whispering voices, to gather the tribes and secret idioms from which I extract something I call my Self (*Moi*).

79. Owen, *Millenial Gazette*, 1:17.

80. Wallace, *Miracles and Modern Spiritualism*, p. 113.

81. Charles Bray, *On Force, Its Mental and Moral Correlates; And on that Which is Supposed to Underlie All Phenomena: With Speculations on Spiritualism, and Other Abnormal Conditions of Mind* (London: Longmans, Green, Reader, and Dyer [1866]), p. 82.

82. *Woodhull and Claflin's Weekly* (September 23, 1871): 13.

83. Quoted in Reuben Briggs Davenport, *The Death-Blow to Spiritualism* (New York: G. W. Dillingham, 1888; rep. New York: Arno Press, 1976), p. 60.

84. Cf. Jacques Derrida's comment, "The 'model' is always the dreamed-of ghost," in "Cartouches," *The Truth in Painting*, trans. Geoff Bennington and Ian McLeod (Chicago: University of Chicago Press, 1987), p. 217.

85. Cf. Barrow's description of spiritualism leading to "what we might call do-it-yourself universe-building (with materials pre-mixed to a varying extent)" in *Independent Spirits*, p. 140.

86. Louisa Lowe, "The Ends, Aims, and Uses of Modern Spiritualism," *"Rifts in the Veil"*, p. 111.

CHAPTER 4

1. Charlotte Brontë, *Jane Eyre*, ed. Jane Jack and Margaret Smith (Oxford: Oxford University Press, 1969), p. 318.

2. Emily Dickinson, "The Only News I Know" [no. 827], *The Poems of Emily Dickinson*, ed. Thomas H. Johnson, 3 vols. (Cambridge: Harvard University Press, 1955), 2:626. Page numbers are given within the text.

3. Robert Owen, *The Life of Robert Owen*, ed. M. Beer (New York: Alfred A. Knopf, 1920), pp. 275–76.

4. George Eliot, *The George Eliot Letters*, ed. Gordon S. Haight, 9 vols. (New Haven: Yale University Press, 1954–78), 6:216–17.

5. Auguste Comte, *Cours de philosophie positive*, in *Auguste Comte and Positivism: The Essential Writings*, ed. with an Introduction by Gertrud Lenzer (New York: Harper and Row, 1975), p. 148.

6. See the analysis of his thought in Robert Darnton, *Mesmerism and the End of the Enlightenment in France* (Cambridge: Harvard University Press, 1968), p. 16.

7. B. Steward and P. C. Tait, *The Unseen Universe or Physical Speculations on a Future State* (New York: Macmillan and Company, 1875), p. 158. Cf. the example of Professor Thury in Geneva, who rejected the spiritualist hypothesis and yet attributed the phenomena in question to "the effect of a special nervous force analogous to the ether of the savants," as reported in Paul Gibier, *Le Spiritisme* (Paris: Octave Doin, 1887), p. 274. On this subject, see the excellent discussion of the role of the ether in the ideology of nineteenth-century science given by Brian Wynne, "Physics and Psychics: Science, Symbolic Action, and Social Control in Late Victorian England," *Natural Order: Historical Studies of Scientific Culture*, ed. Barry Barnes and Steven Shapin, Sage Focus Editions, no. 6 (Beverly Hills, CA: Sage Publications, 1979), pp. 167–86. See also Logie Barrow's analysis of the legacy of Newtonian science to the nineteenth century, especially in regards to the conception of imponderables, which "was a license either to invent or to disbelieve hypotheses, or at least to

proliferate forces which often remained even more mysterious than the phenomena they had been invented to explain," in *Independent Spirits: Spiritualism and English Plebeians, 1850–1910* (London: Routledge and Kegan Paul, 1986), p. 73. The Baron von Reichenbach's "odylic force" was the most famous of these hypotheses in the early years of spiritualism, one which was accepted even by some avowed disbelievers in the spiritualist movement, such as Asa Mahan. See his *Modern Mysteries Explained and Exposed* (Boston: John P. Jewett and Company, 1855).

8. Quoted in Alexandre Aksakoff, *Animisme et spiritisme: Essai d'un examen critique des phénomènes médiumiques*, trans. [from the Russian] Berthold Sandow, 4th ed. (Paris: Librarie des Sciences Psychiques, 1906), p. 41. Aksakoff quotes from an 1872 issue of *Photographic News*; in *Chronicles of the Photographs of Spiritual Beings and Phenomena, Invisible to the Material Eye. Interblended with Personal Narrative* (London: E. W. Allen, 1882), Georgiana Houghton approvingly quotes the same photographer, a Mr. Beattie, from his argument about the ether in an issue of the *Spiritual Magazine*.

9. Théophile Gautier, *Spirite: Nouvelle fantastique, Oeuvres complètes*, 9 vols. (Paris: Charpentier, 1882; rep. Geneva: Slatkine Reprints, 1978), 4:165.

10. Robert Hare, M. D., *Experimental Investigation of the Spirit Manifestations, Demonstrating the Existence of Spirits and their Communion with Mortals, etc.*, 4th ed. (New York: Partridge and Brittan, 1856), p. 160.

11. Charles Beecher, *Spiritual Manifestations* (Boston: Lee and Shepard, 1879), p. 16.

12. George Sexton, "Scientific Materialism Examined and Refuted," *The Medium and Daybreak* 5 (September 25, 1874): 609. See also the poem from *Punch* on "Science and Superstition" quoted in *The Medium and Daybreak* 4 (January 24, 1873): 41, in which superstition answers the charge of credulity by accusing science of the same, as in the following stanza: "If my bright imagination / People space with airy shapes, / What of your dull brains' creation, / Hairier forms; ancestral apes?"

13. See Dr. Justinus Kerner, *Die Somnambülen Tische: Zur Geschichte und Erklärung dieser Erscheinung* (Stuttgart: Ebner und Seubert, 1853); [Samuel Guppy], *Mary Jane; Or, Spiritualism Chemically Explained, with Spirit Drawings. Also, Essays by, and Ideas (Perhaps Erroneous) of "A Child at School"* (London: John King and Company, 1863); William Gregory, *Letters to a Candid Inquirer on Animal Magnetism* (Philadelphia: Blanchard and Lea, 1851), especially his discussion of the theory of the Baron von Reichenbach on p. 119; Alfred Russell Wallace, *Miracles and Modern Spiritualism* (London: G. Redway, 1896; rep. New York: Arno Press, 1975), especially p. 44; Frederic W. H. Myers, *Human Personality and Its Survival of Bodily Death*, 2 vols. (New York: Longmans, Green and Company, 1903), especially 2:262; and Johann Carl Friedrich Zöllner, *Transcendental Physics: An Account of Experimental Investigations from the Scientific Treatises*, trans. and ed. Charles Carleton Massey, 4th ed. (Boston: Colby and Rich, 1888; rep. New York: Arno Press, 1976).

14. Adin Ballou, *An Exposition of Views Respecting the Principal Facts, Causes and Peculiarities Involved in Spirit Manifestations: Together with Interesting Phenomenal Statements and Communications* (Boston: Bela Marsh, 1852), pp. 22, 76.

15. T. Grant, "A Scientific View of Modern Spiritualism," *The Medium and Daybreak* 4 (January 31, 1873): 50.

16. "My Name: 'The Medium and Daybreak,'" *The Medium and Daybreak* 1

(April 18, 1870): 4; and "The Medium to Its Readers and Spiritualists Generally," *The Medium and Daybreak* 3 (January 5, 1872): 1.

17. Lizzie Doten, "The Mysteries of Godliness," *Poems from the Inner Life*, 3rd ed. (Boston: William White and Company, 1864), pp. 145–46. See also the interpretation of Poe as a medium in Sarah Helen Whitman, *Edgar Poe and His Critics* (New York: Rudd and Carleton, 1860; rep. New York: AMS Press, 1966). Also, on this issue of mediumship, cf. Jean Baudrillard's description of the "implosion *of the medium and of the real*, in a sort of nebulous hyperreality, in which even the definition and the distinct action of the medium are no longer locatable," in "L'Implosion du sens dans les media," *Simulacres et simulation* (Paris: Éditions Gallilée, 1981), p. 126. (Baudrillard's recent writings might well be seen as a twentieth-century counterpart to the writings of the spiritualists, resembling the earlier works in terms of vulgarity, millenarianism, and pretensions to revealed authority – lacking only their conscience and charm.)

18. David Hume, *An Enquiry Concerning Human Understanding, Enquiries Concerning Human Understanding and Concerning the Principles of Morals*, ed. L. A. Selby-Bigge, 3rd ed., ed. P. H. Nidditch (Oxford: Oxford University Press, 1975), p. 34.

19. Fine distinctions were sometimes made in the first half of this century between those who called themselves biologists and those who identified themselves as mesmerists, as a more important distinction was made later in the century between the theories of mesmerism and hypnotism; but these are not essential to the present argument.

20. Wallace, *Miracles and Modern Spiritualism*, pp. 260, 262.

21. G. H. Lewes, *The Study of Psychology: Problems of Life and Mind*, 3rd Series, *Significant Contributions to the History of Psychology 1750–1920*, Series A: Orientations, 6, ed. Daniel N. Robinson (Boston: Houghton, Osgood and Company, 1879; rep. Washington, DC: University Publications of America, 1977), pp. 7, 27, 158, 162, and 156.

22. Myers, *Human Personality*, 2:218.

23. Elizabeth Barrett Browning, *The Letters of Elizabeth Barrett Browning*, ed. Frederic G. Kenyon, 2 vols. (London: Smith, Elder, and Company, 1897), 2:422. The "Strauss" referred to is of course David Friedrich Strauss, whose *Life of Jesus* was frequently cited for its principled refusal to entertain the possibility of miracles.

24. G. W. F. Hegel, *The Phenomenology of Mind*, trans. and ed. J. B. Baillie (New York: Harper and Row, 1967), p. 86.

25. Paul K. Feyerabend, *Realism, Rationalism and Scientific Method, Philosophical Papers*, vol. 1 (Cambridge: Cambridge University Press, 1981), p. 76; and *Problems of Empiricism, Philosophical Papers*, vol. 2 (Cambridge: Cambridge University Press, 1981), p. 19.

26. W. E. H. Lecky, *History of the Rise and Influence of the Spirit of Rationalism in Europe*, 2 vols. in 1 (New York: George Braziller, 1955), p. xv; and William B. Carpenter, *Mesmerism, Spiritualism, &c. Historically and Scientifically Considered* (New York: D. Appleton and Company, 1877), p. 3. Feyerabend, as it happens, cites Lecky as an admirable predecessor in his line of thought in *Realism, Rationalism, and Scientific Method*, p. 32.

27. *Preliminary Report of the Commission Appointed by the University of Penn-*

sylvania to Investigate Modern Spiritualism in Accordance with the Request of the Late Henry Seybert (Philadelphia: J. B. Lippincott Company, 1887), p. 4.

28. Emma Hardinge Britten, *Nineteenth Century Miracles, Or Spirits and their Work in Every Country of the Earth* (New York: W. Britten, 1884; rep. New York: Arno Press, 1976), p. 123.

29. Beecher, *Spiritual Manifestations*, pp. 52–53.

30. Walt Whitman, "Mediums," *Complete Poetry and Collected Prose*, ed. Justin Kaplan (New York: The Library of America, 1982), p. 590.

31. A. Leah Underhill refers to the Broadway tune in *The Missing Link in Modern Spiritualism* (New York: Thomas R. Knox and Company, 1885; rep. New York: The Arno Press, 1976), p. 128; the polka is mentioned by James Laver, *Victoriana* (Princeton: The Pyne Press, 1975), p. 127.

32. Mark Twain, *Schoolhouse Hill, Mark Twain's Mysterious Stranger Manuscripts*, ed. William B. Gibson (Berkeley: University of California Press, 1969), p. 201.

33. Emma Hardinge [Britten], *Modern American Spiritualism: A Twenty Years' Record of the Communion Between Earth and the World of the Spirits* (New Hyde Park, NY: University Books, 1970), pp. 481–82.

34. See [Epes Sargent], *Planchette; Or, The Despair of Science. Being a Full Account of Modern Spiritualism, Its Phenomena, and the Various Theories Regarding It, With a Survey of French Spiritism*, Handy-Volume Series, no. 3 (Boston: Roberts Brothers, 1869), p. 326.

35. George Barlow, *The Medium and Daybreak* 5 (May 22, 1874): 331.

36. [William E. Aytoun], "Modern Demonology," *Blackwood's Edinburgh Magazine* 97 (January 1865): 194, 198.

37. See, for instance, Edward Bulwer-Lytton's comparison of the drawings made by Lilian, his clairvoyant heroine, to Blacke's illustrations for Edward Young's poems, in *A Strange Story, Bulwer's Novels*, 32 vols. (Boston: Estes and Lauriat, 1892), 24:351. It is important to note that many mediums, such as Andrew Jackson Davis, earned their living as orators and writers without producing any sort of physical manifestations. The relation between spiritualism and theater is an issue in Nathaniel Hawthorne's *The Blithedale Romance* and is often noted in contemporary accounts.

38. Alphonse Cahagnet, *Arcanes de la vie future devoilé*, 2 vols., 3rd ed. (Paris: Librarie Vigot Frères, 1896), 2:233; J. M. Gully, as quoted in D. D. Home, *Incidents in My Life*, (New York: G. W. Carleton, 1863), p. 224; Browning, *Letters*, 2:395; Myers, *Human Personality*, 2:203; and Warren Chase, *Forty Years on the Spiritual Rostrum* (Boston: Colby and Rich, 1888), p. 160.

39. "Spiritual Manifestations," *Blackwood's Edinburgh Magazine* 73 (May 1853): 642; "Spiritualism, as Related to Religion and Science," *Fraser's Magazine* (January 1865): 40; Lewes, "Seeing is Believing," *Blackwood's Edinburgh Magazine* 88 (October 1860): 385; Robert Browning, "Mr. Sludge, 'The Medium,'" *Poetical Works 1833–1864*, ed. Ian Jack (London: Oxford University Press, 1970), p. 857; John Nevil Maskelyne, *Modern Spiritualism: A Short Account of its Rise and Progress, with Some Exposures of So-Called Spirit Media* in *The Mediums and the Conjurors*, ed. James Webb (London: F. Warne, 1876; rep. New York: Arno Press, 1976), pp. 165–66; and John Hay, *The Bread-winners: A Social Study* (New York: Harper and Brothers, 1884), pp. 107–8. One might compare to Hay's account a particularly

interesting (and extreme) "nonfictional" account of spiritualism's supposed relation to sexual depravity—written, from his own sad experience, by B. F. Hatch, M.D.; his work is titled *Spiritualists' Iniquities Unmasked, And the Hatch Divorce Case* (New York: Published for the Author, 1859).

40. Elizabeth Barrett Browning, *Letters of the Brownings to George Barrett*, ed. Paul Landis and Ronald E. Freeman (Urbana: University of Illinois Press, 1958), p. 180.

41. Charles Baudelaire, "Salon de 1859," *Oeuvres complètes*, ed. Y.-G. Le Dantee, rev. and with an Introduction by Claude Pichois (Paris: Éditions Gallimard, 1961), p. 1038. Significantly enough, in this same article (p. 1040) Baudelaire approvingly quotes a remark on the imagination by Catherine Crowe, the author of *The Night Side of Nature*, a book arguing for the historical reality of ghosts that was much read by spiritualists.

42. See Roland Barthes's analysis of "that rather terrible thing which is there in every photograph: the return of the dead" and his description of the photograph as "a modest, *shared* hallucination" in *Camera Lucida: Reflections on Photography*, trans. Richard Howard (New York: Hill and Wang, 1981), pp. 9, 115.

43. On this relation between spiritualism and literature, see also Darnton, *Mesmerism and the End of the Enlightenment in France*, chapter 5, "From Mesmer to Hugo," especially pp. 150–59.

44. Browning, "Aurora Leigh," *The Complete Poetical Works of Elizabeth Barrett Browning*, ed. Harriet Waters Preston (Boston: Houghton Mifflin, 1900), p. 266.

45. Eliot, *Adam Bede, The Personal Edition of George Eliot's Works*, 12 vols. (New York: Doubleday, Page and Company, 1901). Page numbers to this work and to "The Lifted Veil," *Middlemarch*, and *Silas Marner* are given within the text.

46. Henry James, *The Bostonians* (New York: Thomas Y. Crowell, 1974), p. 11.

47. Graham Hough, *The Mystery Religion of W. B. Yeats* (Brighton, Sussex: The Harvester Press, 1984), p. 18.

48. Brontë, *Jane Eyre*. Page numbers are given within the text.

49. Emily Brontë, *Wuthering Heights*, ed. Ian and Jane Jack (Oxford: Oxford University Press, 1969). Page numbers are given within the text.

50. Alfred, Lord Tennyson, "In Memoriam A. H. H.," *The Poems of Tennyson*, ed. Christopher Ricks (London: Longmans, Green and Company, 1969). Page numbers are given within the text.

51. Nathaniel Hawthorne, *The Blithedale Romance, The Centenary Edition of the Works of Nathaniel Hawthorne*, ed. William Charvat et al., 14 vols. (Columbus: Ohio State University Press, 1964). Page numbers to this work and to "The House of Fantasy" and *The House of the Seven Gables* are given within the text.

52. See especially Sigmund Freud's treatment of the double in "The 'Uncanny,'" *The Standard Edition of the Complete Psychological Works of Sigmund Freud*, ed. James Strachey et al., 24 vols. (London: The Hogarth Press and the Institute of Psycho-Analysis, 1955), 17:234–36 *et passim*. As should be evident, my analysis implies criticism of as well as support for Freud's; see my consideration of the uncanny in the concluding chapter of this book.

53. Joseph Conrad, "The Secret Sharer," *Complete Works*, 26 vols. (New York: Doubleday, Page and Company, 1925). Page numbers are given within the text.

54. Lecky, *History of Rationalism*, 1:183.

CHAPTER 5

1. Elizabeth Barrett Browning, *Aurora Leigh, The Complete Poetical Works of Elizabeth Barrett Browning*, ed. Harriet Waters (Boston: Houghton Mifflin Company, 1900), p. 332.

2. L. Alph[onse] Cahagnet, *The Celestial Telegraph: Or, Secrets of the Life to Come, Revealed through Magnetism, etc.*, 2 vols. in 1 (New York: Partridge and Brittan, 1855): 1:159.

3. William Howitt, *The History of the Supernatural in All Ages and Nations and in All Churches Christian and Pagan Demonstrating a Universal Faith*, 2 vols. (Philadelphia: J. B. Lippincott and Company, 1863), 2:220.

4. Friedrich Nietzsche, *The Will to Power*, ed. Walter Kaufman, trans. Walter Kaufman and R. J. Hollingdale (New York: Random House, 1967), p. 144.

5. Geoffrey K. Nelson, *Spiritualism and Society* (New York: Schocken Books, 1969), pp. 8–9.

6. Henry Spicer, *Sights and Sounds: The Mystery of the Day* (London: Thomas Bosworth, 1853), pp. 188–89; John Hindle, "Address of Congratulation to Robert Owen," *Robert Owen's Millenial Gazette*, 3 vols. in 1 (London: Published by the Author, 1856–58; rep. New York: AMS Press, 1972), 1:13; [Epes Sargent], *Planchette; Or, The Despair of Science. Being a Full Account of Modern Spiritualism, Its Phenomena, and the Various Theories Regarding It. With a Survey of French Spiritism*, Handy-Volume Series, no. 3 (Boston: Roberts Brothers, 1869), p. 290; and Henry James, *The Bostonians* (New York: Thomas Y. Crowell, 1974), p. 122. Cf. William James's comment on this subject (in a work in which he also discusses spiritualism):

> [T]here is a whole race of beings to-day whose passion is to keep their names in the newspapers, no matter under what heading, 'arrivals and departures,' 'personal paragraphs,' 'interviews,' — gossip, even scandal, will suit them if nothing better is to be had. Guiteau, Garfield's assassin, is an example of the extremity to which this sort of craving for the notoriety of print may go in a pathological case. The newspapers bounded his mental horizon.

In *The Principles of Psychology*, 3 vols., *The Works of William James*, ed. Frederick H. Burkhardt et al. (Cambridge: Harvard University Press, 1981), 1:294.

7. Q. K. Philander Doesticks, P. B. [Mortimer Thomson], *Doesticks: What He Says* (New York: Edward Livermore, 1855), pp. 63, 65.

8. Quoted in Janet Oppenheim, *The Other World: Spiritualism and Psychic Research in England, 1850–1914* (Cambridge: Cambridge University Press, 1985), p. 99.

9. Éliphas Lévi [Alphonse Louis Constant], *La Clef des grands mystères: suivant Hénoch, Abraham, Hermés Trismégiste et Salomon* (Paris: Félix Alcan, 1861), p. 142. "Éliphas Lévi" was the pseudonym of the former Abbé Constant (originally, Alphonse Louis Constant), who was expelled from the church for heresy. He was a "traditional" occultist; in the passage I have quoted, he was referring to the case of Daniel Home, whom he thought misunderstood by those who accused him of fraud, although his own explanation differed from that of spiritualists, to whom he was hostile. (He attributed Home's effects to "a natural [psychological] influence similar to that of hashish" and to "magnetic force" [p. 194].)

10. S. B. Brittan, ed., *The Spiritual Telegraph*, 4 (n.s.) (New York: Partridge and Brittan, 1854), p. 65.

11. Thomas Hardy, *Jude the Obscure*, in *The Works of Thomas Hardy in Prose and Verse*, 22 vols. (London: Macmillan and Company, 1920), 3:406. For Nietzsche's comment on the spirit, the interpretation of sacred text, and popular forces in relation to Luther and the Reformation, see *Human, All Too Human: A Book for Free Spirits*, trans. Marion Faber and Stephen Lehmann, ed. Marion Faber (Lincoln: University of Nebraska Press, 1984), pp. 310–13.

12. John Hay, *The Bread-winners: A Social Study* (New York: Harper and Brothers, 1884), p. 111.

13. Cf. the moment in Immanuel Kant's thought in which he considers that judgment, which is of the understanding and through which reason comes into relation with experience, is a kind of "gift of nature" that can be improved but not established by education. *Kritik der Reinen Vernunft, Sämmtliche Werke*, ed. G. Hartenstein, 18 vols. (Leipzig: Leopold Voss, 1867), 3:139.

14. Gerald Massey, *Concerning Spiritualism* (London: James Burns [n.d.]), p. 86.

15. Quoted in Herbert W. Schneider and George Lawton, *A Prophet and a Pilgrim* (New York: Columbia University Press, 1942), p. 52.

16. Blaise Pascal, *Pensées, Oeuvres complètes*, ed. Jacques Chevalier (Paris: Éditions Gallimard, 1954), p. 1109.

17. David Hume, *An Enquiry Concerning Human Understanding, Enquiries Concerning Human Understanding and Concerning the Principles of Morals*, ed. L. A. Selby-Bigge, 3rd ed., revised and edited by P. H. Nidditch (Oxford: Oxford University Press, 1975), p. 111.

18. Hume, *An Enquiry Concerning Human Understanding*, p. 113.

19. [Robert Bell], "Stranger than Fiction," *Cornhill Magazine* 2 (August 1860): 211.

20. [Robert Bell], "Stranger than Fiction," p. 211n.

21. See H[ermann] Ulrici, *Ueber den Spiritismus als wissenschaftliche Frage: Antwortschreiben auf den offenen Brief des Hernn Proffessor Dr. W. Wundt* (Halle: C. E. M. Pfeffer, 1879), p. 8.

22. Immanuel Kant, *Critique of Pure Reason*, trans. J. M. D. Meiklejohn (London: J. M. Dent and Sons, 1934). Page numbers are given within the text.

23. [G. H. Lewes], "Seeing is Believing," *Blackwood's Edinburgh Magazine* 88 (October 1860): 393.

24. Harriet Beecher Stowe [in a letter to George Eliot], *Life and Letters of Harriet Beecher Stowe*, ed. Annie Fields (Boston: Houghton, Mifflin and Company, 1897), p. 337.

25. Comte Agenor de Gasparin, *Les Tables tournantes*, 4th ed. (Paris: Michel Lévy Frères, 1889), p. 147.

26. George M. Beard, "The Psychology of Spiritism," *The North American Review* 129 (July 1879): 70.

27. Charles Carleton Massey, "Appendix A. The Value of Testimony in Matters Extraordinary," in Johann Carl Friedrich Zöllner, *Transcendental Physics: An Account of Experimental Investigations from the Scientific Treatises*, trans. and ed. Charles Carleton Massey, 4th ed. (Boston: Colby and Rich, 1888; rep. New York: Arno Press, 1976), p. 210; Alfred Russel Wallace, *Miracles and Modern Spiritualism*

(London: G. Redway, 1896; rep. New York: Arno Press, 1975), p. 15; Emma Hardinge, *Modern American Spiritualism: A Twenty Years' Record of the Communion Between Earth and the World of Spirits* (New Hyde Park, NY: University Books, 1970), p. 441; and Edward M. Cox, *Spiritualism Answered by Science* (New York: Henry L. Hinton, 1872), p. 443. Cox, it may be noted, was arguing that the phenomena of spiritualism were real but that they represented a natural "psychic" force, not a spiritual reality. This was a common fallback position, which was shared, for instance, by Edward Bulwer-Lytton, and late in the century by many of those involved in the Society for Psychical Research.

28. Hume, *An Enquiry Concerning Human Understanding*, pp. 113, 158–59.

29. Quoted in *The Medium and Daybreak* 1 (September 7, 1870): 213.

30. Cf. the analysis of how mesmerism became a way of exploring and disseminating radical political ideas in prerevolutionary France, as described by Robert Darnton throughout *Mesmerism and the End of the Enlightenment in France* (Cambridge: Harvard University Press, 1968). See in particular his discussion of the problem eighteenth-century philosophers had in defining competent or respectable witnesses in relation to mesmerism (p. 61). Also, for a wonderful analysis of the conceptions of testimony, representation, and subjectivity in the Salem witch trials, in many ways apposite to the present analysis, see Ross J. Pudaloff, "Witchcraft at Salem: (Mis)representing the Subject," *Semiotica* (forthcoming).

31. Dr. Justinus Kerner, *Die Somnambülen Tische: Zur Geschichte und Erklärung dieser Erscheinung* (Stuttgart: Ebner und Seubert, 1853), p. 34.

32. Cf. Walter Benjamin's analysis of the alienation effect in Bertolt Brecht's dramatic theory, which he advances through the illustration of "a stranger" entering a house and by this entrance turning "ordinary scenes of middle-class life" into "a startling picture," in "What is Epic Theater?", *Illuminations*, ed. Hannah Arendt, trans. Harry Zohn (New York: Schocken Books, 1969), pp. 150–51.

33. Reuben Briggs Davenport, *The Death-Blow to Spiritualism* (New York: G. W. Dillingham, 1888; rep. New York: Arno Press, 1976), p. 68; Rev. Charles Maurice Davies, *Mystic London: Or, Phases of Occult Life in the Metropolis* (London: Tinsley Brothers, 1875), p. 304; Warren Chase, *Forty Years on the Spiritual Rostrum* (Boston: Colby and Rich, 1888); and Arthur Symons, "Dante Gabriel Rossetti," *Strangeness and Beauty: An Anthology of Aesthetic Criticism 1840–1910*, ed. Eric Warner and Graham Hough, 2 vols. (Cambridge: Cambridge University Press, 1983), 2:218.

34. Thomas Lake Harris, quoted in Schneider and Lawton, *A Prophet and a Pilgrim*, pp. 34–35.

35. Logie Barrow, *Independent Spirits: Spiritualism and English Plebeians, 1850–1910* (London: Routledge and Kegan Paul, 1986), p. 247.

36. Brittan, *The Spiritual Telegraph* [vol. 4], p. 394.

37. Quoted in *Report on Spiritualism of the Committee of the London Dialectical Society, Together with the Evidence, Oral and Written, and a Selection of the Correspondence* (London: Longmans, Green, Reader and Dyer, 1871; rep. New York: Arno Press, 1976), p. 184.

38. Herman Melville, "The Apple-Tree Table," *The Apple-Tree Table and Other Sketches*, ed. Henry Chapin (Princeton: Princeton University Press, 1922), pp. 18–19.

39. See Logie Barrow's description of how it was "quite easy to translate from

ILP [Independent Labour Party] to spiritualist idiom" in *Independent Spirits*, p. 112; to the same effect but from the opposite perspective, see William Hepworth Dixon's castigation of the third National Convention of Spiritualists in 1866 for its resolutions on "the Labour question" in *New America*, 2 vols. (London: Hurst and Blackett, 1867; rep. New York: AMS Press, 1971), 2:164–65.

40. Owen, *The Life of Robert Owen*, with an Introduction by M. Beer (New York: Alfred A. Knopf, 1920), p. 41.

41. Harriet Martineau, *Autobiography*, ed. Gaby Weiner, 2 vols. (London: Virago Press, 1983), 1:232.

42. Owen, *The Revolution in the Mind and Practice of the Human Race or The Coming Change from Irrationality to Rationality, with a Supplement 1849* (London: Effingham Wilson, 1849; rep. Clifton, NJ: Augustus M. Kelley Publishers, 1973), p. 39.

43. Owen, *Life*, pp. 111–12, 41.

44. Owen, *Millenial Gazette*, 1:26.

45. Owen, *Life*, p. 316.

CHAPTER 6

1. Paul Gaugin, quoted in Richard Hobbs, *Odilon Redon* (Boston: New York Graphic Society, 1977), p. 99.

2. Georges Ribemont-Dessaignes, quoted in Maurice Nadeau, *Histoire du surréalisme* (Paris: Éditions du Seuil, 1948), p. 44.

3. Robert Desnos, "Pygmalion et le sphinx," *Nouvelle Hébrides et autres textes: 1922–1930*, ed. Marie-Claire Dumas (Paris: Éditions Gallimard, 1978), p. 466.

4. Immanuel Kant, *Critique of Judgment*, trans. Werner S. Pluhar (Indianapolis: Hackett Publishing Company, 1987), p. 87.

5. Kant, *Critique of Judgment*, p. 77. Cf. Edmund Husserl, "Philosophy and the Crisis of European Humanity," *The Crisis of European Sciences and Transcendental Phenomenology: An Introduction to Phenomenological Philosophy*, trans. and ed. David Carr (Evanston: Northwestern University Press, 1970), p. 290:

> Reason is a broad title. According to the old familiar definition, man is the rational animal, and in this broad sense even the Papuan is a man and not a beast. He has his ends and he acts reflectively, considering the practical possibilities. The works and methods that grow [out of this] go to make up a tradition, being understandable again [by others] in virtue of their rationality. But just as man and even the Papuan represent a new stage of animal nature, i.e., as opposed to the beast, so philosophical reason represents a new stage of human nature and its reason.

Cf. also, in the same volume, "The Attitude of Natural Science and the Attitude of Humanistic Science," pp. 321n, 325. There is a history to be written of the use of the foreigner and of racist anthropological examples in philosophy. A particularly interesting text in this regard, for the assumptions it puts forward about women, national characters, races, and the like, is Kant's *Anthropology from a Pragmatic Point of View*, trans. and ed. Mary J. Gregor (The Hague: Martinus Nijhoff, 1974).

6. Charles Baudelaire, "L'Amour du Mensonge," *Oeuvres complètes*, ed. Y.-G. Le Dantee, revised Claude Pichois (Paris: Éditions Gallimard, 1961), p. 95. On this

question of Kant's aesthetics, see especially the analysis of the "arche-pleasure" conditioning knowledge in *The Critique of Judgment* in Jacques Derrida's *Truth in Painting*, trans. Geoff Bennington and Ian McLeod (Chicago: University of Chicago Press, 1987), p. 113.

7. Kant, *Critique of Judgment*, p. 68.

8. André Breton, "Avis au lecteur pour 'La Femme 100 têtes' de Max Ernst," *Point du jour* (Paris: Éditions Gallimard, 1970), p. 64. In the 1950s and 1960s, Breton's term, diversions (*"détournements"*), was reappropriated by members of the Situationist International, as was the surrealist habit of wandering city streets (the Situationists' *dérive*); the latter group also seemed to imitate the surrealists' internecine feuds and ostracisms.

9. Friedrich Nietzsche, *On the Genealogy of Morals*, trans. Walter Kaufmann and R. J. Hollingdale, in *On the Genealogy of Morals and Ecce Homo*, ed. Walter Kaufmann (New York: Vintage Books, 1967), p. 103. Nietzsche may have been remembering Dante's description of Satan as "the guilty worm that pierces the world." See *The Divine Comedy: Inferno*, trans. and ed. John D. Sinclair (New York: Oxford University Press, 1939), pp. 425–26. See also Nietzsche's reference (*On the Genealogy of Morals*, p. 112) to "the *physiology of aesthetics.*"

10. Sigmund Freud, *Three Essays on a Theory of Sexuality, The Standard Edition of the Complete Psychological Works of Sigmund Freud*, ed. James Strachey et al., 24 vols. (London: The Hogarth Press and the Institute of Psycho-Analysis, 1955), pp. 156n, 160–61, 150.

11. Leonora Carrington, "Uncle Sam Carrington," *The House of Fear: Notes from Down Below*, with an Introduction by Marina Warner, trans. Katherine Talbot and Marina Warner (New York: E. P. Dutton, 1988), p. 65; and Salvador Dali, "De la Beauté terrifiante et comestible, de l'architecture modern style," *Minotaure* 3/4 (December 1933): 76.

12. See Kant, "Speculative Beginning of Human History," *Perpetual Peace and Other Essays on Politics, History, and Morals*, trans. and ed. Ted Humphrey (Indianapolis: Hackett Publishing Company, 1983), p. 52.

13. Nietzsche, *The Will to Power*, ed. Walter Kaufmann, trans. Walter Kaufmann and R. J. Hollingdale (New York: Random House, 1967), p. 435.

14. André Breton, "Second manifeste du surréalisme," *Manifestes du surréalisme* (Paris: Éditions Jean-Jacques Pauvert, 1972), p. 135.

15. Jean Baudrillard, *Pour une critique de l'économie politique du signe* (Paris: Éditions Gallimard, 1972), p. 233.

16. On the relation between surrealism and primitivism, see James Clifford, "On Ethnographic Surrealism," *The Predicament of Culture: Twentieth-Century Ethnography, Literature, and Art* (Cambridge: Harvard University Press, 1988), pp. 117–51; on the modern attraction to madness in art, see the excellent essay by Ann Temkin, "Wöfli's Asylum Art," *Art in America* 3 (March 1989): 132–41, 162.

17. Tristan Tzara, "Essai sur la situation de la poésie," *La Surréalisme au service de la révolution* 4 (December 1931): 16; Tzara, "Dada manifeste sur l'amour faible et l'amour amer," *Oeuvres complètes*, ed. Henri Béhar, 4 vols. (Paris: Éditions Flammarion, 1980), 1:378.

18. Charles Baudelaire, "Hymne à la Beauté," *Oeuvres*, pp. 23–24.

19. Kant, *Critique of Judgment*, p. 83.

20. Algernon Charles Swinburne, "Some Pictures of 1868," in *Strangeness and*

Beauty: An Anthology of Aesthetic Criticism 1840–1910, ed. Eric Warner and Graham Hough, 2 vols. (Cambridge: Cambridge University Press, 1983), 1:247.

21. Baudelaire, from a projected preface for *Les Fleurs du mal*, in *Oeuvres*, p. 185.

22. Comte de Lautréamont [Isadore Ducasse], *Les Chants de Maldoror*, in *Oeuvres complètes*, ed. L. Genonceaux et al. (Paris: Librarie José Corti, 1963), p. 134.

23. [Guillaume] Apollinaire, *Le Poète assassiné*, in *Oeuvres en prose*, ed. Michel Décaudin, 2 vols. (Paris: Éditions Gallimard, 1977), 1:256.

24. Baudelaire, "Le Fou et la Vénus," *Oeuvres*, p. 237; J.-K. Huysmans, *A Rebours*, ed. Rose Fortassier (Paris: L'Imprimerie Nationale, 1981), p. 90.

25. T. W. Adorno, *Aesthetic Theory*, ed. Gretel Adorno and Rolf Tiedemann, trans. C. Lenhardt (London: Routledge and Kegan Paul, 1984), p. 76; and The French Surrealist Group, "Manifesto of the Surrealists Concerning *L'Age d'or*," *The Shadow and its Shadow: Surrealist Writings on Cinema*, ed. Paul Hammond (London: British Film Institute, 1978), p. 115.

26. Baudelaire, "Exposition Universelle – 1855 – Beaux-Arts," *Oeuvres*, p. 956.

27. Francis Picabia, "L'Art," *Littérature* 13 (May 1920): 12.

28. G. W. F. Hegel, *Aesthetics: Lectures on Fine Art*, trans. T. M. Knox, 2 vols. (Oxford: Oxford University Press, 1975), 1:68.

29. Breton, "Position politique de l'art d'aujourd'hui," *Manifestes*, p. 237.

30. Max Ernst, "Notes pour une biographie" and "Les Mystères de la forêt," *Écritures* (Paris: Éditions Gallimard, 1970), pp. 15, 223.

31. Baudelaire, "Déjà!", *Oeuvres*, p. 287.

32. Robert Desnos, *Deuil pour deuil* (Paris: Éditions du Sagittaire, 1924), pp. 29–30.

33. Paul Eluard, "Peintres [1]: Je parler de ce qui est bien," *Oeuvres complètes*, ed. Marcelle Dumas and Lucien Scheler, 2 vols. (Paris: Éditions Gallimard, 1968), 1: 943; Breton, *L'Amour fou* (Paris: Éditions Gallimard, 1937), p. 26; Breton, *Nadja* (Paris: Éditions Gallimard, 1963), p. 190; and [Louis] Aragon, *Le Paysan de Paris* (Paris: Éditions Gallimard, 1948), p. 251.

34. Breton, "Manifeste du surréalisme," *Manifestes*, p. 43; René Crevel, "Révolution, surréalisme, spontanéité," *Révolution, surréalisme, spontanéité*, ed. Jean-Michel Goutier (Paris: Éditions Plasma, 1978), p. 18; Paul Eluard, "Les Dessous d'une vie ou la pyramide humaine," *La Révolution surréaliste* 8 (11 December 1926): 20.

35. The quotation, which praises Aragon's writing, is attributed to an otherwise unidentified Professor Curtius in René Crevel's *L'Esprit contre la raison* (Paris: Tchou, 1969), p. 44.

36. Breton, "Manifeste du surréalisme," *Manifestes*, p. 25n.

37. Maxime Alexandre, *Mémoires d'un surréaliste* (Paris: La Jeune Parque, 1968), p. 108.

38. Baudelaire, "Salon de 1859," *Oeuvres*, pp. 1043–44.

39. Michel Leiris, "Quant à Arnold Schoenberg," *Brisées* (Paris: Mercure de France, 1966), pp. 23–24.

40. Breton, *Le Surréalisme et la peinture* (Paris: Éditions Gallimard, 1965), p. 2.

41. Comte de Lautréamont, *Les Chants de Maldoror*, in *Oeuvres*, p. 296.

42. Eluard, "Yves Tanguy," *Oeuvres*, 1:385.

43. Salvador Dali, "Objets surréalistes," *La Surréalisme au service de la révolution* 3 (December 1931): 16, 17.

44. Hans Bellmer, "L'Anatomie de l'amour," *Le Surréalisme en 1947* (Paris: Éditions Pierre à Feu, 1947), p. 108.

45. Baudelaire, "Le Miroir," *Oeuvres*, p. 292.

46. George Eliot, *Adam Bede*, in *The Personal Edition of George Eliot's Works*, ed. Thomas Pinney (London: Routledge and Kegan Paul, 1965), p. 183.

47. Nietzsche, *Human, All Too Human: A Book for Free Spirits*, trans. Marian Faber with Stephen Lehmann, ed. Marian Faber (Lincoln: University of Nebraska Press, 1984), pp. 134–35.

48. Friedrich Schiller, *On the Aesthetic Education of Man: In a Series of Letters*, trans. and ed. Reginald Snell (New Haven: Yale University Press, 1954), p. 27.

49. Tzara, "Note sur la poésie," *Oeuvres*, 1:405.

50. Kandinsky, of course, was not a surrealist, but his example is relevant to theirs, not only in terms of his art but also in the way his interest in theosophy, the occult, and mysticism in general resembled the interests of the surrealist movement. The spiritual or spiritualist motivation among other modernist artists is also relevant here.

51. Walter Benjamin, "Surrealism: The Last Snapshot of the European Intelligentsia," *Reflections: Essays, Aphorisms, Autobiographical Writings*, ed. Peter Demetz, trans. Edmund Jephcott (New York: Harcourt Brace Jovanovich, 1978), p. 179.

52. Lautréamont [Isidore Ducasse], "Poésies," *Oeuvres*, p. 386.

53. Victor Crastre, "Explosion surréaliste," *Clarté* 74 (May 1925): 9. *Clarté* was a generally procommunist journal, though not an official party organ; this article was written shortly before the surrealists and the *Clarté* group began to meet in what eventually turned out to be a failed attempt to reconcile their aims.

54. Aragon, "La Peinture au défi," *Écrits sur l'art moderne*, ed. Jean Ristat (Paris: Éditions Flammarion, 1981), p. 37; Ernst, "Au-delà de la peinture," *Écritures*, pp. 244–45.

55. Nietzsche, *Beyond Good and Evil: Prelude to a Philosophy of the Future*, trans. and ed. R. J. Hollingdale (London: Penguin Books, 1973), p. 50.

56. Breton, *Le Surréalisme et la peinture*, pp. 20–21.

CHAPTER 7

1. Antonin Artaud, "La Rue," *Oeuvres complètes*, 9 vols., rev. ed. (Paris: Éditions Gallimard, 1970), 1:287.

2. For a fine analysis of the "irrationality" of the perspectives and other elements in de Chirico's paintings, see William Rubin, "De Chirico and Modernism," *De Chirico*, ed. William Rubin (New York: Museum of Modern Art, 1982), pp. 55–79.

3. Paul Eluard, "Une pour toutes" and "Réel," *Cours naturel, Oeuvres complètes*, ed. Marcelle Dumas and Lucien Scheler, 2 vols. (Paris: Éditions Gallimard, 1968), 1: 807, 806.

4. Invented in 1925, according to Breton, the *cadavre exquis* was the surrealist game in which two or more persons successively contributed words to a sentence without having seen what those before them had written; they knew only what part of the sentence (subject, verb, predicate complement) had been given. (The first example was said to be "Le cadavre—exquis—boira—le—vin—nouveau" [The exquisite corpse will drink the new wine].) Collaborative drawings were also produced in the same fashion, with body parts substituting for parts of grammar.

5. Having taken the name, surrealism, from Guillaume Apollinaire (who had used it in 1917 in a program note for Erik Satie's *Parade* and as a subtitle for his own *Mamelles de Tirésias*), Breton had to wrest it away from what he saw as Apollinaire's rather inferior intention in coining it. He also had to contend with Paul Dermée and Ivan Goll, who tried to form their own, unrelated movement around this term; with Georges Bataille, who pursued themes that Breton feared might be confused with his; with Jean Cocteau, whom the surrealists viewed as a ripoff artist; and with various surrealists who came to be regarded as betrayers or apostates (one of the most famous among them being Salvador Dali, for whom Breton devised the anagram "Avida Dollars"). In this respect, one might note that the Belgrade group of surrealists, at the very moment of its formation as a group, protested against the "appropriation of this term [surrealism] by usurpers." (See Hanifa Kapidzic-Osmanagic, *Le Surréalisme serbe et ses rapports avec le surréalisme français* [Paris: Société les Belles Lettres, 1968], p. 157.) Moreover, after the Second World War, a group called the Revolutionary Surrealists organized and tried to claim the name for themselves, to Breton's outrage.

In thus being vexed continually and from the very beginning by the problem of guarding its identity against threats from without and within, surrealism has been seen as resembling those other late nineteenth-century and early twentieth-century movements with which it allied itself: Marxism and psychoanalysis. Of more interest here is the way this problem of group identity is also a problem of identifying the implications of representations.

6. Some of those who gathered around Bataille and *Documents*, the journal with which he was associated in the late twenties, were "dissident" surrrealists who had lost or rejected the favor of the orthodox. These included, for instance, Michel Leiris and Roger Vitrac.

7. Gerard de Nerval, "Aurélia," *Oeuvres*, ed. Albert Béguin and Jean Richer, 2 vols. (Paris: Éditions Gallimard, 1966), 1:363.

8. Eluard, "Déclaration de 27 Janvier 1925," *Oeuvres*, 2:987. (This "Declaration" was signed by several members of the group, as was the custom, but was written by Eluard, according to his editors.)

9. Slightly misquoted, this passage appears as an epigraph in René Magritte, "L'Art pur: défense de l'esthétique," *Écrits complèts*, ed. André Blavier (Paris: Éditions Flammarion, 1979), p. 20. (Victor Servranckx coauthored this essay.)

10. André Breton, "Manifeste du surréalisme," *Manifestes du surréalisme* (Paris: Jean-Jacques Pauvert, 1972), p. 28.

11. Eluard, "L'Evidence poétique," *Oeuvres*, 1:521.

12. Charles Baudelaire, "Mademoiselle Bistouri," *Oeuvres complètes*, ed. Y.-G. Le Dantee, revised by Claude Pichois (Paris: Éditions Gallimard, 1961), p. 303.

13. Breton, "La Confession dédaigneuse," *Les Pas perdus* (Paris: Éditions Gallimard, 1969), p. 11.

14. Schwitters said his signature term, "Merz," derived from one of his collages, in which it was the remnant of the printed word "Kommerziel" (Commercial), part of the name of a bank. Whether or not chance made this poetic choice all on its own, as Schwitters implied, the selection was significant in that dada and surrealism were both defined in large part by their symbolic destruction of commercial values in art and society. For an interesting perspective on this relation between commerciality and art, see Tristan Tzara's description of weather-worn commercial posters in "Le

Papier collé ou le proverbe en peinture," *Oeuvres complètes*, ed. Henri Béhar, 4 vols. (Paris: Éditions Flammarion, 1980), 4:359–60. This example is especially interesting because of the widespread interest in commercial posters among participants in dada and surrealism; this interest is relevant to my comments below on collage.

15. Philippe Soupault, *Les Dernières nuits de Paris* (Paris; Éditions Seghers, 1975), pp. 25–26.

16. [Louis] Aragon, *Le Paysan de Paris* (Paris: Éditions Gallimard, 1948), p. 18.

17. On this topic see Marie-Claire Bancquart, *Paris des surréalistes* (Paris: Éditions Seghers, 1972). On the relations that bound together Parisian streets, *disponibilité*, chance encounters, and surrealist aesthetics, see also Dawn Ades, "Photography and the Surrealist Text," in Rosalind Krauss and Jane Livingston, *L'Amour fou: Photography and Surrealism* (Washington, DC: The Corcoran Gallery of Art; New York: Abbeville Press, 1985), pp. 153–89; and cf. Michel de Certeau, "Walking in the City," *The Practice of Everyday Life*, trans. Steven F. Rendall (Berkeley: University of California Press, 1984), pp. 91–110.

18. Aragon, *Traité du style* (Paris: Éditions Gallimard, 1928), p. 69.

19. Edmund Husserl, *The Crisis of European Science and Transcendental Phenomenology: An Introduction to Phenomenological Philosophy*, trans. and ed. David Carr (Evanston: Northwestern University Press, 1970), p. 137. Cf. Marc Eigeldinger's argument that Breton "elaborated a veritable *phenomenology* of the imagination" in *André Breton*, ed. Marc Eigeldinger (Neuchâtel: Les Éditions de la Baconnière, 1970), p. 178.

20. Breton, *L'Amour fou* (Paris: Éditions Gallimard, 1937), p. 122.

21. Robert Bréchon, *Le Surréalisme* (Paris: Librarie Armand Colin, 1971), p. 48; Clifford Browder, *André Breton: Arbiter of Surrealism* (Geneva: Librarie Droz, 1967), p. 79.

22. Cf. André Thirion's acerbic comment on the first attempt of Breton and some others to join the French Communist Party, as he described it in *Révolutionnaires sans révolution* (Paris: Éditions Robert Laffont, 1972), p. 126:

> In the end, the *disponibilité* for a militant life among most of the surrealists was mediocre: girls, the cinema, and the excursions of a young bourgeois in those crazy years dangerously rivaled political meetings. Everything conspired, then, to justify the orderly retreat that took place in the spring of 1927.

Although Thirion had a personal ax to grind in this case (at the time of which he writes, he was more politically orthodox than most of his surrealist friends), his comment is accurate enough and relevant to my conclusion about the role of chance in surrealism.

23. Breton, *L'Amour fou*, p. 39.

24. Baudelaire, "Les Sept viellards" and "A une heure du matin," *Oeuvres*, pp. 84, 240.

25. Breton, *Nadja* (Paris: Éditions Gallimard, 1963), pp. 133, 68.

26. See Gaston Bachelard, "Le Surrationalisme," *Inquisitions* 1 (1936): 1–6.

27. Husserl, *Cartesian Meditations: An Introduction to Phenomenology*, trans. Dorion Cairns (The Hague: Martinus Nijhoff, 1973), pp. 78, 139; and Husserl, *The Crisis of European Science*, p. 197.

28. Paul Nougé, "Les Images défendues," *Histoire de ne pas rire* (Bruxelles: Éditions de la Revue les Lèvres Nues, 1956), p. 258. (In this passage Nougé was writing

of the work of his friend, René Magritte.) Virtually everyone who has written about surrealism has dealt with its conception of the object, but see, for example, Marcel Jean, *The History of Surrealist Painting*, trans. Simon Watson Taylor (New York: Grove Press, 1960), pp. 227–56; Jean Baudrillard's comments on the surrealist object in comparison to Bauhaus aesthetics in *Pour une critique de l'économie politique du signe* (Paris: Éditions Gallimard, 1972), pp. 240–43; J. H. Matthews, *The Imagery of Surrealism* (Syracuse: Syracuse University Press, 1977), chapter 5, "Object Lessons," pp. 116–224; Haim N. Finkelstein, *Surrealism and the Crisis of the Object* (Ann Arbor: UMI Research Press, 1979); T. W. Adorno's analysis of the surrealist "perception that art is preponderant over the work of art" in *Aesthetic Theory*, ed. Gretel Adorno and Rolf Tiedemann, trans. C. Lenhardt (London: Routledge and Kegan Paul, 1984), p. 37; and Matthews, *Languages of Surrealism* (Columbia: University of Missouri Press, 1986), chapter 10, "The Language of Objects," pp. 177–94.

29. In a nice irony, Man Ray's *Gift* was stolen when it was first exhibited in Paris at Soupault's Librarie Six. That it *could* be stolen suggests that surrealist objects may not have been as pure or as perverse as my description at this point allows them to have been, but of course my description here is only provisional, as will become clear below. (In terms of my argument, it is unimportant that Ray made this object before surrealism was formally launched; like Duchamp's ready-mades, de Chirico's *Melancholy and Mystery of a Street*, and Ernst's *Oedipus Rex*, it was taken to be surrealist *avant la lettre*; chronology, in this context, is less important than mythology.

30. Breton, *Entretiens (1913–1952)*, rev. ed. (Paris: Éditions Gallimard, 1969), p. 71. In an article, "Il y aura une fois," in *La Surréalisme au service de la révolution* [hereafter *SASDLR*] 1 (July 1930): 2, Breton wrote, "Imagination is not a gift but *par excellence* an object of conquest." As should be evident, this statement does not really contradict my characterization of this movement in terms of "the gift," for as I have emphasized, the world as gift appears only if one has the venturesome, totalizing or "conquering" imagination that springs from *disponibilité*.

31. Aragon, "La Peinture au défi," *Écrits sur l'art moderne*, ed. Jean Ristat (Paris: Éditions Flammarion, 1981), pp. 40, 43–44.

32. Breton, *Le Surréalisme et la peinture* (Paris: Éditions Gallimard, 1965), p. 10. See also Breton's argument for a "work-of-art event" in "Prestige d'André Masson," *Le Surréalisme et la peinture*, p. 152.

33. Breton, "Manifeste du surréalisme," *Manifestes*, p. 47.

34. G. W. F. Hegel, *Aesthetics: Lectures on Fine Art*, trans. T. M. Knox, 2 vols. (Oxford: Oxford University Press, 1975), 2:968, 971.

35. Sigmund Freud, "Constructions in Analysis," *Collected Papers*, ed. James Strachey, 5 vols. (London: The Hogarth Press and the Institute of Psycho-Analysis, 1950), 5:371.

36. Tzara, "A Propos de Joan Miró," *Oeuvres*, 4:431.

37. "We are the guests of the Comte de Lautréamont!" Breton is reported to have shouted (with rather more humor than he usually showed) as he and his friends broke up the festivities. See Thirion, *Révolutionnaires*, p. 244.

38. Breton, "Idées d'un peintre," *Les Pas perdus*, p. 93.

39. Breton, "Ce que Tanguy voile et révéle," *Le Surréalisme et la peinture*, p. 178.

40. Comte de Lautréamont [Isadore Ducasse], *Les Chants de Maldoror*, in *Oeuvres complètes* (Paris: Librarie José Corti, 1963), pp. 35–36.

41. Eluard, "Défense de savoir," *Oeuvres*, pp. 223, 224.

42. "Le Cadavre exquis," *SASDLR* 4 (December 1931): 12.

43. Breton, "Les Mots sans rides," *Les Pas perdus*, p. 141. In "Résumé d'une conférence," *SASDLR* 3 (December 1931): 36, René Crevel remembers Breton using a similar phrase during the *temps des sommeils*.

44. Michel Leiris, "Glossaire," *La Révolution surréaliste* 3 (15 April 1925): 7.

45. In a draft for one of the footnotes to an article on Dali, "Le 'Jeu lugubre,'" Georges Bataille expressed violent disdain for the way the surrealists turned Isidore Ducasse (among others) into "an abominable poetico-religious idol" (Bataille, *Documents*, ed. Bernard Noël [Paris: Mercure de France, 1968], p. 222). This was a common criticism, often associated with accusations of idealism and authoritarianism.

46. Breton, "Second manifeste du surréalisme," *Manifestes*, p. 135.

47. Breton, *Le Surréalisme et la peinture*, p. 47.

48. Aragon, "Programme," *Le Mouvement perpétuel: Précedé de Feu de joie et suivi de Écritures automatiques* (Paris: Éditions Gallimard, 1975), p. 59.

49. Rubin also points out that de Chirico borrowed this figure of a girl with a hoop from Georges Seurat's *Sunday Afternoon on the Island of the Grande Jatte*. See "De Chirico and Modernism," *De Chirico*, pp. 60–61.

50. Aragon, "Contribution a l'avortement des études Maldororiennes," *SASDLR* 2 (October 1930): 22. Cf. Breton's oft-quoted statement, "'Transform the world,' said Marx; 'change life,' said Rimbaud: for us, these two calls to order are as one," in "Discours au congrès des écrivains," *Manifestes*, p. 251; and his comparison of Lenin and Lautréamont in his open letter to Henri Barbusse, in *Documents surréalistes*, ed. Maurice Nadeau (Paris: Éditions du Seuil, 1948), pp. 56–71.

51. On this point surrealism makes an interesting comparison to the works of Mikhail Bakhtin and especially to his conception of dialogism, which also describes an unsettling dialectic that serves to emphasize the embattled and violent conditions of communication. One might also look to the way much contemporary critical theory is preoccupied with images of war, violence, and transgression; the writings of Jacques Derrida and Michel Foucault would be cases in point.

It should be noted that in a few instances surrealists were accused of actual crimes. For instance, in 1930 Georges Sadoul was prosecuted for having written an antimilitarist letter to a student training to be an officer at the School of Saint-Cyr, and Aragon was threatened with prosecution for "Front Rouge," a poem in which he appeared to advocate assassination. Although instances such as these were isolated and never came to much, the surrealists did not take chances only on paper or canvas.

52. Breton, *Nadja*, p. 133.

53. Artaud, "Nouvelle lettre sur moi-même," *La Révolution surréaliste* 5 (15 October 1925): 23.

54. See Arthur Rimbaud's letters to Georges Izambord (13 May 1871) and Paul Demeny (15 May 1871), *Oeuvres complètes*, ed. Antoine Adam (Paris: Éditions Gallimard, 1972), pp. 349–51.

55. This reference to the retina as the traditional screen of painting was general; it appears, for instance, in a 1954 interview with Duchamp that Breton quoted in "Présent des Gaulles" (*Le Surréalisme et la peinture*, p. 366) and in Ernst's comments on the impressionists in "Avec Robert Lebel," *Écritures* (Paris: Editions Gallimard, 1970), p. 419.

56. See the comparison Breton draws between surrealism and Baudelaire's *Artificial Paradises* in "Manifeste du surréalisme," *Manifestes*, pp. 44–45; Rimbaud, "A George Izambard" and "A Paul Demeny," *Oeuvres*, pp. 249, 250; and Breton and Soupault, *Les Champs magnetiques*: suivi de *Vous m'oublierez* et de *S'il vous plait* (Paris: Éditions Gallimard, 1967), p. 42. Cf. Pierre Naville's surrealist work, "Les Reines de la main gauche," collected in *Le Temps du surréel* (Paris: Éditions Galilee, 1977), p. 445: "I tell you that the author has not managed his effects, adopted a language: he does not speak, he is spoken." One might also compare these images to the argument in Martin Heidegger's later writings that "language speaks man."

57. Baudelaire, "Le Voyage," *Oeuvres*, p. 127.

58. Artaud, *Le Pèse-nerfs, Oeuvres*, 1:104; *Fragments d'un journal d'enfer, Oeuvres*, pp. 137–38.

59. Breton and Eluard, "Notes sur la poésie," *La Révolution surréaliste* 12 (15 December 1929): 53. In *Mémoires d'un surréaliste* (Paris: La Jeune Parque, 1968), Maxime Alexandre points out that this work is a parody of the aphorisms on literature that had been published recently by Paul Valéry.

60. Breton and Soupault, *Les Champs magnetiques*, p. 78.

61. On this point see J. H. Matthews, *Languages of Surrealism* (Columbia: University of Missouri Press, 1986), chapter 3, "Grammar, Prosody, and French Surrealist Poetry," pp. 38–58.

62. Breton, "Usine," *Littérature* 7 (September 1919): 12. This line also appears in Breton's and Soupault's *Les Champs magnetiques*, p. 82.

63. Breton, *Nadja*, p. 69.

64. An exception is Philippe Soupault's article on Raymond Roussel, *Littérature*, n.s., 2 (1 April 1922), in which he notes (p. 16) that Roussel is wealthy and so has been in a position "to observe the others, beasts, people, or machines, agitate themselves. Not all men can interest themselves in this game, in these labors." This is particularly interesting in light of the fact that Soupault was eventually excluded from the group in large part because of his taking up of employments, such as journalistic work, that were considered to be degrading. See also the bitter reply that Robert Desnos wrote to Breton's "Second manifeste" after he had been excluded from the movement. Much of Desnos's anger in this "Troisième manifeste du surréalisme" (*Documents surréalistes*, pp. 157–62) focuses on what he sees as Breton's bad faith in criticizing his work of earning a living. (Breton, who married a rich woman, was unabashed in advising others to do the same, explaining that it was easy to do so and a much better choice than working for a living.)

65. Friedrich Nietzsche, *The Gay Science: With a Prelude in Rhymes and an Appendix of Songs*, trans. Walter Kaufmann (New York: Vintage Books, 1974), pp. 224, 217.

66. Roger Vailland, *Le Surréalisme contre la révolution* (Paris: Éditions Sociales, 1948), p. 23.

67. Breton, *Nadja*, pp. 132–35.

68. See Alexandre's comment in his *Mémoires* (p. 68) that the surrealists, "in creating the myth of the woman-child, opposed it to the petit-bourgeois ideal of the woman at work, knowing better how to read and calculate than how to be a woman." See also Margaret Cohen's argument that prostitution "indicates the limits of Breton's social critique" in her "Mysteries of Paris: The Collective Uncanny in André Breton's *L'Amour fou*," *Dada/Surrealism* 17 (1988): 108; Xavière Gauthier's analysis of the

representation of desire in surrealist works, which leads to the conclusion that "mad love" can appear "only outside of society and especially outside of the working class," in *Surréalisme et sexualité* (Paris: Éditions Gallimard, 1971), p. 198; Susan Rubin Suleiman's analysis of the passage I have quoted from *Nadja* as showing Breton's rejection of "female 'otherness'" in "Nadja, Dora, Lol V. Stein: Women, Madness, and Narrative," *Discourse in Psychoanalysis and Literature*, ed. Shlomith Rommon-Kenan (London: Methuen, 1987), especially pp. 140–41; and Gloria Feman Orenstein, "*Nadja* Revisited: A Feminist Approach," *Dada/Surrealism* 8 (1978): 91–106. For an account of women's participation in surrealism, which also considers their relations with the men in the movement, see Whitney Chadwick, *Women Artists in the Surrealist Movement* (Boston: Little, Brown and Company, 1985).

69. Michel Carrouges, *André Breton and the Basic Concepts of Surrealism*, trans. Maura Prendergast (University, AL: University of Alabama Press, 1974), p. 185.

70. Breton, *Entretiens*, p. 135.

71. V. I. Lenin, *What Is to be Done?, Selected Works*, ed. J. Fineberg, 12 vols. (New York: International Publishers, n.d.), 2:180–81.

CHAPTER 8

1. Paul Eluard, "Premières vues anciennes," *Oeuvres complètes*, ed. Marcelle Dumas and Lucien Scheler, 2 vols. (Paris: Éditions Gallimard, 1968), 1:532–33.

2. All references to *Troilus and Cressida* are taken from *The Complete Signet Classic Shakespeare*, ed. Sylvan Barnett (New York: Harcourt Brace Jovanovich, 1963). Citations are given within the text.

3. René Descartes, *Meditations on First Philosophy*, in *The Philosophical Works of Descartes*, trans. Elizabeth S. Haldane and G. R. T. Ross, 2 vols. (Cambridge: Cambridge University Press, 1968), 1:156. All further references to this work, abbreviated *MFP*, will be included in the text.

4. Roland Barthes, "Writers, Intellectuals, Teachers," *Image-Music-Text*, ed. and trans. Stephen Heath (New York: Hill and Wang, 1977), p. 191.

5. Ludwig Wittgenstein, *On Certainty*, ed. G. E. M. Anscombe and G. H. von Wright, trans. Denis Paul and G. E. M. Anscombe (Oxford: Basil Blackwell, 1974), p. 39e. Further references to this work, abbreviated *OC*, will be included in the text.

6. René Crevel, "Révolution, surréalisme, spontanéité," *Révolution, surréalisme, spontanéité* (Paris: Éditions Plasma, 1978), p. 13.

7. Eugène Ionesco, *La Leçon*, in *Théâtre*, with a Preface by Jacques Lemarchand, 4 vols. (Paris: Éditions Gallimard, 1954), 1:72.

8. [Louis] Aragon, *Le Paysan de Paris* (Paris: Éditions Gallimard, 1948), pp. 8–9. Cf. the comparison of Descartes and Salvador Dali in Alain Grosrichard's "Le Langue de Dali: 'Introduction au discours de la méthode paranoïaque-critique,'" *Regards sur Minotaure: La Revue à tête de bête* (Geneva: Musée d'art et d'histoire, 1987), pp. 121–37.

9. Edmund Husserl, *The Crisis of European Sciences and Transcendental Phenomenology: An Introduction to Phenomenological Philosophy*, trans. and ed. David Carr (Evanston: Northwestern University Press, 1970), p. 74.

10. Cf. Wittgenstein, *On Certainty*, p. 7e, where he describes consciousness as being "*as it were* a tone of voice in which one declares how things are" even though "one does not infer from the tone of voice that one is justified."

11. Giorgio de Chirico, "Manuscript from the Collection of Jean Paulhan," in *Surrealists on Art*, ed. Lucy R. Lippard (Englewood Cliffs, NJ: Prentice-Hall, 1970), p. 71.

12. Friedrich Nietzsche, *The Will to Power*, ed. Walter Kaufmann, trans. Walter Kaufmann and R. J. Hollingdale (New York: Random House, 1967), p. 189.

13. André Breton, "Second manifeste du surréalisme," *Manifestes du surréalisme* (Paris: Jean-Jacques Pauvert, 1972), p. 133.

14. Georges Hugnet, *Pleins et déliés: témoignages et souvenirs 1926–1972* (La Chappelle-sur-Loire: Éditions Guy Authier, 1972), p. 125.

15. Breton, "Situation surréaliste de l'objet," *Manifestes*, p. 271.

16. Husserl, *The Crisis of European Sciences*, p. 162.

17. Comte de Lautréamont [Isidore Ducasse], *Les Chants de Maldoror*, in *Oeuvres complètes* (Paris: Librarie José Corti, 1963), p. 250.

18. Breton, *Les Vases communicants* (Paris: Éditions Gallimard, 1955), p. 160.

19. Eluard, "Premièrement," *Oeuvres*, 1:242.

20. Sigmund Freud, *The Interpretation of Dreams*, in *The Standard Edition of the Complete Psychological Works of Sigmund Freud*, ed. and trans. James Strachey et al., 24 vols. (London: The Hogarth Press and the Institute of Psycho-Analysis, 1953), 5:567.

21. Nietzsche, *The Gay Science: With a Prelude in Rhymes and an Appendix of Songs*, trans. Walter Kaufmann (New York: Vintage Books, 1974), p. 38. Schiller's "The Veiled Image at Sais" was a kind of touchstone for the reactionary idealism of nineteenth-century anti-realist works. For instance, it is quoted in epigraphs in Edward Bulwer-Lytton's *Zanoni* and in Villiers de l'Isle-Adam's *L'Eve future*.

22. Antonin Artaud, "Correspondence de la momie," *Oeuvres complètes*, rev. ed., 9 vols. (Paris: Éditions Gallimard, 1970), 1:361–62. Also, cf. "L'Automate personnel," *Oeuvres*, 1:177–82.

23. Michel Leiris, "Métaphore," *Brisées* (Paris: Mercure de France, 1966), p. 25.

24. Eluard, "L'Évidence poétique," *Oeuvres*, 1:518–19.

25. Eluard [with Max Ernst], "Des Éventails brisés," *Oeuvres*, 1:132. This poem was first published in 1922, before surrealism had claimed its name, but Ernst cited it as an example of fruitful surrealist collaboration in "Au-delà de la peinture," *Écritures* (Paris: Éditions Gallimard, 1970), p. 266; and two lines of it appeared in the *Short Dictionary of Surrealism* as a definition of the crocodile.

26. Breton, "Position politique de l'art d'aujourd'hui," *Manifestes*, p. 220.

27. Lautréamont, *Les Chants de Maldoror*, in *Oeuvres*, p. 296; Crevel, "Notes en vue d'une psycho-dialectique," *La Surréalisme au service de la révolution* 5 (May 1933): 48. See also the passage on psychoanalysis in Crevel's *Êtes-vous fous* (Paris: Éditions Gallimard, 1929), pp. 115–23; and his criticism that psychoanalysis is involved with racism in "De la volupté coloniale au patriotisme de l'inconscient," *Le Clavecin de Diderot* (Paris: Jean-Jacques Pauvert, 1932), pp. 95–100.

28. René Char, *Artine*, in *Oeuvres complètes*, ed. Jean Roudant (Paris: Éditions Gallimard, 1983), p. 19.

29. G. W. F. Hegel, *Aesthetics: Lectures on Fine Art*, trans. T. M. Knox, 2 vols. (Oxford: Oxford University Press, 1975), 1:11. See Roger Vitrac's comments on what he regards as the sense and nonsense of Hegel's consignment of art to the past in *Georges de Chirico* (Paris: Éditions Gallimard, 1927), p. 9.

30. Crevel, "L'Enfance de l'art," *Révolution, surréalisme, spontanéité*, p. 44.

31. Aragon, *The Peasant of Paris*, p. 252.

32. Aragon, "Sommeil de plomb," *Le Mouvement perpétuel: Precédé de Feu de joie* et suivi de *Écritures automatiques* (Paris: Éditions Gallimard, 1975), p. 66.

33. Aragon, "Du Décor," *Écrits sur l'art modern*, ed. Jean Ristat (Paris: Éditions Flammarion, 1981), pp. 8–9. See also Aragon's characterization of modernity in terms of mechanicity or automatism in "Introduction à 1930," *La Révolution surréaliste* 12 (15 December 1929): 63–64.

34. Breton, "Lettre aux voyants," *Manifestes*, p. 199.

35. Breton, *L'Amour fou* (Paris: Éditions Gallimard, 1937), p. 15.

36. Breton, "Manifeste du surréalisme," *Manifestes*, p. 37.

37. Nietzsche, *Human, All Too Human: A Book for Free Spirits*, trans. Marion Faber with Stephen Lehmann, ed. Marion Faber (Lincoln: University of Nebraska Press, 1984), p. 237.

38. See Freud, *The Interpretation of Dreams, Standard Edition*, 5:356. See also Breton's Freudian interpretation of Lautréamont's chance meeting of a sewing machine and an umbrella on an operating room table in *Les Vases communicants* (Paris: Éditions Gallimard, 1955), p. 67.

39. Nietzsche, *The Gay Science*, p. 38: "Perhaps her name is—to speak Greek—*Baubo*?"

40. Breton, "Giorgio de Chirico," *Littérature* 11 (January 1920): 29.

41. Crevel, "Le Patriotisme de l'inconscient," *Le Surréalisme au service de la révolution* 4 (December 1931): 4.

42. [Julien Offroy de] La Mettrie, *L'Homme-machine*, ed. Paul-Laurent Assoun (Paris: Éditions Denoël/Gouthier, 1981), pp. 145, 47.

43. Eluard, "Dors," *Oeuvres*, 1:360.

44. Aragon, *Le Paysan de Paris*, p. 44.

45. *Le Surréalisme au service de la révolution* was published from 1930 to 1933, following *La Révolution surréaliste* (1924–29) and the dada and protosurrealist *Littérature* (1919–24).

46. All quotes are from Crevel, "La Grande mannequin cherche et trouve sa peau," *Révolution, surréalisme, spontanéité*, pp. 57–61.

47. See Erwin Panofsky's account of Bellori in *Idea: A Concept in Art Theory*, trans. Joseph J. S. Peake (Columbia: University of South Carolina Press, 1968), p. 110.

48. E. T. A. Hoffmann, "The Sandman," *Selected Writings of E. T. A. Hoffmann*, ed. and trans. Leonard J. Kent and Elizabeth C. Knight, 2 vols. (Chicago: University of Chicago Press, 1969), 1:149.

49. Philippe Soupault, *Mémoires de l'oublie (Première parte)* (Paris: Lachenal and Ritter, 1981), pp. 71–72n.

50. Breton, "La Confession dédaigneuse," *Les Pas perdus* (Paris: Éditions Gallimard, 1969), p. 14. For some other discussions of the surrealist mannequin, see Rosalind Krauss, "Corpus Delicti," in Rosalind Krauss and Jane Livingston, *L'Amour fou: Photography and Surrealism* (Washington, DC: The Corcoran Gallery of Art; New York: Abbeville Press, 1985), pp. 55–100; William Rubin, "De Chirico and Modernism," *De Chirico*, ed. William Rubin (New York: Museum of Modern Art, 1982), pp. 55–79; and Peter Webb (with Robert Short), *Hans Bellmer* (London: Quartet Books, 1985), p. 46.

51. *La Révolution surréaliste* 2 (15 January 1925), recording responses to its inquiry about suicide ("Is suicide a solution?"), noted that when Kokoschka received the questionnaire, he had just finished a self-portrait in which he portrayed himself as a dead man, an image *LRS* reproduced (p. 11) along with the comment, "We insist on the *miraculous* character of this coincidence."

52. All references are to Oskar Kokoschka, "Der Fetish," *Kunstlerbekenntnisse: Briefe/ Tagebuchblätter/ Betrachtungen Leutiger Künstler*, ed. Paul Westheim (Berlin: Prophläen-Verlag, n.d.). Page numbers are given within the text.

53. Robert Desnos, "Les Mystères de New York," in *Les Surréalistes et le cinéma*, ed. Alain and Odette Virmaux (Paris: Éditions Seghers, 1976), p. 130.

54. Hegel, *Aesthetics*, 1:38, 26.

55. See Jacques Derrida's analysis of Kant's aesthetics and the issue of frames in *The Truth in Painting*, trans. Geoff Bennington and Ian McLeod (Chicago: University of Chicago Press, 1987).

56. Charles Baudelaire, "Le Cadre," *Oeuvres complètes*, ed. Y.-G. Le Dantee, revised by Claude Pichois (Paris: Éditions Gallimard, 1961), pp. 37–38.

57. Aragon, *Le Paysan de Paris*, p. 218.

CHAPTER 9

1. Jacques Baron, *L'An 1 du surréalisme* (Paris: Éditions Denoël, 1969), p. 66.

2. See Pierre Mabille's fascinating psychoanalytic essay on the incident of Victor Brauner's injury, "L'Oeil du peintre," *Minotaure* 12/13 (1939): 53–56. Mabille points out that Brauner painted many works that involved injuries to or transformations of eyes, including one that could be taken to foretell Oscar Dominguez's involvement in the affair; he argues that Brauner's "whole life was converging on that mutilation." Also, on the subject of friendship and group relations in surrealism, see Maurice Blanchot, "Le Demain joueur," *La Nouvelle Revue Française* 172 (1 April 1967): 866–68.

3. See Louis Aragon and André Breton, "Petite contribution au dossier de certains intellectuals à tendances révolutionnaires," *Variétés* [special issue] (1 June 1929): ii.

4. Comte de Lautréamont [Isidore Ducasse], "Poésies," *Oeuvres complètes* (Paris: Librarie José Corti, 1963), p. 386.

5. André Breton, *Nadja* (Paris: Éditions Gallimard, 1963), p. 96.

6. André Masson, "Propos sur le surréalisme," *Médiations* 3 (1961): 34.

7. Victor Crastre, "André Breton et la liberté," *André Breton*, ed. Marc Eigeldinger (Neuchâtel: Les Éditions de la Baconnière, 1970), p. 144.

8. P. E. [Paul Eluard], "Les Philosophes," *La Révolution surréaliste* (15 January 1925): 32.

9. See Mary Douglas, *Purity and Danger: An Analysis of Concepts of Pollution and Taboo* (London: Routledge and Kegan Paul, 1966).

10. René Crevel, "Mort, maladie et littérature," *Le Surréalisme au service de la révolution* 1 (July 1930): 6.

11. Arthur Rimbaud, "Jeunesse," *Oeuvres complètes*, ed. Antoine Adam (Paris: Éditions Gallimard, 1972), p. 148.

12. Breton, "Pour dada," *Les Pas perdus* (Paris: Éditions Gallimard, 1969), p. 79.

13. Breton, "Alfred Jarry," *Les Pas perdus*, p. 51.

14. Breton, "Situation surréaliste de l'objet," *Manifestes du surréalisme* (Paris: Jean-Jacques Pauvert, 1971), p. 272.

15. Philippe Soupault, *Mémoires de l'oublie [Prèmiere parte]* (Paris: Lachenal and Ritter, 1981), p. 143. On this point and others related to this chapter, see Philippe Audoin, "Le Surréalisme et le jeu," *Entretiens sur le surréalisme*, ed. Ferdinand Alquié (Paris: Mouton, 1968), pp. 455–69.

16. [Louis] Aragon, *Aragon parle avec Dominique Arban* (Paris: Éditions Seghers, 1968), p. 65.

17. Breton, *Les Vases communicants* (Paris: Éditions Gallimard, 1955), p. 157.

18. Salvador Dali, "De la Beauté terrifiante et comestible, de l'architecture modern style," *Minotaure* 3/4 (December 1933): 71.

19. Breton, "Le Bouquet sans fleurs," *La Révolution surréaliste* 2 (15 January 1925): 25.

20. Like the difference between Tzara and Breton, this difference, too, is characteristic: Duchamp was idolized by many surrealists but kept his distance from their movement.

21. Breton, "Du Temps que les surréalistes avaient raison," *Manifestes*, pp. 255–56.

22. The article in question is Jacques Rivière's "Reconnaisance à dada," *La Nouvelle Revue Française* (15 August 1920): 216–37.

23. The remark was made in Crevel's reply to the inquiry on suicide (from which the following quotations are also taken), *La Révolution surréaliste* 2 (15 January 1925): 8–13. In this regard, see Crevel's reference to this inquiry and his argument for the value of such "demoralizing interrogations" in the title essay of his volume, *L'Esprit contre la raison* (Paris: Tchou, 1969), p. 16. Also, see J. B. Pontalis's remarks on surrealism's double compulsion "toward synthesis and toward permanent rupture" in his preface to Xavière Gauthier, *Surréalisme et sexualité* (Paris: Éditions Gallimard, 1971), pp. 11–12; and Octavio Paz's comment, "Each one of the surrealist exhibitions gravitated around an axis of contradiction: scandal and secret, consecration and profanation," in "André Breton ou la recherche du commencement," *La Nouvelle Revue Française* 172 (1 April 1967): 611.

24. Maxime Alexandre, *Mémoires d'un surréaliste* (Paris: La Jeune Parque, 1968), p. 56.

25. Friedrich Nietzsche, *The Gay Science: With a Prelude in Rhymes and an Appendix of Songs*, trans. Walter Kaufmann (New York: Vintage Books, 1974), pp. 289–90. See also Nietzsche, *Thus Spoke Zarathustra*, in *The Portable Nietzsche*, ed. and trans. Walter Kaufmann (New York: The Viking Press, 1954), p. 126: "Man is a rope, tied between beast and overman—a rope over an abyss. A dangerous across, a dangerous on-the-way, a dangerous looking-back, a dangerous shuddering and stopping."

26. Breton, "Second manifeste du surréalisme," *Manifestes*, p. 153n.

27. William Rubin, "André Masson and Twentieth-Century Painting," *André Masson*, ed. William Rubin and Carolyn Laucher (New York: Museum of Modern Art [1976]), p. 43.

28. René Char, "Bel édifice et les pressentiments," *Oeuvres complètes*, ed. Jean Roudant (Paris: Éditions Gallimard, 1983), p. 11.

29. Breton, "Second manifeste du surréalisme," *Manifestes*, p. 157.

30. V. I. Lenin, *What Is to Be Done?*, in *Selected Works*, ed. J. Fineberg, 12 vols. (New York: International Publishers, n.d.), 2:27–70. This epigraph from Ferdinand Lasalle was paraphrased approvingly in David Gascoyne's pioneering English-language introduction to surrealism, *A Short History of Surrealism* ([London]: Cotsden-Sanderson, 1935), p. 81. This work is also notably hilarious in its earnestness, as when Gascoyne says of *L'Age d'or* (p. 96), "It is impossible to imagine what would happen were this film to be shown in England, even to a Film Society audience."

31. As in "Du Temps que les surréalistes avaient raison," *Manifestes*, p. 261:

> We maintain that the free affirmation of all points of view, the permanent confrontation of all tendencies, constitutes the most indispensable ferment of the revolutionary battle. "Everyone is free to say and to write what suits him," Lenin affirmed in 1905: "liberty of speech and of the press must be complete." We consider any other conception reactionary.

32. See Patrick Waldberg's characterization of surrealist excommunications as a virtually unparalleled example of "intolerance allied with puerility" in *Surrealism*, trans. Stuart Gilbert (London: Thames and Hudson, 1965), p. 133. However, there remain many apologists for the history of excommunications in surrealism; see, for example, Philippe Audoin, *Les Surréalistes* (Paris: Éditions du Seuil, 1973).

33. Max Ernst, "Après la mort d'André Breton," *Écritures* (Paris: Éditions Galli-mard, 1970), p. 415. One might argue that in "nonreciprocity" Ernst chose the wrong term to describe the game; at least Breton characterized what he sought in precisely the opposite term in *L'Amour fou* (Paris: Éditions Gallimard, 1937), p. 120, where he hoped that "the absolute gift of one being to another, which cannot exist without reciprocity, may in the eyes of all be the only natural and supernatural bridge thrown over life."

34. Paul Nougé, "Récapitulation," *Histoire de ne pas rire* (Bruxelles: Éditions de la Revue les Lêvres Nues, 1956), p. 144.

35. Robert Desnos, "Rrose Selavy," *Corps et biens* (Paris: Librarie Gallimard, 1930), p. 23. "Rrose Selavy," a phonetic play on "eros, c'est la vie," was the name Duchamp had invented for the purposes of a feminine, punning masquerade; there exists a Man Ray photograph of him dolled up in his costume.

36. Nietzsche, *The Will to Power*, ed. Walter Kaufmann, trans. Walter Kaufmann and R. J. Hollingdale (New York: Vintage Books, 1967), p. 170.

37. Immanuel Kant, "Idea for a Universal History with a Cosmopolitan Intent," *Perpetual Peace and Other Essays on Politics, History, and Morals*, trans. and ed. Ted Humphrey (Indianapolis: Hackett Publishing Company, 1983), p. 32.

38. Sigmund Freud, *Group Psychology and the Analysis of the Ego*, in *The Standard Edition of the Complete Psychological Works of Sigmund Freud*, trans. and ed. James Strachey et al., 24 vols. (London: The Hogarth Press and the Institute for Psycho-Analysis, 1953), 18:77–80. In these descriptions, Freud was referring to the work of Gustav Le Bon, but he was also expressing his general agreement with him.

39. Nietzsche, *The Will to Power*, p. 171.

40. Tristan Tzara, *Monsieur Aa l'antiphilosophe*, in *Oeuvres complètes*, ed. Henri Béhar, 4 vols. (Paris: Éditions Flammarion, 1980), 2:304.

41. See, for example, Breton, "Poisson soluble," *Manifestes*, p. 102: "It is the

sweet and always available evasion called 'the future' that reabsorbs the stars that hang over our distress in the meantime."

42. Maurice Blanchot, "Réflexions sur le surréalisme," *La Part du feu* (Paris: Éditions Gallimard, 1949), p. 97.

43. Breton, *Entretiens (1913–1952)*, rev. ed. (Paris: Éditions Gallimard, 1969), p. 93.

44. Lautréamont, "Poésies," *Oeuvres*, p. 374.

45. Aragon, *Aragon parle*, p. 134.

46. Lautréamont, *Les Chants de Maldoror, Oeuvres*, p. 327. Literary mottos could also be given a visual form; a notable example is the emblem the surrealists devised for use in some of their publications, based on an image in *Maldoror*: "Take yourself away from the side where the lake of swans is found, and I'll tell you later why there happens to be one among the flock that is completely black and whose body, which supports an anvil surmounted by the putrefying corpse of a crab, inspires a justifiable mistrust in its other aquatic comrades."

47. [Roger Vitrac], *Georges de Chirico* (Paris: Éditions Gallimard, 1927), p. 7.

48. Breton, *Le Surréalisme et la peinture* (Paris: Éditions Gallimard, 1965), p. 16.

49. See the account in Marcel Jean, *The History of Surrealist Painting*, trans. Simon Watson Taylor (New York: Grove Press, 1960), p. 136.

50. Paul Eluard, untitled note, *La Révolution surréaliste* 8 (1 December 1926): 7.

51. For some examples of the butterflies, see Maurice Nadeau, ed., *Documents surréalistes, Histoire du surréalisme*, 2 vols. (Paris: Éditions du Seuil, 1948), 2:23; all references to "152 Proverbes" are taken from Eluard [with Benjamin Péret], *Oeuvres complètes*, ed. Marcelle Dumas and Lucien Scheler (Paris: Éditions Gallimard, 1968), pp. 153–61. Eluard published a short-lived journal, *Proverbe*, from February 1920 to July 1921, and the "152 Proverbes" were written before the formal advent of surrealism; but they are still characteristic of the surrealist penchant for sloganeering. Thus, in addition to the other examples I mention, one could compare this work to "L'Immaculée conception," which Eluard wrote with Breton in 1930. It contains such mottos as "Correct your parents," "Don't drink water," "Perform miracles in order to deny them," and "Trace the disinterested games of your ennui in the dust" (Eluard, *Oeuvres*, pp. 353–55). Relevant to this point is Tzara's "Proverbe dada" (which first appeared in *Proverbe*), *Oeuvres*, 1:411: "The motif of the popular proverb is observation, experience, while that of the dadaist proverb is a spontaneous concentration that insinuates itself into the forms of this other and can arrive at the same stage and result: the small collective folly of a sonorous pleasure." Also, on this subject, see J. H. Matthews, *The Imagery of Surrealism* (Syracuse: Syracuse University Press, 1977), pp. 108–15.

52. Benjamin Péret, "Pieds et poings liés," *Oeuvres complètes*, 4 vols. (Paris: Librarie José Corti, 1987), 1:94; Rimbaud [Letters to Paul Demeny dated May 1 and May 15, 1871], *Oeuvres*, pp. 249–50; and Thomas De Quincey, *Confessions of an English Opium-Eater*, in *Confessions of an English Opium-Eater and Other Writings*, ed. Grevel Lindop (Oxford: Oxford University Press, 1985), p. 135.

53. The monocle was a favorite affectation among the dadaists and surrealists, the notable wearers including Tzara and Breton; in this object as in the artworks and writings I have mentioned, there was a "slogan." The monocle was at least in part a statement about pure artificiality, inutility, and illogicality.

54. Aragon, quoted in Jacqueline Chénieux-Gendron, *Le Surréalisme et le roman: 1922-50* (Lausanne: Éditions l'Age d'Homme, 1983), p. 24n.

55. *Malediction* is a prominent term in surrealist rhetoric, as in the writings of Lautréamont and Baudelaire. Breton comments on this term (and on its relation to *Les Chants de Maldoror*) in the "Second manifeste du surréalisme," *Manifestes*, pp. 180-81:

> This question of the malediction, which hitherto has generally lent itself only to ironic or thoughtless commentaries, is now of more topical interest than ever. Surrealism has everything to lose if it should wish to distance this malediction from itself. Here it is important to reiterate and to maintain the "Maranatha" of the alchemists, placed at the threshold of the work to ward off the profane.

The notion of the divisive threshold here is another instance of what I discuss as the problem of the public.

56. Breton, "Manifeste du surréalisme," *Manifestes*, p. 44. For another treatment of many questions addressed in this chapter, including the issue of words as performatives and the problems of group animation and adhesion, see Julian Gracque's insightful and provocative study, *André Breton: Quelques aspects de l'écrivain* (Paris: Librarie José Corti, 1966). Also, on the surrealist use of words, see Judi Freeman, *The Dada and Surrealist Word-Image* (Cambridge: The MIT Press; Los Angeles: Los Angeles County Museum of Art, 1989).

57. Breton, "La Confession dédaigneuse," *Les Pas perdus*, p. 12.

58. Breton, "Manifeste du surréalisme," *Manifestes*, p. 18. In evaluating this attitude toward Valéry, one should take into consideration the considerable impact made upon the young Breton by Valéry's *Monsieur Teste*. Indeed, the surrealists' sense of purity is strikingly prefigured in the titular character in this work, for whom there can be no satisfaction, and only the most tortured pleasures, because he sees in all things — including the ideal — the mockery that *is* the ideal, whose existence is everywhere assumed and thus commanding even though its perception and expression are impossible. Cf. the attitude Breton assumed in relation to Guillaume Apollinaire in the first "Manifeste du surréalisme" (*Manifestes*, p. 34). He noted that he and Soupault adopted the name of their movement in homage to the recently deceased Apollinaire, but he also said that Apollinaire had possessed only "the letter, still imperfect, of surrealism" and had showed himself "incapable of giving it a theoretical insight" that he and his associates provided.

I should note that the surrealist attitude toward the novel was much more complex than I can indicate here; on this subject, see Chénieux-Gendron's extensive treatment in *Le Surréalisme et le roman*.

59. See Salvador Dali, "Intreprétation paranoïaque de l'image obsédante 'L'Angelus' de Millet," *Minotaure* 1 (1933): 65-67.

60. See, for instance, E. Tériade, "Documentaire sur la jeune peinture, IV. — La réaction littéraire," *Cahiers d'art* 5 (1930): 69-77.

61. Charles Baudelaire, "Notes et documents pour mon avocat," *Oeuvres complètes*, ed. Y.-G. Le Dantec, revised by Claude Pichois (Paris: Éditions Gallimard, 1961), p. 181.

62. Char, "Migration," *Oeuvres*, p. 55; Soupault, "L'Ombre de l'ombre," *La Révolution surréaliste* 1 (1 December 1924): 25; Breton, "Second Manifeste," *Manifestes*, p. 138.

63. Breton, "Avertissement pour la réédition du second manifeste," *Manifestes*, p. 124.

64. See Renée Riese Hubert, "Surrealist Women Painters, Feminist Portraits," *Dada/Surrealism* 13 (1984): 70–82; and Whitney Chadwick, *Women Artists and the Surrealist Movement* (Boston: Little, Brown and Company, 1985). Also, see Mary Ann Caw's excellent essay on the treatment of women in surrealist art, "Ladies Shot and Painted: Female Embodiment in Surrealist Art," *The Female Body in Western Culture: Contemporary Perspectives*, ed. Susan Rubin Suleiman (Cambridge: Harvard University Press, 1986), pp. 262–87.

65. Breton, *L'Amour fou*, p. 176.

66. Gisèle Prassinos, quoted in Jeanine Warnod, "Entretien avec Gisèle Prassinos en janvier 1987," *Regards sur Minotaure: La Revue à tête de bête* (Geneva: Musée d'art et d'histoire, 1987), p. 250.

67. See, for instance, Breton's comments in the roundtable discussion, "Recherches sur la sexualité," *La Révolution surréaliste* 11 (15 May 1928): 32–40.

68. Lenin, "'Left-Wing' Communism, an Infantile Disorder," *Selected Works*, 10: 76.

69. Aragon, "Introduction à 1930," *La Révolution surréaliste* 12 (15 December 1929): 62.

70. Breton, "Avertissement pour la réédition du second manifeste," *Manifestes*, pp. 124–25.

71. Freud, "The 'Uncanny,'" *Works*, 17. Page references are given within the text. For a good analysis of surrealism's debts to contemporary psychological, psychoanalytic, parapsychological, and spiritualist thinking, see Jean Starobinski, "Freud, Breton, Myers," in *André Breton*, ed. Eigeldinger, pp. 153–71.

72. Freud, *Group Psychology and the Analysis of the Ego, Works*, 18:78.

73. Breton, "Caractères de l'évolution moderne et ce qui en participe," *Les Pas perdus*, p. 170.

74. Breton, "Position politique du surréalisme," *Manifestes*, p. 208.

75. Victor Brauner, "Avertissement," *Le Surréalisme en 1947* (Paris: Éditions Pierre à Feu, 1947), p. 26.

76. Dali, *La Conquête de l'irrationnel* (Paris: Éditions Surréalistes, 1935), p. 147.

77. See André Souris, "Paul Nougé et ses complices," *Entretiens sur le surréalisme*, pp. 438–39.

78. See Georges Hugnet's description of the surrealist meeting convened in February 1934 to consider the possible expulsion of Dali in "Petite contribution à la vie secrète de Salvador Dali," *Pleins et deliés: témoignages et souvenirs 1926–1972* (La Chappelle-sur-Loire: Éditions Guy Authier, 1972), pp. 251–64. (The meeting ended inconclusively, and Dali remained affiliated with the group until the late 1930s.) While Dali's inclination toward fascism was condemned by Breton and the others around him, their difficulty in dealing with it was perhaps a telling mark of a weakness in the movement. On this point see Rene Passeron's comments on Dali's place or nonplace in the movement in "Le Surréalisme des peintres," *Entretiens sur surréalisme*, pp. 251–52. In the same volume ("Contre-attaque," p. 160), see also Robert Stuart Short's consideration of an occasion on which the surrealists, through their short-lived liaison with Georges Bataille and the Counterattack group, gave at least indirect approval to a seeming apology for Hitler's aggression.

79. The allusions in this statement to gestures that had been made by Jacques

Vaché and Arthur Craven and, beyond them, to the First World War make this all the more clearly a surreal, nonfunctional, statement; for a description of these allusions, see William S. Rubin, *Dada, Surrealism, and their Heritage* (New York: The Museum of Modern Art [1968]), pp. 12, 15.

80. Rimbaud, "Guerre," *Oeuvres*, p. 146.

81. Aragon, "Lorsque tout est fini," *Le Libertinage* (Paris: Éditions Gallimard, 1924). Page references are given within the text. This work is based on the exploits of the Bonnot gang, famous in France about ten years before the 1924 date of the story. Cf. Chénieux-Gendron's analysis of this story in relation to dada and to the surrealist reading of Lautréamont, *Surréalisme et le roman*, pp. 68–69.

82. For a more detailed, generally Freudian analysis of this painting, see Dawn Ades, "Between Dada and Surrealism: Painting in the *Mouvement flou*," in Dawn Ades et al., *In the Mind's Eye: Dada and Surrealism* (Chicago: Museum of Contemporary Art; New York: Abbeville Press, 1985), especially pp. 39–41.

83. Aragon, *Le Paysan de Paris* (Paris: Éditions Gallimard, 1948), p. 83.

Index